Rethinking the Welfare St

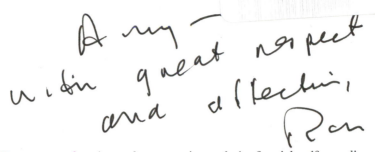

This book offers a comprehensive and comparative analysis of social welfare policy in an international context, with a particular emphasis on the US and Canada. The authors investigate the claim that a decentralized delivery of government-supported goods and services, enables policy objectives to be achieved in a more innovative, efficient and responsive manner. They also examine the effectiveness of the voucher system as a solution to problematic welfare concerns.

The voucher system, which includes all forms of government subsidy, whether in the form of tax deductions, credits or means-tested consumer entitlements, places the resources directly into the hands of citizens and allows them, rather than a government agent, to determine which goods they will consume from competing private suppliers. While this system has shown much promise in improving welfare, there have been problems for institutions unable to attract enough voucher-assisted consumers to ensure their survival.

In this context the authors examine major social programmes such as food stamps, low-income housing, legal aid, health care, early childhood education, primary and secondary education, post-secondary education and job training and other active labour market policies. This book will be of interest to students of comparative politics, social policy and economics.

Ronald J. Daniels is Dean and James M. Tory Professor of Law at the Faculty of Law at the University of Toronto. His research and teaching interests encompass law and development, corporate law, law and economics, the professions, and privatization of government services. **Michael J. Trebilcock** is University Professor and Professor of Law and Economics at the University of Toronto and Director of the Law and Economics Programme there. His principal research interests relate to contract theory, competition policy, economic and social regulation, international trade regulation, and law, institutions and development.

Rethinking the Welfare State

The prospects for government by voucher

**Ronald J. Daniels
and Michael J. Trebilcock**

Routledge
Taylor & Francis Group

LONDON AND NEW YORK

First published 2005
by Routledge
2 Park Square, Milton Park, Abingdon, Oxon, OX14 4RN

Simultaneously published in the USA and Canada
by Routledge
270 Madison Ave, New York, NY 10016

Routledge is an imprint of the Taylor & Francis Group

Typeset in Baskerville by
HWA Text and Data Management, Tunbridge Wells
Printed and bound in Great Britain by
MPG Books Ltd, Bodmin

British Library Cataloguing in Publication Data
A catalogue record for this book is available from the British Library

Library of Congress Cataloging in Publication Data
Daniels, Ronald J. (Ronald Joel), 1959–
    Rethinking the welfare state : government by voucher /
Ronald J. Daniels and Michael J. Trebilcock.
        p.   cm.
    Includes bibliographical references and index.
1. Social policy. 2. Welfare state. 3. Public welfare. 4. Subsidies.
5. Canada–Social policy. 6. United States–Social policy–1993–
I. Trebilcock, M. J. II. Title.
    HN18.3.D36 2005
    361.6′1–dc22   2004020323

ISBN 0–415–33776–3 (hbk)
ISBN 0–415–33777–1 (pbk)

Contents

Preface

This book is the by-product of a longstanding interest we have shared for several decades in the goals and instruments of the modern welfare state. Our interest in the welfare state has first and foremost been shaped by our scholarly commitment to law and economics analysis, and, in particular, to the issue of how the state can realize its goals, however defined, in the most efficient manner. In considering this issue, we have been extremely fortunate to have had a number of different opportunities to test and enrich our theoretical understandings of the modern welfare state in the crucible of applied policy experience. Indeed, our earliest collaboration (when Daniels was a student of Trebilcock's) involved a study undertaken for the MacDonald Royal Commission on Canada's Development Prospects (in the early 1980s) that sought to determine how the state could respond in a targeted and humane manner to the transition costs inflicted on certain stakeholders as a consequence of welfare increasing trade liberalization.

Since that time, we have grappled separately and together with the prospects for strengthened delivery of government-financed goods and services in areas as diverse as state-owned enterprises, public infrastructure, professional regulation, education, telecommunications, legal aid, corporate and securities regulation, university education, occupational health and safety regulation, and energy market structure and regulation. We have undertaken this work on behalf of governments and within and outside of Canada. Most recently, we jointly directed a blue ribbon panel established by the Premier of Ontario that was charged with the task of examining the future role of government in the province.

In the course of this journey into the interstices of the modern welfare state, we have been forced to confront and understand a number of different exogenous and endogenous challenges that have been leveled against the modern welfare state, and which emanate from, *inter alia*, changing technology, fiscal capacity, and citizen preferences. We have studied and advised governments as they sought to respond to the various policy movements that were triggered by these challenges, including: privatization, de-regulation, government re-invention, contracting-out, and, finally, re-regulation. And through all of these changes, we have remained committed to understanding whether core and received rationale(s) for public intervention had changed, or, whether, in fact, the argument for government change was less about basic goals and more about more effective means of delivery (i.e., instrument choice). And, to the extent that reform was focused on the latter, was it reasonable to expect that significant change could occur on the scale often imagined (particularly in relation to ostensible cost-savings) without compromising the realization of core governmental goals.

Our perspective on these and many other issues is more measured than many other commentators who have tackled the issue of the role and responsibilities of the modern welfare state. Both of us are strongly committed to the role that the modern welfare state has played (and continues to play) in supporting liberal democracy and market capitalism. Further, both of us remain somewhat skeptical about the prospects for, as well as the desirability of, radical government abandonment of time-honoured public goals and responsibilities. Yet, this skepticism does not imply reflexive commitment to the existing modalities of the social welfare state. Indeed, quite the contrary. As the title of this book suggests, we do believe that there is value in considering the broad implications of the applicability of the voucher instrument in vindicating public goals and responsibilities in a number of different policy areas.

In mounting this thought experiment, we have, over the years, benefited enormously from conversations around the prospects of the welfare state with a wide array of colleagues and friends at the Faculty of Law, University of Toronto. One could not imagine a more stimulating or supportive intellectual environment in which to consider these issues. We also have been enriched by the conversation (sometimes quite animated) that we have had with students at the Faculty of Law who have, over the years, enrolled in our upper year seminar course devoted to the changing role of the modern welfare state.

This project has greatly benefited from the superb research assistance offered by the following students (some of whom are themselves now legal academics): Malcolm Thorburn, Benjamin Alarie, Thomas Ringer, Graham Mayeda, Kathleen Grandy, Mandeep Dhaliwal, Jeffrey Torkin, Adam Samarillo and Leah Theriault. Not only did these students provide invaluable assistance in developing the various policy case studies that are included in this book, but their contributions also allowed us to refine and enrich the theoretical framework that shapes this inquiry. We are in their debt. We are also much indebted to Nadia Gulezko for the administrative and secretarial responsibilities she assumed in relation to this study and to the editors at Routledge for their professional attention to all details of the publication process.

Ronald J. Daniels
Michael J. Trebilcock

1 Introduction

This book is in part a thought experiment. In it we seek to consider the prospects for government by voucher. We ask: What would the state look like if, instead of delivering public goods and services itself, the government were to rely on voucher-financed delivery of these goods and services by private actors? In this world, vouchers would not be confined to one or two discrete policy areas, but rather would be the predominant instrument of public policy. With the exception of a few areas like national defense or policing, governments would discharge their responsibilities by creating or, at least, supervising markets in which citizen beneficiaries would use publicly financed vouchers to determine their consumption of a range of different goods and services supplied by private actors.

Such a scenario is not as far fetched or fanciful as it seems. Many industrialized democracies have, in fact, adopted voucher-based programs in discrete policy areas, including: education, health care, social services, housing, pensions, and legal aid. In some cases, these voucher-based programs are relatively narrow experiments which have only operated for a short period of time. In other cases, however, vouchers have a well-established pedigree, and have operated successfully for decades. Although we know of no single government anywhere that has as yet adopted the voucher across the broad spectrum of services provided by the modern welfare state, we can identify a rich vein of experience with the voucher from a number of different jurisdictions that enables us to imagine what the state might look like if all of these programs and experiments were, in fact, concentrated in a hypothetical "government by voucher."

Many commentators, we acknowledge, will be inclined to denigrate or dismiss this enterprise of thinking about "government by voucher." The fact is that there are few ideas in modern public policy that seem to elicit as much criticism, acrimony and passion as vouchers. Why is this so? It is indeed perplexing that a policy instrument would engender so much visceral antagonism. As we define it, the voucher is a tied demand-side subsidy, and the fact that we are talking about the conferral of subsidies should assuage concerns that the voucher is antithetical to time-honored goals of the social welfare state. After all, by creating and distributing vouchers, the state is responding to some legitimate set of interests and values through targeted financial assistance.

We would argue that there is nothing inherent in the voucher instrument that is irreconcilable with the goals of the modern social welfare state. Indeed, quite the opposite. It is, as we will discuss, open to governments to use vouchers any way they want. The voucher can be the means by which a government expands or contracts the contours of the welfare state. The voucher is equally consistent with a universal welfare state as with a residual one. The voucher can be generously or poorly endowed. The voucher can be used as a substitute or a complement to existing governmental programs. In other words, a decision by government to invoke the voucher instrument to achieve public goals in a specified policy area does not in itself reveal much about the underlying character of the policies being pursued by the sponsoring government.

That is not to say that reliance on vouchers is bereft of any normative content whatsoever. In deciding to pursue the realization of public goals through vouchers, governments will certainly be sensitive to the relative strengths and weaknesses of the voucher instrument as against other instruments of public policy, for instance, public delivery of public services. As against alternative instruments, the case for the voucher is straightforward: once governments have decided to intervene in a given policy area (for a host of different rationales, including equity, efficiency, and distributional goals), by conferring explicit, targeted subsides on individual citizens, decisions regarding the consumption and production of public goods and services will be made more efficiently. This results from the fact that vouchers place resources directly into the hands of citizens, where they, rather than a govern-mental agent, will determine the precise goods and services that will be consumed from among a number of competing suppliers, thereby increasing the likelihood that citizen preferences in the consumption of publicly supported goods and services will be more effectively vindicated. Specifically, the voucher concept introduces the prospect of economic exit and hence failure on the supply-side (e.g. bankruptcy) for institutions that are unable to attract and retain sufficient voucher-assisted consumers to ensure their survival and thus face a discipline that is markedly absent from many current government programs that depend exclusively or primarily on political voice to ensure accountability.[1]

However, the case for vouchers is not based solely on efficiency rationales. Because vouchers enable (and, indeed, promote) citizen choice in the consumption of publicly funded goods and services they increase the scope for individual autonomy. In Julian Le Grand's terms, vouchers convert citizen beneficiaries of the welfare state from pawns, the least powerful piece on the chess board, to queens, the most powerful.[2] Thus, vouchers demonstrate considerable promise in terms of their ability to realize public goals. Indeed, given this potential, the adoption of voucher programs may be able to mute, or even obviate, the great efficiency–equity trade-off of which Arthur Okun wrote so eloquently in his celebrated essay by that title.[3]

Despite these claims, many commentators remain highly skeptical of the voucher's virtues, and are unwilling to see the voucher as following, rather than shaping, government's underlying goals. For them, the voucher is deeply hostile to a compassionate welfare state. Vouchers are regarded as implying the unalloyed triumph of individualism over community, of markets over governments, of private greed over public obligation, and of consumerism over citizenship. Vouchers, on this view, do not promise more efficient, more dynamic, or more accountable public services, but only fewer public services, of a lower quality, and overseen by smaller and more mean-spirited governments.[4]

The depth of the antipathy to the voucher instrument cannot be exaggerated. In many cases, the mere identification of a new program initiative with the voucher, particularly where the voucher is designed to substitute for existing programs that involve direct government provision of goods and services, is sufficient to provoke considerable public consternation. In fact, in many cases, the intensity of public opposition to proposed voucher programs has forced sponsoring governments to abandon the idea altogether. And, in those cases where vouchers have been adopted, sponsoring governments have often done so only after overcoming stiff, sometimes excoriating, political opposition and, even then, find that they are often constrained in establishing programs large enough to reap the benefits of competition. We can illustrate these points by reference to a number of different voucher initiatives.

Vouchers and politics

Primary and secondary school vouchers

Without doubt, the most intense and protracted debate over vouchers has been in relation to elementary and secondary school choice experiments in the United States. Over the years, governments from Colorado to Florida have drafted and, in several cases, enacted legislation implementing choice programs, and, in the course of so doing, have confronted virulent opposition. For instance, in 1993, a coalition against Proposition 174 in California, which would have introduced education vouchers, waged a US$6 million television advertising war against the proposed state legislation, leading to its eventual defeat. Despite widespread support for greater school choice and general recognition of the failures of the public education system, particularly in inner-city areas, polls revealed antipathy among suburbanites towards the voucher concept on the grounds that it would "import to the suburbs the problems of *ghetto* and *barrio* education."[5]

While various stakeholder groups, like the National Education Association, a major teachers' labour union, have been active in lobbying against voucher initiatives,[6] the legislature is not the only forum for their activities. Courts, too, have been an important site for opposition to vouchers, where opponents have alleged that proposed voucher programs violate the Constitution's non-establishment clause because public funds will ultimately be directed towards sectarian institutions. Vouchers have also been challenged on the basis of their inconsistency with state constitutional requirements. A *Wall Street Journal* editorial wryly frames an emerging pattern: "As surely as night follows day, education reformers can expect that any expansion of school choice will be followed by a lawsuit."[7]

Primary and secondary school vouchers have fared no better in our home province, Ontario. In 2001, when the Conservative government of Premier

Michael Harris introduced a budget that proposed partial subsidization of private school education at both the primary and secondary level through an "Equity in Education Tax Credit" (essentially a flat-rate voucher), the public response was swift and determined.[8] A broad cross-section of journalists, politicians, policy-makers and union leaders contended that the "Harris Agenda" was tantamount to the destruction of public education.[9] The claim was made that the government's initiative would "erase a 100 year history of support for public schooling."[10] Further, the program was characterized as sectarian, elitist, segregationist and socially corrosive. The Chief Commissioner of the province's Human Rights Commission went so far as to warn that the voucher program would "ghettoize the education of our children."[11] Interestingly, in defending the measure, the government studiously refused to characterize the program as a voucher for fear of further heightening public hostility.[12] Although the measure was adopted, one year later, the Conservative government was defeated and the incoming Liberal government abolished the program retroactively.

Post-secondary vouchers

The university reform programs recently introduced in Australia (1996) and Britain (2003–4) are also indicative of the daunting political challenges surrounding vouchers. In both cases, incumbent governments were seeking to address problems of deteriorating program and facility quality that had long afflicted publicly financed universities.[13] They did so by relaxing longstanding restrictions on tuition pricing, while simultaneously adopting a voucher-based system of conditional grants and income contingent loans.[14] As we will discuss later in the book, there are strong efficiency and equity arguments that favour students paying higher fees for their university educations, particularly in light of the significant private benefits that are derived from these opportunities. The critical issue is how to ensure that students from financially disadvantaged families, who are traditionally under-represented in universities, are not deterred from applying to, and enrolling in, university as a result of higher tuition fees. Vouchers in the form of means-tested grants and income contingent loans are certainly a plausible way of responding to this concern. Nevertheless, in both countries, tuition de-regulation, coupled with vouchers, provoked considerable public outrage.

In Australia, the reforms unleashed a hailstorm of student protest, described by the press as "scenes of rage."[15] Students alleged that the reforms were designed to limit access to university education to only the most advantaged members of society. The reforms were viewed as part of a slippery slope towards privatization. In response, some student leaders urged "militant action" as it was "the only way we are going to be able to achieve our aims … boycotting upfront fees next year, shutting down the administration and not allowing them to process results or to process applications."[16] In fact, students did storm university offices, occupied senior administrative offices, and engaged in walk-outs to protest the reforms. Further, the National Tertiary Education Union council funded an intensive campaign against the sitting government, which included "a national strike, the targeting of certain marginal seats, protests, endorsements and polling."[17]

The situation was not much different in Britain when the Blair government introduced its university reform program. As in Australia, the reforms led opponents to charge that British higher education was becoming elitist because higher education would be priced out of reach of financially needy students.[18] Not only was there criticism and protests from students, but, significantly, there was vehement opposition from within the ranks of Blair's Labour Party. Indeed, so intense was the internal opposition to the reform package that there was speculation (prior to the vote in the House of Commons) that the government may well be defeated over the measure. Although the bill passed on the first reading, it did so only narrowly – by 5 votes as against the government's usual margin of 161 votes, inflicting significant damage on the Prime Minister's reputation and on the cohesiveness of the Labour Party.[19]

Housing vouchers

In the United States, the Clinton administration faced similar challenges with the voucher when it sought to place greater reliance on housing vouchers, as opposed to government owned housing, in meeting the needs of the urban poor. Section 8 housing vouchers were originally introduced by the Nixon administration, and have been a "staple of federal housing policy for three decades."[20] The Clinton administration sought to expand the program by increasing the number of voucher allocations designated for rental (300,000 vouchers) and ownership subsidization (50,000 vouchers).[21] At the same time, the administration proposed demolishing some of the worst public housing in its portfolio. The administration argued that vouchers would promote more efficient delivery of subsidized housing, while encouraging more socio-economically and racially integrated neighborhoods.[22] Nevertheless, the expansion of the voucher program was criticized for its adverse impact on established communities[23] and for its naïve reliance on the markets. Critics claimed that the voucher program would increase homelessness or unsafe living conditions. One critic likened the voucher program to the "beginning of a national policy of racial cleansing."[24] Another observed that: "People are excited and worried about this (voucher) issue … It'll force more people on the street, and that means more of everything – more crime, more insurance, more money needed for other social programs."[25]

Refugee vouchers

The British Labour government's recent experience with vouchers earmarked for social services for refugees constitutes another case in which political opposition subverted the adoption of the program. In that case, the government wanted to replace cash subsidies designed to subsidize the provision of social services to refugee claimants with a voucher entitlement. The proposal faced effective opposition from a broad cross-section of British interest groups, who were concerned about the magnitude of the voucher entitlement (set at 70 percent of the poverty level) and the stigma associated with presenting vouchers for food in supermarkets.[26] Vouchers were viewed as an insidious form of racial segregation because "refugees will be the foreign-looking ones holding up the queue (in the grocery store), getting free stuff."[27] Vouchers would make some "of society's most vulnerable groups even more exposed to potential hostility."[28] In reaction to the initiative, a number of boycotts and protests were launched, and several NGOs declined to participate in the proposed scheme.[29] By 2002, the government was forced to revoke the scheme and to return to a system of cash benefits.[30]

Health care

Indeed, it is noteworthy that even when proposed voucher initiatives are responsive to normatively compelling public policy concerns that are not being addressed through some other instrument, the political challenges confronting these programs are not trivial. The ill-fated Clinton managed health care initiative (the Health Security Act (HSA)) illustrates this point. In his first week in office, President Clinton inaugurated the Task Force on Health Care Reform, chaired by Hillary Clinton. In a few months, the Task Force had drafted the HSA, a massive bill of some 1,500 pages. The HSA would provide universal coverage for all Americans not already privately insured, employer mandates requiring employers to provide coverage to their employees, and allow for the formation of alliances under which groups of companies could purchase policies collectively, thus ostensibly reaping bulk discounts.[31] Whilst allowing alliances and individual employers their choice of insurers, the HSA also stipulated certain minimum comprehensive coverage standards in the form of a "benefits package," including (among many other items) "hospital services, services of health professionals, emergency and ambulatory medical and surgical services, clinical preventive services, mental health and substance abuse services."[32] The HSA provided flexibility for state governments and employers, including the option (for states) of going to a single-payer system, and (for corporations) of forming alliances with other bulk insurance purchasers. It also represented a (highly regimented) tied demand-side subsidy scheme, assuring low-income Americans the same choice of health care providers available to all other insured persons – albeit not the same choice of insurers.[33]

Despite the fact that the program would have provided health care coverage for all Americans not having health care insurance, the program was uniformly opposed by Republicans and even by many conservative and liberal members of the President's Democratic party.[34] The acrimonious and divisive debate over the HSA in Congress was mirrored by a similarly heated debate in public *fora*. The Health Insurance Association of America, concerned about the increased liability they would face due to restrictions on refusing high-risk clients and the costly comprehensive minimum coverage rules, unleashed a multi-million dollar television advertising campaign condemning the bill, a campaign that stretched on for nearly 10 months.[35] Physicians, largely alienated from the HSA drafting process and concerned about the delegation of health-related decision-making powers "from MDs to MBAs,"[36] also opposed the bill.[37] The US Chamber of Commerce, the National Association of Manufacturers and the National Federation of Independent Business, and a Business Roundtable of some 300 businesses of various sizes, all concerned about the costs of the employer mandate portion of the HSA, directed their support, and their lobbying resources, behind a much more modest initiative.[38] As a consequence of these efforts, as well as of the war of rhetoric accompanying the bevy of competing alternative bills, public interest in health care reform gradually eroded and gave way to cynicism and confusion.[39] By the spring of 1994, only 12 percent of Americans expected to see a net gain for themselves under reform "through some combination of lower costs and increased quality of care."[40]

Although there is little doubt that the HSA suffered from critical design problems, including, ironically, a tendency for excessively centralized decision-making and planning, nevertheless, the role played by vested interests, ranging from physicians' groups to business lobbies, in scuppering the HSA and its voucher-based initiatives should not be underestimated. As one commentator noted, the single most intractable obstacle to health care reform was the limited political support for a program perceived to be inherently redistributive, i.e. predicated on moving resources from higher wealth quintiles to lower.[41]

The promise of vouchers

In all of these cases, vouchers became a lightning rod for public disaffection with policy reform. In fact, the intensity of the political reaction to contemporary voucher proposals was predicted by Friedman several decades ago. Friedman viewed the voucher as a demonstrably superior form of delivery of public goods and services, but lamented the dismal prospects for its adoption as a result of concerted opposition from various stakeholder groups, mainly public sector unions, whose welfare would be adversely affected by shifting from monopoly public provision to competitive delivery of publicly financed goods and services by private actors. In accordance with the dictates of classic public choice analysis, vouchers would fail in the political market given the power and interests of concentrated and incumbent public suppliers as against the scattered and uncoordinated interests of prospective suppliers and consumers of voucher-based services.[42]

We do not wish to entirely dismiss Friedman's bleak prediction as to the political economy challenges confronting policy-makers contemplating adoption of the voucher instrument. Vouchers, particularly when they unseat (or, at least, threaten to unseat) existing public suppliers and complementary bureaucracies will elicit formidable and vocal political opposition. Nevertheless, while acknowledging the existence of political economy constraints, we do not subscribe to the view that policy-makers and citizens more generally will always succumb to them. When artfully implemented, democracies have proven themselves remarkably adept at surmounting concentrated and articulate interests in the service of adopting welfare-enhancing policy reforms. Accordingly, we think that there is good reason for believing that if sponsoring governments demonstrate appropriate and sincere fidelity to legitimate public policy goals both in their design and implementation of voucher programs, then the prospects for government by voucher are promising.

We argue in this book that the degree of congruence between efficiency and equity that government by voucher promises critically depends on a number of central design issues that arise in any voucher program, the resolution of which is likely to prove both technically complex and politically and normatively highly contentious and which explain, in large part, why government by voucher has not yet proven to be the panacea to important policy concerns that voucher proponents have often represented it to be. More specifically, we argue that voucher systems cannot eliminate the tension between efficiency and equity but only change the nature of the trade-offs. We argue, as well, that movement from a system of direct governmental provision to one in which private suppliers compete to earn citizen patronage turns out not to be an unalloyed triumph of markets over politics, but rather a more complex policy shift in which markets are substituted for politics in only certain dimensions and politics assumes a larger role in other dimensions, in particular in the financing and regulatory roles of government even where it has withdrawn from its role as direct provider.

This argument is developed in several stages. In this chapter, we discuss the context for the voucher instrument by reviewing briefly the various goals that undergird the modern welfare state. In Chapter 2, we examine the design challenges for government in mounting voucher programs. In particular, we draw on the insights of agency theory and incomplete contracts to illuminate the various challenges that government confronts in the delivery of social services. Against this backdrop, we then proceed to discuss the voucher against other policy instruments, and focus on the various design challenges that inhere in establishing principled and workable voucher programs. In Chapters 3 through 10, we pursue the technical and normative complexities raised by these central design issues by examining them in a wide range of specific programmatic contexts. These programs cover many important social services, although they by no means exhaust the actual or potential domains of voucher systems. We also do not explore systematically the inherent limits of voucher systems in ensuring access to public goods or services: the natural monopoly characteristics of some public goods or services, e.g. national defense, highways, airports, which may render irrelevant voucher systems that critically depend on fostering demand-side choice and supply-side competition; in other cases even though supply-side competition is feasible, we do not want demand-side choice, e.g. correctional services. However, in order to render our domain of inquiry tractable, we have confined our focus to the major social programs reviewed herein. Chapter 11 draws together some conclusions from our programmatic reviews for the critical design issues raised by all voucher systems.

The goals of the welfare state

What is the normative case for the panoply of programs and policies associated with the modern welfare state? Although the precise contours of the social welfare state, and the goals which animate it, are contestable, we believe that a careful review of the normative literature surrounding the welfare state, as well as consideration of the policies that have actually been adopted in a number of industrialized economies, evidences support for the five following ends or goals of the welfare state:

1   Regulation of public morality.
2   Building social solidarity.
3   Insuring individual risk.
4   Promoting economic stability.
5   Providing an equitable distribution of resources.

Regulation of public morality

The initial function of social welfare programs was to regulate public morality. Until the beginning of the twentieth century, it was a commonly held view that socio-economic disadvantage was an effect, rather than a cause, of social problems. Moral failings, lack of self-motivation and poor education were counted among the causes of this disadvantage.[43] In England, the consequence of this view was that social services for the poor provided under the Poor Law were separated from those available to other citizens. The services were to be unattractive in order to make dependence on them unappealing,[44] thereby providing an incentive for the poor to abandon an immoral lifestyle. In this two-tiered system, the class of "paupers" was denied the rights and privileges of ordinary citizens. Marshall points out in *Citizenship and Social Class* that the British Poor Law was not about the protection of citizens, but about creating a separate class of the "poor" who had fallen below the level of citizenship:

> The Poor Law treated the claims of the poor, not as an integral part of the rights of the citizen, but as an alternative to them – as claims which could be met only if the claimants ceased to be citizens in any true sense of the word. For paupers forfeited in practice the civil rights of personal liberty, by internment in the workhouse, and they forfeited by law any political rights they might possess. [...] The stigma which clung to poor relief expressed the deep feelings of a people who understood that those who accepted relief must cross the road that separated the community of citizens from the outcast company of the destitute.[45]

The result of the label of moral inferiority attached to the poor was that there was little government involvement in the delivery of social services. On the European continent, the provision of social services generally fell to family, the community and the Church.[46] The role of the government was confined to a local level, and focused on the control and regulation of the poor, particularly by means of workhouses and the criminal law. These institutions served not only to stigmatize the poor, but also served to emphasize the relative positions of the middle and working classes within the social hierarchy. As Christian Marzahn points out, the workhouses ensured that the free working classes understood their place within this hierarchy by reinforcing certain norms and values:

> At the ideological level, workhouses and prisons demonstrated and spread in a pedagogical manner the orientation and norms which, once internalized by the free working class, made them useful and valuable to the middle classes.[47]

Building social solidarity

A second important goal of the emerging welfare state has been to foster social solidarity and national identity, and reinforce shared or common values. Albert Weale, for instance, regards social solidarity as one of the primary functions of the insurance reforms of Bismarck's Germany. In his view, the provision of state insurance programs tempered the attraction of German socialist movements by demonstrating the benevolence of the German state.[48] In England, promoting social solidarity was one of the principal benefits of state involvement in education. The *Education Act* of 1870 made primary education free, universal and compulsory, and in so doing, it enabled the development of a literate society that was capable of peaceful self-government.[49]

In the United States, the first widespread system of social welfare came about with the creation of Civil War pensions. As Theda Skocpol points out, the impact of the Civil War, which on the Union side alone involved approximately 2,213,000 men,[50] played a substantial role in the development of a social program that eventually expanded to the point where, by 1910, about 28 percent of American men over the age of 65 were receiving benefits.[51] The creation of the Civil War pensions was thus intimately connected to one of the core aspects of the identity of the United States: mass mobilization during the war.[52] A similar nation-defining event – the French Revolution and subsequent Napoleonic Wars – also gave rise to a complex program of pensions in France. In the case of both the United States and France, pensions for war veterans served to structure national identity, but also to reinforce the social value of supporting those who had fought for their country and their dependants.

The role of social programs in reinforcing social cohesion and national identity has continued throughout the twentieth century and is still present today. For instance, Marshall argues that in Great Britain, post-Second World War social programs reflected the unity brought about by the experience in the war as "the Welfare State came to be identified with the war aims of a nation fighting for its life."[53] Likewise, core social programs such as universal health care have come to be the hallmark of Canadian identity.

Insuring individual risk

Another goal of the welfare state is to manage risks to individual citizens.[54] In many cases, government provision of insurance addresses the failure of individual citizens to secure appropriate levels of private insurance for the risks that they confront, and which can inflict serious economic hardship on them in the event that they materialize.[55] There are two principal reasons for this failure. The first is individual misperceptions of risk that reflect incomplete information respecting the nature and magnitude of risks, the limited cognitive ability of individuals to assimilate this information, and, finally, a lack of personal willpower to act on information respecting future risks (even if known and properly interpreted).[56] To the extent that these problems systematically cause individuals to under-insure against non-trivial risks, a role for government is mandated by making certain types of private insurance mandatory, or by providing universal coverage itself.[57]

However, even if individuals were able to accurately assess the true level and character of risk, and would seek to secure appropriate levels of insurance against these risks, there is no assurance that the desired levels of insurance will be available. Insurance markets are characterized by endemic information problems. Insurers have difficulties identifying the true risk profile of each insured and insureds, who typically have better information on their risk profile than insurers, face incentives to misrepresent this risk in order to secure a lower premium. This is often referred to as the problem of adverse selection. Indeed, in the face of an actuarially fair premium for a general class of insureds (both high and low risks), low-risk insureds (i.e. those insureds whose expected loss is lower than the premium) will decline to purchase the insurance contract, and the level of risk borne by the insurer in relation to the premium charged for the remaining insureds will increase. In extreme, this process continues until the insurer will decline to offer any insurance to a specified class of risks for fear of insuring only high-risk insureds ("lemons") at economically insufficient premium levels.

In contrast to private insurance schemes, public insurance programs facilitate mandatory pooling of insurers (both high and low risk), which attenuates the scope for unraveling as a result of successive rounds of exit by low-risk insureds. Old-age pension schemes are a good example of how the state can pool risk across the whole population in spite of the fact that some citizens will live longer than others. What makes the insurance scheme function effectively is the predictability of the average life-expectancy for the population and the assurance that adverse selection will be countered by universal participation.

Promoting economic stability

Another public goal embedded in social welfare policies and programs is the promotion of economic stability. By and large, recognition of, and support for, the role of government in deploying social welfare as an instrument for economic stabilization can be traced to the devastating harm suffered by citizens during the Great Depression. In particular, the depth and magnitude of the Depression caused economists to reconsider whether economic instability and not economic stability was the norm.[58] The classical view had been based on an economic model which considered the business cycle to be capable of self-correction, with a natural equilibrium point of full production and employment.[59] As it became apparent that economic downturns were more common than had been previously thought, receptivity grew to the desirability of government economic intervention.[60] Indeed, "[i]t was realized that social policy must be conceived as allied to general economic policy, and not as a separate area of political action governed by principles peculiar to itself."[61] This shift towards viewing social policy as an instrument of economic stabilization was reflected in the establishment of government works projects, whose purpose was to inject money directly and indirectly into the economy.

Providing an equitable distribution of resources

As T.H. Marshall famously argued, a central goal of welfare is the promotion of equal citizenship. For Marshall, citizenship meant focusing not only on civil rights, which secure the ability of the *individual* to advocate for greater entitlements, but also on social rights, which are achieved when *groups* exercising political power claim an "absolute right to a certain standard of civilization which is conditional only on the discharge of the general duties of citizenship."[62] According to Marshall, this claim for social rights is primarily aimed at eliminating the "nuisance of destitution in the lowest ranks of society."[63]

During and after the Second World War, this distributional claim was given increasing recognition by industrialized democracies. For instance, in 1942, the British *Beveridge Report* (1942) argued that "[s]ocial insurance should aim at guaranteeing the minimum income needed for subsistence."[64] By ensuring uniformity of contributions and benefits among all citizens, the risks of particular industries could be distributed across all sectors, and social services could be accessed based on need, rather than by means-testing.[65] The system proposed by Beveridge, however, encompassed more than just the alleviation of unemployment. It was aimed at the five "giants on the road of reconstruction," which included: want, disease, ignorance, squalor and idleness.[66]

Conclusion

Our brief review of the various rationales for public intervention in the modern welfare state underscores a central point for our study of the prospects for government by voucher, namely that, despite the oft-made and illogical connection between means and ends, there is, in fact, no innate or inexorable linkage between certain ends of the welfare state and instrument choice. Public subsidies on the demand-side and private delivery of services on the supply-side can respond at least as well as public provision to all of the goals that have been enveloped by the social welfare state. Indeed, as we shall see, in many cases, it can be demonstrated that private provision of publicly financed goods and services is superior on a number of different dimensions to conventional public provision. We now turn to a systematic exploration of this issue.

2 The case for vouchers

Introduction

This chapter will survey the intellectual origins of the voucher concept. It will begin with the somewhat contentious matter of defining vouchers, and will then compare the voucher system with the continuum of alternatives – purely public provision or supply-side subsidization on the one hand and untied tax-and-transfer policies on the other. Our primary claim, as stated earlier, is that choice on the demand-side and competition on the supply-side, with public money following consumers, not suppliers, is often the most effective way of providing social services (relative to public provision or supply-side subsidies). To the extent that this claim is not borne out by the evidence in particular programmatic contexts, this is often because of design failures, hence underscoring the importance of taking design challenges more seriously than has often been the case.

The perspective of our comparison will be that of incomplete contracts, and our approach will be to examine the different modes of social service provision in terms of the networks of contractual relationships which undergird them, including those between the government, its citizen-consumers, and service providers, be they public agencies or private contractors.[1] Many of the problems relating to inefficient and poor quality delivery of services under different modes, whether semi-private or purely public, originate in these contractual relationships, and a contractual perspective helps to illuminate why voucher programs have the potential to work better than their alternatives in certain domains, particularly those in which a wide range of consumer choices and strong incentives towards efficient and innovative service are especially desirable. Finally, we will conclude with a general discussion of the design challenges alluded to in our secondary claim.

Defining vouchers

It is widely held that the concept of a voucher system – the use of a state-funded demand-side subsidy to purchase social goods in a competitive market as an alternative to pure public provision of such goods – was pioneered by Milton Friedman, notably in his seminal 1962 work *Capitalism and Freedom*, where he outlines a limited voucher scheme for education.[2] In point of fact, as Mark Blaug observes,[3] the education voucher concept and the use of the particular term 'voucher' to denote it appeared a few years earlier, in a 1959 article by J. Wiseman for the *Scottish Journal of Political Economy*,[4] and the education voucher was even tendered as a serious proposal in the French parliament of the 1870s.[5]

Although Wiseman appears to have coined the use of the term "voucher" to refer to demand-side subsidies, tracing the origins of the voucher concept itself is greatly complicated by the fact that, as Blaug notes, when it comes to vouchers, "it all depends on what you mean,"[6] since, in Bradford and Shaviro's words, "there are no platonic vouchers."[7] Does the Canadian health care system, where the government is billed directly for health services without any financial exchange between provider and consumer, constitute a voucher scheme? Are co-payment plans for higher education voucher schemes? Should taxable benefits be regarded as voucher mechanisms? None of these questions can be answered by comparing the case in point against an established standard of "voucher-ness."

The debate over the definition of "voucher" is not of crucial import, since in a public policy context, what matters most is what a particular plan actually does or is likely to do. Nor, as it is important to remember, did voucher programs themselves originate from scholarly debate about vouchers. Rather, numerous voucher-like programs, such as food stamps and rent subsidies in various jurisdictions in the United States and health insurance and legal aid in Ontario, predate the contentious debate touched off by education vouchers.

In any debate, however, it is useful to have a working definition of what is being disputed, and to this end a number of scholars have attempted to develop a model for identifying and classifying voucher schemes. Blaug proposes a "voucher tree," with "limited, fixed-value" coupons redeemable against uniform fees at the summit and "unlimited, supplementable," fee-indexed and income-scaled vouchers at the base (see Figure 2.1).[8] Barr defines vouchers generally as social good provision plans where production and choice about individual consumption are private, while finance is entirely, or almost entirely, public.[9]

It is often taken for granted, as in Barr and Blaug, that voucher schemes assume private "production." However, Shaviro and Bradford provide an expanded definition which includes systems in which vouchers are redeemed in a market of competing public providers, such as a scheme where public schools are "de-zoned" and must then compete for student enrollment. According to Shaviro and Bradford's more flexible definition, vouchers are policy programs which tend to possess, in varying degrees, four "voucher-like" characteristics: grant[s] to consumers based on personal or household characteristics; intermediate choice (some choice within the "favored category," such as between schools, doctors and alternative expenditures that fit the definition of medical care); supplier competition (the allowance of competition between suppliers); and declining marginal rate of reimbursement (it is argued that uncapped programs are not considered as providing vouchers).[10] Perhaps the most flexible definition of all is proffered by Bridge, who characterizes vouchers as "limited authorizations to spend public funds."[11]

Like Bridge, we favour a straightforward and inclusive definition of the voucher, and have chosen to define a voucher as a *tied demand-side subsidy*, where public dollars follow consumers rather than suppliers, with the objective of fostering competition

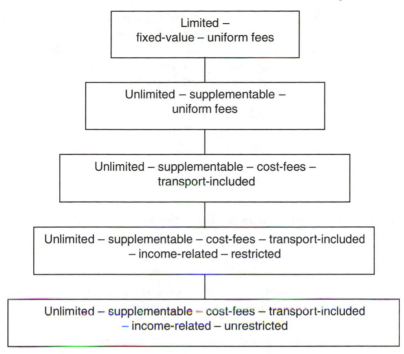

Figure 2.1 One proposed model for comparing different voucher schemes: Blaug's "voucher tree"

on the supply-side and choice on the demand-side in order to improve efficiency in the delivery of classes of social goods and services, and enhance autonomy on the part of consumers of those goods and services. By "tied," we mean that the voucher can only be redeemed to purchase a particular class of good or service – it is not "cashable," and may be subject to other restrictions as well. For instance, food stamps in the United States may not be spent on restaurant food or on alcohol. By "demand-side," we emphasize that vouchers are intended to improve consumer choice by providing them with the purchasing power and the ability to influence the supply-side of the market and the "menu" of services provided to meet their evolving wants and needs. This creates both supply- and demand-side incentives: suppliers must compete for the "voucher dollar," thus providing encouragement for more efficient, responsive, innovative and high-quality service, while consumers have an incentive to make more informed and cost-effective decisions about their choice of provider. On our definition, vouchers can be universal, but need not be; they can be progressive (i.e. inversely related to income), but can also be flat; they can be supplemented ("topped up" with private funds to purchase goods beyond the value of the voucher) or comprehensive; and they can be fixed, capped or proportionate to fees, depending on what design challenges are presented in each context.

Our definition, like any other, is not without its shortcomings. It will no doubt exclude some voucher-like programs, and include others (such as the Canadian health care system) which Bradford, Shaviro and others do not consider voucher-like. We contend, however, that it manages to capture what is unique, from a policy innovation perspective, about voucher initiatives: their emphasis on consumer choice and on improved efficiency in the supply of a limited set of goods or services. As such, our definition responds to the two main arguments against pure public provision: the inefficiency of monopoly public provision, and the lack of consumer choice. Since these criticisms are precisely why options like voucher schemes are being sought out as alternatives to pure government provision, a definition which addresses them directly is both appropriate and timely.

Contractual relationships and the delivery of social services

The context

As Osbourne and Gaebler have observed, since the birth of the welfare state "political debate in America [and, indeed, elsewhere] has centered on questions of ends: what government should do, and for whom."[12] However, these questions are now eclipsed by intense debate about the ability of the government to actually meet these ends; that is, to do what it and the electorate to whom it is ostensibly responsible have decided to do. The perceived crisis, according to Osbourne and Gaebler is that while "we have new goals [...] our governments cannot seem to achieve them. The central failure of government today is one of *means*, not *ends*,"[13] a failure which the instrumental use of private providers through contracting-out, voucher programs and other policy alternatives is hoped to rectify. A strong formulation of the case for private provision is offered by Shleifer, who considers that:

> [t]he benefits of private delivery – regulated or not – of many goods and services are only beginning to be realized. Health, education, some incarceration, some military and police activities, and some of what now is presumed to be "social" insurance like Social Security, can probably be provided more cheaply and attractively by private firms. It is plausible that 50 years from now, today's support for public provision of these services will appear as *dirigiste* as the 1940s arguments for state ownership of industry appear now. A good government that wants to further "social goals" would rarely own producers to meet its objectives.[14]

Despite Shleifer's strong rhetoric, the idea that private firms can do a better job of delivering social goods than the state and that governments are better at "steering" rather than "rowing" is not a partisan contention, but rather one around which many commentators from both the left and the right have converged to varying degrees. Even certain contemporary socialists have rejected the very idea of a command economy.[15] So persuasive is the idea of public-private partnerships that Martha Minow chose the following secondary title for her recent article on the topic: "Accounting for the New Religion."[16]

A rather different justification for the limited withdrawal of government from the business of producing social goods and services is provided by Cass, who argues that government providers and their private counterparts actually pursue fundamentally different objectives. "In essence," contends Cass, "private enterprise is used to produce goods and services cost effectively and public enterprise is used to produce in-kind wealth transfers cost effectively."[17] That is, public providers have a certain wealth redistribution and income equalization mandate which does not apply to private suppliers and which may compromise their ability to deliver particular social goods in a cost-effective manner. Correspondingly, private providers' focus on cost makes them unsuitable for effectuating wealth transfers. On this argument, private enterprises and public enterprises are better suited for different tasks and should not be thought of as competing alternatives. It is important not to assume that the case for privatization is a *fait accompli*.[18] But the case for at least exploring a reduced role for government in the actual provision of social goods and for the instrumental use of private providers (both for- and non-profit) in this regard seems clear.

This new paradigm is often called "privatization," but the term is construed in so many radically different ways that, in the context of any debate about it, it is always imperative to ask "what kind of privatization?" Barr's overview of private versus public provision schemes reveals not a binary opposition of "public" and "private" but a continuum, with varying degrees of privatization from one end to the other. He compares different provision schemes according to four different features: production, regulation of production, decisions about individual consumption and finance (see Table 2.1). As Barr's account helps to illustrate, grouping different plans under the single rubric of "privatization" often conflates significant distinctions with respect to these and other features. There are substantial differences between programs which use tax dollars to purchase services from private contractors, and those in which consumers must use their own personal income to purchase social goods in a private market; yet both are forms of privatization.

The rhetoric of comparative efficiency, however, obscures some important structural differences between public and private modes of delivery, differences which we consider can be best understood from the point of view of the network of contracts alluded to earlier. Rather than viewing public and private provision as inherently either more or less efficient, we consider it important to recognize that public services are goods which must be contracted for, and that contractual relationships possible under public provision and privatization differ insofar as they are able to provide different incentives for and control over (or accountability for) outcomes. These differences in turn give rise to qualitative and quantitative differences between the public and private provision of social services. A detailed analysis of these contractual relationships will provide us with a more sophisticated understanding of why some provision schemes are more successful than others, and what drawbacks the various modes of delivery actually present.

Table 2.1 Tabular comparison of different degrees of public and private provision: Barr's "Public and private provision: a more compltex view"

Type of allocation	Production	Regulation		Finance	Examples
	(1)	Decision about total production (2)	Decision about individual consumption (3)	(4)	
1. Pure private	PRIVATE	PRIVATE	PRIVATE	PRIVATE	Food purchased out of non-transfer income
2. Private market pluse state finance (income subsidy)	Private	Private	Private	Public	All consumption of privately financed goods purchased out of transfer income: food stamps, Medicare and Maedicaid (USA)
3. Private market plus regulation					
(a) regulation of individual consumption	Private	Private	Public	Private	Mandatory automobile insurance
(b) regulation of total suppply	Private	Public	Private	Private	Health care (Canada approx.)
4. Private production, state regulation and finance					
(a) supply wholly private	Private	Private	Public	Public	Education vouchers
(b) total supply determined by state	Private	Public	Public	Public	Inputs for NHS and national defence
5. Public production, private allocation and finance					
(a) total supply determined by private demand	Public	Priavte	Private	Private	Public transport
(b) supply wholly public	Public	Public	Private	Private	NHS pay beds
6. Public apart from private finance	Public	Public	Public	Private	National insurance (UK), health-care insurance (Canada approx)
7. Public apart from private consumption decision	Public	Public	Private	Public	Post-compulsory education
8. Pure public	PUBLIC	PUBLIC	PUBLIC	PUBLIC	NHS, national defence

The perspective of incomplete contracts

According to Hart, Shleifer and Vishny, all contracts between governments and providers, be they public ministries or private firms, are incomplete: it is not possible to specify fully certain elements of the desired outcomes.[19] Moreover, because externalities (the unintended but consequent positive or negative effects on those outside the contract, e.g. the general public) cannot always be taken account of in a contractual agreement, some publicly important dimensions of a transaction cannot be contracted for. For instance, one recurrent objection to the privatization of public services is its potential cost to societal cohesion, a value so ephemeral that it can hardly be safeguarded by a clause in a contract. The incompleteness of contracts also makes it difficult to achieve certain policy objectives, such as a guarantee that public services will remain universally available and accessible.

A contractual perspective also explains other problems in the delivery of social services. On this view, for instance, the problem of efficiency originates in the impossibility under certain contractual arrangements of providing proper incentives to either or both parties – the provider and the consumer – to produce or consume efficiently. The lack of innovation in the menu of public services can also be seen as a consequence of the failure to provide adequate contractual incentives for innovation, as well as of the very structure of certain contractual arrangements, as for example in situations where the precise terms of service provision must be negotiated *ex ante* and cannot change to meet the actual preferences of consumers.

Agency costs

There are also a set of challenges called *principal–agent problems*: scenarios in which one party (the agent) acts on behalf of another (the principal), such as when a government (the agent) contracts with a private company to provide services to consumers (the principals). In such scenarios, problems will arise for two major reasons: it is impossible for even the most well-informed agent to have complete knowledge of the principal's interests and preferences; and the preferences of principal and agent may be divergent, sometimes radically so.[20] The former problem is sometimes described (most famously by Friedman[21]) as *paternalism*; that is, the arrogation to the agent of the right to decide what is in the best interests of a rational and self-aware principal who may actually be in a far better position to discern what is best insofar as his or her own welfare is concerned. The latter problem can manifest itself in a variety of forms, from the development of policies which are unpalatable to consumers, to overt conflicts of interest, such as patronage and bribery.

Modes of accountability

As serious as certain principal–agent conflicts can be, a variety of mechanisms or *modes of accountability* operate in both the public and private sectors to align the interests of principals and agents. These mechanisms become particularly important in scenarios which are not explicitly covered by the terms of contract. However, these mechanisms are not all equally effective, and can give rise to agency costs, such as "the cost of structuring the contract so as to require the agent to perform the desired service as a proxy for the principal [and] the cost of enforcing the contract."[22] As Trebilcock observes, "[d]ifferent organizational arrangements have different inherent incentive structures that yield different agency costs."[23]

For instance, in organizations with a diffuse body of principals, such as publicly traded companies with a large number of stockholders, the principals face a problem in asserting control over the company, since they can only exert pressure on their agent (the company's management) by acting collectively. At the same time, however, the "market for managers" and the fact that the hiring of management is often based on the track record of candidates with respect to stock performance, can help to align the interests of the principals and their agents.[24] Furthermore, remuneration in the form of stock or stock options creates a direct incentive on the part of management to improve the company's market performance, and the wealth of stockholders along with it. Public enterprises, however, are not as directly affected by management markets, and must rely on still other modes of account- ability, with different forms of agency costs.

Some commentators opine that market-driven modes of accountability are insufficient and that consumers' "dollar votes" or diffuse demand-side pressure will not be enough to ensure that public demands are met in uncontracted-for circumstances. Minow, for instance, is unsure whether democracy will remain vibrant as citizenship is gradually redefined in the direction of "consumership." She poses a number of challenging questions about the civic consequences of privatization:

> If the language of competition and consumption overtakes social provision in education and welfare, what will be the effect on civic commitment? Will people learn to be consumers rather than citizens, with a reduced sense of collective commitment? [...] If the accountability measures do not capture these kinds of effects, then they are not themselves accountable to the public values of democracy, equality, and even public safety. [...] Testing account- ability requirements in the light of public values is not a task to be contracted out to a private enterprise. For it is through the process of participatory inquiry into the values that it uses to govern that the polity constitutes itself.[25]

Trebilcock and Iacobucci, however, respond that "[t]he agency problems that afflict public provision also afflict public accountability mechanisms. Furthermore, public accountability exists for the most part through reliance on certain process values, like the right to hearings and the right to information. [...] Because of this reliance on process, agencies are often free to pursue a substantive agenda that may or may not advance the public interest."[26]

Freeman also offers an alternative view of privatization as the continuation of public accountability through alternative means, offering the possibility of, as the title of her commentary puts it, "extending public law norms through privatization." "Instead of seeing privatization as a means of shrinking government," considers Freeman,

I imagine it as a mechanism for expanding government's reach into realms traditionally thought private. In other words, privatization can be a means of "publicization," through which private actors increasingly commit themselves to traditionally public goals as the price of access to lucrative opportunities to deliver goods and services that might otherwise be provided directly by the state. So, rather than compromising democratic norms of accountability, due process, equality, and rationality – as some critics of privatization fear it will – privatization might extend these norms to private actors through vehicles such as budgeting, regulation, and contract.[27]

Normative questions about the relationship between privatization and democratic accountability are not susceptible to simple solutions, and the debate over the relative merits of public and private modes of accountability is not yet exhausted. Our analysis from the perspective of principal–agency problems, however, allows us to begin to compare both private and public modes of accountability and assess the degree to which they succeed, under different modes of public service delivery, in reconciling the interests of providers (agents) and consumers (principals). It is not that public accountability and private accountability are equivalent, but rather that they present similar challenges when considered from the point of view of principals and agents with both conflicting and congruent interests.

Using the perspective of contractual problems elaborated above, we propose to compare the range of modes of service provision, from pure public provision to tax-and-transfer schemes. It will become apparent that each of these modes will produce different "trade-offs" between the various areas of contractual difficulty. For instance, supply-side subsidies in the form of "contracting out" of services formerly provided directly by the state will be expected to lower agency costs in virtue of the effect of market forces on management behaviour; however, it can be expected to exacerbate certain principal–agent problems, as the interests of the consumer (high-quality services) and the producer (the accumulation of residuals) may be radically divergent. Tied demand-side subsidies represent the preferable alternative in many situations, because of their potential to reconcile the interests of principals and agents, provide strong incentives for efficient delivery and consumption, and reduce the incidence of certain forms of moral hazard. Our analysis will also reveal potential contract problems endemic to voucher arrangements, and discuss possible remedies.

The four principal modes of social service delivery: a critical comparison

Purely public provision

The contractual arrangements which undergird purely public provision are rather complex. Since the government arranges for the provision of services and contracts for them on the behalf of its citizen-consumers, it takes on the role of agent with respect to them as principals. At the same time, however, it is also the principal in another relationship: its contract with the agency, employees or union which will actually be providing the service, who acts as its agent in the transaction.

In situations where the services are provided by an agency which is a department of the same government which is purchasing the service, the state is effectively contracting with itself.[28] This represents a trivial solution to one set of principal–agent problems: if the government is both the principal and the agent, the interests of both will always be coterminous. On the other hand, the interests of the consumer-as-principal (which are paramount) and government-as-agent can still diverge, sometimes radically. From the perspective of incomplete contracts, a major drawback of public provision is its inability to provide contractual incentives which can reconcile the latter set of interests.

In the first place, a primary mode of contracting between governments and agents takes the form of employment contracts with civil servants – often collective agreements with public sector workers – contracts which can stipulate inputs (e.g. in the case of public school teachers: salary, hours, duties and basic standards, etc.) but which cannot assure outputs (e.g. quality of teaching, efficient use of time, involvement in extracurricular activities, etc.). Such contracts can often be of fairly long duration, and may not provide adequate mechanisms for disciplining unsatisfactory performance.

In the second place, government employees have no claim on residuals arising from efficient "production." As Trebilcock and Iacobucci note, "The government is the residual claimant of its operations [...] Allocating the residual claim to the government, however, does not create incentives in any agent to maximize value."[29] Residuals simply accrue in the form of budget underruns, which cannot ordinarily be "cashed out" for redistribution. While the principal, i.e. the taxpayer, has a personal interest in cost-effective service delivery because of the ultimate effects of waste (rising taxes or the cancellation or reduction of services), the agent does not.

Furthermore, the absence (in most regimes) of markets for the securities of a particular government enterprise makes performance-based compensation incentive schemes, such as stock grants or options, difficult, if not impossible, to implement in the public sector.[30] In fact, under certain budgetary schemes, there is a perverse disincentive against dollar-efficient delivery, since under-budget delivery sometimes results in a commensurate reduction of the budget in the following time period.

As Trebilcock and Iacobucci further illustrate, assuring accountability in uncontracted-for circumstances is problematic under public provision, since control is diffused among a large number of principals (all citizens) who stand to receive only a fraction of the residuals, and can only exert indirect control over an under-performing public agency through their elected representatives.[31] As compared with individual bureaucrats, ministerial officials and elected representatives, consumers have a very limited role in the oversight of services which pertain directly to them and, in some cases, to the quality of their daily lives. As a result, there is little incentive for consumers to assert their preferences vigorously, and little incentive for public agencies to be highly responsive to them. This presents a high likelihood of "incomplete market[s]" – the failure "to provide a good or service even though the cost of providing it is less than what individuals are willing to pay;"[32] that is, markets in which certain services, however much desired or needed by consumers, are not "on the menu," while other undesirable or unsatisfactory services remain on offer.

To remedy these "incentive deficits," more intensive regulation and oversight is often necessary under public provision to assure quality output and cost-effectiveness. As Stiglitz notes, however, bureaucratic vigilance can give rise to another set of constraints on productivity: "restrictions on personnel, procurement and budgeting; [...] [further] principal agent problems, such as the pursuit of bureaucratic objectives; excessively high levels of risk aversion leading to a focus on following procedures (red tape)."[33] Whatever the efficiency outcomes of these measures, however, the basic principal–agent problem endemic to public provision remains: under public provision, the interests of providers and government agents are not strongly aligned with those of consumers as principals, and this is to say nothing of other distortions which need to be considered in the case of public provision, such as the influence of the political interests and ambitions of government officials, and their electoral agendas, forces which have considerable potential to divert full attention from the interests of consumers.

Supply-side subsidies

Supply-side subsidies refer generally to programs in which the state "contracts out" the provision of public services to private companies. Stiglitz cites the example of private adult correctional facilities in the United States, where the government pays a private corporation to operate prisons, often with considerable savings and even "improved" services.[34]

"Contracting-out" is simple in principle, if not always in practice.[35] Essentially, like a firm hiring a web designer on contract or a homeowner looking for the best price on a renovation, the government tenders a contract for a particular service on the open market. Private corporations make offers, and the government chooses the bidder who makes the best offer, according to the relevant criteria. This introduces competitive pressure into the market: contractors have an incentive to lower their dollar costs and to introduce new and more creative services. Innovation can be rewarded. Contractors who fail to deliver do not see their contracts renewed. Those who do not provide a good "product" are never hired, and are forced to "exit" the market. This aspect of market efficiency is often referred to as "the competition effect," which Hrab, following Vickers and Yarrow, defines as:

> the generally held belief that the market discipline provided by competition between firms is conducive to an organization that is customer oriented, efficient, technologically superior and better able and willing to adapt to change [because of] internal efficiency and allocative efficiency as firms seek to lower costs in order to offer a lower price to consumers than competitors and gain market control.[36]

In addition to the operation of competitive pressure, contracting-out creates incentives on the part of the provider in favour of efficient service delivery in the form of residual claims (the "ownership effect"). As Shleifer points out:

> [Ownership of production and distribution assets by the actual provider] gives the owner control and bargaining power in situations where contracts do not specify what has to be done. As a consequence, ownership strengthens the owner's incentives to make investments that improve the ways or reduce the costs of using the assets, because the owner has the power to reap more of the rewards of these innovations [...] An owner of a postal business who invents a better way to deliver mail can implement this innovation and profit from it. In contrast, if the government or someone else owns the business, the inventor needs the agreement of the owner to implement the innovation, and thus must share the benefits of the invention with this owner. Without the bargaining chip provided by ownership, the incentives to invest and innovate are lower.[37]

The transfer of this "bargaining chip" to the private provider creates incentives on the part of the provider to maximize profit through cost-effective delivery, but also provides more discretion to innovate and invest, since the provider now has the authority to make decisions in uncontracted-for circumstances.

Private enterprises also have recourse to more effective means of disciplining managers. Unlike public enterprises, private firms face "hard" budget constraints.[38] Funds must be raised through new equity or debt investment, and if resources are wasted, investment sources will dry up, and the firm will eventually fail.[39] Even private, nonprofit corporations "remain exposed to the risk of being wound up"[40] if they squander resources. Hrab, again following Vickers and Yarrow, refers to the efficiencies arising from "market discipline through product prices, profits, stock prices, [and] the threat of hostile takeover or bankruptcy" collectively as "the ownership effect."[41]

The mechanisms of accountability related to "the ownership effect" help to harmonize the interests of the agents and one principal (the government): governments want dollar-effective delivery; and companies want profit. The profit motive drives down costs to the benefit of the provider, which in turn drive down prices to the benefit of the government. So far, at least, as the government and the provider are concerned, their interests are much the same.

Yet the interests of consumers are not precisely the same as those of the government. While consumers have some stake in cost-effective delivery because of the effect of ballooning costs on taxes, the residual interest of consumers in cheaper service provision remains as limited in this case as it did in the case of pure public provision. In other words, the cost advantages of privatization are, from the perspective of the individual consumer, rather limited. Furthermore, these advantages accrue regressively: citizens with higher incomes who consequently pay more taxes will benefit from tax savings far more than their less wealthy counterparts.

Unlike their government agents, consumers are apt to be deeply and directly concerned about the quality of the actual service delivered because of the direct impact of many services on their quality of life (education and health care furnishing the most obvious examples). This presents a contractibility problem: while it is eminently possible to contract for a guaranteed price, it is not always possible to guarantee the quality of service delivered, or the absence of negative externalities. Nor does the consumers' proxy agent – the government – have perfect incentives to secure such guarantees when contracting with the provider.

In the first place, the consumer cannot withdraw his or her tax dollar if he or she does not find a service contract satisfactory, and thus has no direct means of influencing the market. Furthermore, his or her non-market options in this respect are limited since, as was discussed earlier in the case of pure public provision, his or her control over contracting-out is diffuse and restricted to the channels of representative government. The transfer of provision from government to private firm does nothing to remedy this. In the second place, in the absence of motivated and persistent political pressure, it remains in the government's interest to favour the latter side of the quality–cost trade-off, since it alone has a claim on the residual proceeds of contracting.

As a result, Hart, Shleifer and Vishny (who are otherwise enthusiastic about privatization) argue that external contracting is contraindicated when cost reductions not preventable through contractual specification tend to have a dramatic and negative effect on the quality of service delivered.[42] One possible example is health care, where it is difficult to anticipate and hence contractually guarantee *ex ante* the cost for the care of any given patient. As a result, uncontracted-for spending is at the sole discretion of the private provider, who has a strong financial incentive to opt for the least comprehensive and therefore cheapest treatment option, regardless of its quality-of-life consequences for the particular patient. In the case of services where quality is extremely cost-sensitive, consumers may favour a different quality–cost trade-off than their proxy, yet possess no direct or effective means of asserting this preference.

Furthermore, while Shleifer argues that private ownership tends to favour innovation, he does not distinguish between forms of innovation which improve quality, and those which improve cost efficiency. While it is true that in some services efficiency is a critical element of quality (consider, for instance, courier services, where faster turnaround benefits both customer and firm), there are others where more efficient service comes at a substantial quality cost. Consumers have an interest in having their preferences met; what better incentives does the contracting out of services give to providers to meet those preferences?

This draws attention to another set of contractibility problems. Let us assume, as is likely to be the case with respect to certain services, that the preferences of consumers are heterogeneous – that is, both varied and variable. The terms of a contract between proxy and provider can anticipate some of these preferences *ex ante*; however, any significant change in preferences will effectively represent an uncontracted-for circumstance. The residual control rights in such situations lie with the provider. This creates a principal–agent divergence, since the agent has no profitable interest in meeting the demands of the consumer (since the contract does not stipulate any remuneration for doing so, and the consumer cannot censure an unresponsive provider by "unsubscribing"). As with purely public provision, supply-side subsidies provide no reliable incentive mechanism through which the consumer can influence directly the content of the market to meet his or her changing demands.

Additionally, as Trebilcock notes, contracting out has the potential to create unintended but persistent monopolies:

> [T]here may be so much flexibility built into [a] contract that the firm can adapt to future changes in such a way as to exercise some monopoly power. The resulting bilateral monopoly becomes a more severe problem as the contract lengthens in duration. [Furthermore,] incumbent contract holders often have a considerable advantage at renewal time over their competitors. Government will not want to cause a disruption by changing contractors. [...] It is in a significantly better position at renewal time than its competitors who must start from scratch in bidding for the contract renewal and must purchase all the necessary assets, often from the incumbent if the assets are highly specific.[43]

Such *de facto* monopolies introduce the risk of driving prices back up above competitive levels, and may counteract the cost-effectiveness advantages imputed to supply-side subsidies in the first place.

Finally, contracting out may invite problems of its own in some contexts. For example, Hart, Shleifer and Vishny view the objective function of a number of government activities as sufficiently complex or contingent that precise specification, by contract, legislation, regulation, or otherwise, of objectives and ready monitoring of the achievement of these objectives are infeasible.[44] An extreme example is the formulation and implementation of a country's foreign or defense policy, where the complexity of objectives and unforeseeable contingencies render delegations of these functions to private actors highly problematic. In contexts such as this, it is unclear exactly what is being delegated.

It is important to point out that some policies which appear, in form, to be supply-side subsidies, actually function as *demand*-side subsidies. For instance, a scheme under which consumers select and patronize the service provider of their choice, and the payment for services purchased is made by the state directly to the supplier is a *de facto* demand-side subsidy (voucher) program. The Canadian health care system provides an excellent example of such a system: rather than hiring doctors, or furnishing consumers with health care vouchers, the state reimburses physicians and other health care providers for "covered" services. The "dollar follows the consumer," and choice on the demand-side is the preponderant feature of such a scheme. In such cases, the fact that the consumer does not tender payment him- or herself is merely an "accounting detail." Similarly, in cases of capitated grants to universities based on student enrolment.

Tied demand-side subsidies (vouchers)

Demand-side subsidies aim to align the interests of consumers and providers by giving providers a stronger market-based incentive to be responsive to consumers' preferences, and giving consumers the means to express those preferences. By arranging the payment for social services so that the funding dollar "follows the consumer," only providers who are supplying a desirable product or service at an appropriate price are able to succeed. Those who find they are able to meet the evolving preferences of consumers and make an adequate profit will flourish, while those who cannot do so will exit the market.

From a contractual perspective, demand-side subsidy schemes give rise to a network of *ad hoc* contracts between providers and consumers for the purchase of particular services. The duration of these contracts is likely to be shorter than in the case of supply-side subsidies. For instance, rather than the government hiring a single physician to supply services to an entire locality for a term of 10 years, a voucher scheme in health care might see physicians remunerated on a fee-for-service basis, with contracts lasting only as long as a particular procedure or treatment. The rapid turnover of contracts allows for a higher degree of *competition within the market*, as opposed to contracting-out, where providers engage primarily in *competition for* (an effective monopoly of) *the market*.

To be sure, there are industries where competition within the market is unlikely to be powerfully operative. Stiglitz uses the market for the supply of fresh water as an example,[45] where the massive "sunk costs" in terms of infrastructure (reservoirs, aqueducts and filtration plants) make it wildly impractical for two rival water companies to install parallel sets of pipes to every single residential block and then compete for individual customers. However, such markets exhibit properties of natural monopolies by design, and in such cases, regulation (according to Williamson[46]) or competition for the market (according to Demsetz[47]) are preferable to a voucher approach. In such situations, however, contractual flexibility is neither highly desirable, nor are preferences likely to be highly varied and variable – consumers' tastes with respect to water are apt to be somewhat similar and stable.

Consider, in contrast, the market for education, where consumers are likely to have highly heterogeneous and changing preferences, and where variety and innovation are among the most desirable features of an ideal supply market. In such industries, where sunk costs are lower and demands are more idiosyncratic (some parents want trade schools, other prefer to see their children receive a liberal arts education; some would value a religious education for their child, while others might prefer a strictly secular one), it makes considerable sense to have many providers competing within a market. The high degree of contractual flexibility available to suppliers under a voucher scheme (since suppliers do not need to guarantee anything *ex ante* before bringing their product to market) allows providers to offer any service which they think is likely to sell on the market, subject to whatever limited government regulations are deemed appropriate and necessary.

Where innovation and variety are desirable, it follows that principals are best disposed to make their own choices, since they are usually best informed about their preferences. Voucher schemes eliminate the need for governments to contract for consumers by proxy: the consumers act as their own agent when "negotiating" with providers. In the actual contracting, market forces align the interests of the principal (consumer) and agent (provider): principals have an interest in purchasing a service that meets their preferences; and agents have a direct interest in providing a service that principals will want to purchase. Principals, since they are now responsible for any costs exceeding the value of the voucher, need to make cost-effective decisions, while agents have an interest in minimizing costs in order to maximize residuals. In principle, then, the "bargaining-chip" of ownership discussed in the case of supply-side subsidies is effectively balanced by the "bargaining-chip" of the consumer's dollar-votes. Thus, the contractual interests of principals and agents tend towards closer alignment.

Even in uncontracted-for circumstances, a number of mechanisms exist to reconcile those interests. First and most obviously, since the providers are private firms, the mechanisms of accountability discussed with respect to supply-side subsidies (such as the market for managers, the threat of being "wound-up," and the use of residual claims as incentives for productivity and innovation) will also be operative in the case of demand-side subsidies. As in the case of supply-side subsidies, the ownership effect is operative, and tends to produce more efficient and cost-effective delivery.

Poor service delivery in uncontracted-for scenarios, in addition to dissuading a particular customer from returning, may also damage a provider's reputation in the market at large. Marginal cost cuts after contracting which have an impact on quality are also contraindicated for much the same reason. The need for suppliers to compete for market share (i.e. for loyal customers) creates an incentive for them to favour a cost–quality trade-off which more closely matches the interests of existing and prospective consumers. At the same time, providers are free to modify, innovate and invent new services as long as they anticipate demand for them, and there is the possibility for a competitive market on the basis of new consumer-oriented service innovations (the competition effect).

This is not to say that principal–agent problems cannot arise under voucher schemes. In the case of monopolies, principal–agent problems will be as preponderant as ever (although as was just discussed, voucher schemes are a poor choice in situations where monopolies are likely to arise). Furthermore, the problem of information failures (contingencies wherein consumers lack sufficient information to make decisions which are in their own best interests) may be significant, and providers who are able to manipulate consumer preferences using misleading information or who engage in outright hucksterism or fraud will gain an unfair advantage at the expense of consumers' interests. Finally, there are other cases where the consumer must purchase on behalf of a party who cannot represent his or her own interests – children redeeming a retirement-home voucher on the part of their elderly parents; or parents choosing a school for their own children – where a new set of agency problems arises: how can proxy agents be assured of choosing wisely for their charges? An overt moral hazard problem presents itself when the agent has a residual interest in choosing a lower-cost option for the principal (i.e. when the agent gets to "keep the difference" between the value of the voucher and the cost of the particular service). These design challenges of vouchers represent some of the most legitimate and enduring objections to voucher schemes, and will be discussed in considerable detail in subsequent chapters.

However, the basic advantage of voucher schemes in many situations, and one which we consider to be substantial from the point of view of consumer choice and autonomy, is its allocation of direct purchasing power to consumers to influence markets and obtain services which meet their needs.

Tax-and-transfer policies

The basic design and principle of tax-and-transfer schemes are essentially the same as those of demand-side subsidies. The goal is to reconcile the interests of the agent providing the service and the principal consuming it so as to obtain better cost, efficiency and quality outcomes. Since the market is open to competing businesses, and since those directly involved in providing the services (i.e. owners and their employees) are the residual claimants, both the ownership effect and the competition effect are operative. Moreover, as with voucher subsidies, there is no "proxy bidding": the principal contracts directly with the provider. The critical difference between the two strategies is that demand-side subsidies stipulate that a voucher must be spent on a *particular* class of services (consumers are issued a voucher which is ear-marked for spending on health care, education, etc.) whereas tax-and-transfer allocations are simple cash grants which, like cash, can be spent on any good or service. Under voucher schemes, consumers exert choice *within* a category of services; tax-and-transfer schemes allow them to choose *between* categories as they see fit.

It is worth noting that some *pro forma* vouchers have the properties of *de facto* cash grants, particularly when the good or service for which the voucher is redeemed is cash equivalent. The most salient example is the food stamp program in the United States, in which the cash equivalence of food stamps has occasioned considerable debate over whether food stamps should simply be "cashed out" – replaced with an equivalent cash grant in order to save the costs of administering the stamp scheme. Giving consumers $200 per month worth of food stamps effectively liberates $200 in cash from their monthly food budget, a sum which need not be spent on food.[48] Where voucher instruments exhibit a high degree of cash equivalence (i.e. where they can be used to liberate cash by replacing expenditures in one budget area, or are otherwise easily fungible) they should be regarded as cash grants.

The proclaimed advantage of cash grants is that they provide consumers with the ultimate degree of choice: consumers get exactly, and only, what they want. Friedman, an early defender of untied cash grants for social services, argues the case from the classical, Millsian libertarian point of view that only the individual is directly concerned with his or her own interests and therefore apt to act vigorously in their service and, moreover, "with respect to his own feelings and circumstances, the most ordinary man or woman has means of knowledge immeasurably surpassing those that can be possessed by anyone else."[49]

Discussing cash grants as compared with public housing, for example, Friedman asserts that: "the families being helped would rather have a given sum in cash than in the form of housing. They could themselves spend the money on housing if they so desired. Hence, they would never be worse off if given cash; if they regarded other needs as more important, they would be better off."[50] Bruce Ackerman and Anne Alstott take the same principle to an even more radical conclusion in their book *The Stakeholder Society*,[51] where they propose that every American citizen who has graduated from high school and avoided significant criminal activity would receive an untied flat grant of $80,000, to be spent exactly as he or she sees fit. A putative advantage is that it creates an incentive on the part of the consumer to spend wisely, since he or she can keep the difference, and must pay out of pocket if he or she goes over budget.

There are several major and credible objections to these schemes. The first and most damaging is its political infeasibility. Few legislators, particularly in an era where austerity is the watchword in most jurisdictions, will be eager to champion the idea of cash giveaways. The second objection is that it exposes consumers to the risks of another raft of information failures. Not only can consumers lack the proper information to choose well *within* a service category, but the untied nature of the cash grant means they may also lack enough information to choose *between* services, and to allocate funds from a single grant appropriately to the various areas of expenditure. Cash grants are also objectionable insofar as they blur the distinction between the provision of social services and income equalization. In effect, a cash grant policy replaces the former by expanding the latter. It is questionable, however, whether income equalization alone will necessarily result in universal access to adequate social services.

Finally, there are the obvious outcomes which most would regard as moral hazards: the squandering of the grant on luxury items or alcohol and other drugs. Of course, from a strictly libertarian point of view, none of these can constitute a "moral hazard," since by definition whatever a person prefers is good for them, so anything he or she spends money on is of benefit to him or her.

However, outside of a purely hedonistic calculus (and instead in a framework where we have some common understanding of what sorts of things are, generally speaking, values and harms) it is clear that such abuse of funds runs contrary to the very purpose of social spending. Moreover, one might well have pause to question the rational autonomy of a drug addict or an alcoholic, particularly when that individual is also responsible for the welfare of the children under his or her care. One might also argue that the government has an implicit contractual responsibility to its taxpayers, who agree to provide money for the public good only as long as it is not spent by recipients on things which actively do them harm.

A final and very substantial moral hazard associated with tax-and-transfer schemes is their potential to create a certain degree of dependency. Since there may be low opportunity cost associated with collecting social assistance, there is no incentive for individuals receiving benefits to invest the time and effort in seeking employment or improving their skills. In other words, from a social perspective, recipients have incentives to devote too much time to consumption and too little to production, even if their consumption choices are rational and well-informed. Rather than treating the poverty which is symptomatic of underemployment, it may be preferable for governments to address the "human capital market problem" directly by adopting active labour market policies (ALMPs) that focus on job search facilitation, job training and remedial education.[52]

Richards directly contrasts "active measures" (ALMPs such as subsidized employment and training) with conventional "passive measures" of simple untied cash grants to eligible welfare recipients.[53] Passive transfers, he considers, ignore "the implicit requirement [...] that social policy design pay more attention to incentive effects and actual outcomes,"[54] notably incentives towards active participation in the labour market and financial self-reliance wherever possible (namely, in the case of able-bodied adults). According to Richards, "[w]hat is known about the effect extended reliance on transfer income has on individuals, families, and communities suggests a strong case for more active policies that more aggressively promote employment."[55]

This is not to say that there is no place in the residual welfare state for social assistance or unemployment insurance, or that ALMPs are appropriate to every case. For instance, cyclical unemployment due solely to downturns in the business cycle cannot be eliminated by retraining, and it may be an inappropriate use of funds to retrain persons who will be reemployed in their preexisting line of work in a short period of time. However, the structurally unemployed – those who are unable to find employment because they lack the skills necessary for available job opportunities – are unlikely to find lasting employment without the acquisition of skills that enhance their productivity and abilities, and in such cases, tied transfer policies such as the stipulation that welfare transfers be conditional on participation in ALMPs may be preferable to untied cash grants.

An overview of voucher design challenges

In this section, we address several crucial design issues that implicate the extent to which the adoption of a voucher scheme is likely to enhance societal welfare. The previous sections have addressed our primary claim; here, we elaborate on our secondary claim that the failure of voucher policies in various programmatic contexts will often be due primarily to inattention to a number of recurrent design challenges, a claim which will also be supported in our examination of the empirical evidence in several program areas in subsequent chapters.

These central design issues can be stated quite briefly. They include:

1   whether to provide means-tested or universal programs;
2   determining the qualifications of suppliers who can compete for voucher-assisted customers;
3   determining the value of voucher entitlements;
4   permissibility of extra-billing;
5   permissibility of cream-skimming;
6   information failures;
7   concerns about the inadequacy of supply-side market responses to vouchering, and the possibility that vouchers, under certain conditions, will simply entrench existing monopolies, or create new ones.

Who should qualify for a voucher: means-tested or universal entitlements?

Assuming that a case has been made for some form of state financing, in particular for a tied form of demand-side transfer, a critically important question then arises as to who should qualify, on the demand-side, for the entitlement. Here the central issue is likely to be, in many contexts, whether the entitlement should be a universal entitlement or whether the entitlement should be means-tested. The case for universal versus targeted or means-tested benefits turns on several factors: first, universal benefits may advance values of social solidarity and equality of life chances. Second, universal benefits may be responsive to incomplete private insurance markets by requiring mandatory pooling. Third, where the risks or contingencies to which the government is responding in a particular program in question are borne more or less universally, this may argue for universal benefits. In contrast, if they are focused on identifiable subsets of the population, some form or targeting or means-testing may be appropriate. Fourth, universal benefits may provide a mechanism of political co-option by harnessing the political voice of articulate citizens in order to ensure adequate program benefits for both themselves and the less well-endowed and less articulate.[56] On the other hand, universal benefits, depending on program design, may constrain individual citizens' choice and autonomy and reduce individual welfare by denying choices that may be more fully responsive to individual preferences. Even where the state has opted for a universal entitlement program, this tension will exist with respect to the availability of partial or complete exit options, such as the right to make additional top-up payments beyond the value of the voucher to secure superior packages of services, or alternatively to opt out of the universal entitlement program altogether and secure private provision.

If a universal entitlement is rejected in favour of a targeted or means-tested entitlement, how means are tested is likely to prove contentious: should it entail a static measure of ability to pay or should it also encompass past circumstances that explain present inability to pay or future prospects of ability to pay? Also, should means be extended to non-financial disabilities such as race and gender (viewing, for example, quota-based affirmative action programs as in effect a form of voucher system)? Even conventional income or asset tests raise significant incentive problems. As Bradford and Shaviro point out,[57] an income test creates a moral hazard problem due to the incentive effect of conditioning the grant on income when earning effort cannot be well observed, although income is presumably a signal of some distributionally important underlying attribute such as low wage or bad luck. Income-conditioned vouchers may exacerbate the resulting incentive problems when they are layered on top of each other and other income-conditioned aspects of the overall tax system. The combined effective marginal tax rate in some cases may approach or even exceed 100 percent. With respect to asset tests, liquid asset tests such as those used in the US food stamps program distort both savings decisions and asset choices by consumers. For example, since homes are not included in liquid assets, food stamps provide an incentive to own a home rather than hold liquid assets and pay rent, even though this choice has a weak relationship if any to the distributional purpose of measuring need. These kinds of problems raise concerns over poverty traps that deprive work and saving of their rewards to low-income households. With respect to household composition, the treatment of household status presents another dilemma in means-testing. One person's income or assets may significantly increase the well-being of others in the same household, but determining tax or transfer consequences at the household level may distort decisions as to whether to form a household (or at least one that is observable). Often the incentive effect is to discourage household formation, despite policy aims that may lie in the opposite direction.

Determining the qualifications of suppliers: who can compete for voucher-assisted customers?

Another central design question is that of who should qualify to compete on the supply-side for voucher-supported consumer demands. While the virtues of vigorously competitive markets often depend on relatively unrestricted entry, in many contexts the normative concerns that motivate some form of intervention in the first place, e.g. paternalism or social externalities, are likely to yield some scepticism as to the ability of consumers to make both privately and socially optimal choices in a totally unregulated market, for example, parents who choose to send their children to schools that propagate sedition or religious, sexual, racial, or other forms of discrimination or intolerance. Responding to these concerns is likely to draw the state back into an active role in managing or regulating the supply-side of the market.

What should be the value of voucher entitlements?

Another central design issue relates to the structure of the entitlement: what exactly does a voucher entitle a holder to? If a voucher provides an unlimited claim to the cost of goods or services to which it relates (a marginal rate of reimbursement of 100 percent), then major moral hazard problems are likely to arise on both the supply- and demand-sides of the market in terms of running up bills at taxpayers' expense, which neither suppliers nor demanders have any incentives to resist. Marginal rates of reimbursement of less than 100 percent (in effect, a form of co-payment system) may induce a higher level of cost consciousness on the part of consumers, but at the risk of being regressive in its impacts on low-income con-sumers.[58] In addition, capped or fixed sum vouchers may create supply-side incentives for under-provision of needed services to many consumers (depending on the value and calibration of vouchers and supply-side elasticities). Related issues arise as to whether vouchers should carry a common fixed value or be calibrated, at least to some extent, to the particular needs of individual recipients or classes of recipients – an exercise that is likely substantially to complicate the design and administration of a voucher system.

Should extra-billing (topping-up) be permitted?

Another central design issue that is particularly likely to arise with fixed sum or capped voucher systems, is whether "extra-billing" or "top-up" payments beyond the value of the voucher should be permitted. If this is permitted, it is likely to raise serious equity concerns if it permits individuals with greater private resources to acquire a larger quantity or better quality of the goods or services in question than individuals with fewer private endowments, perhaps also attenuating political voice in maintaining the value of voucher entitlements. On the other hand, it may be argued that fixed-value or capped vouchers are designed only to ensure that all citizens receive some basic or core level and quality of the goods or services in question and that it is inappropriate to prevent other individuals with the resources or inclination to choose to augment their spending beyond the value of a voucher on the activities to which the vouchers relate. Moreover, it will be argued that prohibiting extra-billing or topping-up undermines the role of the price system as a signal of and reward for superior quality.

Should "cream-skimming" be permitted?

A further central design issue relates to whether competitors should be able to minimize their costs by screening voucher-supported consumers to whom they choose to supply services, more specifically by "cream-skimming," "cherry-picking" or "discriminating," so that they choose only to service those consumers who entail fewer costs or present lower risks for them (an issue rendered more acute if the value of vouchers is not calibrated in some way to reflect differential costs or risks). To the extent that this form of screening or supply-side selective servicing is permitted, equity concerns will arise with respect to citizens who are screened or selected out in this process, who may be amongst the most disadvantaged or needy members of the constituency at which the voucher program is targeted. In order to preclude "cream-skimming," some form of mandatory pooling of recipients is likely to be required, which will pose major challenges in regulatory design and enforcement if it is to be effective in constraining countervailing incentives. However, if the state not only regulates entry on the supply-side into the class of activities in question, and constrains or prohibits extra billing or top-up payments, but also imposes constraints on whom amongst the voucher-supported population suppliers may choose to do business with, by for example adopting some form of mandatory pooling, it will have taken on major roles in managing the supply-side of these voucher-supported markets. This is both at variance with the simple, stylized virtues of voucher systems advanced by "reinventing government" proponents and, at the limit, may also raise questions as to whether an intensively state-managed form of competition is likely, in practice, to yield the efficiency properties often claimed for unconstrained competitive markets.

Information failures

A major concern with respect to the implementation of voucher programs relates to the quality and quantity of information that citizens have in making consumption choices with their assigned voucher. Many critics of voucher systems argue that consumers lack the information necessary to make fully informed decisions, and, as a result, the assumption of informed individual citizen choice in the consumption of publicly desired goods and services is unrealistic. To support this claim, critics of voucher systems argue that it is difficult to make robust *ex ante* determinations of the quality of many of the goods and services typically provided by government which are "experience" or "credence" rather than "search" goods (indeed, this may be an argument for government provision in the first place),[59] and that uninformed consumers are likely to make systematic and severe mistakes in consumption. This argument is strengthened when vouchers are distributed on a means-tested basis, and the recipients of the voucher tend to be the least educated and sophisticated members of society.

However, while acknowledging the potential for information deficiencies in a voucher market, it is important not to overstate their significance. While it is true that consumers may not possess perfect or even good information respecting the quality of services provided within the voucher market, there are a number of different ways in which these information problems can be mitigated. First, as in the case of markets for other goods and services, suppliers will have strong incentives to develop credible *ex post* bonding mechanisms (such as brand names, guarantees, etc.) that ameliorate *ex ante* information deficiencies. Second, for citizens to spend their vouchers rationally, it is not necessary for them to have perfect information about the goods and service in question, but simply for them to have the capacity to observe the decisions of other more informed citizens and to be able to secure the good or service in question on the same terms. Third, if these two conditions do not hold, there still is scope for governments to reduce information asymmetries through tailored consumer protection requirements (e.g. mandatory certification, information disclosure, and/or warranties) or by explicit monitoring and measurement programs that would provide meaningful information to citizens.

Inadequate supply-side market responses and monopolies

As has already been discussed, one of the putative advantages of voucher programs over their alternatives is the stimulus they provide for competition between suppliers in the market. The conversion from pure public provision to a system of demand-side subsidies is intended to create a new market of consumers, for whose patronage suppliers must compete. Moreover, where the supply market is not already saturated, new suppliers can be expected to enter the market as long as barriers to entry are low. Vouchering should ideally generate a supply-side response characterized by new entry and the obviation of monopolistic behaviour.

Such a response, however, will depend on a number of market conditions. Consider a market, such as that for rental housing in a major metropolitan area, where demand exceeds supply, and the barriers to entry for new suppliers are high.[60] Such markets are "inelastic;" that is, changes in demand are unlikely to generate significant increases in supply. Where affordable housing is scarce, for instance, the issuing of a rental voucher to low-income families is more likely to result in a rent increase on the part of existing suppliers rather than in the entry of new suppliers, with consumers no better off.

An inadequate supply-side response might also be elicited in a remote rural community where there is only sufficient demand to support a single supplier for a given service, and where the entry of new suppliers is unlikely due to the limited scope of the market. In such communities, where vouchers can only be redeemed at one supplier, the voucher program becomes a *de facto* supply-side subsidy, issued *via* consumers to a monopoly provider of an essential service. Where this is the case, one major proclaimed advantage of vouchering – "competition on the supply-side" – is neutralized. Inadequate competition, in turn, neutralizes the cost advantages of vouchering, as well as its advantages for consumer choice. It also greatly diminishes the accountability of private providers to individual consumers because the ownership effect is not counterbalanced by the competition effect: where there is only one provider, customers cannot threaten to "take their business elsewhere."

While there may be some force to this concern, in the sense that small communities typically possess many fewer commercial suppliers of most goods and services than more densely populated areas, it is important not to overstate economies of scale in most of the social services that are the focus of this study and hence impediments to new entry. For example, one might readily imagine alternative schools to the local public school opening up in unconventional facilities (e.g. church halls, basements or community centres). In addition, by providing consumers with vouchers that can be redeemed at any provider in any community, not simply at designated "in-district" suppliers, voucher programs have the potential to broaden the supply market available to consumers, thus enhancing choice. Broadening the "catchment area" of voucher programs, however, may importantly require that vouchers be set and financed at higher levels of government than local governments, weakening the local voice option in exchange for arguably less effective political voice at higher and more distant levels of government.

Such concerns about the likely effect of voucher programs on the supply-side markets in their various domains of potential application need to be taken more seriously than has sometimes been the case. As will be consistently emphasized in our discussions of specific programmatic areas, policy problems do not begin or end with a choice of instrument. Instead, the success of any given mode of delivery depends not only on the characteristics of the instrument itself, but also on the market conditions in which it will be operative.

Interest groups, normative legitimacy and the political acceptability of social program reform

There are two different elements to be considered in assessing the political acceptability of social policy reforms such as the implementation of voucher schemes or the modification of existing voucher programs. These elements are:

1   the interests of stakeholders; and
2   the normative legitimacy of a public policy choice.

When making changes to government policy, the interests of incumbent and potential goods and service providers, the interests of political actors and bureaucrats, and the interests of political interest groups and the media, all play an important role in determining the acceptability of proposals for new public policies. As well, various stakeholders can benefit from externalities generated by particular policy choices. These benefits play an important role in the political acceptability of policy decisions. Against this background of interests, there is also a process of normative justification involved. Advocates and critics of a particular social policy change must be able to justify their positions in terms of reasons that have normative legitimacy in the public forum.[61]

Interests of stakeholders

The interests of stakeholders have increasingly been recognized as influential in the outcome of political decision-making. The Public Choice school in particular has applied an economic understanding of how individuals act to increase their individual welfare in competitive markets to the "marketplace" of public policies. As Mercuro and Medema explain, the purpose of public choice theory is to "describe and explain political results in terms of rational, utility-maximizing behavior of individuals and groups of individuals as they participate in the political process."[62] Generally, public choice theorists consider three groups of interests: those of politicians, those of bureaucrats, and those of political interest groups. However, Trebilcock *et al.* also add the media to this list.[63] The stakeholders involved in the delivery of social policy programs are: politicians, government bureaucrats, the media, incumbent and potential service providers, consumers, and issue-specific political interest groups (e.g. public education advocates, housing policy advocates, etc.).

According to Public Choice theory, each of these groups plays the interest group game according to certain "rules." These rules are the factors that determine the interests of each group. Politicians are concerned with acquiring the necessary votes to ensure them political power. The interests of bureaucrats include job security, the maintenance of personal and departmental prestige and power.[64] Finally, political interests are also at play. The interests of suppliers in a profitable business and those of consumers in low-cost, high-quality goods have an important impact on decisions about the provision of social services.

Various interest groups can also benefit from externalities of public policy decisions. As Barr points out, in-kind or tied provision of social services by means of vouchers often give rise to consumption externalities. For instance, donors or taxpayers may derive greater utility from financing particular types of consumption rather than untied cash transfers even if in-kind or tied transfers are more costly in financial terms.[65] Consideration of these positive externalities is important from a political perspective because donors and taxpayers often have publicly unjustifiable interests and preferences that nonetheless must be taken into account in order to garner public acceptance of a social program.

For example, while the cash-equivalency of vouchers might be an argument against their use in a particular social program area (for example, food stamps), vouchers might nonetheless be preferable (as is likewise the case for vouchers that are not cash-equivalent) because of the externalities that they generate. The public, in their role as taxpayers and donors, might not accept a direct cash transfer for paternalistic reasons based on the belief that recipients would "fritter it away" on goods and services of which taxpayers would not approve. However, by targeting transfers to particular areas such as food, education or health, it is possible to secure public empathy. As Kelman points out, donors and taxpayers are more likely to empathize with the specific needs of recipients in particular contexts relative to financing "one big cash transfer."[66] A second externality is generated by vouchers because in many cases they are *de facto* subsidies to producers and suppliers of particular goods and services. When they are not cash-equivalent, food stamps, housing vouchers and similar voucher programs benefit food suppliers, housing developers, schools and so on by increasing spending on the goods they produce and distribute. This second source of externalities is an important consideration in the design of public policy, since the interests of suppliers can be enlisted in support of voucher programs.

While we have focused primarily on the Public Choice model, other models of the welfare state also depend in part on an analysis of the interests served by public policy choices. The Public Choice model holds that democracy pursues what the majority or winning coalition of salient political interests demands, resulting in intense competition amongst political interests to align the interests of the median voter with their own.[67] However, class-based theorists, while recognizing the importance of interests, see these interests as aligned along divisions between social classes. Thus instead of politicians, bureaucrats, the media and the public, these theorists see social welfare structures as serving the competing interests of social classes. Equality-promoting social welfare policies are thus either the result of the mobilization of the working classes, or in more recent theories, they are the result of coalition building among the working classes and other social groups such as farmer organizations or white-collar workers.[68] Thus while Public Choice theory correctly observes that "political choices are determined by the efforts of individuals and groups to further their own interests"[69] and that these interests are more or less effective depending on the degree of organization of these groups,[70] class-coalition theorists disagree as to the identity of the groups in competition. The public is neither a group of isolated individuals nor a homogeneous "mass," but rather it is divided into groups whose interests align along the lines of social class.

Normative legitimacy

In addition to the interests involved, normative justifiability plays an important role in the making of social policy decisions. While some social policies may represent bargains struck between various interests, the fact that the bargains must ultimately be justified on the basis of the public interest demonstrates the role that normative legitimacy plays in limiting the scope of possible interest group bargains. The bargains struck must not only be rational, they must also be *reasonable*, i.e. the parties at the table must take into account the consequences of their bargain for others, including those not represented in the bargain.[71] Some public choice theorists have come to recognize the important place that ideas have in the making of social policy. For instance, Trebilcock acknowledges that the Public Choice model "obscures the importance of a range of non-economic and non-self-interested values that commonly motivate various participants in collective decision-making processes, including notions of distributive justice, corrective justice, due process, communitarianism, racial and gender equality etc."[72] Thus a social policy will only be viable if, in addition to satisfying the interests of salient political interests, it also relates to important public value positions that underlie and justify the existence of the welfare state and its policies.

Some will argue that normative justifications for social policies are mere "window dressing" that disguise political rent-seeking as normatively justifiable policy. However, a more positive approach would be to see norms against the background of interests. In this way, the genuineness of normative arguments can be judged against the interests involved:

> [I]deas and interests will interact in relation to particular issues, but the terms of discourse, or the rhetoric, of public debate may often disguise the true interests and ideas at play. For example, it will often be strategic for an interest group to disguise its self-interest under the rubric of a broader normative idea in order to engage the support of other members of the political community who may share the idea but not the interest. Similarly, those who espouse particular ideas that are unappealing to other members of the community may disguise those ideas (e.g. racist values) under the rubric of other values (e.g. cultural homogeneity) that are more appealing to a broader segment of the community. Thus, an understanding of the real ideas and interests at play in each epoch requires *a careful interpretation of the rhetoric of public discourse.*[73] (emphasis added)

In this regard, voucher programs have the advantage of providing greater transparency for the public about the interests that underlie social policy decisions. From a Public Choice perspective, one of the significant political attractions of government supply is that it allows governments to obscure differential entitlements that are predicated on politically contentious cross-subsidies. In contrast, because vouchers place government subsidies in the hands of citizens, there is a need for government to be more explicit in defining the precise nature of the benefit conferred. And although the government need not go as far as imputing a precise monetary value to the voucher, the relative levels of voucher entitlements will have to be expressed in some manner. In this way, the conferral of vouchers provides citizens with greater information respecting the distribution of government benefits, and, in particular, it facilitates critical evaluation of whether the distribution of benefits accords with legitimate normative principles or is simply the outcome of unprincipled political rent-seeking.

Conclusion

As we have discussed, the principal advantage of tied demand-side subsidies over other alternatives is their ability to reconcile the interests of principals and agents using market mechanisms of accountability, and without relying on coercive regulation. While retaining the many efficiency incentives of supply-side subsidies, including the dual effects of ownership and competition, demand-side subsidies provide the means for consumers to influence markets directly according to their preferences. While it presents some forms of moral hazard, it precludes others, such as government patronage in the tendering of contracts. Moreover, it rewards those innovations which benefit consumers the most directly, and empowers those individuals who are most directly concerned with the delivery of high-quality, innovative services: consumers themselves. Insofar as voucher programs have produced unfavourable or ambiguous results, design defects have often been largely responsible for these outcomes, a claim which our examination of the empirical evidence in numerous program areas in subsequent chapters will attempt to support.

It will be evident from this brief reprise of the advantages and disadvantages of voucher schemes and of critical design issues that the potential for intense debate and disagreement, even among disinterested analysts, over the normative wisdom of the voucher concept in various policy contexts is likely to be substantial. Moreover, ideas alone do not drive the policy-making process. In assessing the viability of using vouchers in a particular area of social service delivery, we must also take into account not only rational arguments about the advantages and disadvantages of voucher schemes in a particular context, but also political factors that work in favour or against the use of vouchers. Political interests might work against or in favour of policy change in a particular program area. The case for using vouchers must also have normative validity, i.e. justifications for their use must align with public values and norms. These political and ideological factors and the weight given to them in particular programmatic contexts are important considerations in the design of a politically acceptable and effective voucher program.

3 Food stamps

Introduction

The US Food Stamp Program (FSP) is a federal program designed to increase the food purchasing power of low-income people and to improve the quality of their diets. Food stamps take the form of coupons valid for food purchases at participating grocery stores, or, as is becoming increasingly common, an electronic benefit transfer (EBT) card, a debit account usable only for food purchases at participating retailers. The purchase of certain products, such as pet food, tobacco, alcohol, soap and paper products, is prohibited, and food stamp purchases are typically exempt from State sales taxes. The US Department of Agriculture (USDA) administers the program nationally, while administration at the State level is handled by a suitable department, such as the department of welfare or social services, who may in turn delegate responsibilities to local offices. The USDA pays for all FSP benefits and a portion of the national and local administrative costs.[1]

The FSP is the largest public assistance program in America that has uniform national standards and is available to all households on the basis of financial need, regardless of age, family type or disability.[2] Unlike its public assistance counterparts such as Temporary Assistance to Needy Families (TANF) and its predecessor, Assistance to Families with Dependent Children (AFDC), the FSP is not designed explicitly to target specific population sub-groups (i.e. children or senior citizens). Rather, the program is open to all in need.[3] As a result, it has reached a staggering size that can best be appreciated numerically: in fiscal year 2001, it paid out over $15.5 billion in benefits, serving an average of 17.3 million people per month.[4] It is also one of the most ambitious, long-lived and popular voucher initiatives in the history of the welfare state. Consequently, as Moffitt observes, "issues that arise in the food stamp program [...] and research discussions surrounding it [...] would be quite relevant should subsidies in other service areas be converted to vouchers,"[5] particularly on a similarly large scale.

Various welfare states have experimented with a variety of hunger interventions across the full spectrum of methods of provision described in Chapter 2, ranging from pure public provision in the form of school lunch programs to untied cash transfers in the form of welfare cheques. The FSP is the only nutritional policy initiative of its size in the world which uses a voucher approach. As such, it occupies an important place in a project of comparative policy.

The Food Stamp Program exemplifies a number of specific and substantial design challenges. The FSP, perhaps more than any other voucher initiative, most closely resembles a "universal, portable, uniform-benefit voucher,"[6] making it an important example to bear in mind when designing or evaluating other universal voucher benefit policies. Moreover, the fungible nature of FSP vouchers calls into question the degree to which demand-side subsidies are generally preferable to cash transfers in situations where vouchers exhibit a high degree of cash equivalency. Indeed, the debate over whether the FSP should be "cashed out," i.e. converted to a system of untied cash grants, is one of the most lively in contemporary American public nutritional policy research.

The rationales for government intervention

The mandate of the contemporary FSP

The official purpose of the FSP is to increase the amount that eligible households spend on nutritious food, ensuring "that low-income households have the opportunity to attain a nutritionally adequate diet."[7] In contrast to the FSP's original intention several decades ago of increasing the sheer quantity of food consumed by poor families, the present nutritional goal of the FSP is to raise diet quality. A number of studies have established a negative relationship between poverty and nutritional intake.[8] This relationship, however, exhibits some complexity.

For instance, one recent analysis employing the USDA's own Healthy Eating Index (HEI), a holistic scale of diet quality, observes that "the estimated effect of household income on [...] diet quality [...] was not significant at conventional levels of statistical significance" among FSP-eligible households, suggesting that when a household income remains below a certain threshold level (namely, the FSP standard for eligibility), marginal increases in income of as much as 20 percent do not produce commensurate improvements in diet quality.[9] The same study, however, finds a positive relationship between the value of FSP benefits received and overall diet quality.[10] Taken together, the two findings suggest that "wealthier" FSP households do not fare better, while those who receive more stamps clearly do. Such findings are the causes of the so-called "cash-out puzzle," which will be discussed in more detail in a subsequent section. Essentially, from the perspective of traditional economic theory, it is perplexing that income differences do not produce corresponding differences in diet quality, while voucher coupons do seem to have a progressively positive effect on diet as the size of the disbursement increases.

Some critics of the FSP contend that "federal feeding programs [which] still operate under their nearly half-century-old objective of increasing food consumption" are contributing to obesity among poor Americans, and that the FSP's half-century-old objective – the prevention of undernutrition – does not match the actual dietary needs of poor Americans in the twenty-first century.[11] Nevertheless, though contentious, the negative relationship between income and dietary quality, particularly insofar as the low consumption of fruits and vegetables and the high intake of cholesterol and animal fats among poorer families are concerned,[12] may present some case for government intervention to assist lower-income families in meeting the requirements of a balanced diet.

A critical perspective on the FSP's original objectives

Strong arguments, however, continue to support the notion that the poor were not the legislators' top priority when the food stamp program was instituted in the 1930s. The features of what has since been termed the "two-stamp program," for example, strongly suggest the higher importance legislators placed on securing the well-being of food producers and retail grocers than the well-being of the poor. To participate in the "two-stamp program" individuals were expected to purchase a minimum set of orange stamps at face value with their own disposable income from the government. Only upon purchase were they supplied with free blue stamps. However, the blue stamps were restricted to food items appearing upon a monthly list of surplus commodities issued by the Secretary of Agriculture. Thus, the blue stamps served the function of subsidizing domestic producers. With respect to retail grocers, the implementation of stamps effectively created transactions that otherwise would not have occurred. The retail grocer was introduced as the middleman in the transactions between the government and benefit recipients. The introduction of redeemable stamps ensured an increase in the volume of goods sold in the grocer's store, while also increasing demand for food products supplied by farmers and food manufacturers.

Many scholars have thus characterized the food stamp program as catering to the interests of producers and retail grocers. Barbara Claffey and Thomas Stuckey have argued that "[a]lleviating hunger never commanded as high a priority as increasing farm income,"[13] while William Boehm *et al.* have conceptualized the program as a surplus removing mechanism.[14] In surveying these arguments, William A. Eisinger observes an interesting result. In seeking to further the interests of farm producers and retailer grocers, the food assistance programs were provided with what he refers to as a "modest protective cover."[15] Because of the self-interested motives of the agricultural lobby groups, the poor were the beneficiaries of an organized political voice. Notwithstanding these arguments, however, an alternative view can be taken. That is, the government had noble intentions when it introduced the food assistance programs but recognized that political support was vital for the adoption of the program. In this light, it can be argued that the well-being of those in need of assistance was achieved by government sensitivity to the interests of food producers.

Working from the perspective on the modern welfare state established in Chapter 1, there are two primary ends which rationalize the FSP in its current form: equitable distribution of resources and economic stability. Humanitarian justifications for the FSP fit under the former rubric, while arguments that adequate nutrition is essential for a thriving labour force are subsumed under the latter. Although we discuss them separately, the two rationales are inextricable. For instance, encouraging labour force participation is humanitarian insofar as it improves people's ability to provide for themselves, while equitable distribution of resources enables people to participate more actively in the economy.

Equitable distribution of resources as an end of the FSP

With the expansion of international markets in the aftermath of World War II, the need to support the agricultural economy with food stamp-driven consumption proved unnecessary. As such, the "two-stamp" program discussed earlier had a short operating life, ultimately ending in 1943.[16] It was not until 1960, when Presidential-aspirant John F. Kennedy committed himself to the reinstatement of food stamps, that government food assistance regained popular support. Kennedy campaigned on issues of state obligation to the hungry and poor[17] and once elected, he followed through on his promises and pilot food stamps programs were initiated in selected states and regions (1961 to 1964). Kennedy's initiative did not end with his assassination. In fact, his successor, Lyndon Johnson, embraced the expansion of food stamps as a part of his "War on Poverty."[18] In furthering Kennedy's food stamp program, the Johnson Administration's language resonated with a sense of humanity, compassion, and responsibility to those in need. Since that time, the FSP has been associated with welfare assistance.

In the political realm, justifying food assistance to the poor in "humanitarian" terms has proven much easier than justifying the provision of government housing or free medical care. Adequate sustenance is viewed as the most basic of human needs. Whether based on religious tenets or social philosophies, if food is regarded as a natural right then it follows that there exists a moral responsibility, or perhaps even a duty, to ensure that all citizens have access to food. Johnson's statement that "we want no American in this country to go hungry" and Ronald Reagan's declaration that "hunger is simply not acceptable in our society" reflect this humanitarian justification.[19]

The acceptance of the humanitarian explanation is further reflected in the nature of the debates on food stamps that have arisen in the United States. The concern has never predominantly focused on whether the government should provide food to the poor. Rather, the debate has revolved around the issues of fraud and abuse of the government food assistance program. This preoccupation with developing mechanisms to limit abuses has played a major role in shaping the FSP.

Economic stability as an end of the FSP

The economic argument – or more precisely the productivity argument – for state-financed food assistance is that the government has a fundamental stake in relieving hunger and ensuring that minimal nutritional requirements are met. The following statement, made before the House Select Committee on Hunger, by social activist Aaron Shirley captures the essence of such an argument:

It is a good investment to see to it that especially our children have adequate nutrition so that they can grow up to be productive citizens, they can be good citizens, they can push the right button on the missile thing.[20]

In these terms, the government receives a return when it invests in the provision of food to the needy, for doing so increases productivity in the home, at school and at work. Further, the threat of criminal activity may be decreased if the view is accepted that anti-social behaviour is linked to economic status. Perhaps, most importantly, the aggregate population will be relatively healthier. As a result, society will not be burdened with individuals suffering from malnutrition and the negative social implications that arise from under-nourishment. Because these are all social advantages that the population enjoys as a whole, the population should collectively bear their cost. The process of tax-and-transfer implicit within government-funded food assistance internalizes this cost.

A policy history of the food stamp program[21]

The two-stamp system: 1939–43

As discussed earlier, despite its current explicit mandate of enriching the diets of poor Americans, the FSP actually originated as an effort to aid two very different but needy groups: unemployed city-dwellers and farmers with unsold surpluses. The first FSP, inaugurated in 1939 by Secretary of Agriculture Henry Wallace, allowed eligible persons to buy orange stamps equal to their normal food expenditures. Along with each dollar coupon, they would also receive 50 cents worth of blue stamps. Orange stamps could be redeemed to buy any food product; however, blue stamps were restricted to the purchase of food which the USDA had listed as surplus. The goal was to help the hungry (typically unemployed urbanites) by providing them with extra food income, while also relieving farmers of their surplus produce. A quote from Milo Perkins, the Program's first Administrator, is illustrative of the FSP's original intentions: "We got a picture of a gorge, with farm surpluses on one cliff, and under-nourished city folks with outstretched hands on the other. We set out to find a practical way to build a bridge across that chasm."[22] The first FSP wound up in 1943, once it was decided that the conditions that created the need for it – unmarketable food surpluses and widespread unemployment – had ceased to exist.

The second FSP and the Food Stamp Act: 1961–80

The next 18 years saw considerable legislative interest in the FSP, and the second pilot FSP was initiated in 1961. While it eliminated the requirement of purchasing special stamps for surplus food, the indirect subsidization of farms remained an important part of the program's mandate, as evidenced by its declared emphasis on increasing the consumption of perishables.

The new FSP allowed consumers to purchase food stamps and receive a subsidy in the form of an additional amount of free stamps sufficient to "shore up" the household's dietary needs. Participation in the FSP grew from half a million in 1965 to over 15 million persons in 1974.[23] In the early 1970s, major concerns arose over the cost of the FSP, which had grown to $1.75 billion by 1971.[24] As the USDA's own "Short History" document observes, "it was during this time that the issue was framed that would dominate food stamp legislation ever after: how to balance program access with program accountability?"[25] Republicans and Democrats both championed the FSP, but advocated very different policy objectives. The Republican initiatives emphasized tighter controls and the targeting of benefits to the very neediest members of society, while Democratic proposals focused on streamlining the approval process and reducing errors. The 1977 Food Stamp Act attempted to meet both sets of priorities. Among other changes, it established the poverty line as the standard for FSP eligibility, undertook to penalize households whose heads voluntarily quit jobs, and required regional authorities to actively encourage participation in the FSP by eligible parties ("outreach" policies). Perhaps the most significant feature of the 1977 Food Stamp Act, however, was that it eliminated the controversial "purchase requirement." Henceforth, recipients were no longer obligated to purchase food stamps in order to receive their subsidy. Rather, they were to receive their entitlement directly, in the form of a book of coupons. By eliminating the obligation to purchase stamps, supporters of the new Act argued that it had removed a significant barrier to participation by needy families.

Modern developments: 1980 to the present day

In the late 1980s, both Congress and the Executive Branch advocated substantial cutbacks to the FSP. Major legislation introduced more stringent eligibility requirements in the form of new income eligibility test (IET) stipulations, prohibited the use of Federal funds for FSP outreach, reduced participation by elderly persons by counting retirement funds as resources, and allowed States to require FSP applicants and recipients to engage in documented job searches. In the mid-1990s, general trends in welfare reform began to effect changes in the FSP. The FSP became subject to the terms of the 1996 Personal Responsibility and Work Opportunities Reconciliation Act, a change which entailed a number of policy alterations for the FSP, including the elimination of eligibility for food stamps for most legal immigrants, placing a time limit on food stamp receipt of 3 out of 36 months for able-bodied adults without dependents (ABAWDs) who are not working at least 20 hours a week or participating in a work program, and freezing certain IET deductions. It also required States to implement electronic benefit transfer systems (EBTs), a debit card-style alternative to the coupon system, by October 2002. Changes in following years continued in the same vein, allowing States to deny food stamps to up to 15 percent of the estimated number of ABAWDs who would otherwise be eligible and cutting administrative funding in view of overlap with other federal assistance programs.

The Farm Bill of 2002 responded to falling participation rates through minor changes which emphasized program access and the simplification of rules. It also indexed the standard IET deduction to inflation, and expanded the existing quality control system which imposes financial sanctions for states with high administrative error rates, a policy structure which at least one commentator has criticized on the grounds that it penalizes poor administration instead of rewarding high participation rates.[26]

Delivery systems

As its uniqueness among international food aid programs illustrates, the American FSP is not the only way to provide nutritional assistance to the poor. Once the state decides to take an interest in supplementing the diets of its poorer citizens, three distinct options are available. The first involves the direct delivery of food by the state to eligible families. This method was the basis of the Commodity Distribution Program (CDP) which was in effect in America during the Great Depression. Under the CDP (1932–9), the government purchased surplus farm products, warehoused them and distributed them directly to needy families.[27] As a system under which the state is responsible for funding and distribution, as well as for the infrastructure to accomplish both, the CDP is representative of the paradigmatic in-kind benefit. Alternatively, the state may elect to provide untied cash transfers. That is, needy families would be afforded monthly income supplements, which in turn could be utilized at their discretion to purchase food. Most Western nations have embraced this policy and, with the notable exception of the United States, do not distinguish between cash transfers for food and welfare support payments, which are intended to subsume the former. The third option is the food stamp or "voucher." This option lies somewhere between the in-kind benefit and the untied benefit. Though the family is provided with stamps to purchase food rather than with actual food, the stamps can be redeemed only for approved food products and nothing else. What follows is a critical analysis of these three options that reveals the advantages and disadvantages of each. It suggests that the untied transfer would be the most effective means of delivering assistance with the voucher method ranking as the next best alternative.

In-kind provision

Although the CDP was replaced many years ago by a food stamp regime, the benefits of the direct distribution of food commodities to households should not be discounted. The most important of these is the alleged assurance that food is indeed consumed by the family. Unlike cash transfers, it is claimed, in-kind benefits provide recipients with no alternative uses for the transfer. Barring the evolution of an elaborate underground economy for food, the recipients must either accept the food they are provided with or go hungry. Given that the goal of the tax-funded assistance is to reduce food inadequacy, it is not unreasonable that the state and its taxpayers expect that assistance be spent on food and not on what they perceive to be less essential forms of consumption. If the claim that recipients of cash transfers would not allocate the entire value of the transfer on food has any merit, then in-kind provision is desirable from a paternalistic point of view.[28] This point is particularly relevant when principal–agent issues arise, that is, when the recipients of cash transfers are parents who choose to under-invest in food for their children. If this under-investment translates into the purchase of low-quality food, though such food may address the immediate concern of hunger, the resultant undernourishment will ultimately lead to long-term costs. A further advantage of an in-kind benefit scheme is its decreased susceptibility to fraud and abuse. Were qualifiers for food assistance simply provided with untied benefits in the form of monthly government cheques, many who do not suffer from food inadequacy may go to considerable lengths to gain entry into the program. However, at least intuitively, it seems rational that fewer individuals would make such false claims if the consequent pay-off were food. Finally, the assurance of consumption and the reduction of false eligibility claims make in-kind transfers politically appealing.

There are, of course, several disadvantages to the direct provision of food commodities, disadvantages that ultimately formed the basis for the replacement of the CDP. First, the implementation of any such distribution program would require a significant investment in infrastructure by the state. Warehouses would have to be built, delivery trucks purchased, and employees hired, all of which would contribute to overhead costs. These costs would be in addition to the administrative costs common to all three regimes (government offices assessing applications and allocating benefits). Second, many food commodities are perishable; thus unlike a cash payment, it would not be feasible to make deliveries only once a month. Instead, the government supplier would have to make food available to each household on a more frequent basis. This too would raise the costs of the program. Though it is true that replacement of home deliveries with centralized pick-up depots would eliminate delivery costs, recipients would be forced to enter lines to accept food, creating a stigma not unlike that associated with soup kitchens or handouts. Many qualified individuals may object to this form of humiliation and choose to forego the benefits. Others may simply not have the means to travel to the site. They may be physically or mentally impaired, too old, sick, or perhaps lack adequate transportation. Consequently, due either to stigma or inaccessibility, the goal of relieving food inadequacy may be undermined.

Cash transfers

The concerns of distribution costs associated with in-kind transfers effectively disappear in the context of cash transfers (also commonly referred to as income maintenance payments). Under a cash transfer regime, the government has a less overt role in the delivery of the good. It simply provides recipients with a benefit in cash, which can then be used to pay for groceries if they so choose. Such a program eliminates the need for the infrastructure required by a benefit in-kind. Additionally, the high degree of stigma associated with queuing for food is eliminated.

Income support payments enjoy much greater flexibility than their in-kind counterparts as well. This flexibility comes in two distinct forms. First, cash transfers allow recipients to choose their level of consumption over time according to their preferences. Recipients no longer have to consume food immediately in the expectation of it becoming spoiled. Second, recipients become the decision-makers with respect to the type of food or other goods they will consume. Although they are ultimately constrained by the amount of the payment, cash transfers still empower recipients to select the types of food or other commodities they prefer. In terms of personal autonomy, then, and all else being equal, cash transfers can be viewed as relatively more beneficial to recipients than the distribution of food of equal value. This argument is similar to the libertarian view of Friedman and others, discussed in Chapter 2, that where their own interests are concerned, individuals are the best arbiters, and that as long as an individual receives what he or she prefers, regardless of its objective value, he or she is still better off than if he or she were coerced into selecting something else.

However, it is this very flexibility (or recipient discretion) which casts a shadow on the allure of cash transfers. As mentioned earlier, the scope for fraud and abuse is a serious concern for social welfare policy-makers. The implementation of a cash transfer program will inevitably attract individuals who are not in need of its services, but who do not stand to lose anything by attempting to apply. Under current FSP regulations, even partially or incorrectly completed applications must be considered, and applications can be made by phone.[29] There is no financial cost for making an application. Given the low opportunity cost of applying for FSP benefits, the fungible nature of benefits creates a *de facto* universal cash incentive to apply repeatedly, overstate need, conceal assets, and traffic in vouchers. Hence the state is confronted with a dilemma. It can raise the cost of the program by increasing the size of the administrative staff in order to better scrutinize applications *ex ante* and monitor the activities of recipients *ex post* or, in the alternative, it can simply choose to ignore the fraud within the system. The government would reduce administrative costs in the latter choice but inevitably the costs of the program would rise as assistance would be provided to successful perpetrators of fraud. Unfortunately, both options lead to a diversion of resources away from those who need them.[30]

A somewhat related concern is the unrestricted purchasing power that the recipients gain with cash transfers. It is unreasonable to think that most individuals will forego food altogether and spend the supplemental income on other commodities. It is, however, reasonable to raise the concern that individuals may not devote a sufficient amount of the income to food – a particularly plausible outcome, for instance, in the case of recipients suffering from extreme drug addiction.[31] This problem is most dramatic in the context of households where the agency concerns with respect to children referred to earlier must be considered. The head of the household is presented with a monthly cash transfer. It is completely up to her discretion as to how much of the income will be devoted to food purchases for her children. If the parent chooses to spend the transfer on goods or services in such a way as to detract from the adequate supply of household food, it is not merely she who may suffer but her children as well. It is this very susceptibility to fraud and abuse that makes cash transfers politically problematic.

At the same time, however, the very parties being considered in the above situation – female heads of households – are also among the most impoverished in American society. Female heads have lower family income, on average, than women as a whole and than married women.[32] Indeed, more than 40 percent of female heads of families with children under 18 live below the poverty line.[33] Moffitt concludes that "future trends [in the use of benefits] are more likely to be driven by growth in female-headedness [of families] than by […] benefit levels." In other words, constraining the use of benefits by needy families, particularly those headed by women, is unlikely to increase the participation of female heads in the active labour force or reduce dependency on benefits. "It follows," Moffitt concludes, "that research on the types of welfare reform best suited to reducing poverty should concentrate […] more on the determinants of female-headedness."[34] This suggests that the policing of fraud and "abuse" of cash transfers is likely to be less effective than programs which address the primary causes of poverty, including most notably the feminization of poor families.

Food stamps

Although somewhat of a compromise between the two schemes, the nature of the food stamp program is itself unique. It cannot be referred to as an in-kind transfer because the recipient does not *prima facie* receive food commodities from the state. However, food stamps cannot be characterized as cash transfers either because, by their very nature, vouchers imply a limitation on use. Essentially, food stamps make the recipient the decision-maker but place constraints on the exercise of her choice.

In comparing food stamps with direct in-kind provision, there are clear advantages. First, in terms of cost, food stamps closely resemble the cash transfer regime in eliminating the daily operating costs associated with direct in-kind transfers. Second, they avoid the stigma associated with food assistance provided through government commodity distribution. Third, stamps do not generate the functional problems created by direct in-kind transfers. Although received on a monthly basis, they can be redeemed at any time. This affords recipients greater ability to allocate consumption over time. Finally, stamps enable the recipient to exercise preferences as to the types and quantity of food purchased within the budget constraint.

In comparing food stamps with cash transfers, it is generally argued that recipient discretion is not as broad as it is under the cash transfer regime for the recipient is only able to redeem the stamps for approved food commodities from approved stores.[35] It is further contended that, given that the purpose of food stamps is to relieve food deficiency, this constrained choice is optimal – government resources are supporting the appropriate form of consumption.[36]

A major criticism of this argument is its failure to recognize the substitution effect that occurs when food stamps are employed. While it is true that recipients must redeem stamps for food, the fact that they can reallocate income previously spent on food in the absence of food stamps is often ignored. As Breunig *et al.* observe, "[t]he standard model of economic theory assumes equivalence between cash income and cash transfers. [...] Consequently, a strong *a priori* case exists for the replacement of the FSP by a system of cash transfers."[37] According to this basic theoretical model,[38] it is clear that food stamps do not represent additional food spending to the household. That is, unless they alter the recipient's overall budget allocation by increasing the amount spent on food, the voucher is essentially equivalent to a cash grant.[39] Furthermore, it is also possible to turn vouchers into cash fraudulently by selling them at a discounted value, or by selling food.

It is not clear, however, that the empirical evidence entirely vindicates this conventional theory. At least one study has found that the marginal propensity to consume food is greater in the context of food stamps than in the context of cash transfers, in spite of the presumed substitution effect.[40] The Department of Agriculture (USDA) estimated in 1991 that if the FSP was "cashed out" (became a cash transfer program), the slippage effect would range from 15 percent to 30 percent of total benefits.[41] That is, given the total benefits paid out, the additional food purchases made by participating households would be 15 percent to 30 percent lower under a cash regime than a voucher regime. Such estimates present a "cash-out" puzzle, the name Breunig *et al.* give to "the large[r] estimated propensity to consume food out of food stamps at the aggregate level, relative to that out of cash income."[42] Some empirical evidence, however, supports the contrary conclusion. Puerto Rico opted to "cash out" in 1982 and there seemed to be no evidence of a change in food expenditures.[43] Fraker's comprehensive 1990 review of the literature, however, cautions that "any prediction made on the basis of findings from those studies [including the one in Puerto Rico] about the effects of cashout on food expenditures by all food stamp recipients would be subject to a very large margin of error."[44] More recent experiments on "cashing out" conducted in both Alabama and San Diego found no changes in food expenditure in the former state and minimal changes in the latter.[45] A retrospective analysis of these experiments found that cashout led to greater undernutrition with respect to only two of 26 key indicators (vitamins E and B6).[46] Such results lend some qualified support to the *a priori* idea of cash equivalence, but have yet to be reproduced in other jurisdictions.

To the extent that empirical evidence is mixed, the FSP "cash-out puzzle" remains an enigma. Breunig *et al.*, however, propose a novel explanation for the puzzle in terms of the decision-making behaviour of multi-adult households. By more closely analyzing the Alabama and San Diego studies in terms of recipient household types, they find that "multi-adult households spend a higher proportion of their food stamp benefit on food than they would with an equivalent amount of cash. In contrast, single-adult households show little difference in food spending between food stamps and an equivalent amount of cash."[47] Their analysis makes use of a sophisticated Cournot game. It finds that the constraint imposed by the inability of any one agent to convert food stamps directly to cash due to the collective holding of vouchers makes it impossible for the agent to divert money allocated by the other agent for food purchases to his/her own private consumption.[48] As a result, no one agent's own discretionary cash income is increased, and only the availability of food from food stamps is improved. The personal utility-maximizing behaviours of multiple agents under the FSP thus constrain their spending behaviours in such a way as to increase marginal spending on food. Conversely, removing this constraint might substantially reduce spending on food. In single-adult households, however, this constraint is not operative: where multiple agents do not compete for resources, food stamp dollars are easily converted by the agent into cash. This explains why single-adult households in the two cash-out experiments show little difference in food spending between food stamps and an equivalent amount of cash. The effect of voucher initiatives like the FSP on recipient behaviour may provide further insight into the desirability of tied over untied subsidies generally. Whether future empirical studies will support this more sophisticated behavioural model remains to be seen.

We conclude that, for the reasons outlined above, there is little dispute that a food stamp program is generally superior to a commodity distribution program. The evidence suggesting that food stamps are superior to untied transfers, however, is rather more contentious. While cash transfers may reduce the administrative costs associated with issuing and distributing coupons and certifying retailers, these savings may be absorbed by the increase in unnecessary and fraudulent participation as cashing out presents a greater fiscal incentive to underreport income and overreport deductions.

Design challenges

Despite the argument that the untied transfer is the preferable delivery mechanism for state financed food assistance, because the FSP remains the primary delivery mechanism employed in the United States at present, we proceed to examine specific design features of the program. It should be noted that although the FSP has been subject to numerous amendments and legislative budget cuts in its history, the primary focus here will not be transitory fluxes but the basic design structure of the voucher program and how it has overcome certain incentive problems while at the same time creating others.

Qualified consumers

In order to qualify for food stamps, households are subjected to both asset and income tests. Assets, gross income, and net income (gross income minus certain permissible deductions, such as monthly shelter costs up to $340) must not exceed specific levels that vary by household size, composition and location.[49] In 2001, the average monthly gross income of FSP households was $624, and over three-quarters were receiving unearned income from sources such as Supplementary Security Income, Social Security and Temporary Assistance to Needy Families.[50] More than 85 percent of all FSP households fell below the national poverty line.[51] Only 26.8 percent of FSP households had any earned income, and nearly 10 percent of all households had no gross income whatsoever.[52]

Clearly, means-testing is a necessary element of the FSP, given that the program, by its very nature, is targeted to households suffering from food inadequacy.[53] By implementing both an asset test and an income test for eligibility, the government has restricted the program to those truly in need. Without the asset test, a household could technically qualify for food stamps without having to liquidate substantial assets that may have been acquired. Correspondingly, if the income test were not applied, the household could simply transfer or hide its assets in order to qualify. The joint tests make the FSP a last-resort measure for the poor.

Means-testing within the FSP, however, has several drawbacks. In targeting the poor, the FSP creates a work disincentive. Like other means-tested benefits, the FSP recipient may not have an incentive to seek employment if unemployed while receiving the benefits. Of course, time restraints limiting the number of months unemployed individuals can receive food stamps can reduce this disincentive.[54] There is, however, credible evidence that the actual effect of benefits with or without time constraints on the reduction of labour participation is very low, particularly in the case of female heads of household, who constitute one of the primary recipient groups. The intuitive argument that cutting benefits will increase labour participation oversimplifies the dynamic at work in labour markets.[55] Moffitt argues convincingly that increasing labour participation rates among certain recipient groups, such as young women with children, is poorly accomplished by constraining benefits.[56]

Another issue that arises is the marginal tax rate on additional income subsequently earned by recipients. Severe work disincentives may arise if assistance is simply taxed away dollar-for-dollar as recipients earn additional income. Further, there is always a question of whether the threshold levels for eligibility are appropriately set and whether the benefit levels are sufficient for eligible households to obtain an adequate diet.

Notwithstanding the large absolute number of participants in the FSP, an on-going concern has been participation rates. Until 1977, households were required to purchase food stamps and were presented with "free stamps" as supplements.[57] The result was low participation rates as many qualified households were unable to meet monthly purchase requirements because of a lack of funds. The elimination of this requirement led to an immediate jump of 3.6 million participants in the ensuing year. Today, it is claimed that among all those eligible for benefits 50 percent fail to receive food stamps.[58] A more conservative estimate is provided by the Survey of Income and Program Participation (SIPP), which found that in 1992 the participation rate was 73.8 percent.[59] Possible factors for non-participation are lack of information, a desire to avoid admissibility disputes, access problems, and stigma.

A General Accounting Office (GAO) survey conducted in the mid-1980s revealed that 14 percent of a sample of eligible but non-participating households cited embarrassment as the main reason for non-participation in the program.[60] Thus, stigma continues to play a factor in non-participation although it can be reasonably assumed that the stigma has been reduced by the displacement of the commodity distribution program by the FSP. Specifically, the program's requirement that the food stamps need to be redeemed at the time of purchase in the grocery store is the source of this stigma.

More significantly, a 1979 study showed that information problems were the largest barrier to participation rates. Forty percent of non-participants, who were otherwise eligible for the FSP, thought that they were not eligible.[61] To combat this problem, the government has tried to eliminate misconceptions – such as, for example, the idea that working individuals or individuals without dependants are ineligible – which act as impediments to the effectiveness of the FSP. Early in the FSP's existence, outreach programs were implemented to counteract the lack of information. Congress had required states to encourage participation and actively seek out non-participants. As an incentive, Congress provided matching funds to support such services.[62] This mandatory program came to an end in 1981 as part of the Reagan administration's public welfare cost cutting, and today the implementation of outreach programs is at the discretion of the states. If the states do offer such services then they can apply for federal supplements. At present, outreach programs exist in only half of the states.[63] Thus, as Eisinger argues, a lack of information combined with application procedures are major impediments to achieving higher participation rates.[64] These barriers become even more formidable because many of the participants are non-English speakers, disabled, elderly, or illiterate. The government is often criticized for not pursuing the goal of alleviating food inadequacy more aggressively. Although this has the effect of reducing program costs, the lack of information provided by the government undermines the FSP's goal of targeting all those in need.

Qualified suppliers

In the design of a food stamp scheme, it would seem that only limited emphasis should be placed on where the stamps can be redeemed. The stamps are coupons after all and thus any retail grocer ought to be able to accept the vouchers in lieu of payment and then be reimbursed by the government. Competition among retail outlets should ensure that collusion will not occur[65] and limited regulation should benefit consumers by increasing the number of destinations where stamps can be cashed in for food. Also, there is typically no scope for supplier price discrimination between subsidized and non-subsidized consumers.

The United States has, however, taken a different course. Retail outlets must gain authorization from the USDA before they are legally entitled to redeem stamps. Two underlying rationales exist for instituting such a policy. First, supplier authorization enables the government to ensure that only certain basic food products are accessible to voucher recipients. For example, restaurants are not eligible for authorization nor are retail stores whose stocks predominantly consist of ready-to-eat prepared foods.[66] Second, the authorization process provides a means of limiting food stamp trafficking. Trafficking typically occurs in two forms.[67] In one, the recipient sells the stamps directly to the retail outlet for cash (usually 50 to 70 cents per dollar face value). The retail outlet redeems the stamps for full value without having sold the corresponding food. In the other, stamps are sold to a "middle-man" at less than face value. Once the middle-man has the stamps, he can either redeem the stamps for food or conduct a similar transaction with the retail outlet. The willingness-to-trade is essentially based on the preferences of the recipient. A household that is truly in need of food would most likely prefer not to trade the vouchers for cash. It is the individuals that falsely make themselves eligible for the program or non-autonomous agents (i.e. alcoholics or drug addicts) that can be expected to engage in trafficking.

Although the USDA oversees the retail outlets that are participating in the program, it remains difficult to measure the precise extent of abuse and fraud within the FSP. One USDA official told *Time Magazine* in 1982 that "the [food stamp] coupons are a second currency. Anything that you can buy with money … you can buy with food stamps."[68] Although this may be an exaggeration, it is plausible to expect that some individuals will be willing to exchange food stamps for less than face value cash payments. Again, the trade-off in trying to reduce such illegal behaviour is the additional cost of doing so. In terms of efficiency, the government must assess the costs of prevention versus the costs of non-prevention. Preventative measures, such as putting the recipient through a rigorous eligibility determination process or stricter authorization guidelines for retail stores, result not only in higher administrative costs but also may reduce participation rates and accessibility.

Notwithstanding the overall authorization process, Robert A. Moffitt notes that there are over 200,000 participating retail outlets in the United States.[69] The large number of authorized outlets indicates that the process is not very restrictive with regards to supermarkets and convenience stores. Given the large monthly pay-outs to recipients, the supply-side enjoys significant benefits from the FSP only if they are not cash equivalent. However, based on data collected in 1987, the USDA estimated that a reduction in the FSP by $1 billion would lead to a loss of 25,000 jobs.[70] Thus, suppliers have a vested interest in the continuance of the FSP.

The value of the voucher

Once a household qualifies for assistance, the value of the food stamps granted is a function of net income. Net income is calculated by deducting expenses such as medical (for elderly and disabled only) and dependent care (if an adult member is working or training and has children) from gross income.[71] The program assumes that the participating household will devote 30 percent of this "net income" to food purchases. The monetary difference between the expected contribution by the recipient and the government-determined cost of purchasing a "nutritionally adequate low-cost diet" given the household size establishes the precise value of the food stamps.[72] Embedded within such a structure is an upper limit or cap on benefits received. For example, a household with an income of zero will receive the maximum level of benefits based on the cost of an adequate diet but no more. The maximum benefit, however, varies according to household size and is adjusted annually for changes in the benchmark diet. In 1995, a single-person household was eligible for a maximum of $115 of coupons per month.[73] For a household of eight, the corresponding benefit was $695.[74]

An important element of the FSP is that the unit of focus is not the individual but the household. The maximum allowable benefit increases as the number of family members increases; however, this increase is not proportional. Each member of a family of four, for instance, does not receive the amount that a single-member household would receive. While at first glance this might seem inconsistent with horizontal equity – the system seems to discriminate against households with multiple members – there is a rational basis for this apparent "discrimination." That is, the average food cost per person decreases as the number of members in a household increases because of economies of scale in the purchasing and preparation of food. The focus on the household thus enables the government to adjust for the decreasing marginal cost of feeding additional household members. A significant drawback of this household unit analysis, however, is its inability to adjust to specific demographics within the household. All things being equal, a household with two teenage boys will receive the same amount of food stamps as a family with two infants.

Political considerations

Notwithstanding its critics, the FSP design has survived numerous presidential administrations, both Democratic and Republican. Nevertheless, two reform proposals, "cost-shifting" and "cashing-out," have been at the centre of debates throughout the 1990s.

Fundamental to a thorough appreciation of the cost-shifting debate is an understanding of the current financing of the FSP. The FSP is a federal program such that 100 percent of benefits are paid for by the federal government out of general tax revenues. However, the program is administered locally by the states, each of which pay approximately 50 percent of local administrative costs. Given that the program has been mandatory since 1973, there have been efforts to shift the responsibility (and a higher burden of costs) on to the states. As such, the federal government would only be responsible for providing set block grants to the states – which by nature do not adjust to economic fluctuations – instead of having to pay the face value of the vouchers.

Not only have social advocacy groups resisted the cost-shifting proposal, but so has the powerful agriculture lobby (both the farming and retail sectors). This latter group stands to lose out in any cost-shifting arrangement for if the states assume greater control of the program, it is likely that they will redesign the program to cut costs. The fear of these interest groups is that the future aggregate expenditure by the states will be less than the current national expenditure on the FSP. This fear may be well grounded; as mentioned earlier, a USDA report in 1995 indicated that a reduction in funding of the FSP by one billion dollars would eliminate 25,000 jobs. It is in part because of the strength of this interest group that the FSP remains one of the last welfare programs wholly financed by the federal government.

The second debated option, "cashing-out," would also involve the provision of block grants by the federal government to the states. Under this scheme, however, the states would not be obliged to continue the FSP. Instead, the state could "cash-out" the program by replacing the stamps with general income assistance. The arguments favouring this option are, of course, lower administrative costs and reduction in stigma.

The political concern with the "cashing-out" option is that it would severely hurt the interests of those in need. Cashing-out the program leaves the states just one step away from amalgamating the food stamp benefits with other state-financed programs such as TANF. In creating one welfare payment, critics argue that the state will be inclined to cut the total benefits allotted. The aggregate benefits to a low-income earner under a lump-sum regime would thus place individuals in more vulnerable positions than they are in now. Given that fewer than 20 percent of food stamp recipient households rely solely on non-governmental sources for income,[75] the cashing-out option would have a detrimental effect on a high proportion of households.

A more immediate concern of cashing-out is the loss of political support for the FSP from the taxpaying population. The program has enjoyed political longevity and public endorsement for over 35 years. Once the limitation to food is lifted, the public perception of the program becomes "just another welfare payment." In a certain sense, the program may lose its political legitimacy. It moves from being a program that directly feeds the hungry to a program that provides general income maintenance support.

Conclusion

The FSP is the largest public assistance program in the United States available to all households based on financial need. Its relative success gives some credibility to the voucher concept as a politically popular means of delivering government-financed goods. Moreover, the constrained choices implicit within the FSP reflect both American society's willingness to provide food for the needy and its concern that public assistance will be abused. At the same time, however, it is important to note that most industrialized countries have consistently preferred the latter option. There thus is no *a priori* reason to believe that social assistance alone cannot meet both these concerns and hence why food stamps are inherently preferable to cash transfers in the form of adequate welfare benefits. As we have seen, evidence that FSP coupons actually increase household spending on food as compared with an equivalent cash grant is equivocal at best, and the effect varies according to household type. Furthermore, the political success of cash-transfer programs in other nations suggests that there is also no *a priori* reason to believe that "cashing-out" cannot gain popular support, particularly where it can be justified on grounds of fiscal efficiency.

Nevertheless, the simple claim that cashing-out will do the same job as the FSP while automatically lowering administrative costs is also not beyond doubt, particularly as there is some reason to believe that cashing-out will create some additional incentive for over-participation, particularly if it becomes clear that FSPs are not entirely cash equivalent. The empirical case for or against cashing-out is still unresolved, and more cash-out experiments are needed to illuminate the debate further. What the FSP example does establish with some certainty is that a few issues common to all voucher initiatives – consumer and supplier qualification, voucher valuation and political concerns – are decisive in determining their economic and political feasibility. It vindicates the view that particular voucher programs like the FSP fail or succeed not because they are voucher initiatives, but because they are able to respond well or poorly to a range of common design challenges as they manifest themselves in a given program area, as well as to local political imperatives.

4   Low-income housing

Introduction

Although the modern state has often assumed the responsibility of providing low-income households with accessibility to basic, reasonably priced housing, poignant statistics point to its failure in realizing this objective. The most publicized illustration of the state's failure in this regard has been the homelessness problem currently plaguing North America.[1] Homelessness, however, is only one indicator of the absence of affordable housing. Another is the fact that in the United States, one in two poor households have housing cost-to-income ratios exceeding the nominally prescribed 30 percent level.[2] In addition, one in four poor households lives in physically inadequate housing.[3]

Nor are such problems confined to North America. Indeed, as McCrone and Stephens observe of the European context, "in all countries, regardless of the average standard of living, there is a large section of the population that cannot afford the full economic cost of what would generally be regarded as an adequate or tolerable standard of housing."[4] Even in European states which have made a substantial commitment to improving housing, misguided policy efforts have in some cases made matters worse. Malpass, for instance, comments on a problem with the basic structure of the United Kingdom's housing policy:

> By making housing tenure [home ownership] seem a mark of social success or failure, "tenure policy" has contributed to the emergence of an acute shortage of affordable housing. The Government's emphasis on the virtues of home-ownership, and the subsequent reduction in the supply of cheap rented housing, has meant that low-income households now find it difficult to obtain suitable accommodation.[5]

Howenstine documents the consequences of a similar policy in the United States, where, since its inception in 1913, the federal income tax code has allowed home owners to deduct mortgage interest payments and property taxes from their gross incomes. Indirect home-ownership subsidies through tax deductions reached an estimated $59.6 billion in 1998, and now apply to mortgages of up to $1 million as well as to second homes, including cottages and other vacation residences.[6] In fact, households with incomes over $50,000 received 52 percent of all housing subsidies in 1998.[7] As Howenstine notes:

> If – as is generally accepted in principle – housing assistance should go to those in most need, such favourable treatment of the middle- and upper-income owners may be regarded as a misdirection of housing subsidies, and as one major explanation why more progress has not been made in reducing the affordable housing gap for low-income households [in jurisdictions where tenure subsidies have been a major part of housing strategy].[8]

Hence, in addition to a sheer quantitative lack of housing assistance, many jurisdictions are also experiencing what van Weesep and van Kempen call "a growing mismatch" of housing assistance and the actual needs of the population.[9] The pervasiveness of homelessness, excessive rent burdens, sub-standard housing and the use of subsidies to subvent middle-class home ownership has created an urgent need in many economically developed nations for a politically and fiscally viable affordable housing policy which targets directly the needs of low-income households.

Affordable housing

Before any housing policy can be examined, however, it is necessary to develop a working definition of the term "affordable housing." According to Peter Salsich, the term is used to describe "decent housing that is within the normal economic reach of families, accounting for the costs of non-shelter necessities, and utilizing income and family size as the defining parameters."[10] Alternatively, government agencies such as the Canadian Mortgage and Housing Corporation (CMHC), define affordable housing as physically adequate housing that does not consume more than 30 percent of household income.[11] For the purposes of this chapter, "affordable housing" will simply represent a sub-market of housing consisting of dwellings which are both physically adequate and financially accessible to low-income individuals. Given this understanding of "affordable housing," the term "unaffordability" can be taken to represent two ideas: first, that there exists an excessive financial burden on those that continue to participate in the housing market which must be offset by household cutbacks on other necessities;[12] second, and relatedly, that many low-income households have been priced out of the market for adequate housing services.

Adequate housing

Adequacy, it should be noted, is a relative property, and one which needs to be assessed according to different subjective criteria in different jurisdictions. For instance, the "sites and services" model, where the state builds a network of roads and sewerage and then allocates spaces for residents to build their own housing from available material as an alternative to squatting on public lands, is usually considered a dramatic improvement over the norm in less-developed countries (LDCs),[13] while the same conditions would of course be regarded as abysmal in the more-developed countries (MDCs) of North America and Europe.

Given the dramatic per capita income differences between LDCs and MDCs, such differences in the quality of housing considered adequate are not surprising. It is surprising, however, to note that adequacy standards vary dramatically even within the broad category of MDCs. In Japan, for instance, the average dwelling space per person irrespective of income group in 2001 was approximately 32.8 m²,[14] while the Ontario community rental housing program stipulates a standard size of 41.8 m² for a low-income bachelor apartment.[15] Furthermore, as McCrone and Stephens point out, generic "fitness" indices often do not adequately cover problems which at best can only be assessed subjectively at the local level, but which have a significant impact on quality of life, such as dampness in Northern European homes, or humidity due to heat in warmer climates.[16] Consequently, we will employ a relative and flexible definition of adequate housing as dwellings in which amenities are in good repair, the premises can be heated and cooled to a comfortable level, residents are protected from exposure to the elements, and in which overcrowding does not exceed a level tolerable according to local standards.

Rationales for government intervention

As Materu observes, there is a wide diversity of opinion among protagonists of housing investment for low-income people as to what its actual merits are.[17] Most claims, however, fall under one or more of the major normative rubrics outlined in Chapter 1, namely, building social solidarity, promoting economic stability and providing for the equitable distribution of resources.[18]

Building social solidarity

While the constituents of social solidarity are more subjective than those of poverty, and are harder to measure empirically, it is possible to speak broadly of some of the features of successful, stable communities: widespread participation in civil society, a sense of belonging and involvement in one's community,[19] relative safety from violence and other criminal activities, and tolerance of ethnic and other differences. Adequate housing is essential to the cultivation of these characteristics. Without a stable housing arrangement, families and individuals are unable to participate fully in the communities in which they reside.[20] The education of children is interfered with when their families must relocate frequently and abruptly, as well as when they are residing in inadequate housing. Individuals who do not develop stable links with their communities through sustained tenure are unlikely to become engaged in the activities of civil society or to advocate for their own political and economic rights. In Latin America, for instance, Castells reports that urban social movements based on the recognition of class interests are important means by which the poor lobby for land rights and infrastructure, means which are not available when communities are highly unstable, as when their constituencies are constantly preoccupied with finding temporary housing.[21]

The poverty of unstable communities where people are not properly housed often results in the proliferation of urban violence, while poorly planned communities geographically reproduce and reinforce preexisting ethnic segregations and tensions. A 1992 study covering 11,793 American housing projects (832,118 units) indicated that occupancy rates were as follows: 37 percent white tenants, 52 percent black tenants, and 11 percent Hispanic tenants.[22] Of the projects studied, 7,093 "drew at least 80 percent of their tenants from one racial group, whites in 4,100 and blacks in 2,973."[23] A 1969 court decision in *Gautreaux v. Chicago Housing Authority*[24] found that the concentration of black residents in poor urban Chicago represented a violation of the Fourteenth Amendment equal protection clause, touching off an ongoing project of litigation based on the claim of many experts that "[p]ublic housing remains [racially] segregated."[25]

Even in the absence of widespread acute homelessness, inadequate and poorly planned housing also presents a considerable threat to social solidarity by jeopardizing its basic determinants: life expectancy, health, and substantive civil and political rights. When the housing needs of low-income groups are not taken into direct consideration, the rapid and disorganized urbanization which has characterized the growth of many societies in the last 70 years often leads to the concentration of poverty and its attendant health and social consequences in certain geographical areas. As a 1996 report by HABITAT, the United Nations Centre for Human Settlements (hereinafter, "the Global Report") observes, there are considerable differences in terms of the principal determinants of social solidarity between those living in "high quality, predominantly high income areas and those living in poor quality, predominantly low-income areas."[26] The Global Report cites a number of studies to illustrate this point. Surprisingly, not all of its starkest examples come from the developing world. In the Easterhouse estate of Glasgow, for instance, the infant mortality rate exceeds 46 deaths per 1,000 births, while the rate in Bishopbriggs, a nearby middle-class suburb, stands at 10 deaths per 1,000 births.[27]

According to the Global Report, the effect of "housing-poverty"[28] on the determinants of social solidarity is often as dramatic as "income-poverty."[29] Conventional poverty studies often overlook the importance of "safe, secure and healthy shelter with basic infrastructure," even though "the proportion of the population living in housing of inadequate quality is often much higher than the proportion with below-poverty-line incomes."[30] The effect of poor housing on communities is both measurable and palpable:

> House values drop, and buildings deteriorate. Urban services departments spend less and less to maintain and upgrade ageing and vandalized infrastructures. [...] Tourists are very careful to avoid venturing into these areas. The juxtaposition of these pockets of poverty and more affluent areas generates envy on [the] one hand and fear on the other.[31]

In terms of its acute effects on individuals and the networks of social relationships which bind them, housing poverty also increases what Chambers calls "vulnerability": "defencelessness, insecurity, and exposure to risk, shocks and stress."[32] Such powerlessness also "weakens people's capacity to bargain for political and legal rights,"[33] an ability which is essential to full participation in the democratic process and hence to social solidarity, broadly construed.

Finally, the lack of affordable housing can lead to the outright failure of communities. In Guadalajara, Mexico, the economic crisis of the 1990s coupled with the absence of affordable housing led to a dramatic increase in emigration to the USA.[34] As the Global Report observes, "migration [also] became more heterogeneous since it now included male and female urban residents from working- and middle-class backgrounds as well as rural males who had previously been dominant in these emigration flows."[35] The stress of community failure is often transmitted to the sometimes only slightly more vibrant communities who must absorb the emigration flow, and who may find their own housing stock depleted, and their social services overwhelmed. The failure of local housing policies can thus have regional, national and (to an increasing degree) international repercussions in the form of economic, social and political destabilization.

Promoting economic stability

Materu, referencing the seminal work of Abrams, Grimes and Drakakis-Smith on the economic effects of low-income housing, particularly in LDCs, enumerates five major economic justifications for low-income housing investment by the state:

Employment: Housing investment can be an important source of employment for newly arrived rural migrants, whose alternative marginal product is low. Rural migrants, who often do not have the qualifications for urban employment, are absorbed in the construction industry, which provides an erratic but important source of jobs.

Income Multiplication: Housing programmes can activate construction-related industries, particularly those concerned with building materials.

Development Planning: Housing development fixes the location of public utilities and facilities. Housing investment can be used as a positive influence in development planning to affect both the pace and direction of growth. Appropriately located housing in relation to jobs in key sectors can lead to massive savings through lower commuting expenses. All these benefits can highly improve the efficiency of the urban economy.

Labour Productivity: Improved housing can lead to rising levels of aspiration. Improved health and greater safety, it is argued, foster individuals' mental and physical capacity for work, which is reflected in increased productivity of workers. Grimes' 1976 study of relocated miners in Korea, for instance, found that the health benefits of improved housing could be measured in a 50% reduction in the number of clinical visits, with an annual cost savings of US$13.94 for each household.

Economic Safety Valve: Well programmed housing investment can be used as a counter-cyclical measure to offset inflationary trends. In times of economic recession in the primary industries, investments flow across to the housing sector; in contrast, when profits are high in industrial operations, construction development all but ceases, as investments are reversed. Housing construction can thus be used to "take up the slack" in investment and employment during periods of recession and also furnish opportunities of expenditure curbs during periods of inflation.[36]

It is important to note, however, that the extent to which a particular housing investment initiative actually meets these objectives will depend on its scale and modalities. For instance, social housing programs where the state finances, builds and maintains ownership of housing units will not act as an inflationary cushion, since private citizens and corporations cannot invest in it. Rent subsidy programs which do not increase the stock of new housing will have little impact on development planning, since they will merely subsidize residency in preexisting communities. Finally, the employment and income multiplication effects of construction will only be experienced by the community being developed if the contractors or government agencies performing the construction recruit directly from the community in question; otherwise, the multiplication effect will likely benefit adjacent, and possibly already more affluent, communities. A major line of criticism with respect to foreign-run community development projects in LDCs holds that they mainly generate jobs for skilled workers from MDCs, and are thus really a form of supply-side subsidy for already-viable economies, a criticism which may also apply to development programs within MDCs.

Materu's appraisal of low-income housing as a form of economic investment is thus somewhat overly optimistic insofar as it fails to see the critical differences that the *kind* of investment can make. Moreover, it is predicated on the Keynesian notion that direct state intervention in markets is the best way of assuring a stable economy. A more *laissez-faire* argument might hold that poorly planned communities with unsustainable economies should simply be allowed to fail, and that subsidizing housing in struggling communities rewards mediocre planning. However, the analogy between communities and markets is a dubious one, particularly since the state has a fundamental role in the lifecycles of communities in virtue of its planning and management functions. Moreover, the social consequences of community failure, as discussed above, can be dire, and may ultimately propagate themselves in the form of widespread economic instability, both regionally and internationally. A qualified and more plausible claim is that certain investments in low-income housing can promote economic stability, but that the scope, scale and roles for state and market need to be considered carefully in each case.

Equitable distribution of resources

As discussed in Chapter 1, two fundamental goals of the modern welfare state have been the establishment of what Marshall termed a "social minimum,"[37] and the elimination of what Lord Beveridge called the "five giants on the road to reconstruction," including want, disease and squalor.[38] Adequate housing is an obvious element of the "social minimum," while the role of sanitary housing conditions in the alleviation of disease and squalor is obvious. Indeed, the Global Report provides extensive evidence of "the enormous health burden of poor quality housing."[39]

In nations such as France, Germany, Britain and the Netherlands, modern housing policies after World War II played a restitutional role, restoring living conditions in war-ravaged areas.[40] The pervasiveness of social democratic ideals in European society in the latter half of the twentieth century has helped to popularize the justification of social housing on equity grounds, a rationale that remains fairly widely embraced. The longevity, scale and cost of these policies bespeaks the continuing importance placed on the provision of adequate housing from the point of view of social equity. Indeed, as McCrone and Stephens observe, "[t]here is [...] no European country, no matter how advanced, where it is considered that housing can be left completely to the free market without state subvention in some form; and it would be unwise to assume that this will change with rising living standards."[41] Even the United States, which began effectively dismantling its National Housing Policy under the Reagan administration, reaffirmed its commitment to a comprehensive housing program with the 1990 Rouse/Maxwell Report, stating that "the Federal Government must reaffirm its role as a leader in finding solutions to the country's housing problems."[42]

It can thus be said that there is some consensus that housing should not be considered merely as a market commodity,[43] but rather as an intrinsic social good. Most societies place a value on housing that extends beyond economic willingness-to-pay schedules. In fact, the equity argument for adequate housing is considered so intuitive that it is now protected as a fundamental international right. Article 25 of the Universal Declaration of Human Rights states:

> [e]veryone has a right to a standard of living adequate for the health and well-being of himself and of his family, including food, clothing, housing and medical care and necessary social services.[44]

However original it may seem to conceptualize housing as a human right, the clause merely states, in the language of what Michael Ignatieff calls "the rights revolution,"[45] a fact which is already enshrined in the housing policies of most states in Europe, North America and Asia: that the absence of adequate housing is beneath human dignity, and an indictment of any society which permits it.

Modes of provision

A survey of housing assistance programs in MDCs reveals that nations can, and do, adopt a range of policy approaches to the problem of inadequate housing. According to Hallett, countries "can be crudely divided, according to their housing systems, into three groups:" comprehensive state socialist nations, more moderate social democratic countries like most Western European nations and the United Kingdom, and "predominantly private enterprise" systems like the United States.[46] However, given the near absence of comprehensive socialist states in the current century, and the broad transnational trends of privatization, deregulation and private-public partnerships, our analysis will continue to rely on the policy spectrum outlined in Chapter 2, which ranges from pure public provision to tax-and-transfer policies, with supply- and demand-side subsidies situated in between. Our analysis will emphasize the tied demand-side subsidy as the basis for comparison, and will attempt to establish the successes and failures of other modes in meeting the housing needs of modern states, with a view towards evaluating whether voucher programs actually present a better alternative.

It merits notice that many states employ a mixture of various instruments, and that classifying certain programs is difficult. For instance, the primary forms of social assistance are welfare benefits programs, which represent straight tax-and-transfer instruments. Participants in the Ontario Works program, for instance, receive a basic Personal Needs Assistance (PNA) allowance, which is supplemented by a Shelter Allowance if the participant is responsible for rent or mortgage payments. Several Canadian jurisdictions, however, also employ rent control measures. Since the two approaches are used in tandem to address a single policy problem – inadequate housing for low-income households – it is difficult to say which rubric the Canadian "solution" falls under, or the extent to which its successes or failures are due to either instrument. In the interest of providing clear comparative evidence, however, such ambiguous cases will not be examined in detail. We have instead favoured, where possible, case studies which clearly represent one of our four classes of policy instruments.

Pure public provision

As in other program areas, the highest degree of "socialization" of housing is found in the states of the European Union (EU). Since the fall of communism, however, there have been no nations in the Western hemisphere where the state is entirely responsible for planning, constructing, managing and regulating affordable housing. Instead, the model of "social rented housing," (SRH) where the state promotes and regulates affordable housing for low-income families but delegates construction and operation to local associations and companies, has been the dominant mode of housing assistance in EU countries.[47] The Netherlands has the largest proportion of SRH in the EU (36 percent in 1994), and its private rented stock has steadily declined since the early post-war years.[48] In Sweden, the majority of rented dwellings are also SRH units.[49] In France, many *habitations à loyer modéré* (HLMs), municipal housing associations designed to help place eligible candidates in low-rent accommodations, are run by local authorities.[50] Spain[51] and Italy[52] represent major anomalies, with just 1 percent and 5.4 percent of their respective housing stocks taking the form of SRH units.

Though it involves extensive participation by the state, SRH is not to be mistaken for publicly provided housing. Even in Sweden, for instance, which has one of the largest proportions of SRH units in its housing stock and maintains what Barlow and Duncan call "a strongly interventionist [housing] regime,"[53] the state restricts itself to funding (either partially or completely), promoting and regulating the construction of new units. Large domestic firms account for the majority of building activity, and sub-contract to smaller firms for certain specialized tasks.[54] In Britain, Italy and Sweden, which represent examples of "liberal," "corporatist" and "social democratic" welfare capitalist regimes, respectively, a high degree of public and private collaboration is (and has long been) the norm.[55]

Given the paucity of empirical evidence and contemporary experience with pure public provision in the case of housing, constructing the putative case in favour of public provision is a highly speculative matter. A major rationale for pure public provision is the decommodification of housing, and the conversion of housing from a market good into a social one. Given its enormous costs, pure public provision of housing only appeals to what Barlow and Duncan call "solidaristic, universalistic and decommodifying welfare system[s]."[56] A quote from the literature of the Housing Program in the defunct German Democratic Republic (GDR) is illustrative:

> The historical social and geographical differences in living conditions are to be eliminated. In this way a basic ideal of socialist development, the gradual attainment of equality between different classes and social groups, will be realized.[57]

The problems with pure public provision of housing are overwhelming, as the signal example of the GDR demonstrates. The massive allocation of new housing construction projects to a few large firms (*Kombinate*) eliminated the local building capacity of many towns and communities, and contributed to their decay, a bitterly ironic outcome for a program intended to revitalize East German communities.[58] The inefficiency of the highly ambitious 1973–90 Housing Program was compounded by the GDR leadership's resolute refusal to "see" inefficiencies endemic to its socialist economy; more fundamentally, the GDR's centrally control-led economy lacked the dynamism and incentive measures required to realize the Housing Program's massive goals.[59] "Architectural monoculture," too inflexible to meet the wide range of housing needs, was a side effect of state monopoly.[60] In the private low-rent housing sector, the steadily shrinking class of property owners was impoverished by the artificial deflation of rents (in rural areas, rents sometimes amounted to less than 0.9 percent of the average household's monthly income), while tenants saw their dwellings steadily deteriorate as landlords could no longer afford to maintain them.[61] Finally, the housing preferences of citizens were mostly ignored, resulting in both drastically over- and under-supplied markets.[62]

While the inadequacy of Marxist-socialist economic planning is ultimately responsible for most of the failures of the GDR's Housing Program, the example of the GDR does help to identify a few principal problems with pure public provision of housing: the absence of strong incentives for efficient production; the inability of a centrally planned housing authority to respond rapidly to diverse and changing local needs and preferences; and the difficulty of fixing affordable and sustainable housing rents without the economic forces operative in a more liberal market system. Centrally planned housing in the GDR and in the United States tended to be concentrated in large public housing projects, which were often far from major centres of employment for low-income earners, resulting in a labour mobility problem and the "ghettoization" of the poor. In contrast, the relative success of the Swedish "interventionist" regime (the most "public" of existing housing systems) in these regards can arguably be attributed to its "private" features; namely, its judicious use of demand- and supply-side subsidies rather than heavy-handed central planning and provision. In 1993, nearly 50 percent of spending on housing subsidies in Sweden took the form of interest-subsidized loans for new private housing units.[63] Twenty-two percent of housing in Sweden is provided by non-profit corporations, who receive construction subsidies from the state but retain local authority over the scale and type of housing.

The only jurisdictions in which centrally planned public provision remains a strongly favourable option are in certain LDCs where high levels of grossly inadequate housing and "informal" residence (squatting and the erection of shanty towns) and an absence of a capital market for low-income housing investment make public housing projects (such as the "sites and services" model discussed earlier) seem viable alternatives. Even in such states, however, public provision is seen as a palliative measure, a temporary solution intended to prevail only until governments are able to establish a market for mortgages and a more robust land-ownership and low-income rental strategy.[64]

Supply-side subsidies

Supply-side subsidies, traditionally in the form of construction and operation funding to private for- and non-profit housing associations, have formed the mainstay of most EU housing programs. In the Netherlands, the SRH sector is divided between housing associations, local authorities and other non-profit institutions who arrange for the construction of, and then manage, housing units, with funding from one of two central authorities (the National Housing Council and the Netherlands Christian Housing Institute).[65] A similar scheme obtains in Britain, although local authorities have somewhat more discretion in terms of the type and location of housing units as compared with other EU nations.[66] Prior to a massive corruption scandal, non-profit housing associations run in a similar fashion conducted "the dominant part of social housing programs" in Germany.[67] Until recently, *habitations à loyer modéré* (HLMs), low-income housing financed by government grants and operated by non-profit bodies and co-operatives, formed a major part of France's low-income housing strategy.

With the notable exception of Sweden, however, such highly interventionist supply-side subsidy programs have declined in breadth and popularity since the mid to late 1970s. For instance, the deregulation of the financial sector in the USA and the UK under the Republican and Conservative governments of the 1980s, coupled with cuts to public expenditures, led to an increasing reliance on the commercial sector to meet the housing needs of low-income households in those states.[68] In other nations, by contrast, the state has remained directly involved in subventing housing, but has changed its principal mode of intervention. In France, for instance, the Housing Act of 1977 introduced a new system of "bricks and mortar" subsidies (PLA) to housing developers to stimulate construction in the low-income rental sector, and rehabilitation grants for the upkeep of both private for- and non-profit low-income rental units (PAH and PALULOS).[69] Rather than undertaking to build low-income housing, the French government has favoured a program of low-interest grants to developers with stipulations such as quality standards and rent controls. The Community Rental Housing program in Ontario, which aims "to remove barriers that increase capital costs for rental buildings and the rents that tenants must pay," grants funding to private developers, provided companies invest their own equity as well, at a minimum of 10 percent of a project's lending value for the first mortgage. The same program also waives equity investment requirements for non-profit groups such as service clubs and religious or charitable organizations who wish to invest in low-income housing.[70]

The supply-side subsidization approach to low-income housing entails many of the benefits of supply-side subsidy programs generally, as discussed in Chapter 2. The competition and ownership effects can be expected to create incentives for cost-effective service provision, while the tied nature of most supply-side subsidies can act as a counterbalance to the profit motive, requiring providers to meet certain quality and accessibility standards. Inefficient or inadequate housing providers will be forced to exit the market. Moreover, supply-side subsidies can also act as a stimulus to the private financial sector, particularly where subsidies to developers include a private equity investment requirement. A further advantage of supply-side subsidies is their ability to target non-profit groups, including those whose services already directly target the needs of low-income groups. As discussed earlier, partially assisting private sector investors can enable the inflationary cushioning effects of investment in building and real estate.

The most cogent argument in favour of supply-side housing subsidies, however, is that they can act as direct stimuli for new construction, thus increasing the available supply of low-income housing. This is particularly salutary in jurisdictions where the existing housing stock is in an advanced state of decay, but where rehabilitation investment on the part of low-income unit landlords is unlikely to furnish a sufficient profit. In such situations, supply-side subsidies which target the construction of new low-income rental units may be preferable to the alternatives. As mentioned earlier, the Swedish example certainly speaks to the effectiveness of such policies, albeit under a limited set of circumstances including low population density, a homogeneous population, and a relatively low level of income polarization.

The major objection to supply-side subsidies, however, concerns "the substitution question," namely, "do [targeted construction subsidies] add to the stock of housing, or do [units constructed through such subsidies] merely substitute for units that would have been produced with other finance sources?"[71] That is, how successful are subsidies at stimulating a sustainable increase in the stock of available low-income housing units?

Malpezzi and Vandell conclude that the critical variable is the price elasticity of housing supply:

> If the market is more or less unresponsive to changes in price, and if the number of low-income households is largely unaffected by the presence of absence of this additional subsidized housing, then the additional [subsidized] housing will have two salutary effects [...] First, the [new] subsidized housing itself will be available for rent, presumably below *ex ante* market rents, so households who participated will presumably benefit from lower rents and possibly better housing conditions. Second, [...] the price of housing will fall in the rest of the market, as [supply increases] and demand for the [previously] fixed stock falls. [...]
>
> On the other hand, if the supply of housing is perfectly elastic [...] an initial fall in the price of housing will lead to a reduction in its supply. Such a reduction will take place until the *ex ante* market price is restored. The total stock of housing will be unaffected *ex post*; but the new [...] units will crowd out an equivalent quantity of unsubsidized housing.[72]

Consequently, there is no reason to assume that construction subsidies will automatically increase the low-income housing stock, particularly where there is reason to believe that the supply market is highly elastic (highly responsive to price changes). Indeed, Murray[73] finds that over a period of roughly fifty years, the construction of subsidized, moderate-income housing (targeted at roughly 80 percent of median income) does not have a statistically significant effect on the total stock of low-income housing. For low-income social housing (targeted at roughly the poverty line), this crowding-out effect does not appear to occur.

Moreover, the critical assumption that an increase in subsidized units will not have an effect on the number of low-income households may not hold true; that is, in an inelastic market, new households could form from the city's existing population as larger households can afford to split up and "doubling up" decreases, while households could also migrate to the city if discouraged by the cost and availability of housing elsewhere. This increase in demand could deplete the housing stock and drive rents back up, thus mitigating the alleged benefits of construction subsidies.[74]

Furthermore, given the relatively small profits to be had through investment in low-income housing, there is no reason to assume that investor interest will necessarily be adequate to meet the demand for new housing units. In fact, a major housing dynamic in urban centres is "filtering (or 'trickling') down," where middle-class dwellings, which eventually deteriorate and become less valuable, eventually filter down to lower-income groups:

> The "trickle down" process is a well recognized concept in the housing market. As a household builds and occupies a new house, existing housing is vacated, making it available for occupancy by lower income households, who in turn liberate their own accommodation as they move up-market. Through this

continuous chain of moves, more housing is ultimately made available for the poor.[75]

In centres where this dynamic is preponderant, subsidies for the construction of middle-class housing may, it can be argued, have a more dramatic effect on low-income housing availability than subsidies which directly target only the construction of low-income housing units, particularly insofar as developers are likely to find the higher profitability of middle-class housing units more attractive. Howenstine, however, cautions that this "trickle down" process slowed considerably in the early 1990s.[76] Moreover, access to middle-class housing, which increasingly takes the form of single-family homes as opposed to rental units, also requires access to the mortgage market, which low-income households (and particularly the poorest among them) may find difficult, if not impossible. There are also geographical problems as far as access to the labour market is concerned – the housing vacated by middle-class families may be in a suburb distant from the areas where the adult members of most low-income households are employed.

In any event, studies such as those conducted by Malpezzi and Vandell cast doubt on the effectiveness of such subsidies in increasing the housing stock. Except in markets where it can be assured that (1) their effect on the number of households will be negligible and (2) the degree of supply elasticity is quite low, supply-side subsidies are unlikely to accomplish their stated objective. In nations such as Sweden, where income polarization and birth rates are low, communities are relatively small, mobility is limited, and housing patterns are stable, these conditions can be met, and may make supply-side subsidies highly attractive. Elsewhere, however, the case is likely to be far more equivocal.

Demand-side subsidies

The nation with the most widespread and recent experience with demand-side subsidies for housing is the United States. Since the Reagan administration, there has been a steady shift in the allocation of housing funding away from construction of affordable, locally managed housing and towards vouchers, which are used to rent in the private sector.[77] By 1993, 1.3 million households were receiving vouchers, about the same number as were then living in traditional public housing projects.[78] The Clinton administration continued this trend of privatization, and from 1993 to 1998, a further 76,000 (or about 6 percent of the total stock) units of Department of Housing and Urban Development (HUD) housing were demolished.[79]

The principal, and simplest, argument in favour of a voucher approach to low-income housing is its cost efficiency. By creating a viable demand market for low-income housing, it is argued, developers can be induced to build facilities and compete for the voucher dollars of low-income families, driving down rents and increasing quality. Where a robust "information market" exists, the reputation of various housing developments will strengthen incentives for quality service provision, and drive inadequate or inefficient suppliers out of the market. Moreover, privatization divests the government of the responsibility for maintaining facilities, as well as for the capital costs associated with construction, and provides a stimulus for the private sector in the construction, building maintenance and financial industries.

Consumer choice is particularly relevant in the case of housing, as place of residence often determines access to schools, job markets and community services. Instead of concentrating low-income families in particular neighbourhoods by requiring them to reside in public housing projects, vouchers give them greater mobility. If low-income households increasingly elect to leave certain neighbourhoods or housing clusters, these projects will eventually fail. Indeed, the mobility of voucher recipients may create incentives on the part of landlords to better maintain their buildings, aware that consumers always retain the option of "taking their business elsewhere." How significant this option is, however, essentially depends on how affordable housing is distributed; there is always the possibility that public housing ghettoes will simply "switch over" into private housing slums. The evidence that vouchers increase dispersion is equivocal. According to Peterson:

> Although there is some clustering of voucher families in practice, voucher tenants are considerably more dispersed geographically than are households living in subsidized housing projects, and are considerably less likely to live in neighborhoods with high poverty rates or homogeneous racial profiles.[80]

As recently as 2000, however, many commentators on the aforementioned *Gautreaux* litigation continue to claim that even after Chicago adopted housing vouchers, low-income households "remain in [racially] segregated areas, simply moving from government owned to privately owned housing."[81]

Such considerations notwithstanding, it is at least plausible that by expanding the demand market, vouchers may be able to stimulate new construction and enlarge the affordable housing stock. As with supply-side subsidies, however, the constraining factor is market supply elasticity, a factor which can have a dramatic effect on the consequences of vouchering for low-income households. Suppose that vouchers are adopted in a jurisdiction where the average low-income rent is $300/mo., and eligible families find they can now afford $400/mo. for housing. There are two possibilities. In an elastic market, suppliers in the $400/mo. range will proliferate. In an inelastic market, however, the number of suppliers will not increase commensurately. As a result, demand will increase without a commensurate increase in supply, and rents will be driven up. Such a demand-side subsidy would be little more than a *de facto* supply-side subsidy to landlords of $100/mo., with no clear incentive to improve quality or quantity of affordable housing.

Susin notes a secondary and more vexing effect:

> [S]ince housing assistance is not an entitlement, but is instead rationed via a waiting list, subsidized renters compete with a large group of income-eligible non-recipients. In fact, about 70 percent of those with incomes low enough to be eligible [for various types of housing assistance] do not receive vouchers, live in housing projects, or receive any other housing subsidy. These non-

recipients will be hurt by vouchers if the increased demand raises market rents.[82]

By itself, it is troubling that demand-side subsidies will simply ramp up the demand and act as an effective cash transfer to landlords with no impact on quality or quantity of affordable housing; it is seriously troubling if demand-side subsidies will act to price non-recipient households out of their homes. To the extent that they do so, vouchers may create a horizontal equity problem, creating arbitrary inequalities within a given income stratum.

Susin's comprehensive study of the effect of the United States' "Section 8" voucher program, where eligible low-income families selected from a waiting list receive a rent voucher scaled to income, seems to vindicate the view that rent vouchers effectively "bid up" market rents without stimulating new construction in the low-income housing sector:

> [L]ow-income households in metropolitan areas with more vouchers have experienced faster rent increases than those where vouchers are less abundant. In the 90 biggest metropolitan areas, vouchers have raised rents by 16 percent on average, a large effect consistent with a low supply elasticity in the low quality rental housing market. Considered as a transfer program, this result implies that vouchers have caused a $8.2 billion increase in the total rent paid by low-income non-recipients, while only providing a subsidy of $5.8 billion to recipients, resulting in a net loss of $2.4 billion to low-income households.[83]

Susin's study is based on so-called "first difference" methodology, which controls for rent-increasing factors affecting all income sectors, such as inflation. It is therefore able to isolate and examine the effect of vouchering on the lowest trecile of households reliably, which makes its results all the more striking, considering that they pertain to a policy which specifically targets assistance to families in that trecile. "Despite its moderate size," concludes Susin, "the effect of the voucher program on rents is surprisingly large."[84]

As Susin affirms, however, the critical issue is low supply elasticity. The major research challenge presented by the findings, argues Susin, "is to distinguish which particular feature of low-income housing markets inhibits their adjustment to demand shocks."[85] He suggests a few such features which may account for this low elasticity:

> [The lack of free exit:] An apartment building yielding low rents cannot be removed from the market except through demolition. There may be landlords in a poor neighbourhood who are earning enough to cover their operating costs, and thus they do not abandon the building. Increased rents would then raise profits, but do nothing to increase entry. [...]
> [Restrictive policies and standards:] Local policies may also restrict the creation of low-income housing, reducing the elasticity of supply. Examples include habitability laws, building codes, and zoning restrictions like minimum lot

sizes and bans on the conversion of single family housing into multiple occupancy units.[86]

These conclusions suggest that voucher programs need to be accompanied by regulatory changes intended to increase supply-side elasticity and allow the supply market to respond to demand-side changes in ways other than simply increasing rents. Ironically, Susin's last remark is that "construction subsidies may do more to improve the housing conditions of the poor"[87] in light of supply-market inelasticities, while Malpezzi and Vandell's article[88] considers supply-side subsidies less effective for precisely the same reason.

One possibility, however, which Susin fails to consider is the explanation that, while vouchers which only increase rental spending power among low-income households by a small amount act to bid up rents, larger or more widely available vouchers may be able to stimulate the entry of new suppliers. According to this theory, it is the valuation of and eligibility for vouchers, and not the basic design of the instrument itself, which needs to be reconsidered. Indeed, according to Mayo,[89] a dollar of spending on social housing produces 37 cents of housing, while the same dollar would have produced 85 to 90 cents of housing with allowances, primarily due to the cost advantage of providing low-income housing through filtering, rather than new construction.

In any event, the Susin and Malpezzi–Vandell studies vindicate the view that housing subsidies depend greatly on the market in which they are intended to operate, and that the particular modalities of a given voucher program need to take factors like supply-side elasticity into careful consideration. Inelastic supply markets mitigate the consumer choice advantage of vouchers and certainly do nothing to increase competition on the supply-side. By reinstituting complex government regulation and oversight to resolve elasticity problems through central planning, however, highly interventionist voucher schemes may actually restore much of the administrative gridlock they are intended to alleviate. Clearly, the balance between the state's tendency to overregulate and the problems of an open market is, in the case of housing vouchers, quite precarious.

Tax-and-transfer policies

As discussed in Chapter 2, where vouchers exhibit a high degree of cash equivalency, they will be considered *de facto* cash grants. The logic is reversible: where cash grants are tied in such a way that a fixed portion will effectively be allocated to a particular prescribed use, that portion should be considered a *de facto* voucher. Most modern welfare states already provide indirect housing assistance in the form of welfare benefits, a large portion of which is assumed to be allocated to lodgings. In fact, since many jurisdictions require recipients to find suitable housing before they become eligible for benefits, a portion of welfare benefits can be thought of as a cash transfer ear-marked for spending on housing, making such tied benefits into *de facto* housing vouchers. This is the case, for instance, in Ontario, where receipt of the maximum individual Ontario Works benefit of $520 per month is contingent on residence in suitable rental accommodation; persons living on the street or in rent-free shelters are not eligible for full benefits, and instead receive only the far more modest Personal Needs Assistance grant. While some jurisdictions, such as Sweden and France, do give welfare recipients a high degree of discretion, no states currently rely on cash grants as the only source of housing assistance; as mentioned earlier, both Sweden and France have fairly extensive SRH programs in place which work to maximize welfare benefits.

The argument against "untying" welfare benefits from their housing requirement is both familiar and obvious. By liberating the lion's share of benefits as cash, a financial incentive is created on the part of the recipient to live in cheap but severely substandard housing, regardless of the consequences for personal or public health. In fact, taken to its logical conclusion, there is no reason why untying benefits in this fashion would not result in an "informal housing boom," given the financial incentive on the part of welfare recipients to live rent-free on public or private land in order to maximize available cash.

Whether or not this scenario is as alarmist as it may sound is not clear, as no jurisdiction has seriously contemplated such a policy. However, it is not difficult to see why political support for the removal of the suitable housing requirement of welfare benefits is likely to be weak at best. Moreover, in the case of those groups for whom adequate housing is most easily justified on humanitarian grounds – families with children – a significant principal–agent problem presents itself as parents have an incentive to spend insufficiently on adequate housing for their children in order to liberate further cash. There is reason to expect that a system which removes the housing requirement of welfare benefits and replaces it with an equal cash grant is likely to be both politically unpopular and ineffective at resolving housing shortages.

Design challenges

Vouchering has obvious advantages over pure public provision, while cash grants do not present a viable alternative. Like supply-side subsidies, however, and in view of the objective of increasing the stock of affordable housing, voucher programs encounter a major difficulty in the form of supply-side inelasticity. A program which fails to produce a sustainable increase in the number of units of affordable housing must be said to have failed to resolve the housing crisis.

The major challenge facing a voucher-based housing policy, then, is to establish how vouchers can best be used to stimulate new construction of affordable housing to meet the needs of a growing population, and to ensure that these units remain accessible to low-income households. It is possible, however, to separate this challenge into two principal design problems: ensuring that low-income households gain access to vouchers, thus creating a stable and adequate demand market for low-income housing; and ensuring that the proper incentive mechanisms are in place to stimulate the supply-side market to provide housing which meets the actual needs of low-income households, including the construction of new units if necessary.

Ensuring a demand-side market: increasing access by low-income households

A major problem with current voucher-based housing initiatives in the United States is the low number of low-income households actually receiving benefits. As Peterson observes:

> Low-end demand financed through a combination of vouchers and household income growth has not kept pace with privately financed middle-income demand resulting from economic growth. Rents in the low-income housing market have risen at approximately the same rate as rents in the rest of the housing market. However, as long as only 36 percent of income-eligible households receive housing assistance, and if household incomes at the lower end of the income distribution continue to lag behind growth in the rest of the economy, housing affordability for unsubsidized households [...] will worsen.[90]

The solution to the horizontal equity problem, in Peterson's view, consists in eliminating the long housing queues associated with housing assistance and making eligibility requirements less restrictive. In order for a voucher initiative to be successful in creating a demand-side market of sufficient size to produce a commensurate response from the supply-side, it needs to ensure more widespread participation; otherwise, vouchers will simply bid up rents and price non-recipients out of the market. It is nevertheless important to note that simply increasing participation without increasing the number of units also has the potential to bid up rents. As discussed earlier, demand-side subsidies must be accompanied by measures which encourage a supply-side response.

Stimulating the supply market

Faced with a sudden increase in the rent budget of the lowest trecile of renters, there are two possible effects on the supply market: either the increase will be met with an increase in suppliers through new developments; or the supply market will maintain its original proportions, driving up rents and increasing profits. Assuming that suppliers act as rational agents, in an unconstrained market, the latter option will be preferred, in view of its lower opportunity cost: where there is sizeable demand (assured by the tied nature of housing vouchers) for a fixed housing stock, it costs landlords nothing to raise rents, as there is no risk of increased vacancy in a market where housing is scarce, which is the case in many major metropolitan areas.

To counteract this tendency towards bidding up rents, incentives need to be established to facilitate the entry option. Supply-side subsidy programs which target new low-income housing construction or conversion projects and encourage partnerships between community groups, private investors and the public sector have an important role to play in resolving the housing crisis. In addition, land-use regulations that create barriers to the construction of low-income rental accommodation or to the conversion of existing housing to multiple units should be repealed. Similarly, property taxes that discriminate in favour of single-family housing and against multiple occupancy rental accommodation should be eliminated. In contrast, rent controls are likely to discourage new suppliers from entering the market and may cause existing units to be withdrawn from the rental market and should be avoided.[91]

Conclusion

We believe that the evidence generally supports the conclusions of William Strange in a recent review of comparative experience with low-income housing policies:[92]

1 Construction subsidies or new publicly built (or social) housing should be targeted at the sort of dwellings used by the most needy. Otherwise, the evidence suggests that privately supported housing will be crowded out by subsidized supply and the total stock of low-income housing is unlikely to increase.
2 If vouchers or other demand-side subsidies are to be provided to some low-income households, they should be provided to the entire population with similar income. Otherwise the price of housing is likely to rise, leaving a group of low-income households actually worse off than before the introduction of the subsidies.
3 The temptation to introduce rent-controls should be resisted. While these may improve affordability in the short-run, they are likely to reduce housing stock in the long-run.
4 Land-use regulations that create barriers to the supply of low-income rental housing should be repealed.
5 Property tax discrimination against rental housing should be eliminated.
6 Because of the mobility of both low-income families and taxpayers, low-income housing issues cannot be dealt with only at the local government level but require regional or central government support.

We also endorse the view of Priemus that in "times of overall housing shortage, property subsidies [that is, supply-subsidies to developers] are recommended as a temporary measure to increase supply. Housing allowances are the instrument of choice in normal situations."[93]

5   Legal aid

Introduction

Essential legal services, despite their overwhelming significance to those who, for example, are confronted directly by the coercive power of the state in the criminal law domain, are not funded or provided universally by any government in the developed world. Instead, legal aid in most jurisdictions consists of a patchwork quilt of legal clinics, duty counsel initiatives and voucher or certificate programs.

The need for legal aid, unlike the need for "universal goods" such as health care and education, is a highly contingent one that is relatively constrained in ambit – only a minority of the population will ever need criminal defence counsel, legal representation at an immigration or custody hearing, or need to contest the cessation of social assistance benefits, services which are generally recognized as basic and essential. Most citizens' encounters with the legal system take the form of personal or commercial transactions and other private litigation, which, while important, can hardly justify the designation of legal aid as a universally essential service.

Yet there is reason to believe that the complete withdrawal of the government from the provision of basic legal services to needy persons would likely be disastrous. If the government abdicated its responsibility for legal aid and attempted to rely only on optional, private insurance markets, for instance, the adequate supply of private insurance would be undermined by the existence of adverse selection problems, since persons who were more inclined to commit crimes would seek insurance to cover the anticipated costs of representation (or to afford better representation than they would otherwise have access to).[1] On the other hand, persons who were unlikely to violate the law would probably not purchase insurance, or would be willing to buy insurance only at a very low premium.

Since there would be no easy (if any) way for insurers to determine reliably whether someone is a high-risk or low-risk individual, the insurance market would fail or would supply such a limited range of coverage that people would have to self-insure to a great extent – a strategy that would be insufficient in the case of complex, serious and lengthy matters, given the extremely high costs of legal advice and representation in such matters. In addition, given society's dedication to the rule of law and the intuitively offensive nature of convicting someone who has not had the benefit of competent legal advice and representation, it would be extremely difficult for governments to remain committed to a policy of not directly ensuring some basic legal advice for an accused who was without counsel because of lack of insurance.

Like any other public service, however, legal aid can be provided by a wide variety of instruments, ranging from a staff of government-employed public defenders to the issuance of vouchers or certificates redeemable for a fixed amount and/or type of legal assistance from private legal service providers. Our objective in this chapter will be to consider the advantages, if any, which a tied demand-side subsidy program offers over the alternatives, and to examine the design challenges encountered by voucher initiatives in this policy area.

The rationales for government intervention

It is crucial to note that the normative rationale invoked to justify the provision of legal services and the actual range of legal services provided are intrinsically linked. Positive egalitarian positions which hold that equal access to justice in all its forms is a basic right will necessarily entail demands for a far more comprehensive menu of publicly provided legal services than will the minimalist libertarian position that the state should avoid interfering in the lives of its citizens to the greatest extent possible. In other words, the legal services that a state deems "essential" correlate not to some universal objective standard, but rather to the grounds on which the provision of legal services is justified in the first place.

Thus, for instance, the Legal Action Group (LAG) in Britain, which places heavy emphasis on the "equal" qualifier of Great Britain's policy of "equal access to justice," argues that "[t]he ultimate policy aim must be that anyone with a legal problem has equal access to its just conclusion so that disputes are determined by the intrinsic merits of the arguments of either party, not by inequalities of wealth or power."[2] Consequently, the LAG recommends the inclusion of several forms of civil litigation as an essential legal service, as well as for extensive alternative dispute resolution to remove the financial barriers to justice presented by the cost of taking matters to trial.[3] As Griffiths points out, this argument contains two hidden premises: that "legal services are a kind of wealth," and that the state's goal is to remedy inequalities in wealth by redistribution, to the greatest extent possible.[4]

This justification will not be acceptable, however, in a more libertarian state, where income redistribution is not seen as a legitimate governmental objective. Such a state is more likely to emphasize guarantees of procedural rather than substantive equality, with a corresponding and more modest scale of public legal services. Luban, for instance, considers that since political legitimacy in such states is grounded on the notion of "equality-of-rights-not-fortune," the primary purpose of access to legal services is to assure the basic equality of legal rights.[5] This argument is consistent with the influential doctrine of Rawlsian liberalism which holds that formal equality (fairness in procedure) as opposed to substantive equality (equality of outcome) should be the guiding principle of the just society.[6] Other positions (e.g. civic republicanism and communal liberalism) exist along the spectrum between the fairly radical stances of egalitarians and libertarians. Such normative nuances account, in large part, for the variety of legal aid policies in place around the world, and make the comparison of different systems more challenging.

There are three broad notions, however, present to varying degrees in most programs of justification for government intervention in the provision of legal services: the importance of equal access to the justice system from the point of view of liberal values and social solidarity; the necessity of access for the survival of the rule of law itself; and the role that the justice system plays in establishing and maintaining patterns of resource distribution. When looking to these rationales we should ask not only whether they are able to justify state funding to legal aid, but also whether they are able to address such questions as: why should some sorts of matters receive funding but not others; and how is legal aid funding different from other state support to the needy, including access to other basic services (like dental services, plumbing, automobile repairs etc.)?

Liberal values and social solidarity

Liberalism respects the equal freedom and dignity of individuals. In addition, the adversarial system of justice that exists throughout the common law world is based on a liberal respect for individual autonomy. That is, the state's role in a trial (in the person of the judge) is limited by the system's faith in the ability of parties to represent their own interests adequately. Rather than paternalistically intervening to determine the "truth of the matter" between the opposing parties, the judge in the adversarial system allows each party to present their own case, and arrives at a judgment that is based (in theory) exclusively on the submissions of the parties, the evidence adduced and the applicable law. Despite this *prima facie* preference for party autonomy, however, a state that is committed to liberal values will seek to ensure that each party has access to adequate and roughly equal legal representation. That is, if the parties are for whatever reason radically unequal in their ability to represent their case (or even worse, in their ability to understand the relevant law), then a liberal state will seek to intervene to help ensure relative equality in this regard.

Moreover, in the context of a pluralistic society which not only tolerates but positively encourages a diversity of moral points of view, the common commitment to fairness or justice – construed as the granting of equal consideration to all perspectives and parties – may be one of the only common values shared by all members of society, and hence an important source of social solidarity in societies where such solidarity does not already exist due to ethnic, cultural or religious differences, or the lack of a moral consensus. Consequently, equal access to the legal system can be seen as a substantive guarantee of an abstract civic value (justice), one essential to societal cohesion. As Michael Ignatieff observes, "It may seem strange to confess a love for something so seemingly legalistic and desiccated as rights. Yet [...] rights create and sustain culture and by culture we mean habits of the heart. Rights create community. [And] [d]efending your own rights means being committed to defending the rights of others."[7] This commitment entails extending to all citizens the means of asserting those rights under the rule of law, instead of through the alternatives of sedition and violence, which can guarantee only the most artificial form of social solidarity: the kind assured by coercion.

The rule of law[8]

The rule of law argument for the provision of legal aid is based on the Hobbesian notion that the publicity of laws is required for the rule of law itself.[9] This view begins from the premise that the rule of law requires that all those subject to the law be able to learn and know its content. This does not require that the state must ensure that everyone is in fact aware of and comprehends the full range of laws to which they are subject. It simply requires that those who are actively engaged in an activity, proceeding or transaction that implicates a particular body of law (whether criminal, family or otherwise) have the opportunity to understand the full import of the law as it relates to them. If they are unable to do so themselves directly (because of their own intellectual limitations or because of the inherent complexity of the law itself), then the state should ensure that they are advised or represented by someone who does, subject to the caveat that assistance will only be granted when they lack the resources to acquire these services for themselves. The lack of resources caveat is due to the fact that the publicity requirement does not give rise to a state obligation to provide legal advice and representation to all citizens with respect to all laws and all legal matters. Actual knowledge of the law is not itself a right (even under the most progressive liberal theory). So long as the publicity requirement for law is met by everyone having the opportunity to know the law, there is no *a priori* reason why it must be met by one means (government-provided legal aid) rather than another (private procurement of legal services).

The "liberal values" argument and the "rule of law" argument are not mutually exclusive. Nevertheless, there is good reason to embrace the "rule of law" argument as the primary justification for supplying legal aid. First, it requires fewer controversial assumptions about the nature of political rights and duties and the content of equality than does the liberal values approach. Second, it is able to provide a principled distinction between legal aid and other essential services. That is, because it is a requirement of the publicity of law, and not merely another form of equalization payment, we can justify transfers to individuals who would not receive them but for their interaction with the justice system. Third, it provides an argument for why some sorts of cases should receive funding over others that is consonant with the values inherent in the legal system. For example, complex matters where the law is more difficult to understand should receive, *ceteris paribus*, legal aid before matters that are straightforward and eminently understandable in their entirety because the law in the former case is less likely to satisfy the publicity requirement for the rule of law in the absence of such aid.

Justice and the equitable distribution of resources

The law plays a considerable direct and indirect role in regulating the distribution of resources. Employment law affects the access of all persons, including low-income earners, to gainful employment. Family law often bears directly on the financial situations and well-being of women and dependent children. Disabled persons "often require remedies against the unscrupulous who take unfair advantage in their dealings with them,"[10] remedies which are frequently sought through civil proceedings. Moreover, in actual practice, access to the legal system often constrains access to other essential services, since rights to such services are legal in nature. A person wishing to protest the withdrawal of his social assistance benefits, for instance, must navigate the legalistic policies of the welfare system, a project which may, in some cases, prove unrealistic without professional assistance. Immigration status, which often determines a person's access to many essential services, is a status conferred by the law, and one which a citizen may require legal assistance in order to establish or contest. Whether they approve or disapprove of it, many commentators regard the legal system as, in the words of former Vice President of the United States Spiro Agnew, "a systematic effort to redistribute social advantages and disadvantages, penalties and rewards, rights and resources."[11]

Legal aid plans often make the *a priori* judgement that any case involving the potential deprivation of an individual's liberty (by imprisonment) is necessarily more serious than one that does not and is therefore more deserving of state assistance. This funding predisposition in favour of criminal law matters, however, has been criticized by many commentators. First, it is not clear that client impact is always most serious in criminal cases. For example, a fine or short prison term may represent less of a disadvantage to some clients than the loss of children or security from domestic abuse involved in family law for others. Further, conferring *a priori* precedence to claims for criminal legal aid over others has the tendency of privileging the interests of men (who are the primary users of criminal defence lawyers) over women (who are more often involved in family law disputes).[12]

The demands of distributive justice require us to take more seriously the less dramatic, but nevertheless significant concerns relating to adequate housing, income-maintenance, occupational health and safety and consumer protection that disproportionately affect the most disadvantaged members of our societies.[13] If access to the means governing the equitable distribution of resources – the legal system – is not itself equitable, then the equity of the welfare state *in toto* is diminished.

This argument must be distinguished, however, from the claim outlined earlier by Griffiths[14] which holds that access to legal services is itself a form of wealth which the state must act to distribute more fairly. Instead, the argument advanced here is that the government's other distributive goals in domains such as health care and education can be hampered by unequal access to justice, and that such procedural inequalities in the legal system may produce actual and arbitrary substantive inequalities in other areas. In fact, this argument most closely resembles the view attributed earlier to Luban and Rawls: that the justice system exists primarily to guarantee rights (which may include the right to socially provided benefits).

Modes of provision

As noted earlier, the organization of legal aid systems varies greatly from country to country.[15] Even amongst provincial and state jurisdictions in Canada and the United States, different legal aid schemes vary dramatically in terms of both scope and structure. In the United States, for instance, most jurisdictions employ a staff of public defenders in criminal trials. However, the federal Legal Services Corporation, the main source of legal aid for low-income Americans in non-criminal matters, mostly allocates grants to local or neighbourhood clinics which focus on particular practice areas (immigration, family law, domestic violence, etc.).[16]

The wealth and variety of legal aid models defies easy categorization. Still, it is possible to group the various schemes loosely under our four conventional headings of pure public provision, supply-side subsidies, tied demand-side subsidies and tax-and-transfer policies. When comparing the four classes of delivery models, it is important to note that the decision about the mode of provision does not obviate some of the more difficult questions about legal aid. The scale, nature and scope of legal aid will depend to a large extent on the normative grounds which are used to justify legal services in the first place, rather than on the instrument or instruments used to deliver them. Moreover, it is unlikely that one mode of service delivery will be effective across the various domains of legal practice in a single jurisdiction or state. There may well be advantages to the use of different modes of provision in different areas of legal service delivery. For instance, a permanent staff of experienced duty counsel hired by the state may be best able to assist citizens with summary matters and small claims, while the granting of legal aid certificates for low-income families to allow them to retain an attorney of their choice in criminal, immigration or family matters may be preferable in such cases. Thus, while our analysis of the different possible modes of provision will use the four modalities of provision described in Chapter 2, it will also take into account that no single mode of provision is likely to be able to meet the complex and variegated legal needs of an entire community. Consequently, our intended goal is not to prescribe a comprehensive and universal solution to the legal aid needs of a state, but rather to evaluate how and in what circumstances tied demand-side subsidies represent a preferable alternative to other modes of delivery.

Pure public provision

As Paterson notes, there are few jurisdictions in which the state itself both funds and delivers essential legal services. A pure staff model (namely, "a system in which the legal aid administration employs salaried lawyers to provide individual advice and case representation"[17]) is more commonly found in jurisdictions in which criminal legal advice and representation take a higher priority for publicly funded legal aid than civil matters. Thus, for instance, most jurisdictions in the United States hire a staff of public defenders in each county to represent respondents in criminal matters who do not have the means to retain attorneys. Where staff lawyers are hired by the government to provide assistance in civil matters, they are often barred from providing services which would place them in competition with the private Bar.[18] As Paterson notes, for instance, "staff lawyers in the Netherlands are usually restricted to providing initial advice to clients before referring them to advocates in private practice,"[19] while salaried employees of the federally funded Legal Services Corporation in the United States are banned from "taking cases to do with school desegregation, abortion, or engaging in political activities such as picketing, striking, lobbying, or working for political campaigns."[20]

One significant advantage of the staff lawyer model is "its ability to offer lawyers with specialized expertise in a given field of legal [...] practice."[21] Moreover, it spares legal aid beneficiaries the burden of selecting an attorney, a matter about which they may lack detailed and useful information.

There are five central objections to the salaried staff model:

- It represents unfair competition with private providers since staff offices do not face the same hard budget constraints as private firms, nor the threat of being wound up. Staff offices in outlying communities can operate indefinitely at a loss, making it impossible for local attorneys to compete, and ultimately making such communities wholly dependent on the state for the provision of certain legal services.
- It limits the use of alternative mechanisms such as the contracting out of cases to private firms or lawyers.
- The salary structure provides only limited incentives for maximum productivity on the part of staff lawyers.
- Since the scale and nature of demand must be anticipated in order to hire adequate staff, staff lawyer programs may be inflexible in responding to changes in demand and, if located in central staff offices, unable to meet the needs of rural or remote communities.[22]
- It denies consumers the right to retain the counsel of their choice.

An additional argument takes account of the principal–agent problem inherent in the selection of counsel by the state on behalf of the individual citizen. As Charendoff *et al.* explain, "[i]t is argued that any staff system, even if the employer is at arm's length from government, is inherently less able to ensure the independent legal advice which legal aid clients, in particular as they are parties often adverse in interest to the state, should receive."[23]

The crux of the problem in models of pure public provision is the lack of a purchaser–provider split. Most governments recognize that there are perverse incentives embedded in a system in which the state both finances and delivers particular services. Indeed, New Zealand recently transferred control over legal aid from the Department for Courts to an independent legal aid agency,[24] as did the Canadian province of Ontario. Similarly, recent reform initiatives in Northern Ireland have focused on the "establishment of a new independent body to administer legal aid."[25] The independence of such an agency is hoped to introduce a greater degree of impartiality and transparency into the administration of legal aid. The report to Parliament states that "the Law Society will no longer be in a position where they might be seen as having a conflict of interest between their responsibility for administering legal aid on the one hand and representing their members on the other."[26]

Under arrangements where legal aid attorneys are employed by the state, the attorney has two allegiances: to her employer, the state, which has a fiscal interest in seeking a settlement as quickly as possible so as to contain costs; and to her client. While the employer has means at its disposal to ensure that its interests are accommodated, the client does not have a voice: his or her preferences do not exert any financial influence on the attorney. Conversely, the staff attorney may face an incentive to draw a case out over a protracted period of time in order to avoid taking on new work, a decision which may not actually be in the client's best interests, and over which the client can exert only limited control. The above characterization is an exaggeration of the likely consequences of the principal–agent dilemma presented by the salaried staff model. It does, however, illustrate the need to assure some accountability on the part of the attorney to her client, accountability which may be assured by giving the consumer direct choice with respect to his or her legal service provider.

Supply-side subsidies

While the basic transaction underlying supply-side subsidization of legal services – the government pays for services provided by a private lawyer or firm, or community clinic – is simple, the range of possible schemes is quite extensive. The government can, for instance, stipulate any number of terms in its contract with its supplier, including:

* the types of cases to be handled (civil litigation by plaintiff or respondent; class-action lawsuits; landlord/tenant disputes; custody; etc., or any combination thereof)
* whether the contract is to assign a "block" of existing cases or for the supplier to receive a certain number of new cases
* whether the number of hours to be spent on a given case is capped or unlimited
* whether the firm should be permitted to pursue test cases
* how the firm must prioritize its caseload
* whether the firm can accept cases on contingency
* who is to receive the residuals from litigation where a financial award is involved.

Because of these and other variables, the category of supply-side subsidization models includes a very broad range of possible and actual delivery schemes.

Community legal clinics

By far the most common model of supply-side subsidization of legal services is that of the community legal clinic model. Indeed, most states support at least some number of legal clinics to assist in specialized areas. Under these alternatives, the legal aid plan issues grants to community legal clinics. The office or clinic and its staff lawyers allocate legal services to those in need of legal aid according to an internal ranking of priorities.

In virtually every Western state, the legal aid clinic movement has its origins in other radical political activities in the 1960s. Indeed, most present-day systems of state-funded legal aid clinics arose around that time as both (1) a government response to a need for legal services by its poorest citizens initially exposed by radical political groups and their independent clinics and (2) an effort by the government to gain control over the highly political "poverty law" movement.

In the United States, for instance, the alliances of concerned jurists forged by the civil rights movement, the anti-draft movement, and class-action lawsuits on behalf of consumer and environmental groups gave rise to an "ambitious series of [...] programs" which addressed problems of social injustice with legal approaches and perspectives.[27] Many existing projects, such as those funded by the President's Committee on Juvenile Delinquency, began to include the provision of certain essential legal services in their mandates.[28] The community legal clinic movement in the United States began as a loose network of privately funded charitable ventures, but, by the 1970s, had quickly evolved in "the direction of the model of the independent, locally-based, neighbourhood law office"[29] funded by the Federal Government through the Legal Services Corporation Act, the model which now prevails.

In the Netherlands in the 1960s, students belonging to the radical socialist movement opened a series of free legal clinics for working class citizens, notably in Tilburg, one of that nation's poorest cities. Through the work of these independent clinics, "unmet legal need was incontrovertibly exposed,"[30] and the government, concerned that this need was "being partially met in a piece-meal and haphazard way by such a volatile and inexperienced section of the community as left-wing law students," began to issue small grants to independent "law shops" which specialized in public interest law and agreed to abide by a series of rules.[31] This effort to both meet the needs of its poorest citizens and at the same time "depoliticize" the delivery of legal services gave rise to the *Bureaus voor Rechtshulp*, the network of government offices now responsible for issuing both "law shop" grants and legal aid certificates.[32]

The advantages of community legal clinics are significant. First, they may benefit from economies of scale and specialization. Because a large number of legal aid cases are very similar to one another (e.g. landlord–tenant disputes), it is more efficient to make use of lawyers that can specialize in a particular type of case or proceeding. Economies of scale and specialization may also permit more efficient utilization of paralegal personnel. Second, under the community clinic model, the lawyers employed in clinics may be more sensitive to the particular needs of a certain class of client – for instance, clinics oriented toward the African-American or Aboriginal populations. For example, in South Africa, "the vast majority of legal practitioners are white (85%), in a population in which the majority are black. Most lawyers work in urban areas, making access particularly difficult for rural people, who are the most impoverished and marginalized segment of the population."[33] In order to address this problem, the South African government has established 'Justice Centres', which are community legal clinics. It is anticipated that these centres will increase access to the legal system because, "they will employ candidate attorneys and paralegals from disadvantaged backgrounds and link up with community-based advice offices functioning as satellites."[34] However, it may not always be the case that community legal centres are better suited to the needs of disadvantaged individuals. For example, Houseman points out that, "many legal services programs and staff are isolated from the communities they are supposed to assist."[35] Therefore, in order to realize the potential social benefits of community clinics, care must be taken to ensure that the location and governance of such clinics truly promotes access. Third, such a model may have superior information properties to other models. Just as in health care, where individuals with little technical background in medicine may find it easier to choose between competing health care plans than between particular doctors, so here it may be that individuals find it easier to choose between clinics rather than between the vast array of individual legal aid lawyers. Finally, clinics may be better equipped to take on particular "test-cases" that have broad systemic implications for their constituencies, even if the stakes for a particular client are limited.

A countervailing consideration is that clinic lawyers are employed on salary and not directly compensated on the basis of outcomes. There are therefore attenuated incentives for enhanced productivity and the attainment of dynamic efficiency. If it makes no difference to clinic lawyers whether they deal quickly and competently with a case, or slowly and merely adequately, they may have incentives to be slower, more methodical and invest less time in improving their skills, time management and efficiency than members of the private bar. Finally, although some practitioners may find the work in community clinics more personally satisfying than private practice, and (given the diminished emphasis on the accumulation of billable hours) less stressful as well, the truncated career ladder that clinic-based models often offer tend to make it difficult for them to attract and retain senior lawyers who possess valuable experience and expertise.

Perhaps one of the most significant, though sometimes overlooked, objections to the community legal clinic model is the degree of control which the state exercises in the setting of clinic priorities. As Cooper observes, "the most serious difficulty brought about by central regulation of public legal services is the reliance that such a system inevitably places upon the goodwill of those who make and enforce such regulations."[36] Thus, in the United Kingdom, the Law Centres' Federation "has been committed to local control of its centres,"[37] and avers itself suspicious of any effort towards centralized regulation and the setting of priorities. The claim of the potential for state interference and the tension between local and central authority is not without foundation. The Legal Services Corporation (LSC) in the United States, for instance, issues operating grants in accordance with a list of accepted priorities, the ordinal ranking of which arguably reflects the social, economic and ideological values and priorities of the government which funds them:

Support for Families: the cohesiveness of the family is not only a time honored value fundamental to our American way of life but also the undergirding of the stability of our American society [...]
Preserving the Home [...]
Maintaining Economic Stability: [...] [T]he prevention of unemployment may obviate a sequence of far greater legal activity [...][38]

Because of such stipulations, clinics attempting to contract for a funding arrangement with the LSC and organizations like it may encounter a principal–agent problem. They must balance their duty to their principal (those in need of legal services) with the necessity of setting priorities which are more likely to attract funding, in order to remain operational. This creates a potential divergence of interests: the interest of the agent (the clinic) in obtaining operational funding and the best interests of the principals (its clients) in having the clinic set priorities which reflect their actual needs. Clinic administrators who sincerely believe that class-action lawsuits against governments or direct political action short of or including civil disobedience are the best strategy to advance the interests of their constituencies, may be dissuaded from such projects in favour of less litigious or radical positions, in order to avoid losing funding.

For instance, the United States' Legal Services Corporation Act, while granting LSC-funded clinics more independence from the government, effectively forbids the participation of community clinics in any law reform activity.[39] Such considerations may undermine the independence of clinics, and dissuade them from adopting the most effective strategies available to them in service of their clients. Finally, there is the brute fact that "commissions or corporations that are [...] funded by central government are liable to be closed down with changes of government,"[40] a reality which may encourage clinics to adopt more neutral or non-partisan stances in order to ensure their longevity.

There are other potential dangers associated with salaried legal aid schemes that are summarized by Goriely. First, there is a high susceptibility to becoming overloaded, "as their staffing and resources fail to keep pace with increased demand."[41] The result of overload is typically a decline in the quality of services delivered. Second, there is a low degree of choice in a community clinic model.[42] Although theoretically, there are many clinics to choose from, there are often only one or two within the reach of a disadvantaged person requiring legal assistance. Further, staff members are typically assigned to cases, thereby leaving the client powerless to choose an attorney with which he or she is comfortable. Third, staff models are likely to be bureaucratic. Aside from the significant start-up costs associated with a staff clinic, staff-based systems, "can also develop their own ineffici-encies. It may, for example, become difficult to dismiss staff who perform poorly."[43]

Other forms of supply-side subsidization

It is interesting to note that, in spite of the variety of potential supply-side subsidy arrangements, very few jurisdictions stray far from the community legal clinic model. The United States experimented briefly with contracting out the handling of indigent criminal defence cases to private lawyers and firms, but abandoned this approach due in part to "the serious quality deficiencies of contracting out."[44] In the late 1980s, the LSC decided that civil matters would benefit from the contract system, but the pilot projects have been, for the most part, unsuccessful.[45] Great Britain's Legal Aid Act of 1988 allows the Legal Aid Board to contract out legal aid work in England and Wales.[46] However, consultations by the Legal Aid Board on the subject of contracting out led them to reject it, in view of the constraints on consumer choice and the access difficulties posed in poor urban or rural areas. Nevertheless, as recently as 1996, the Lord Chancellor indicated his desire for more expansive use of competitive tendering of blocks of cases.[47]

It is worth considering why alternative supply-side subsidy options such as block allocation remain underused. One possibility is that, in markets where demand for legal services exceeds the supply, the price commanded by legal professionals exceeds what the government is willing to pay. Another related explanation is that the sorts of cases for which the government is prepared to contract (immigration, custody, injured worker's compensation) are insufficiently lucrative to attract the attention of a competitive number of highly qualified firms.

As compared with demand-side subsidies, supply-side subsidy schemes represent a certain advantage from the point of view of information failures. It may be the case that an individual consumer, endowed with a voucher, faces serious information problems in choosing between an assortment of individual practitioners and firms. It may be that government officials, with more training and expertise, are better qualified to contract with a firm to supply services to all qualified consumers, and then to simply direct the consumer to the appropriate firm: firm I for immigration matters, firm C for custody claims, firm W for worker's compensation claims, and the like. In markets where the typical consumer's choice about a critical matter (such as the choice of one's attorney) is uninformed, the alleged consumer choice advantage of demand-side over supply-side subsidies may be attenuated.

However, the success or failure of a supply-side subsidization scheme to provide legal services in a more cost-effective manner will depend ultimately in large part on some of the modalities listed earlier. For instance, a "block" allocation system through competitive tendering where a firm agrees to handle a certain number of cases for a fixed price allows the government to negotiate a price *ex ante*, ideally for a sum less than it anticipates it would cost to devolve the same block of cases to a publicly funded legal clinic or to issue legal aid certificates to private practitioners on a case-by-case basis. For the firm's part, however, it will now be in its best interests to calculate the optimal number of billable hours and resources to be expended on any given case based on the price negotiated *ex ante*, since additional time or cost related to the disposition of any one case cannot be reimbursed by seeking a higher price *ex post*. Thus, it is in a firm's best financial interests to settle a case as soon as the number of hours or quantity of resources expended on it approaches that optimal number, regardless of whether or not a settlement is actually in the client's best interests. Furthermore, since no additional income can be generated by providing service of a quality higher than that stipulated in the initial contract for the block of cases, and, equally, since there are no strong economic sanctions for providing lower-quality service provided that it meets any baseline standards stipulated in the contract, it seems likely that a quality–cost trade-off will also be sought. While such a trade-off may satisfy the interests of both the firm (profit) and the government (cost-effective service delivery), the interests of the client him- or herself may be sacrificed in the process.

Tied demand-side subsidies

Judicare

Apart from community clinics, programs of legal aid vouchers or certificates (often referred to as "judicare") are the major system of publicly funded legal service delivery. Indeed, virtually all legal aid to low-income respondents in criminal cases in Canada and the United Kingdom is provided in the form of judicare. In Sweden, comprehensive legal aid is also available for plaintiffs and respondents in civil litigation in the form of government-issued fee waivers indexed to income.[48]

The advantages of this model are not inconsiderable. First, because clients choose their lawyers in much the same way that paying clients do, it provides them with a high degree of both choice and dignity. Further, its incentive structure in terms of choice of counsel is correct in principle because it is the very individuals who are receiving the service who select their representative. The private provider's claim on residuals creates an incentive for more cost-effective service delivery, while the discipline of reputation, as well as the possible additional mechanism of mandatory review of participating firms by professional regulators in order to retain the right to accept voucher clients, create an incentive for adequate quality of service delivery.

On the other hand, a judicare or certificate system may be afflicted both by supplier-induced demand, which leads to unnecessary tasks being undertaken, and asymmetric information problems, which impede client choice of the most appropriate service provider *ex ante* and preclude the effective monitoring or evaluation of the quality of the service provided *ex post* – that is, at the time of delivery. There is reason, moreover, to believe that information deficiencies and supplier-induced demand are not discrete phenomena, but instead are intrinsically related.

Matthews defines supplier-induced demand as "advice to the client to incur expenses on professional services [...] that are in fact unnecessary."[49] As Bevan observes, however, this definition is inadequate:

> [It] mis-specifies the nature of the economic problem. Who defines what is "unnecessary" and on what basis? Are "unnecessary" services those which incur costs but are of no value? Or are they services where the cost exceeds the value? And who defines value or cost: the principal or the agent? The problem of supplier-induced demand in professional services arises precisely because of the difficulty of answering these questions.[50]

Bevan considers that the operative issue (one which Matthews, in using a less sophisticated and more colloquial definition of supplier-induced demand, overlooks) is information asymmetry. Supplier-induced demand is only possible when the client lacks sufficient information to properly identify the value and costs of different aspects of legal services. Therefore, as Bevan points out, supplier-induced demand actually "occurs when the agent supplies more services than [the] principal would pay for if the principal had the agent's knowledge."[51]

The impact of supplier-induced demand in a context in which impartial and detailed information about the value of legal services is not widely available is considerable. According to Blankenberg, for instance, "the relatively high expenditures of the Legal Aid Board [in Great Britain] have more than doubled since 1990" due in no small part to "British solicitors' ability to draw a considerable income from the scheme."[52] Research conducted in England and Wales by Gray *et al.* found a high degree of "professional autonomy" in the market for legal services; namely, the tendency on the part of solicitors "to manipulate the volume of [...] cases (especially civil ones), and to choose the level of input, independently from [sic] the preferences of either their clients or the Legal Aid Board, in its capacity as a third party reimburser."[53] The authors conclude that "the prevailing methods of remunerating legal work [namely, judicare certificates] did provide solicitors with incentives and opportunities to protect their incomes, notably when their residential conveyancing income fell sharply during the late 1980s."[54] It is important to note that the incidence of supplier-induced demand can be manipulated to some degree by the payment structure that is utilized. For example, in a system in which lawyers are remunerated solely on an hourly basis, there will be a significant incentive to engage in behaviours that create supplier-induced demand. The use of fixed fees will mitigate the tendency to engage in such behaviours by ensuring that there is, "no financial incentive to work additional hours"[55] than are required by the case. However, fixed fees "do not remove the incentive to get new clients into the legal aid system."[56] The most promising method of payment for reducing the incidence of supplier-induced demand is an hourly rate that is capped at a particular number of hours, depending on the type of case, although there will then be incentives to truncate service once the limit or cap has been reached.

Gray *et al.* consider that the problem of professional autonomy is intractable enough that simply changing delivery mechanisms may not resolve it.

> [Professional autonomy] is not, by its nature, going to disappear with a change in the payment mechanism [...] If subsidized services are paid for prospectively, there will still be an incentive for professionals to look to a combination of public and private work in order to maximize profits. This may lead them to find ways of minimizing effort on public work in order to maximize income from private work.[57]

Consequently, in jurisdictions where judicare programs are otherwise preferable to the alternatives, the problem of professional autonomy is not reason enough to change the basic paradigm of service delivery from demand-side subsidization to another model. Instead, it seems preferable to devote more attention to the design challenges presented by information asymmetry and the related problems of professional autonomy and supplier-induced demand, topics which are addressed in more detail below.

Although there are strong arguments both for and against supply-side and demand-side subsidies, in order to make a meaningful choice as to which of these alternatives is superior, one must weigh the evidence pertaining to the effectiveness and efficiency of each system in practice. The Ontario Legal Aid Task Force surveyed a number of studies and concluded that, "most of the controlled, comparative studies completed in both Canada and the United States conclude that there is no significant difference in cost between a staff and a judicare mode of delivery."[58] However, others have suggested that staff schemes are generally less expensive than judicare systems.[59] In South Africa, the Legal Aid Board has estimated that the move from a judicare model to a mixed model in which staff clinics are heavily relied upon will lead to a savings of R153 million in a three-year period.[60] Goriely finds that salaried lawyers are often cheaper because they tend to spend less time per case than do private lawyers. She hypothesizes several reasons as to why this might be the case: staff offices may select easier cases, staff lawyers may be more specialized, staff offices may enjoy economies of scale, and the different payment structures may induce private lawyers to spend more hours on a particular case.[61] None of these possibilities has been conclusively determined to be the main factor, and it is likely that they all play a role in creating this phenomenon. The crucial question arising from this discussion is whether or not quality suffers as a result of staff lawyers spending less time per case. There is some evidence from Canada that staff lawyers and private lawyers achieve similar outcomes. For example, "the Burnaby and Manitoba studies found that staff clients were convicted no more often and were less likely to receive a prison sentence. Client satisfaction was much the same."[62] However, Goriely points out that this does not seem to hold true for all jurisdictions. She postulates that, "staff lawyers can only be expected to make efficiency gains where there is already inefficiency in the system."[63] Therefore, it is premature to draw conclusions about which type of service is more cost-efficient, and whether staff and private lawyers achieve comparable results.

Stronger evidence is presented by the Canadian National Council of Welfare (NCW) in favour of staff models. It is pointed out that the legal aid expenditure per person (total legal aid expenditure divided by population size) in Ontario was $29.74 in 1992, in comparison with a $15.73 expenditure in Quebec.[64] The NCW concludes that the reason for this discrepancy is that whereas Ontario relies primarily on judicare, Quebec utilizes a large number of staff lawyers in local clinics.[65] Although this explanation is plausible, the report provides no basis for ruling out other possibilities. For example, the costs in Quebec may be lower because fewer people use the system, the means-test is more stringent, the quality of service is poorer etc. Therefore, one should not uncritically accept the NCW's conclusion that the difference in cost can be attributed entirely to the different delivery methods of legal aid.

As to the effectiveness of staff and private lawyers, the NCW looks at criminal cases and finds that, "staff lawyers pleaded their clients guilty more often and more quickly."[66] The report goes on to say that this tendency produces positive results, both from the perspective of the client and society. Clients who plead out early are less likely to go to jail. Additionally, by pleading out, the case is disposed of more quickly, thereby reducing the amount of resources used.[67] However, it should be pointed out that the merits of this pattern only hold true if the client is, in fact, guilty. The NCW recognizes this in stating that, "overworked legal aid staff lawyers may be tempted to pressure their clients into pleading guilty when they have a valid defence to avoid the time and trouble of going to trial."[68] The real problem is that there is no way for anyone to know whether or not a particular defendant has a valid defense and whether or not he or she is guilty. Therefore, it is virtually impossible to determine whether or not staff lawyers are acting efficiently or negligently.

Although this is also the case in the context of evaluating private lawyers, it is argued that the concerns are more pronounced when staff lawyers are involved. The future income of a staff lawyer is not contingent to the same degree as that of a private lawyer on the satisfaction of the client. Legal aid clients, under a staff model, have no choice but to seek assistance at a staff office. Staff lawyers are subsequently assigned to particular cases. Even if a staff lawyer has a reputation for losing cases, unless she is fired, she will continue to be assigned to clients and will continue to receive the same salary. Private lawyers, on the other hand, are not assigned to clients. They depend on the clients to come to them, and therefore have greater incentives to provide a satisfactory service in order to preserve their reputations.

The South Australian Legal Services Commission has also reported finding that staff lawyers are less expensive than private practitioners.[69] However, the results of this study have also been criticized for failing to take into account the differences in the type of cases that were handled by staff and private lawyers. It has been suggested that, "the files that were retained in-house were of a routine and repetitive nature whereas the more complex matters were referred out."[70]

The use of staff lawyers does not alleviate the principal–agent problem mentioned earlier; it simply changes the nature of the agency relationship. Stephen points out, "Performance-related pay or promotion related to performance against objectives are ways of encouraging an employee's efforts to be directed toward the employer's objectives."[71] Thus, the agent (the staff lawyer) will have incentives to direct their efforts towards measurable components of performance, such as the number of cases dealt with in a particular time frame. This may, however, induce lawyers to under-supply their services to each client in order to process a higher number of clients. Stephen concludes that, "this results in the public defender responding to incentives in much the same way as a financially motivated independent supplier who is paid a fixed fee by a third party payer."[72] Therefore, both types of schemes have perverse incentives embedded within them.

Legal expenses insurance

One alternative to judicare which is growing in popularity in a number of jurisdictions (notably in Scandinavia, Germany and the Netherlands) is mandatory private legal expenses insurance (LEI). Under such schemes, individual citizens are required to subscribe to an insurance plan which provides coverage of legal fees in the event of litigation or prosecution. One can envision a program under which the state either insures citizens itself, or issues a voucher for the purchase of an LEI plan. This model constitutes a form of indirect demand-side subsidy, since the consumer, after receiving an LEI "payout," chooses which legal services provider he or she will contract with. The mandatory nature of LEI subscription obviates the adverse selection problems mentioned earlier in the case of optional private insurance, through pooling of diverse risks, while also guaranteeing a demand-side market large enough to stimulate a supply-side response favouring competition and innovation.

In Sweden, which has experienced considerable success with LEI programs, LEI is "built in" to the standard universal household insurance policy issued by the government. Under the Swedish LEI scheme, the state directly insures its citizens against the cost of legal proceedings. The LEI coverage scheme, introduced in the 1970s, was specifically designed to "fill the gaps in the legal aid scheme rather than to compete with it [...] LEI covered legal problems that legal aid did not; protected the groups who were excluded by legal aid [...]; and included legal costs ignored by legal aid, particularly the costs awarded by the courts in unsuccessful civil cases."[73] Since extensive legal aid cutbacks in 1997, however, LEI has come to replace many of the services formerly provided through judicare, and is now the primary mode of assistance for plaintiffs and respondents in most civil litigation.

LEI as a mode of demand-side subsidy shows considerable promise, in that most of the objections raised against it by its critics have to do with the extent of its coverage rather than with its basic *modus operandi*.[74] These criticisms can likely be met by expanding coverage to include a wider range of claims. Another concern is that there are no special waivers for low-income earners who cannot afford the deductibles on LEI, and that the lack of coverage for basic, non-trial legal advice creates an incentive to litigate matters which might not otherwise go to court.[75] These drawbacks, however, represent specific design challenges as opposed to fundamental critiques of the structure of LEI as a viable demand-side subsidy scheme for the provision of essential legal services. More research is necessary on the viability of private markets for the provision of LEI in other jurisdictions, since the adoption of LEI would represent a major policy change from the norm in most English-speaking nations, where conventional judicare and clinic systems still preponderate. It is worth noting, however, that the United States did experiment with a similar policy in the 1960s and 1970s, and at least one major Canadian trade union, the Canadian Auto Workers (CAW),[76] provides LEI to its members. One major question in such states, however, is likely to be whether or not LEI should be mandatory for all citizens and subvented in the case of low-income persons or an optional market good, for which vouchers can be issued to those

who cannot afford it. These questions are complex, and require a more comprehensive analysis of private insurance markets than is feasible here. Notwithstanding
such issues, however, the limited experiments with LEI suggest that LEI is at least
a feasible, if unorthodox, solution.

Tax-and-transfer policies

As Griffiths observes, the use of legal services correlates closely with wealth.[77] The
question, then, naturally presents itself: "Why not intervene to redistribute wealth
and the distribution of legal services will take care [of] itself?"[78] As Goriely and
Paterson observe, "[G]iven that in 1994–5 the English legal aid scheme cost around
£130 a year for every household eligible for help [...] [i]f people were allowed to
choose for themselves whether they spent their £130 on legal expenses insurance
or in some other way, one suspects that few would opt for the insurance policy.
[...] Why should the state make the decision for them?"[79]

As the discussion of tax-and-transfer policies in other chapters has shown, the
conventional libertarian position is that if people elect not to spend their own
resources (or, alternatively, the welfare cheque to which they are entitled) on legal
services, it is because these services are not desirable; and whatever is not considered
desirable by a person is not of value to him or her. It is quite possible that individuals
would rather spend their income or welfare benefits on other goods than on legal
services.

The justice of forcing people to spend their income on legal expenses insurance,
or on retaining an attorney, in order to insure that the "publicity" requirement of
the rule of law is met, and to preserve the normative legitimacy of the legal system,
is debatable. The matter requires the balancing of the individual's authority over
the disposition of her resources against the state's obligation to make the law fair
and understandable by all. Should a person who has squandered the portion of
his resources intended for legal services or insurance and cannot afford legal
representation be denied it? Or can the state legitimately force people to insure
themselves, or act as an insurer on their behalf by using tax revenue to issue vouchers
and/or support community clinics? Is the state, at any point, entitled to decide
that an individual has repudiated his right to representation because he has consistently preferred to spend his income on something else, or does justice require the
provision of a "safety net" that even protects those who have refused to insure
themselves?

These questions are normative in nature, and go to the fundamental role of the
state and the conception of justice. It is telling, however, that not even the United
States has embraced a policy of non-intervention in the provision of basic legal
services. It seems that the symbolic and institutional importance of basic access to
the law has exempted legal aid from the intense criticism leveled at other social
programs. Goriely and Paterson argue that a commitment to universal access to
justice "can provide a glimmer of hope to the poor and some legitimacy to the
state."[80]

Design challenges

Qualified consumers

There is good reason in the context of legal aid to means-test the provision of benefits. If we take the rule of law as the central justification for the provision of legal aid, then there is every reason to expect that those who through their own "wit or wealth" have the ability independently to understand the law or have the financial means to obtain their own legal advice will do so. If they do not, so long as they have the *opportunity* (through their "wit or wealth") to "know" the law and thereby satisfy the publicity requirement, it is not the role of government to intervene on their behalf to ensure that they do. A universal entitlement with respect to legal aid services is also unlikely to co-opt the voices of the politically influential in maintaining the value or universality of the benefits in any event. This is the case because legal aid is a highly contingent benefit whose value to those covered depends, to an important extent, on having been charged with a criminal offence. Those who exercise the greatest political voice are likely to have a far lower stake in the level of benefits provided to accused individuals because they will rarely, if ever, be unable through their own "wit or wealth" to learn and know the law themselves or acquire advice from someone who understands the relevant law. Moreover, most politically influential individuals will rarely if ever confront directly the coercive power of the state. Besides criminal law, other contexts in which legal aid benefits are important include child custody disputes, refugee determinations, and the maintenance of social assistance benefits. The limited import of these concerns to the politically influential also mean that the case for extending benefits universally to co-opt the voices of the politically influential is weaker here than it is in many other contexts.

It is necessary to consider, however, how stringent a means-test should be applied. Some systems employ a very generous means-test, with the aim of ensuring that both the poor and the middle-class can receive legal assistance. In other jurisdictions, legal aid is limited to the extremely economically disadvantaged population. For example, the Dutch system of legal aid is available to almost 45 percent of the population, whereas in Germany, legal aid is available to only about 15 percent of people.[81] Similarly, income limits in Canadian legal aid systems range from a low of $8,865 in Quebec, to a high of $15,800 in Ontario.[82] The decision of whether to employ a stringent or generous means-test is often the result of a particular jurisdiction's ideology regarding social welfare. As well, this decision will be influenced by the budget constraints on the legal aid system. For example, the per capita costs of legal aid in the Netherlands are more than three times as high as those in Germany.[83]

Qualified suppliers

No one arrangement of providing legal aid services, be it judicare, a community clinic, a staff office or duty counsel system, is best at providing all forms of legal aid services. In order to take advantage of the benefits of each type of system, we should encourage mixed modes of service delivery to be made available in the system and allow consumers to choose between them. This would allow individuals to choose individual lawyers by voucher when this is appropriate and the services of legal clinics or staff offices that would be funded to a large extent through capitated supply-side grants or contracts (*de facto* vouchers) when that alternative is suitable (e.g. when it addresses the special needs of a community). Entitling all those who qualify to choose from among those members of the bar participating under different organizational structures provides the benefits of competition and diversity while preserving access to justice.[84] It also allows organizational experimentation, innovation and competition with respect to delivery models. These freedoms are especially valuable because no firm consensus currently exists as to the relative efficacy of delivery modes in particular contexts, even though the general strengths, weaknesses and limits of each delivery mode are well known. It may be that through this type of competitive arrangement the efficient role for each delivery mode will emerge spontaneously in the market for legal aid services.

The means by which quality of legal representation can be monitored both institutionally and by consumers of the legal aid system varies from delivery mode to delivery mode and is critical in assessing whether access to justice goals are being realized. Four basic elements[85] are required in any quality control program for legal aid. First, clear standards for qualifying as a specialized individual legal aid provider in a particular class of legal matter should be developed. These standards might include a graduated system of accreditation whereby points are earned by members of the Bar for various indicia of expertise. A minimum degree of experience in a field would be necessary to undertake cases of deemed complexity. Indicia could include the specific types and numbers of courses taken in law school, engagement in ongoing education in relevant areas, and extent of past practice experience in the field. Second, a mechanism for detecting quality problems on an ongoing basis should be developed so that the provision of poor-quality services cannot become entrenched in the system. This can be done by using better mandatory reporting and technology systems than currently exist that can serve to raise flags when signs of deficiencies arise. The system could be set up to detect, *inter alia*, abnormal billing practices, patterns in case outcomes that indicate potentially negligent or deficient provision of services, and blatant supplier-induced demand. Third, when problems or abuses are detected, there must be a well-functioning mechanism to ameliorate the deficiencies in conduct. This mechanism could include mandatory remedial education, increasingly serious sanctions for repeat offenders, and greater coordination between the legal aid administrators and the disciplinary authorities of the legal profession. Finally, there must also be ongoing experimentation with the development of detailed performance standards as they are appropriate to particular practice areas so that quality can be monitored effectively.

The recent reforms to the legal aid system in the Netherlands provide some insight into how quality monitoring may work in practice. In order to increase the quality of legal services provided to recipients of legal aid, reforms in 1994 introduced both quality requirements and an increase in lawyers' remuneration.[86] In theory, the quality requirements were to include a maximum number of certificates in a specific area of law that a lawyer is allowed to handle; a maximum number of areas of law in which a lawyer is allowed to handle certificates; and a commitment to continued investment in education and professional training.[87] However, the Legal Aid Boards have largely failed to implement these standards. Klijn speculates that the reason for this failure is that, "the Boards disliked the consequences to be expected from enforcing these rules."[88] The expected consequence was that in most areas of practice, about 50–70 percent of lawyers would not meet the standards.[89] Although an independent agency should be responsible for accrediting lawyers and monitoring quality, care must be taken to ensure that the proposed regulations are not overly stringent. If virtually unattainable quality standards are imposed, the risk is that either there will not be enough qualified lawyers to meet the demand for legal aid or that the agencies responsible for monitoring quality will turn a blind eye to infractions.

Value of voucher

A lump-sum voucher per class of case (absent reputational effects that can increase or decrease relative demand for an individual supplier) creates incentives for providers to chisel on-costs by resolving matters as quickly as possible (e.g. pleading clients guilty or settling civil matters quickly when they should be contested). An hourly prescribed tariff, on the other hand, creates opposing incentives – to over-service clients by prolonging matters unnecessarily (as in fee-for-service health care models). A prescribed hourly tariff up to some capped limit will partially address these problems but will lead to under-servicing once the cap has been reached, even though the complexity or merits of the matter may warrant further expenditure of effort on the part of the provider. Providing for voucher increments to cover such cases, including meritorious appeals, may address this problem, but at the cost of greater administrative complexity and expenditures.

Extra-billing, for good reason, is not permitted under most existing legal aid programs. The specific nature of the normative rationale behind the provision of legal aid casts doubts on the extra-billing issue because the central idea for providing legal aid is to facilitate access to legal advice and representation among those who would otherwise lack the resources to access the law. Allowing extra billing while maintaining fixed voucher valuations would reduce the supply of legal assistance to citizens in need, which is the problem legal aid seeks to address. However, this does not rule out the possibility that a legal aid scheme could mandate client contributions when income exceeds a prescribed limit. By requiring that clients who have moderate means make a contribution based on their level of income, it is possible to make legal aid much more widely available. For example, as has been mentioned, legal aid is available to upwards of 45 percent of the population in the Netherlands. However, individual clients are often required to make a means-tested contribution to the costs of the services they receive. In some cases, a person's income will be so low that the contribution is waived.[90] This maintains the integrity of a system in which the government purports to ensure access to the legal system for everyone. However, people with higher incomes (although still relatively low) are required to make contributions on a sliding scale.[91] In Canada, legal aid does not require any individual contributions. However, a much smaller proportion of the population is able to benefit at all from legal aid. Thus, many people who are not destitute, but who are of moderate means, cannot afford the costs of legal representation. In the Canadian system, this segment of the population is over-looked. They are not wealthy enough to hire a lawyer, but they are not poor enough to qualify for legal aid. It is argued that a system like the one in the Netherlands can help to alleviate this "plight of the lower middle class" by increasing the legal resources available to them.

Another alternative involves assigning different voucher values to lawyers of various practice experience. For instance, in Ontario there is a sliding scale of remuneration associated with judicare vouchers depending upon how many years the participating lawyer has been practising. The pay scale has three levels. The lowest level of pay is reserved for lawyers with fewer than four years of experience. Lawyers with five to ten years of experience and greater than ten years of experience receive vouchers of higher value, respectively. In this way, the system builds in an added incentive for more experienced lawyers to provide legal aid services. Of course, such an arrangement is imperfect because experience is only crudely related to quality of representation, but it is likely better than ignoring the role of experience altogether.

Cream-skimming is less problematic in the context of legal aid than in other social programs. First, it is essential that community clinics be allowed to choose their clientele in order to preserve their community links and promote their specialized knowledge. In addition, however, all lawyers should be allowed to choose their clients on the basis of both specialty and ethics. So long as we can maintain a relatively close correlation between the time and expense of a particular class of case and the value of the corresponding voucher, there will not be strong incentives to select one client over another.

Government's post-design role

The state's primary post-design role after the implementation of a legal aid voucher scheme overseen by an independent multi-stakeholder body would be in providing adequate funding to the responsible body. The multi-stakeholder body, which would not be a direct government agency but would rely on state funding, would be responsible for overseeing, monitoring and fostering different delivery modes for legal aid. Thus, the *ex post* role of government would be aimed at negotiating adequate, long-term budgets with the multi-stakeholder oversight body.[92]

Friedland notes that, in the context of a constrained budget, "the most important consideration is the need for innovation and experimentation"[93] in the delivery of legal services in order to arrive at the best "mix" of judicare, clinics and other delivery mechanisms. Consequently, governance of the legal aid system needs to be independent from the legal profession and other groups whose interests are implicated, and yet also be responsive to their concerns as well. As Friedland observes, "The stronger the independent component of [the governing body], the more confidence the government may have in it and the less likely it may be to try to influence the operation of the institution."[94]

Friedland proposes that funding be allocated by the government, but that the allocation of funds via a mix of instruments be at the discretion of an independent board comprising lawyers, government representatives, community clinic staff members and persons with management expertise.[95] This body would assume many of the tasks that the government or Law Society would otherwise be responsible for, including monitoring the quality of legal aid provided in the system, ensuring that people in need of legal aid are actually receiving assistance, and taking a proactive role in experimenting with new delivery modes and engaging in pilot projects. Friedland also advocates a rigorous system of accountability mechanisms including reporting, audits, inspection and a complaint process. Community clinics would be required to have at least one board member appointed by the legal aid board and to abide by certain guidelines set by the board in order to qualify for funding. The Legal Aid Board system in England and Wales compares favourably with Friedland's model, although the Lord Chancellor's office, to whom the Board is ultimately accountable, retains considerable control over the setting of priorities.[96]

Political considerations

Clearly the most formidable lobby relating to legal aid is lawyers. The other principal interest group is legal aid clients, but these are generally amongst the most vulnerable and voiceless members of society, not only because they are poor but because they also very frequently have been charged with a criminal offense, and the general public is unlikely to be disposed to favour their interests with large-scale expenditure programs. Lawyers, as an interest group, are likely to favour a generously compensated judicare form of legal aid program of the kind that exists in many (but far from all) jurisdictions. There are reasons for supposing that this is not always the most efficient form of delivery of legal aid services, and that in a wide range of contexts duty counsel and community legal clinics may be more appropriate delivery vehicles. However, the private Bar will likely be opposed to assigning a substantial role to these alternative delivery mechanisms because of their self-interest in the judicare/certificate system, although the fact that many jurisdictions extensively employ these mechanisms, and the fiscal constraints facing those that do not, suggest that the private Bar's opposition to a more broadly cast voucher system that provides consumers with a choice of delivery mechanism is in many contexts unlikely to be insuperable.

Conclusion

As was noted above, mixed systems show the most promise in meeting the need for basic legal services in an age of more restricted social spending. Models which rely either entirely or principally on community clinics present governance challenges and raise concerns of unfair competition with the private Bar, while the competition and ownership effects operative in private practice are muted. Moreover, they are likely to meet with vigorous opposition from professional associations. Furthermore, clinic-intensive models generally entail a high degree of government involvement in priority setting, creating a principal–agent problem to the extent that clinics must realign their priorities to meet those of their funding agency. Clients under clinic-based models cannot choose where to take their business, and may have little say in the processes of governance. Clinics which provide inadequate service can be disciplined only indirectly by clients through the channels of representative government, even though unsatisfactory legal service can have direct consequences for a particular client.

Conversely, systems which rely entirely on demand-side subsidies may experience the problems of supplier-induced demand, or monopolistic behaviour in communities where the choice of practitioners is limited. The model of mandatory legal expenses insurance, as an alternative to judicare certificates, also needs to be examined in more detail. The challenge for legal aid governance bodies will be to find which blend of community clinics and demand-side subsidies functions best in their particular jurisdictions, although participation in the governance of any legal aid scheme by all stakeholders must be assured.

6 Health care

Introduction

Health care – like primary and secondary education – is vital to human flourishing. This notion underlies the World Health Organisation's definition of health as "a state of complete physical, mental and social well-being and not merely the absence of disease or infirmity."[1] That is, health is not simply a consideration that surfaces only when we are stricken by illness or injury; rather, health is a state that pervades every aspect of our lives. It is fundamental to our ability to work effectively, to participate in the life of our families and community, and to enjoy our leisure time. Moreover, to suffer ill-health is not merely to experience an immediate disutility (such as physical pain), but also to be deprived of the very grounds for the effective exercise of autonomy itself. In this light, health care cannot be viewed as a benefit that can be straightforwardly allocated in accordance with an individual's preferences (as reflected by his or her willingness to pay for it). Instead, it must be conceived of as a necessary condition for human fulfilment in all aspects of life and hence a Rawlsian primary good.[2]

Because good health has generally been recognized as essential to our overall well-being and autonomy, most Western countries have elected to regulate the provision of health care services and concomitant health care insurance in order to guarantee at least a minimum level of this necessary good to all. In part this reflects precepts of distributive justice and in part concerns about limitations of private insurance markets that are likely to screen out the highest risk or sickest individuals from coverage. Removing the provision of such services from the discipline of the market, however, introduces a number of perverse incentives for both providers and purchasers and, as will be demonstrated through a discussion of three different models of health care reform, these perverse incentives are not easily addressed. We will argue that a universal but limited voucher system may be the most appropriate means of resolving this tension. In such a system, the government would provide every citizen with a voucher with which health care services could be purchased in the health care market. Essentially, a market in health care would be created with government funding. As we shall see again, however, striking the right balance between efficiency and equity is an extremely difficult enterprise.

The goals of health care policy

Distributive justice

Because good health is vital to one's autonomy and general well-being, it is a central concern for distributive justice or the equitable distribution of resources, as we articulate this objective of the welfare state in Chapter 1. Fundamental to the liberal model of individual free choice is a universal guarantee of its necessary conditions.[3] That is, it is not liberty simpliciter that is the central feature of contemporary liberalism, but equal liberty to all. Although there will always exist some disparities among individuals that result from their personal choices, each individual's initial position should be roughly the same.[4] Accordingly, those benefits that are central to one's health must be made available to all, and those disadvantages that are the result of the poor health of certain individuals[5] (such as physical disabilities, diseases, age, etc.) must be minimized. One must not, however, assume that equal access to health care services in itself will ensure a fair allocation of health. Other determinants of health besides health care services include biological factors, physical environment, lifestyle and social environment. Furthermore, socio-economic status along with access to social welfare services and education may have a greater impact on health than the consumption of health care services.[6]

Individual autonomy

The central importance of health, both to individual well-being and to the possibility of autonomous choice itself, underscores the importance of assuring the good health of all citizens. However, not only is a basic level of health a necessary condition for autonomous choice, its provision should, in turn, be the subject of autonomous choices as well. Although most patients do not have the information required to make highly technical decisions about how, precisely, to carry out their treatment, considerations of value (such as whether or not to proceed with a certain form of treatment at all) must be left up to patients themselves. Because it is one's own body and mind that are the subject of health care decisions, such decisions are necessarily private and personal. However, as these decisions involve information that is highly technical, it is also crucial that patients be fully informed of the consequences of their choices.[7]

Efficiency

In 1997, per capita spending on health care in the United States equalled $3,925, with total expenditures representing 13.5 percent of the country's GDP[8] (twice the amount spent on education and approximately three times that spent on national defence).[9] Canada spent $2,095 per capita on health care in that year, the total expenditure representing 9.0 percent of its GDP.[10] By way of comparison, the OECD median per capita expenditure in 1997 was $1,728 with an average total expenditure representing 7.5 percent of GDP.[11]

The percentage of GDP that a country spends in any particular sector is an important figure to consider for it is suggestive of opportunity costs. That is, if a large proportion of GDP is spent on health care services, this may "crowd out" resources available for other goods and services. It is noteworthy that between 1960 and 1997, no OECD country was able to limit growth of health care spending to growth in GDP.[12] The escalation of total health care expenditures has been the result of a variety of factors including the increasing proportion of the elderly in the population and rapidly changing technology with respect to drugs, equipment and products.[13] For example, by 2002 Ontario's forecast health spending per capita was $3,393 (1997 dollars), up from approximately $1,745 in 1975 – 39 percent of total provincial program spending in 2002 compared with 29 percent in 1977.

Apart from the efficient allocation of resources between the health care sector and other sectors (allocative efficiency), dynamic efficiency within the health care sector is another important goal. Health care is, by its very nature, a dynamic enterprise: a vast number of new therapies – pharmaceuticals, surgical techniques, alternative health maintenance measures – are constantly emerging. No system is able to take advantage of these innovations, even where cost effective, quickly enough. As well, health care provision is often highly bureaucratic: it has a tendency to resist change – technological or organisational.

Preservation of public health

Perhaps the most basic rationale for government intervention in the domain of health care is the preservation of the state of health of the population as a whole. Although there is a vast range of factors that affect the status of every individual's personal health, many of those factors are related to interactions with others. In particular, infectious diseases – from the common cold to flu to chicken pox to HIV – spread across populations with little regard for age, ethnicity, or economic status. Unfortunately, because of the costs of health care services, or due to general myopia as to the long-term benefits of investment in health care, or due to collective action or free rider problems, many members of society fail to take sufficient precautions to safeguard their own health and hence the health of others. Thus, it is in the interests of those with the requisite resources to ensure that suitable health care services are available to all and to promote the benefits of those services, for doing so reduces every individual's risk of infection.[14]

Redressing insurance market failure

Health care services are an unusual commodity in that, for most part, it is difficult to predict when they will be required. Unlike the need for food, education, or housing, the need for health care services is contingent upon the onset of an illness, the contraction of a disease, or the suffering of an injury – all events that could occur at any time. Coupled with the high cost of health care services, the uncertainty of whether or when to expect these occurrences makes health care insurance the only means of preparing for future need.

Insurance market failure stems from the fact that insurance providers are particularly wary of high costs and uncertain need. Because these providers are private entities seeking to maximize profits, it is vital to their success that they minimize both of these variables. They do so by risk-rating individuals according to age, disability, and lifestyle and avoiding those individuals whom they consider to be high-risk and therefore costly patients. For many, the result of this profit-seeking behaviour is an unaffordable insurance premium or no coverage at all. Ironically, the result is a health care system that discriminates against those who are most in need of care. This problem has the potential to become even more acute as genetic screening technology develops that will allow insurers more carefully to pinpoint high-risk individuals. Government intervention in the health care domain is likely the only means of addressing this concern. Untied cash transfers to individuals of modest means will not resolve this concern because the premiums they are likely to face if they are revealed as high health risk individuals are likely to exceed such transfers; high-risk individuals of more adequate means are likely to face similar problems of insurability

On the demand-side, private insurers must contend with problems of adverse selection and moral hazard; adverse selection entails patients concealing the risks they present to prospective insurers in order to secure coverage or reduce premiums, while moral hazard entails over-consumption of services once coverage has been provided. Both of these factors are likely to increase the costs or reduce the availability of private health care insurance.

Problems with existing systems

In the last decade, as governments have come under mounting pressure to reduce budget deficits and public debt, no public policy issue has been more vigorously debated than the organization of health care services. In this context, health policy analysts are increasingly invoking the experience of other countries in contemplating reforms. For the sake of simplicity, these reforms can be generalized into three types: (i) single payer/fee for service (as in Canada); (ii) purchaser/provider split (as in Britain and New Zealand); and (iii) managed competition (as proposed by President Clinton in his first mandate and as adopted, at least in part, in Germany and the Netherlands). Below, each of these three systems of reform are examined as a means of identifying the different approaches that governments have employed in their efforts to reform their respective health care systems and of highlighting the challenges they continue to face. It should be noted that one of the greatest difficulties in conducting a comparative analysis of various health care systems is that most standard outcome measures – such as life expectancy or infant mortality – are only crude indicators of health status and are not very sensitive to changes in health care financing and delivery systems.[15] Thus, this discussion will focus less on actual health outcomes and more on the ability of a system to provide sound incentive structures to producers and consumers of health care as a means of meeting the health care goals outlined above .

Single payer/fee for service

In Canada, provincial governments (with federal government cost-sharing) provide insurance to all individuals for all hospital services deemed "medically necessary" and for all "medically required" physician services. In effect, residents are provided with an unlimited voucher for essential medical services. Unlike most other countries, private insurance companies are generally prohibited from competing in this sector.[16] Decisions as to what constitutes "medically necessary" or "medically required" are largely left to the discretion of health care professionals, typically those in private practice. With respect to financing, hospitals (which are nominally "private" in that they are owned by private non-profit organizations but fully publicly funded)[17] are allocated capital and operating budgets by governments on an annual basis. Physicians, whether they work independently or through a hospital, are for the most part remunerated on a fee-for-service basis. That is, for each procedure performed they or their hospital employer bill the provincial insurance plan at the prescribed rate, which is periodically negotiated between provincial governments and provincial physicians' associations.

Perhaps the most significant flaw with the single-payer/fee-for-service system is the incentive structure that it yields. For the consumer, there is an incentive to seek health care services even in cases where the marginal health benefits are small relative to the costs of providing the services. The obvious reason for this is that the expected private benefits (that is, those to the individual consumer) are still greater than the private (but not the public) costs of the service. Although policy-makers have sometimes raised the possibility of implementing a user fee co-payment system to curb patient abuse, the notion is a highly contentious one in Canada, although most of the "universal access" nations in the OECD apply user fees or co-payments of some sort.[18] Critics argue that rather than targeting abusers of the system, user fees discriminate against the poor who will be more price sensitive. Moreover, they argue that there is little evidence that patient-driven demand for unnecessary medical services accounts for a significant percentage of overall health care expenditures and that severe information asymmetries between patient and physicians render the latter the key decision-making agents in health care utilization decisions.[19]

The perverse economic incentives faced by physicians in a heavily subsidized, fee-for-service environment are of central concern. Because physicians are paid solely for the services that they provide to their patients, they face incentives to increase the number of those services as a means of enhancing their revenues or to externalize costs to other elements of the system through, for example, unnecessary referrals, because they do not bear these costs.[20] The result has been an increase in in-patient hospital care, an overuse of testing, a sharp increase in billings by specialists, and an over-prescription of pharmaceuticals, all of which are expensive services for which more cost-effective alternatives often exist.[21] Thus, despite their designated role as gatekeepers to the health care system, in a pure fee-for-service system, general practitioners have few economic incentives to be sensitive to the cost-effectiveness of the various services they supply or recommend.[22] The long-term effects of this perverse incentive structure include the over-use of health care services, unduly high costs, and a growing concern over the resultant rationing of services through queuing (especially for secondary care and specialist services where capacity constraints are more binding).

Finally, there are perverse incentives facing hospitals in the Canadian variant of the single-payer/fee-for-service model as well. Because hospitals are allocated annual prospective global budgets on the basis of their previous operating budget and capital costs, it is advantageous for them to operate at maximum capacity, even if the medical benefits do not justify the costs.[23] Recently, this concern has led some provinces to adopt "case-based" funding systems, which attempt to reimburse hospitals for the mix and volume of cases they actually treat.[24] On a larger scale, there continues to be ongoing debate in Canada regarding the effective governance of publicly funded health care institutions, the need for improved accountability with respect to public spending, and the need for more community input into decision-making processes.[25]

Having identified the frailties of the single-payer/fee-for-service system, it is important not to overlook its benefits. First, the system largely eliminates concerns of insurance market failure. Because health care providers receive government funding for every citizen or resident whom they treat there is no incentive to screen out high-risk patients. In turn, the government as sole supplier of health insurance benefits from the ability to pool costs. That is, the costs of providing care to costlier patients are spread over the whole of the population. A single-payer system is also likely to involve significantly lower administrative/transaction costs than a multi-payer system.

Another benefit of the system is that it is more attentive than others to distributive justice concerns because every citizen or resident is formally entitled to whatever medically necessary services they require. However, the Canadian experience suggests that this claim should not be overstated for there are a variety of health care related goods and services that are not consistently publicly funded. The most significant of these are prescription drugs required in non-hospital settings and nursing and other medical services needed in the home, medical devices such as artificial limbs, ambulance services, and dental and vision care.[26] It has also been argued that constraints on government funding have resulted in a deterioration of health care provision in remote areas.[27] Moreover, a recent study finds that socio-economic status may impact on one's likelihood of accessing health care services.[28]

A final benefit of the single-payer/fee-for-service system is that it maximizes individual autonomy. Every individual is free to seek as much medically necessary attention as they desire and individuals are further free to choose their own family physician. Despite this domain for choice, however, there are features of the system that continue to constrain exercise of effective patient autonomy. A central concern with the current system is the lack of adequate collection, management and use of information. Canada spends a tremendous amount on health care, yet has surprisingly little information on factors such as the costs and benefits associated with providing various services, the expected outcomes for different procedures and the lengths of waiting lists. Such information is often spread across different components of the system, but is central to ensuring accountability and efficient resource utilization within the health care system. Patients also lack information about the quality of particular doctors or hospitals and, as a result, cannot make informed choices. Doctors lack information on the health histories of patients, such as records from visits to other doctors or hospitals, and on the efficacy of advances in medical knowledge. Without this information, physicians and other health care professionals may not be able to provide appropriate care or may offer duplicate or unnecessary services.[29] A public information strategy should include publicizing the status of waiting lists by institution and reporting on individual physicians with regard to wait times, outcomes and volume of various procedures, since evidence suggests higher volumes are tied to better outcomes. Governments should ensure easy access to all such information, via the Internet. Such detailed information is a fundamental aspect of encouraging individuals to exercise effective choice in the area of health issues.

Evaluation of research and technology is also important. Advances in health technology have tremendous potential for increasing the quality of care, but they come at a price. In a publicly funded system governments must ensure that the returns on health technology warrant the significant financial investment required. Evaluating clinical and cost effectiveness of treatments while reviewing new and existing technology can ensure greater quality control for services provided. By emphasizing evidence-based decision-making, health practitioners and consumers can be more confident that the services they provide and consume are effective.[30]

A second limitation on patient autonomy in the Canadian system is the prohibition on opting out of the system. Many provinces make it illegal to sell private insurance covering medically necessary physician and hospital services and all provinces require physicians to be in or out of medicare – that is they cannot operate in both the public and private spheres. The only available alternative is to seek care in another country but for most citizens this alternative is prohibitively expensive.

Purchaser/provider split

Prior to the introduction of major reforms in 1989, the British government employed a "command-and-control" approach to health care.[31] That is, the state was responsible not only for the financing of health care services but for the management of the delivery of those services as well.[32] At the top of the governing hierarchy was the Secretary of State for Health. The Secretary appointed Regional Health Authorities (RHAs) which in turn delegated duties to District Health Authorities (DHAs) and Family Practitioner Committees (FPCs). The DHAs were responsible for supplying their respective districts with public hospital services. Each of the approximately 145 DHAs directly managed hospitals that provided care to the district's population, which, on average, amounted to about 250,000 people.[33] In turn, the FPCs were responsible for provision of general medical, dental, ophthalmic, and pharmaceutical services. Every individual in the UK was enrolled with a general practitioner (GP) whom they were free to select from the National Health Service (NHS) list. These GPs acted as gatekeepers, limiting patient access to more expensive entry-points in the health care system such as hospital or specialist services.[34] Although publicly financed, GPs were treated as independent private contractors who were compensated through a mixture of three methods: (i) salary, (ii) capitation payment per registered patient, and (iii) specific fee-for-service payments for particular preventative services.[35]

While it might appear that the pre-reform UK system had strong state control over the NHS, in fact a hybrid model of governance existed.[36] While it is true that the state administered the NHS through the hierarchical tiers of administrative bodies outlined above, the organized medical profession, primarily the British Medical Association (BMA), played a key role in the corporatist regulation of the health care system. The BMA negotiated health policy with the Department of Health and the profession administered the health services in conjunction with health authorities. This left individual physicians with a significant degree of autonomy and power.

The driving force for change in the NHS arose out of heightened public perceptions that the service was on the brink of collapse. The basis for the intense and pervasive sense of crisis incorporated three inter-related factors: (i) budget constraints, (ii) increased demand for health care services, and (iii) pressure on providers to increase efficiency.[37] As a result of the troubled state of the British economy in the 1980s the government was committed to keeping health care expenditures in check, choosing to focus on increasing efficiency rather than dedicating an increasing proportion of its budget to the NHS. At the same time, however, demand for health care services was growing; the NHS's notorious waiting lists grew from 700,000 to nearly 1,000,000 and the number of individuals opting for private health insurance rose from 3.5 million at the beginning of the decade to almost 6 million at the end.[38] Recognizing the impact that reform initiatives would have on their livelihoods, members of Britain's medical profession exploited public concerns as a means of protecting themselves. They questioned budgetary constraints and denounced the inadequacy of the NHS. Finally, in 1987 when the presidents of the Royal Colleges representing the prestigious specialists issued a public statement warning that the NHS was facing ruin, Prime Minister Thatcher announced her review.[39]

Major proposals for the reform of Britain's National Health Service were advanced at the beginning of 1989 in a White Paper produced by Prime Minister Thatcher's government entitled *Working for Patients*.[40] The reforms introduced in the paper, primarily advocating the creation of an internal market in the NHS, were legislated one year later in the National Health Service and Community Care Act 1990[41] and came into effect on April 1, 1991.

At the heart of Thatcher's reform program was the creation of an internal market in the NHS that entailed a severance of the role of health care purchaser from the role of health care provider. While prior to 1991 the DHAs were responsible for directly managing the hospitals in their charge, once the reforms were implemented their role became limited to that of health care purchasers.[42] It was now their function to seek out and bargain for the best services they could from the variety of sources that existed. That is, DHAs could contract for care with their own hospitals (Directly Managed Units), with other NHS hospitals, with the private sector or with NHS hospital trusts, a new category created that, under certain conditions, allowed hospitals to turn themselves into self-governing trusts giving them considerable freedom to determine their own policies and salary scales, as well as to raise capital, provided they attracted enough patients to generate sufficient income.[43,44] The underlying idea of the purchaser–provider split was that it would foster competition by encouraging hospitals to offer quality services in a cost-effective manner and that the money would follow the patients to those that did so.[45]

Another key feature of the reform program was the creation of a new purchasing entity, the GP Fundholder. Fundholders are GP practices with more than 5,000 patients that would apply to receive budgets with which to purchase pharmaceuticals and specified hospital services for their patients from either NHS or private hospitals. They were allowed access to approximately 20 percent of hospital and community services encompassing specified diagnostic tests and elective surgical procedures for which long waiting lists exist.[46] It was the reformers' belief that Fundholders would put an end to the power imbalance favouring specialists over GPs and help to make specialists more receptive to patient needs. Further, reformers hoped to shift the emphasis of the NHS away from more expensive acute care toward more cost-effective outpatient and primary care.[47]

The putative benefits of the reforms to the NHS were fairly straightforward. First, the re-worked system seemed to avoid the agency problems inherent in the Canadian single-payer/fee-for-service model. Because physicians and Fundholders are funded on a modified capitation basis, there is an incentive for them to minimize costs in order to retain a surplus from their allocated budgets for reinvestment in their practices (and hence in enhanced quality of service).[48] These incentives further serve to counterbalance excessive demand for services by consumers who remain insulated from their own health care costs. The concern that doctors might under-service their roster of patients as a means of cost minimization was mitigated by the fact that patients were free to select any general practitioner from the NHS list (and by medical malpractice laws and professional self-regulation). Because the system was designed such that the money follows the patients, and patients are unlikely to choose doctors with reputations for poor service, the doctors would have an incentive to run their practices competitively but in a manner attentive to patients. With respect to the provision of secondary care, hospitals and other institutions, which must compete amongst each other for contracts with local health authorities, would face greater incentives to reduce costs and enhance service quality. Because decisions regarding resource allocation are made by purchasers who maintain a closer eye on costs rather than by providers with incentives to maximize costs, the system ought to be more allocatively efficient than the Canadian model.

Despite the careful engineering of the reforms, however, the NHS continues to demonstrate shortcomings that have severely limited the realization of the above benefits. Perhaps the most significant of these is the failure of real competition to materialize among health care providers. One reason for this failure is the restricted capacity for meaningful competition given the limited number of hospitals in many localities.[49] Another are the high transaction costs associated with writing, executing, and enforcing contracts in the health care context and the significant capital costs that act as a barrier to entry in much of the acute care sector.[50] A final impediment to the emergence of effective competition is the persistence of relationships between many purchasers and providers that predate the internal market reforms. The purchasers and providers who make up the new market were created by the division of established entities and thus it is far easier from an administrative perspective for them to perpetuate established patterns of activity.[51] In fact, the NHS initially promoted this behaviour by permitting the use of simple block contracts between purchasers and providers as a means of facilitating a smoother transition to the contracting mode with the objective of increasing the degree of specificity of contracts and the degree of performance monitoring over time. Unfortunately, once the requirement was implemented that DHAs move to greater use of more specific "cost and volume" contracts, prescribing the number of treatments to be provided for a given price, in practice block contracts continued to be used albeit in a more sophisticated manner.[52]

A further problem that stems directly from the persistence of block contracts is the continued reliance of the NHS on bureaucratic decision-making. While much of the emphasis of Thatcher's *Working for Patients* was on making the NHS "more responsive to the needs of the patient," in fact hospital services have stopped well short of allowing consumer demand to drive supply.[53] There are at least two problems with such an arrangement. First, it remains unclear what incentives local authorities have to make prudent purchasing decisions that are in the best interests of the patients they serve. Second, local authorities making large-scale purchasing decisions are unable to be responsive to idiosyncratic service requirements of individual consumers. Finally, block contracts also create an incentive for purchasers to pass any blame for inadequate performance on to providers.[54] Because fixed sums of money are paid to providers for unpredictable quantities of services, purchasers essentially retain their power of control while shedding their responsibility. That is, purchasers remain responsible for stipulating the services to be provided yet not for the direct provision of those services. As such, they can set unreasonable goals for providers and then suggest that any shortfalls that arise are the fault of the provider. It should be noted that in the absence of sophisticated information, providers can also take advantage of the system, either by seeking extra reimbursement on a per case basis or by simply omitting to provide the required service without being detected.[55]

With the insights gained from both its success and failures, the British NHS continues to evolve. In December of 1997, Tony Blair's newly elected Labour government released another White Paper detailing reforms to the NHS that promised to dismantle the internal market and shift from an emphasis on competition and choice to an emphasis on cooperation[56] and much more extensive reporting of performance measures by physicians and hospitals. Medical audits are now the norm across almost all major health disciplines.[57]

The Labour government's reforms comprise a number of different initiatives but the most significant is the abolition of GP Fundholders and the creation of

"Primary Care Groups" (PCGs). The latter are to be large groups of general practitioners and community nurses, which in addition to managing the budgets for primary and community care will also, eventually, be responsible for purchasing services from the NHS Trusts. On average, a PCG includes 50 to 60 general practitioners from 20 or so different practices. PCGs being formed cover populations ranging from 50,000 to 200,000 people but the average is anticipated to be around 100,000 people each.

Each PCG will have available their population's share of the available resources for hospital and community health care services, the budget for prescribing by general practitioners and nurses, and the budget which reimburses general practitioners for the cost of their practice staff, premises and computers. The PCGs will not control payments to general practitioners for the services they provide and general practitioners will retain their "independent contractor status" under the new reforms.

The difference from the previous system is that people had a choice, even if it were rarely exercised, to leave one Fundholder for another or for a non-Fundholding general practitioner. Now, for better or for worse, people have no choice but to rely on their PCGs to make good decisions. Also of concern is that whereas previously general practitioners determined themselves whether or not they wanted to be Fundholders, now general practitioners and community nurses are being forced to assume clinical and financial responsibility for purchasing a wide range of health care services. The other key difference between PCGs and Fundholders is that general practitioners who were Fundholders had a much stronger financial incentive to purchase cost-effective care. With PCGs any savings made by one general practitioner would have to be shared amongst 50 to 60 general practitioners and, indeed, may be offset by overspending by other members of the PCG over whom the practitioner has little or no control.

It seems that the Labour government has been less than satisfied with its impact on the NHS. In its March 2000 budget the government announced an injection of £19.4 billion into the NHS over the next four years. This expansion of funding likely reflects a mixture of motives from genuine commitment to the NHS to frustrated impatience with the failure of New Labour's policies so far to achieve the hoped-for transformation. According to the prime minister, the NHS still "needs fundamental reform."[58]

Managed competition

US

In 1992, Bill Clinton campaigned for the presidency of the United States on a platform that included as a key plank an ambitious reorganization of the health care delivery system. His vision was for the country to adopt a system that ensured universal access to a comprehensive range of health care services in a manner roughly analogous to the managed competition model being implemented in Germany and the Netherlands.[59] Although Clinton's Health Security Act appeared to address the significant problems that had prompted the need for national health reform – concerns of the uninsured[60] and cost containment – the plan nevertheless failed. While partisan politics, the strength of the health care lobbies, the inexperience of the Clinton administration, and the complexity of the plan all played a role in the its demise, Sherry Glied has asserted that these factors alone cannot account for the failure of the effort. Rather, she argues that the real basis for the plan's failure stemmed from three distinct sources.[61] First were the irreconcilable differences between the two main groups of reformers, supporters of single-payer reform and supporters of market-oriented, managed competition. While the former believe that health care has a unique quality that distinguishes it from other goods and services and thus cannot be allocated by way of the market, the latter view health care as a good like any other and favour delivery by way of the market. In the end, although the two groups were brought together to attempt to find a compromise between the two ideals, neither was willing to yield to the other. Second were the false assumptions about health care spending and the health sector made by these two groups. The supporters of single-payer reform failed to recognize that a centrally organized health care system would be too inflexible and would respond too slowly to inevitable and desirable changes in health care technology and patient preferences. Supporters of market-oriented, managed competition, however, were unable to acknowledge that the market solution has difficulty addressing the distributional concern, namely that it cannot guarantee adequate universal coverage and health security. Finally, neither group was able to address successfully the financing of health care reform. Although Clinton's proposed reforms were never implemented, certain features may have been viable and are thus worth examining for the purposes of a comparative analysis.

The Clinton model of managed competition would have been superimposed upon a predominantly private health care services and insurance system (although it should be noted that over 40 percent of the US health care system is publicly funded). Mandatory coverage would be provided to employees and their dependents primarily through employer mandates (with employers meeting 80 percent of costs and employees 20 percent) and public subsidies for low-wage firms and low-income individuals to assist in the purchase of health insurance. Employer-provided health insurance would continue to be non-taxable as an employment benefit and deductible as a business expense by employers. Clinton's plan required government-appointed sponsors (referred to in the initial proposal as "Health Insurance Purchasing Co-operatives" and in subsequent amendments as "Regional Alliances") to act as intermediaries between consumers and insurers.[62] Funding from government, employers and consumers would be funnelled through the Alliances, which would consolidate the purchasing power of individual consumers and smaller employers in purchasing health care insurance from private insurers.[63] The idea was that with only one Alliance permitted in any particular region, each would control enough of the market to negotiate affordable insurance plans that would meet minimum quality requirements. With respect to competition among insurers, Clinton's proposal required that individuals would have an opportunity to choose a new insurer on an annual basis if they so desired. To facilitate effective decision-making, citizens would be provided with information on the performance of each insurer in terms of the satisfaction levels of their enrollees, their ratings on nationally approved quality indicators, and any restrictions within their policies on choice of and access to providers.[64] Additionally, it would be the responsibility of the Alliances to ensure that insurers were competing on price and quality rather than on their ability to avoid high-risk patients. In fact, insurers would be prohibited from risk-rating patients and charging higher premiums to those with higher ratings except with the express permission of the Alliance.[65]

The features of President Clinton's health proposal outlined above clearly distinguish it, in various ways, from either the Canadian or UK models. First is its resulting incentive structure – one that is arguably superior to those in either of these other two countries. As previously discussed, the single-payer/fee-for-service model creates perverse incentives for consumers, physicians, and hospitals. The purchaser/provider split model has also been criticized for failing to create effective incentives for the DHAs to purchase services from those providers who are most efficient. With managed competition, however, private health plan providers are extremely conscious of costs and will constrain primary and secondary care providers with whom they in turn contract accordingly, yet at the same time they are obligated to provide a state-defined minimum level of services. Thus, it may be more likely than the other two models to reach an optimal balancing of cost-reduction and allocation of needed services.[66] A second issue that may be more effectively dealt with by the managed-care system is that of the effective generation of competition. The single-payer/fee-for-service model has done little if anything to foster efficiency through competition and unlike the purchaser/provider split model, Clinton's proposal ensures substantial competition because health plan providers or insurers are competing directly for the dollars of the end-users rather than relying on historical relationships with DHAs. Insofar as preferences are accounted for, the single-payer/fee-for-service model clearly provides the most choice in that it places no restrictions on which doctor a user must see. Among the other two systems, each has its strengths and weakness. While the purchaser/provider split model has until recently allowed patients to choose any GP from the NHS list, choice among hospitals and specialists is more limited. In contrast, the managed-competition model allows users to switch insurers annually but these insurers may limit their choice of doctors to a specified list. Finally, perhaps one deficiency of Clinton's proposals is the lack of encouragement of the use of GPs as gatekeepers to the health care system. Both the Canadian and British health care systems have heavily emphasized primary care as a means of containing health care budgets but the US system has always allowed for direct access by patients to more expensive specialists; the managed-competition plan does nothing to change this. However, managed-competition does promote efficiency through competition and it is likely that health care providers themselves will choose to place a greater emphasis on primary care as a means of increasing the efficient delivery of services.

While these features of the managed-competition model are attractive, other features are more problematic: constraining cream-skimming by health plan providers to screen out high-risk patients, which requires administratively complex policies either to compel mandatory pooling of patients or differentiated risk-rated subsidies directly or indirectly from government to mitigate the incentives faced by the health plan providers to screen out high-risk patients. These policies in a decentralized, multi-payer system are likely to increase administrative/transactions costs, offsetting to an important extent the adaptability, flexibility, and dynamism of a more decentralized, competitive system.

Germany

The German health care system has been described as "the prototype of the European social insurance-based health care system."[67] In the German model, individuals pay a premium that operates like a payroll tax, in that it is collected by the government and redistributed to insurers on the basis of the number of enrolees.[68] Insurers are free to enter and exit the market and as of 1996, each individual is allowed to choose among existing health care providers.[69] This availability of choice has substantially increased the competitive incentives among insurance providers.

Although various market incentives exist within the German system, Germany still outspends most of its European counterparts in terms of both per-capita expenditures and health care spending as a proportion of the GDP.[70] In recent years, the German government has made attempts to contain costs by increasing patient cost-sharing,[71] altering the payment structure to health care providers and insurers,[72] and removing inefficient services from the bundle of entitlements provided to patients.[73]

Although insurers (known as sickness funds) are theoretically private entities, they have become increasingly subject to government regulation. The government mandates individual contribution levels, which are currently set at approximately 13 percent of each person's salary (half of which is paid by the individual and half of which is paid by the employer).[74] For those who are unemployed or who receive social assistance, the government subsidizes the insurance contributions normally paid by individuals.[75] In addition, citizens with salaries exceeding a fixed amount are free to opt out of the public system and purchase private insurance. An important feature of both the public and private insurance systems that operate in Germany is that insurers are not permitted to refuse clients. This ensures that high-risk individuals do not face prohibitive costs in obtaining comprehensive insurance.[76] However, there exists some suspicion that sickness funds may engage in more subtle forms of cream-skimming by adopting an insurance system that is more likely to attract high-income and/or healthier individuals.[77]

The Netherlands

The Dutch health care insurance system encompasses many of the structural features found in the German system, but differs from it in several design particulars. For example, the income threshold (for opting out of the public system) is much lower in the Netherlands, and 30 percent of the population has opted for private insurance as opposed to 10 percent in Germany.[78] Another important variant in the Dutch system is the existence of separate insurance schemes for ordinary medical insurance and so-called "catastrophic" health insurance. Ordinary medical insurance is provided via sickness funds and the payment mechanism is similar to that operating in Germany,[79] but the average contribution in the Netherlands is only about 1 percent of wages, as opposed to 13 percent in Germany. However, this does not necessarily translate into a 12 percent difference, because the German contribution covers all health risks, whereas the Dutch contribution covers only ordinary health risks. Catastrophic insurance coverage is mandatory for all individuals who are required to participate in the public insurance system, and is financed via the income tax.[80]

The rationale for maintaining two systems is that for the very costly "catastrophic" risks, citizens are pooled in the largest possible risk pool (the entire country), whereas for ordinary risks, the existence of a number of insurers allows consumers to have a choice of providers and introduces competitive incentives into the insurance market. Indeed, with respect to "catastrophic" risks (including long-term care and mental health care), van Doorslaer and Schut argue that competition would not be appropriate because effective pressure from the demand-side is lacking: this is either because most people who need such care do not have the ability to make a trade-off between price and quality, or because the likelihood of people needing such care during the next contract period is so small that they do not concern themselves with the quality of the providers selected by the insurer.[81]

Although the Dutch health care system provides comprehensive and universal coverage, concerns have emerged with respect to its efficiency. One of these is the lack of incentives for sickness funds to contain costs. Funds were fully reimbursed for all medical expenses, and thus had no incentive to be efficient in their spending. In an attempt to alleviate this problem, the government altered the reimbursement scheme, making it partially prospective and partially retrospective. Thus, rather than being reimbursed at the end of the fiscal period for all expenditures, each fund receives a fixed block grant at the beginning of the period and is required to use these funds to purchase services. If expensive services are purchased, then the fund will be left with no surplus, or may go into deficit. In order to mitigate any perverse incentives that may arise from this structure (e.g. under-provision of services), funds can be reimbursed *ex post* where they can show that the expenditures were made in response to actual patient need. It is estimated that this change has increased the financial risk for the sickness funds to more than 40 percent of their expenditures.[82]

Designing a voucher system

The voucher concept has a large potential realm of application to the health care field. Universal single-payer/fee-for-service health care systems such as in place in Canada form one potential mechanism of implementation. However, as explained above, such systems create moral hazard problems on both the supply-side and demand-side of the market. We believe that these problems can be substantially mitigated, as we outline below.

Qualified consumers: value of vouchers

We argue that an equitable, efficient, high-quality and financially sustainable health care scheme would be universally available and would operate via an uncapped voucher system in the form of a health card. However, unlike the current Canadian system, citizens would make contributions based on individual usage of the health care system through the existing tax system.[83] These contributions would be made on a sliding scale according to income, such that individuals with the lowest incomes would be exempt from the contribution, and all other persons would be assessed for their contribution according to income level. Contributions would only exist, however, up to a specified cap. Beyond this income-contingent ceiling, a catastrophic insurance system would apply, relieving patients of the obligation to make co-payments. This will ensure that individuals who suffer from unexpected and expensive health problems are not put in precarious financial positions.

There are three principal methods for altering demand-side incentives.[84] First, the government could institute user fees for health care services. User fees are out-of-pocket costs imposed on consumers upon point of contact with the system. Advocates argue that fees deter unnecessary use of the system. However, for these fees to be effective, they must deter only inefficient and unnecessary use and not necessary and appropriate use. While most empirical studies find that user fees do reduce use, they show that lower-income individuals tend to be those most affected. Other evidence suggests that user fees translate into poorer health outcomes for lower-income patients, and deter both efficient and inefficient use.[85]

A second approach for modifying health care services is through medical savings accounts (MSAs). Although numerous types exist, a typical government MSA would be to allocate each individual or family a yearly health care allowance, such as $4,000 for a family of four. Over the year, the family would access the account to pay for health care services. Any expenses above the yearly allowance would be paid out of the family's income, up to a catastrophic threshold like $8,000. Beyond this threshold, all health care expenses, including prescription drugs, would again fall to the government. At year's end, left-over money could be rolled over into the family's account for the following year, or returned directly to them as a tax credit or cash. This policy provides a natural incentive for a family to use services most efficiently.

Unfortunately, little empirical evidence exists to indicate whether or not MSAs do, in fact, reduce overall health care spending. The system may encourage low-intensity health care users to avoid over-utilization, but the majority of MSA policies leave the savings with the individual, not lowering overall government costs at all. Moreover, high-intensity users experience no incentive, under this program, to alter behaviour, since government covers all health care costs once catastrophic coverage is reached. In fact some argue it is a "tax on the sick," particularly for those with persistent high-cost health care usage below the catastrophic coverage threshold and that, given patient–physician information asymmetries, patients are not well-placed to make informed decisions about their utilization of the health care system.[86]

A third, more promising option for improving demand-side incentives is a tax-based health care utilization charge. This charge comes in many forms; some involve a tax credit, others provide a taxable benefit. Aba, Goodman and Mintz propose in a Canadian context that individuals using a covered health care service receive a receipt detailing the full cost of the service.[87] At the end of the year, the government would issue individuals a TH form listing all the health care services used over the year, with 40 percent of the total cost included as income for tax purposes. Under this system, the maximum a family could pay a year would be 3 percent of any annual income above $10,000. Families with an income below $10,000 would not be taxed. Aba, Goodman and Mintz estimate that 60 percent of all health care system users would pay the maximum fee allowed under this plan. For those earning less than $10,000 per annum, 100 percent would pay the maximum of $0; between $10,000 and $30,000, 95 percent would pay the maximum, averaging individual contributions of about $280; and between $60,000 and $100,000, only 4 percent would pay the maximum, averaging contributions of about $797. As a result of the incentive to reduce utilization, the authors estimate that Canada's total public expenditure on health care in 2000 alone would have fallen from $46.7 billion to $40.4 billion, a saving of 13.5 percent. In the same year, the new tax would have raised $6.6 billion in revenue across the country. Aba *et al.* make a simple, yet persuasive, argument regarding the implementation of a tax-based user fee. They state that, "our rationale [for requiring co-payments] is that a certain proportion of an individual's expenditures on health care ought to be regarded as a basic consumption expenditure, akin to food and shelter."[88] As noted earlier, most universal access OECD health care systems apply user fees or co-payments of some sort.

Tax-based health care co-payments offer advantages over traditional user fees and MSAs. Using the existing tax system, the plan would be relatively easy to administer. It would include a built-in exemption for low-income families, minimizing the negative effects of encouraging reduced utilization and so payments would be scaled both to utilization and income levels. Unfortunately, similar to MSAs, high-volume users receive no incentive to alter treatment patterns, as they continue to face the maximum health tax annually – again seemingly a "tax on the sick."[89] Again, critics argue that because of patient–physician information asymmetries, patients are poorly placed to regulate their own utilization levels.

Qualified suppliers; mode of remuneration

The benefits of a voucher system are contingent on maintaining a broad scope for individual consumer choice. Accordingly, as open a market as possible ought to be maintained for health care providers. A major issue in Canada in this respect is the so-called "privatization" of the health care sector – to which there has been much public opposition. This issue unfortunately conflates the questions of who should provide health care services with who should pay for them. Over 30 percent of total health care services are already privately paid for and provided. Physicians and specialists operate private for-profit practices; pharmaceuticals are produced and dispensed by for-profit providers; most medical technology is supplied by for-profit firms; laboratory testing is done by for-profit providers; much institutional care is provided by for-profit entities. Only the hospital sector is the exclusive preserve of public or non-profit entities. We see no reason why for-profit entities should be prevented from participating in this or indeed any other segment of the health care sector. The issue of what health care services the state should pay for is an entirely distinct issue and is discussed below. Nevertheless, in a sector that provides services so fundamental to the well-being of the population, certain regulations are necessary. Traditionally in Canada, there has been a tendency toward passivity by provincial governments in their regulation of health care quality, and malpractice laws and professional self-regulation have been the primary mechanisms used to ensure the quality of health care services supplied to the public. Similarly, the assurance of quality in hospitals has been through a voluntary accreditation process. This relatively passive role of the government stems from the formidable information barriers faced by regulators with respect to patients' health needs and furthermore from the near impossibility of effectively monitoring the treatment of all patients. These informational challenges have recently become more tractable as governments are now able to collect information about treatment and referral patterns and to compare this information with studies showing optimal treatment and referral patterns, and many governments have begun to institute various physician and hospital auditing procedures, although much more needs to be done to provide consumers with the information required to make effective choices among physicians, hospitals, and other health care institutions. However, the major driver of cost-effective behaviour by physicians is the system of remuneration. The three major options are fee for service (FFS), capitation, and salary.

FFS most clearly exposes the information asymmetries inherent in a physician–patient relationship. Patients generally rely on their physician to diagnose problems and recommend treatments. From a purely economic perspective, physicians have an incentive to supply as many services as possible in order to maximize their incomes or to ignore externalities that their behaviour imposes on other elements of the health care system. However, economic theory predicts that individuals seek to maximize utility both in personal income and lifestyle. As a result, physicians may, in fact, work less but perform more expensive services.[90] A study comparing 19 OECD countries found that on aggregate, all else being equal, FFS increased health care spending by 11 percent.[91]

Numerous alternatives exist for paying physicians. The two most prominent options are capitation and salary. Under capitation, physicians receive a lump sum for each patient managed over a given period of time. Although, in the short term, this system appears to create incentives for physicians to minimize the number of services provided to each patient, it institutes long-term incentives by encouraging health care specialists to keep their enrolled population healthy through preventative services. A patient falling ill in the future poses high service costs to a medical caregiver. If physicians are charged with the long-term care of their patients, this higher cost will create immediate incentives for continued preventative treatments (assuming they are responsible for long-term costs and cannot shift these to other payers).

Capitation would replace the incentives under FFS of offering increased services to a larger number of patients, with a sharper focus on overall patient health. However, it may be inefficient for a physician to insure against the potential high costs of one of her patients becoming extremely ill. As a result, any capitation payment scheme would have to require or encourage groups of physicians to form cooperative group practices in order to diversify risk. Further, if capitation were implemented through practice groups, including physicians and other health professionals, systemic incentives would ensure that each professional used his or her skills fully and in the most appropriate settings. Physicians have the most thorough information regarding the health of their patients, and the risks and consequences of various illnesses and treatments. Capitation creates an incentive for these physicians or practice groups to emphasize preventative treatments and primary care.[92] However, there is now a risk that some health care professionals will "cream-skim" for the lowest risk patients, who are less costly to service. Any capitation scheme must incorporate mechanisms to safeguard against this possibility, for example, through mandatory pooling or risk-adjusted capitation payments, although either mechanism is likely to entail substantial additional administrative complexity and transaction costs. Moreover, capitation by itself may exacerbate incentives to externalize costs to other elements of the health care system, so that encouraging the emergence of group practices with global patient-capitated budgets may be desirable, perhaps covering all medically necessary services other than catastrophic risks.[93]

The practice of salaried remuneration simply provides a yearly income for physicians, independent of services provided or the number of patients seen. The risk with salary is the disconnect between payment received and services issued, creating incentives to under-provide treatment. In addition, no incentive exists for physicians to supply the most cost-effective service. For example, the most economical approach to an illness may involve treatment and follow-up consultations with one doctor. However, a salaried physician might be influenced to refer the patient to a specialist. On the other hand, if physicians were employed in group practices, competition could arise between groups for patients.[94] The employer of a physician group could hire specialists with a similar approach to medicine – perhaps a focus on preventative and primary techniques rather than more intensive and invasive procedures – if this was believed to provide effective patient service. Incentives could be calibrated to peer reviews and promotions, with bonuses available for performance and prevention targets achieved.

Studies show a correlation between payment methods and health care use. Physicians paid by FFS see more patients and have higher billings than physicians paid by capitation or salary.[95] They also exhibit higher hospital admissions than physicians paid by capitation.[96] Salaried doctors conducted fewer tests, saw fewer patients and had fewer referrals than those paid by either FFS or capitation.[97] Further, physicians paid by capitation or salary tend to transfer their work to others, increasing their numbers of prescriptions and referrals.[98]

Due to the varied incentives, some systems now employ a mixture of FFS and capitation. Britain utilizes a mixed payment scheme, under which compensation for general practitioners is composed of capitation and basic allowances (65 percent), FFS (25 percent) and target payments (10 percent).[99] The most innovative suggestions for mixed payment schemes involve tying compensation to outcomes. The UK and parts of the Ontario system use a similar blended approach tied to outcomes and measures such as vaccination rates.[100] This sort of approach deserves further exploration.

Based on existing evidence, significant supply-side incentive gains are likely to be realized by embracing some form of capitation system for physicians within a structure of group practices. Capitation would encourage greater use of incentives for long-term patient care including prevention. It would also promote a more efficient use of services, such as the provision of 24-hour availability seven days a week through the group rather than through higher-cost emergency hospital rooms. The incentive to cream-skim could be avoided either by weighting capitation payments to compensate physicians for higher-risk patients or some form of mandatory patient pooling (although both entail significant additional administrative complexity).

As the comparative experience reviewed above suggests, capitation systems are likely to function best when health care providers (e.g. GP fund holders in the UK) or health plan providers (e.g. sickness funds in Germany and the Netherlands or HMOs in the US) (a) are large enough to diversify risks, but not so large that consumers are denied effective choices amongst providers or plans; (b) the capitation payments internalize most of the costs of health care provision to service or plan providers so as to minimize incentives to engage in cost shifting to other elements of the health care system; and (c) mandatory patient pooling or risk adjusted capitation payments are adopted to minimize cream-skimming.

While these features of a capitation regime improve incentives on the supply-side of the health care market, they leave unaddressed moral hazard problems on the demand-side of the market, although there is controversy over how serious these problems are. While physicians would no longer derive marginal private benefits from providing additional services to patients, patients would still derive marginal private benefits from demanding them. A tax-based health care co-payment system would improve incentives on the demand-side of the market while being sensitive to the regressive impact of co-payments and the problem of catastrophic health care needs. Decoupling the issues of how health care providers should be compensated from the issue of how the health care system should be financed presents similar features to the economic analysis of liability for accidents. While making defendants wholly liable to plaintiffs for the latters' losses may create appropriate incentives for injurers, they remove any incentive for plaintiffs to take self-precautionary measures. Ideally, both parties to an injury-causing interaction should face the full social costs of their causal contribution to the negative outcome. In bilateral tortious interactions, this is difficult to achieve but in health care financing it is feasible, in principle, to decouple what health care providers get paid from what patients should pay. Under a capitation system obviously some cost-accounting mechanics would need to be resolved in order to attribute a cost or value to services received by consumers and hence treated as a taxable benefit.

While this may entail an element of arbitrariness, it is not clearly a more arbitrary exercise than prescribing fees for services under a fee-for-service regime.

In short, in principle, moral hazard problems on both sides of the health care market need to be addressed if a better efficiency–equity trade-off is to be realized than is evident in most health care systems today.

Scope of the voucher entitlement

A major challenge inherent in identifying the appropriate scope of a health care voucher is defining precisely the distinction between essential and non-essential health care services. In Canada, for example, the ambiguity of the term "medically necessary" has resulted in differing interpretations in each province as demonstrated by the differing policies towards prescription drug coverage, long-term care, eye care and dental care.[101] The difficulty of this task is further demonstrated by recent attempts in the Netherlands, New Zealand, and the state of Oregon in the US to define what constitutes "core" services.[102] In New Zealand for example, the National Advisory Committee on Health and Disability has found it impossible to develop a specific list of priorities in treatment. As a result, significant discretion has been left in the hands of the Regional Health Authorities who have largely resorted to maintaining pre-existing service patterns. The question of what services should be covered and which should not is indeed a difficult challenge and requires recurrent revisitation in response to technological developments and new evidence of health service costs and benefits, raising institutional issues of who should decide these questions, on what criteria, and following what kind of decision-making process.

With the aging of the population in many countries, the provision of long-term care (LTC) raises the issue of scope of coverage in one of its most acute forms. LTC comprises a wide range of services including medical care, assistance with activities of daily living (ADLs), which includes assistance with mobility, using the restroom and eating, and assistance with instrumental activities of daily living (IADLs), which includes assistance with household chores, taking medication and money management. LTC can involve institutionalization in a hospital or nursing home, the use of adult day care facilities, or home visits. While the medical components of LTC are often treated as health care benefits, non-medical components are generally viewed as "social" benefits, hence not attracting the same level of government support.

The policy rationalization for this distinction seems to be that LTC services that are not "medically necessary" fall outside the ambit of the Rawlsian justification for universal access to health care. In our view, a comprehensive and efficient system of health care should include many LTC services. First, most non-medical LTC services are required as a direct consequence of medical conditions. For example, an elderly person with severe arthritis may require help with household chores because of her medical condition. The distinction between a "medical" service and a non-medical service that is required as a direct consequence of a medical condition is tenuous, and the denial of a benefit to a person requiring the latter conflicts with values of distributive justice and personal autonomy.

In many countries, only those with extremely low levels of assets are eligible for government funding of non-medical LTC services.[103] This means-testing is often normatively justified on the basis that these services are akin to welfare benefits, and thus should only be provided to those who are seriously impoverished. However, it fails to recognize that the costs of LTC are often prohibitive, even for those people with moderate income/asset levels. In many countries, individuals are required to "spend down" their assets in order to meet eligibility requirements for state-funded LTC,[104] at which point they will then be eligible for state-financing but will then find themselves in a state of poverty.

Another concern is that the strict separation of medical and non-medical services serves as a source of inefficiency in the health care system. Hospitals may simply discharge patients requiring chronic care to nursing homes or to the community, thereby divesting themselves of the costs. Alternatively, hospitals may be under pressure to keep patients in high-cost, publicly financed chronic care units even when a more efficient but unfunded alternative exists.

Finally, there does not seem to be a coherent theoretical reason for the reluctance to finance LTC primarily through a public insurance system. Feder and colleagues argue that, "we typically rely on insurance to deal with costs that are potentially catastrophic and unpredictable. Long-term care satisfies both criteria."[105] It would seem, therefore, that LTC is as suitable for a public insurance system as is health care. It would therefore be more equitable, and more efficient, to require that all members of the population share in the risk, rather than to simply finance services on a means-tested basis as is now typically the case.

An interesting model of LTC provision is the new German model. In 1994, Germany enacted a universal-coverage social insurance program for long-term care.[106] This program is mandatory and is financed partially by the government and partially through individual contributions. The benefits are extensive and pertain to nursing home and home-care services for "people of all ages without regard to financial status."[107] Thus, eligibility for benefits is contingent solely on meeting criteria relating to functional status; specifically, to qualify, a person must show that he or she requires assistance with at least two ADLs and some assistance with respect to IADLs.[108]

Once an individual is deemed to qualify for the receipt of benefits, he or she may choose to receive a voucher for the approved services, or may choose to receive a cash payment instead. Those who choose the latter receive less than half the value of the service benefits, but the use of cash is unrestricted.[109] As well, expenditures per person are capped at levels that vary by disability level and institutional status.[110] There are three "grades" of disability, by which recipients are categorized. The cash payments vary according to the grade of disability experienced.[111] In addition to these cash benefits, informal caregivers (friends and family members) can attend free care-giving training courses.[112] The costs of this program have remained relatively low, largely due to the cap placed on per-person expenditures and the overwhelming preference for cash benefits (which are less expensive for the government).

Individuals electing to receive vouchers are free to choose from among a variety of suppliers who have contracts with the sickness funds. One of the benefits of this new program is that the number of suppliers has increased substantially, thereby providing more choice to consumers, and introducing a greater element of competition into the market. In addition, regulatory measures have been put in place to ensure that minimum standards are being met. A national quality framework was introduced in 1995 that, "specifies standards and review procedures for institutions and home-care providers participating in the long-term care program."[113] These standards require that providers implement internal quality assessment programs, and provides for external reviews when complaints are made.

In our view, consumers should be enabled to choose their suppliers and change suppliers as they see fit, thus enhancing both the quality and cost-effectiveness of LTC service provision. We envision a system in which eligibility is assessed on a needs basis. Those requiring LTC services would apply to an independent case-management agency that would be responsible for determining the level of assistance required. Individuals would be encouraged to utilize home-based services where appropriate in order to contain costs, as well as to foster individual autonomy and community participation by the elderly. Individuals would bear the full costs of services purchased beyond the average cost of the recommended care, in order to mitigate moral hazard problems. Tax-collected user fees (based on a sliding income scale) would apply to covered services and would be integrated with our proposed tax-based user fees for other health care services. However, the extent of this integration would be qualified by the extent to which LTC services comprise housing and other living expenses that would otherwise be borne by every individual with no disabilities. In other words, individuals who require institutional care will be responsible for paying the portion of the costs related to the non-service components of the care (shelter, food, etc.) either on their own or with the assistance of social welfare or pension benefits, rather than through the tax-based system and LTC government assistance.

Thus, the system would operate as follows for consumers of institutional care. The cost of the care would be divided into two amounts, representing the service components and the non-service components. The service component would be financed in the same way that home-based care is financed – that is, the government will subsidize a certain percentage, and the individual will pay the remaining percentage through the tax-based collection system. Regarding the non-service component, the individual will bear the full costs independently of the health care system. However, low-income individuals may be eligible for subsidization of these costs through social assistance or pension benefits.

Normatively, the justification for drawing a dividing line between the service components and non-service components of institutional care is straightforward. Taxpayers should not be required to pay for the basic living expenses of LTC consumers under the guise of health care expenditures. The services that should be provided with some level of government assistance on a needs-tested basis are limited to those that are necessary for enabling individuals to perform daily living tasks that otherwise could not be performed. Living expenses are properly subsidized by a means-tested social assistance program. In Germany, for example, the federal government is responsible for LTC services, while local governments are responsible for social assistance. Thus, individuals who require financial assistance in addition to LTC benefits must apply to the local government.[114] Another policy reason for this division relates to horizontal equity among LTC consumers. Individuals receiving home-based services are required to pay for their own living expenses, and thus subsidizing the living expenses of those using institutional resources would create inequities in the treatment of the two groups. Moreover, by creating a windfall for individuals utilizing institutional care, perverse incentives would be created. LTC recipients would be encouraged to use higher-cost institutional care, even when they are capable of remaining at home. From both a personal autonomy standpoint and an economic perspective, this is an undesirable result. Empirically, only two countries actually separate the medical and housing costs of LTC – Belgium and France.[115] Both operate successfully, fiscally and socially.

The successful operation of the proposed program requires that providers are able to freely enter and exit the market. For example, Hjertqvist reports that, in Sweden, "privatized nursing homes have reduced costs by 20–30 percent,"[116] suggesting that the introduction of competition has increased cost-efficiency. Further, it has been found that competition can also increase service quality. Zinn finds that when there is greater bed availability in nursing homes (meaning that consumers have more options, and therefore that competition between providers is increased) there are "fewer violations of nursing home licensure code require-ments."[117] This finding suggests that, "higher quality may be one outcome of increased competition."[118]

However, concerns regarding the health and safety of beneficiaries mandate that the government ensure that service providers are competent. To reconcile these goals, it is necessary to establish a baseline set of requirements that providers must meet in order to redeem the government funding. The need for baseline safety and quality standards is of particular importance in the domain of LTC, as consumers are, by definition, vulnerable. Further, as Geron notes, "for those con-sumers who are unable or ill-prepared to take on these tasks [choosing providers], too much choice may not result in greater independence – but rather in a sense of powerlessness."[119] A regulatory framework for setting baseline standards will help to alleviate the concern that these individuals will receive inadequate care in a consumer-directed system.

Geron suggests that an appropriate LTC delivery model should contain both regulated standards of safety and quality as well as consumer-derived quality measures. This would include the implementation of sector-wide safety standards because "quality problems are not eliminated when consumers are given the responsibility to determine the quality standards for their care."[120] However, consumers should be able to control their care to a large extent, particularly in the case of non-medical home-based services where concerns about safety are limited, by defining their own standards of quality and retaining the freedom to hire and fire caregivers pursuant to these standards.

Extra billing

A final issue that arises in designing a voucher regime is that of extra billing or "topping up." Here the issue to be confronted is whether individuals should be free to negotiate for services above the minimum standard (assuming a minimum standard can be defined). Specifically, the question arises as to whether patients should be permitted to use voucher entitlements as a credit towards higher quality, more expensive or more expeditious essential services and pay the difference themselves, or alternatively opt out of the system altogether. Again, the familiar efficiency versus equity trade-off arises. Prohibiting extra billing for basic covered services suppresses the price system and its value as a signal of and reward for superior quality, although permitting it is likely to seriously compromise equality of access goals and perhaps attenuate the political efficacy of voice in maintaining the value of basic voucher entitlements. Extra billing has traditionally been prohibited in Canada out of concern that those with the ability to do so would essentially exit the publicly financed health care system in favour of a superior, largely privately financed one. The public system left behind would then lose the support of those individuals with the political voice necessary to ensure the maintenance of high-quality health care delivery. Conventional wisdom in Canada asserts that forcing the entire population to put their health in the hands of the public system ensures that those with sufficient political voice will use it to ensure their own well-being and thus, by extension, the well-being of all. In this respect, the system is seen as an important expression of social, even national solidarity. Although this line of reasoning has some cogency to it, it is arguable that at least some tailoring of services to meet individual preferences could be permitted without compromising the quality of the publicly financed system – especially given that in some ways, a two-tiered system already exists in Canada as the wealthy can pay for additional services, for example, private nurses, private hospital rooms or traveling to the United States and making use of US facilities and physicians.[121] Implementing a "topping up" tax, for example, as suggested by Sherry Glied[122] is one means by which this could be achieved. With such a tax in place, individuals who choose to do so would be permitted to purchase health care services whose value exceeded the value of their personal voucher but they would be taxed on the difference between the cost of that expenditure and the value of their voucher. The proceeds of the tax would then be re-invested in the underlying voucher program.

There are many reasons why the institution of a "top up" tax scheme may be beneficial to the health care system. First and foremost it would increase the amount of funding available for health care expenditures. Second, it would create a means by which the level of sustainable national health care spending would be determined at least in part by individual citizens rather than simply being imposed by government. Finally, it would provide concrete evidence of the adequacy or inadequacy of the state-financed health care. That is, the extent to which citizens choose to top up their personal expenditures on health care would indicate the level of satisfaction they have with the existing spending levels of the state. Thus, the greater the degree of topping up, the greater would be the pressure on the state to improve the program.

Political economy

In Canada and the US, the political dynamics of health care provision are significantly different. Canada already has a government-financed, voucher-like system for primary and secondary care. By contrast, in the US there is no broad-based government health care voucher program. The Canadian voucher-like system for health care provision has weak incentive properties on both the demand- and supply-sides in terms of cost-effective utilization of health care services, and in several jurisdictions (including the US) recent health care reform proposals attempt to reconcile the objectives of universal access with cost-effective service provision through some form of managed competition among health insurance or health plan providers. As the failure of the Clinton Administration's health care reform proposals illustrate, this form of voucher system is likely to engender opposition from many sources, including employers (especially smaller employers) to the extent that it is financed through mandatory employer contributions; health insurance or health plan providers to the extent that demand-side purchasing power is concentrated in the hands of a relatively few purchasing agents; and physicians and hospitals who will resist the constraints imposed on their medical autonomy by cost considerations. While about 40 million Americans are currently uninsured, as poorer or more disadvantaged citizens they are unlikely to constitute an effective political counter-weight to the interests arrayed against this kind of health care reform. While Canada contemplates reforms from a different starting point, patients/consumers will be difficult to persuade to forego the relatively unconstrained form of universal access that they currently enjoy for cost-constrained universal access, despite its potential but speculative benefits to them as taxpayers, and providers will be reluctant to forego fee-for-service forms of remuneration for capitation-based systems that may entail more risk for them and more potential conflicts with patients in refusing to provide or recommend unnecessary medical services.

Conclusion

We believe that a universal voucher regime in health care provision, if properly designed, can provide effective, if bounded, choices to consumers, effective competition by health care or health plan providers for consumer patronage, and effectively address concerns over equitable access to health care services. While the politics of moving to such a system in countries with long histories of alternative delivery systems, and concomitant entrenched vested interests or expectations, are challenging, some universal access health care systems already exhibit many of these properties, and increasingly severe fiscal imperatives to prevent public health care expenditures escalating to the point of crowding out many other classes of socially valued public expenditures or raising tax burdens to unsustainable levels, suggest that a better efficiency–equity trade-off may be more realizable than many health care systems currently exhibit. Better information and better incentives are key to achieving this goal.

7   Early childhood education

Introduction

In recent years, concern over the scope and quality of child care services has become salient primarily as a consequence of the growing participation of women in the paid labour force and the need to ensure appropriate and stimulating care for pre-school children.[1] Interestingly, whereas virtually every continental European country has implemented a broad program for the funding (and in many cases, the provision) of child care in order to respond to this challenge, to date this has not been the case in either Canada or the United States.[2]

This chapter explores whether the introduction of a voucher instrument is an appropriate form of intervention for government in the provision of child care, and if so, how a child care voucher instrument should be designed. We first examine the desired ends of child care and canvass rationales for government intervention in this area. From the rationales for intervention we then proceed to investigate the problems that currently exist with the provision of child care. Finally, we examine how a voucher scheme might operate so as to provide a stronger efficiency–equity trade-off than is currently manifest in government-provided child care programs.

The ends of child care and the rationales for government intervention

The term early childhood education and care ("child care") has a wide ambit. Often understood as "all arrangements providing for care and education of children under compulsory school age, regardless of setting, funding, opening hours, or program content," child care can include parental leave benefits, regulated and unregulated care, and care provided by both public and private agents.[3] We understand child care more rigorously as containing some component of early childhood education – necessarily so, in order to encompass aspects of the ends and rationales we see as valid arenas for government policy. The literature identifies many ends of such child care, including: increasing the labour market participation of mothers; promoting equal opportunities for education among both children (through child care) and parents (through the opportunity to pursue employment or human capital investments); fostering the overall development of children; and "maintaining social integration and cohesion."[4] Because child care has the potential to alter such a broad range of potentially competing inputs and outcomes, child care policy is complex.[5] The result is often highly variegated systems of design: "One person's well-designed policy is another's worst nightmare; typically the origin of these different perspectives lies in the different underlying policy objectives being pursued."[6]

There is significant evidence supporting the long-term private (and public) benefits of child care programs. Early childhood development contributes to the future well-being of society by making infants more independent, more socially adept and more self-confident.[7] "It is widely agreed that the experiences and environment faced by children in the preschool years have an important influence on their subsequent development."[8] A Swedish study focusing on academic achievement among 13-year-olds concluded that academic performance was highest among "children who entered child care before the age of one and lowest among those with home care only. For those entering child care in their second year of life, school performance is higher by 11 percent at 13 and by 19 percent for those who enter at 9–12 months."[9] A French study determined that children who received early childhood education outperformed their counterparts in a broad range of subjects, including language and mathematics, at every level of primary education and throughout secondary school.[10] The positive impact of early childhood education was particularly marked among low-income students.[11] In the United States, empirical evidence clearly supports the medium-term benefits of early child care programs like Head Start, but is more equivocal on the long-term benefits realized from these interventions.[12]

There is also significant empirical evidence for the role that child care programs play in promoting labour market participation, particularly for working class women. Over the past several decades, most developed countries have seen substantial increases in the number of women participating in the paid labour force,[13] but despite these trends many mothers do not work. For some, this choice is based on personal preference, but for others the unavailability of affordable, reliable child care precludes employment. For women with lower earning capacity, the average cost of market-based care, estimated at between US$3,000 and $5,000 annually, is prohibitive.[14] "More than 70 percent of four-year-olds from affluent families were enrolled in a center or preschool in 1995, compared with 45 percent of those from low-income households."[15] Many women must become dependent on social assistance, rely solely on their spouse's income and remain in poverty, or reluctantly place their children in sub-standard care while they work. None of these options is acceptable. Lemke *et al.* found that marginal reductions in the cost of child care result in significant reductions in parental unemployment.[16] In a landmark study, Berger and Black found that an "average weekly subsidy of $46 induced an increase in maternal employment of 8.4 to 25.3 percentage points."[17] Blau and Tekin found that the receipt of a child care subsidy is associated with a 13 percent increase in the likelihood of employment and a 2 percent increase in the likelihood of attending school.[18] All of these studies found that the receipt of a child care subsidy is positively correlated with a higher probability of working. Surveys report that over a quarter of mothers with children under age 5 would enter the labour force if they had access to satisfactory child care at reasonable costs.[19] Sheila Kamerman found that "the countries with the most generous ECEC [Early Childhood Education and Care] policies and the most extensive coverage tend to have higher rates of female labor force participation."[20]

In light of the substantial benefits associated with child care, what is the rationale for government intervention in this area? Put differently, why is public action necessary in order to realize the promise of early childhood education and care? Ron Haskins, for instance, has argued that the vast majority of the benefits and burdens from the care of children are internalized by parents, and therefore we can be confident that parental child care choices will approach optimality.[21] According to this line of reasoning, significant intervention by government is not required beyond the provision of a child care tax credit for low-income families, so allocated for reasons of distributive justice.[22] There are several possible responses to this argument.

Information failures

As discussed in other policy contexts, endemic information asymmetries between consumers (parents) and suppliers of child care services justify some form of government intervention aimed at ensuring that parents make fully informed choices. The child care market offers a wide assortment of care. Services range from "protective custody" (or more pejoratively, "child storage"), to care that emphasizes children's development, education and socialization. Since parents cannot easily observe the child care environment or monitor quality, there is a significant problem – both theoretically and empirically – with sub-standard provision of services, especially among for-profit providers in jurisdictions with very little regulatory oversight in the provision of child care.[23]

Paternalism

Even assuming that information asymmetries could be redressed, a second rationale for government intervention sounding in paternalism relates to the character of the fully informed choices that some parents may make for their children. Because children cannot make decisions respecting the consumption of child care services, they are dependent upon their parents to make these decisions for them. Generally, it can be assumed that parents will act to vindicate their children's best interests, but there may be situations where the child care decisions of parents may be driven more by cost considerations, convenience, and whether parents share the values of the child care provider than by the best interests of their child.[24]

"Second-best" intervention

Government intervention in the provision of child care may also be regarded as a necessary corrective to distortions created by other forms of government intervention. For instance, the fact that governments typically tax labour income but not the imputed income of self-performed child care will distort optimal private decisions. As a result of this asymmetry, it may be privately irrational for parents to continue working in the wage economy for pre-tax dollars and to pay for formally provided child care with after-tax dollars, resulting in a misallocation of resources dedicated to child care that is biased towards the use of self-performed care or informal care provided by relatives and friends.[25] Further, government social assistance programs may also distort optimal private decisions by subjecting parents who leave welfare rolls to high marginal rates of taxation. As a consequence, parents in receipt of welfare assistance may decline to look for work or obtain job training because there is little financial advantage to working and paying the costs of child care services compared with receiving assistance and caring for one's own children. Lisa Powell determined that a single mother in a typical Canadian province in 1989 would have had to earn over twice the minimum wage in an employment setting to attain the level of disposable income available to her if she did no paid work at all, when all taxes and probable child care expenses are taken into account.[26] In 1998, Gordon Cleveland and Douglas Hyatt conducted a similar analysis and found that, "Any mother whose employment earnings are lower than $12,000 per year is worse off when employed after full child care costs are deducted [than when unemployed]. Even a mother who earns $20,000 is only better off by $3,000 per year."[27] If the state generously subsidizes the child care expenses of those on social assistance, then recipients will experience a stronger economic incentive to look for work outside the home and increase their long-term prospects of becoming economically self-sufficient. Moreover, the subsidization of child care may be an effective means of breaking the chain of intergenerational welfare dependency by modifying the impressions imparted to children by parental behaviour. "If children growing up in homes where no parent regularly participates in the labour market are then themselves less attached to labour markets, a pattern of intergenerational welfare dependency may emerge."[28] The converse implication, of course, is that if parents do engage in the labour market, intergenerational welfare dependency is less likely to develop.

Externalities

A further rationale for government intervention in the child care arena is based on the social externalities generated by child care programs. Martha Friendly enumerates a wide variety of the external public benefits to be derived from effective early childhood development,[29] including the promotion of equity for children with special needs, the reduction of poverty, crime prevention,[30] future educational and employment success by children, social cohesion and the development of a competent citizenry.[31]

Despite the demonstrated existence of positive social externalities associated with child care, it is important to emphasize that these benefits only accompany *quality* child care. Low-quality child care has impacts upon children that are as negative as the impacts of high-quality child care are positive. That is, early care can be as damaging as it can be ameliorative of the later well-being of children.[32]

Some of the indicators of high or low quality are the age-appropriateness of the programming, care provider/child ratios, staff wages, work conditions, quality of staff and staff turnover rates.[33] The conclusion that high-quality care is resource intensive and therefore more expensive (at least in the short term) to provide than low-quality child care is intuitively unsurprising.

In the presence of positive and negative externalities along the quality continuum, sub-optimal choices are likely to be made by consumers. Because positive externalities result from high-quality child care, parents (who do not experience the full range of benefits flowing from quality care, but who do pay the full costs) will under-invest systematically in quality care. Since negative externalities result from low quality, "warehousing" type child care, parents (who do not experience the full costs of *low*-quality care) will *over*-invest systematically in low-quality care. These externalities ground at least two cases for government intervention. The positive externalities associated with quality child care support a case for the public subsidization of quality child care. The negative externalities associated with poor-quality child care militate in favour of regulation imposing some minimum standards on the quality dimensions of child care services.

Equality and social solidarity

A final rationale for intervention relates to those benefits discussed in subsequent chapters in connection with the "citizenship" model of primary and secondary education (social solidarity). Universal access is of course fundamentally necessary in order to generate an engaged and active citizenry. In this respect, the ends of distributional equity and equality of opportunity are also obviously well served when early childhood development is encouraged across the population. "For children, the key equity argument relates to providing children with an equal start in life, by ensuring that they enter school ready to learn."[34]

Modes of government intervention: problems in the present system

Cleveland and Colley identify five general categories of child care provision: kindergarten, regulated child care, cash benefits paid to parents, support services and unregulated child care.[35] As indicated earlier, in the United States and Canada, government intervention in child care is fairly shallow. By and large, the costs of child care are remitted to parents, with modest means-tested subsidies being conferred on some families. In the United States, the largest source of federal funding to child care is the child care expense tax credit whereby parents may receive between 20 and 30 percent of their expenditures on child care up to a maximum of $2,400 per child (maximum $4,800 total per family).[36] Additionally, the first $5,000 of employer-provided child care is not considered a taxable benefit.[37] For particularly needy families, the federal Head Start program is designed to provide child care services. The majority of child care costs, however, are left to parents. In Canada, the federal government expends roughly $600 million per year on child care, about half of which is administered by the provinces. The other $315 million goes toward the child care expense tax deduction of up to $7,000 per child for the lower-paid parent.[38] The provinces, by contrast, allocate most of their child care resources to needy families as targeted subsidies.[39] Quebec, somewhat anomalously in North America, offers a public $7 a day child care service to all children aged 0–4, with reductions down to $0 for low-income families.[40]

Internationally, the breadth and quality of child care services is superior to that available in North America. Many European countries guarantee full public child care for children aged one and up, with parental contributions based on income until mandatory school age (at between 4 and 6 years of age).[41] The United Kingdom has focused on support for low-income families, offering "Sure Start" public day care for needy children from birth to age 3.[42] Belgium and Australia employ demand-side subsidies, but to very different degrees. In Australia, child care from birth to age 4 is privately delivered with voucher support from the government, but crippled by low funding and low enrollment.[43] Belgium employs demand-side subsidies for ages 1–2½, followed by universal access to public pre-schools from 2½ onwards.[44]

There has been a great deal of debate – in both political and scholarly arenas – concerning the reform of child care service delivery and funding. Criticisms of the *status quo* generally focus on two fundamental aspects of the current regimes – accessibility (including financial accessibility) and quality.[45] These two concerns appear to cut across methods of child care service provision. Nor are quality and accessibility problems limited to the North American context. Quality appears to be a universal worry, with many European states making trade-offs between quality and accessibility. Disparities in the accessibility and quality of child care, particularly the sharp dichotomy between "warehousing" and education-based models, become less tolerable as we begin to view early childhood education as a natural extension of primary and secondary education. We investigate these problems below.

Accessibility

Accessibility to child care has two aspects. The first is the availability or supply of child care. The second is the affordability of the child care that is supplied. The supply of child care services varies greatly depending on location, the age of the children seeking care and the dominant socio-economic level of local residents. Most OECD countries struggle to maintain an adequate supply of child care despite a significant increase in spaces in some jurisdictions.[46] However, the chief obstacle to accessibility is affordability. Even where child care services are available, many parents cannot afford access to high-quality day-care programs – often as a result of one of many faulty modes of government financing.

Low-income access to well-regulated centres is usually possible only through targeted government subsidies with onerous means-tested thresholds.[47] In the alternative, tax credits (as per the US) and tax deductions (as per Canada) do little to alleviate affordability problems for disadvantaged children. Tax deductions are only valuable to individuals who earn enough to pay taxes at a high marginal rate in the first place, and are therefore worth little to parents with modest incomes.[48] The result is perversely regressive: child care expenses are subsidized less for the poor and the middle class than for the wealthy. Purely public provision of child care also has its pitfalls. Many public child care systems continue to experience waiting lists, despite high spending levels.[49] Public care also poses accessibility problems for certain citizen groups. For instance, public child care services often run on a Monday to Friday daytime model, with significant summer breaks and other vacation periods.[50] So-called "atypical" parents whose work schedules do not conform to this pattern may be left with no government support whatsoever.[51] Solutions to the "atypical" parent problem include both direct cash benefits and employer participation. Direct cash benefits are offered by many European countries to offset child care costs. Unfortunately, "the parents most likely to use this cash benefit and stay at home with their children are lone mothers, mothers with several children, and mothers in low-income one-earner families."[52] These parents may prefer cash in hand to child care, short-changing on the early education of their children. High levels of employer–employee provision of day care services, as in the Netherlands,[53] may address "atypical" accessibility concerns as well as inject employer funding into child care services. However, employer programs are, at base, a tax on employers and therefore on employment. This also creates new tiers of accessibility, as between the employed and the unemployed, and as between employees whose employers may vary in their commitment to early childhood education. Private provision in the absence of government support is little better and arguably worse. In the United States, for example, the average annual cost of child care services per child is $4,500 (Canadian), unaffordable for low-income families.[54]

Clearly, lack of accessibility poses an obstacle to reaping the private and public goods generated by early childhood education and care. The central importance of child care to future success[55] suggests that ensuring a universally accessible basic level of child care to all may be the most effective and minimally intrusive means of promoting equality of opportunity.

Quality

There are competing understandings of quality in the delivery of early childhood education and care. At its most basic level, quality refers to the caliber and "character of interactions that occur in the classroom."[56] A variety of measures of quality have been developed and tested by trained observers, including the Early Childhood Environments Rating Scale (ECERS); the Infant-Toddler Environments Rating Scale (ITERS); and the Family Day Care Rating Scale (FDCRS).[57] There is very little consistency in quality across child care programs. For instance, many at-home providers are unlicensed and have no formal child care training. Furthermore, providers have incentives to take on too many children because of the low remuneration available for child care, which often leads to a child to care-giver ratio that is too high for children to reap much benefit developmentally. At the other end of the quality continuum, there are many formal, tightly regulated programs that are highly child-centred, have low child/caregiver ratios and explicitly focus on early childhood education and development.

The quality of child care in the OECD is mixed. In Canada, a small minority of jurisdictions provide "good" care according to FDCRS measures, but most provide only "minimal" quality.[58] The lowest scores in the FDCRS study are typically in "learning activities" associated with the principal gains of early childhood development and staff training in this area is generally inadequate.[59] In the United States, "Only 14 percent of centres and 13 percent of family child care homes are estimated to be of good quality."[60] In Finland, the government lacks a comprehensive regulatory or monitoring system, unable to afford such a key government function while maintaining a guarantee of universal access to public child care.[61] This is despite the fact that Finland spends almost twice as much on early childhood education as Canada.[62] In general, child development experts believe that much child care is of poor developmental quality because of low wages, high staff turnover, poor regulation, and untrained providers.[63]

In contrast, Sweden, Portugal and Denmark all maintain public programs with strict staffing and training requirements.[64] However, in each of these jurisdictions high levels of spending are necessary to maintain this level of quality, particularly in Denmark, and accessibility problems remain. Moreover, the Finnish experience (high levels of spending and low-quality public care) demonstrates that despite a significant commitment of government funding, exclusive reliance on public delivery can create quality concerns that might be ameliorated by competition. A multiplicity of providers in a competitive market might better address the need for quality child care, particularly given that many countries may be reluctant to fund early childhood education at the same high levels as the Danish. Demand-side subsidies and competition may be a more realistic delivery mechanism, but system design to date has been poor and support for voucher systems half-hearted.

Designing a new system

The foundation for any re-design of the child care system should be predicated on a commitment to child care as a form of early childhood education rather than as some form of protective custody. Simply, child care absent pedagogically sound forms of education lacks many of the public and private goods that motivate government intervention. Given this starting point, the parallel between early childhood education and primary and secondary education is obvious. In the primary and secondary education context, for instance, a strong case will be advanced in subsequent chapters for voucher entitlements and it is difficult, as a matter of principle, to discern any justification for treating child care differently. A key characteristic of this argument, that *enhanced* choice should also be *bounded* choice, applies here as well. In arguing for parental choice of child care provider, we are not supporting subsidies for low-quality care. Government vouchers should only subsidize those parental choices which are in keeping with the goal of high-quality early childhood development. As in the case of other policy areas that we have considered, the key to effective delivery is good program design: ensuring adequate regulation, providing adequate funding, and accounting for market failures.

Qualified consumers

We focus here on whether child care vouchers should be provided on a universal or means-tested basis. In the primary and secondary education context, we will establish a case for universal rather than means-tested voucher entitlements. Similarly, we believe that child care should be supported by a universal voucher entitlement. While means-testing reduces the overall costs of government expenditures, there are several reasons to believe that a universal child care subsidy would be preferable. First, a significant minority of children enter the primary school system with cognitive or behavioural difficulties that could be greatly alleviated by early childhood education. However, these difficulties are rooted in indicators which are very difficult to identify in advance and are not necessarily determined by socio-economic status.[65] The most relevant predictors of cognitive and behaviourial difficulties include: poor parenting skills, recent immigrant status, stay-at-home mothers (a remarkable divergence from the traditional "family values" arguments), maternal depression, dysfunctional family life, single parenthood (a point in favour of "family values"), and teenage parenthood.[66] Many of these measures are probably very difficult, not to mention expensive, to adequately evaluate. Such findings severely undercut arguments in favour of means-testing: the children in most need of early childhood development are not exclusively or even largely from low-income families.

Moreover, means-tested voucher eligibility militates against many of the ends we view as most important in justifying government intervention in child care. "Universal programs provide a natural integration of different types of children, a desirable social goal in its own right" and a key indicator of social solidarity.[67] Many working families may be relatively poor, but not below the cut-off level for means-tested subsidies. If the costs of high-quality child care remain prohibitive for these families, then mothers may either leave the work force in order to care for their children or be forced to put their children in a child care facility of low quality. Neither is a desirable social outcome. Middle-income parents may have the fiscal resources to purchase child care, but not high-quality child care of the kind essential for capturing positive externalities and avoiding negative ones. For example, Fuller finds that, "based on structural characteristics, the quality of centers attended by middle-class children was worse, on average, than the quality of centers attended by poor children."[68] Fuller speculates that this is largely the result of the disparities between government expenditures in poor and middle-class neighborhoods, respectively. This suggests a need for additional resources to be allocated to middle-income families so that they can purchase higher-quality care for their children. And, fundamentally, the positive externalities generated by quality early childhood development are latent in all children, not just the poor: "Once we start considering ECEC as the first stage of most children's education, the motivation for universal services becomes clear."[69]

Problems with program under-inclusiveness are manifest in the recently introduced reforms to the Australian child care system. In place of direct operational subsidies, the government introduced Childcare Assistance (CA) and the Childcare Rebate (CR) as voucher subsidies for families.[70] Although these subsidies eased some of the burden of child care expenses, their design did not significantly facilitate the purchase of child care for many parents. Both the CA and the CR are paid up to a specified amount, independent of the actual fee charged. In places where child care fees are higher, there is a substantial gap fee which must be paid by parents regardless of income – and only a handful of parents can afford to pay. The CA is the more progressive of the two subsidies, providing greater assistance to low-income and multi-child families, but is still insufficient to address affordability problems for all parents.[71] In response to mounting concerns over the accessibility of child care services, the government later introduced the Childcare Benefit, which increases the fee subsidies given to parents using *approved* services. These increases are directed disproportionately at low-income, single parents.[72] Child care in Australia suffers from significant quality problems.[73] At base, Australia simply does not spend enough on subsidies to encourage broad participation, and where spending is increased parental choice is reduced to a limited range of services. A well-designed voucher system must avoid these pitfalls.

Qualified suppliers

The design challenges of qualified supply in child care are twofold: ensuring good quality care and avoiding information failures which would undermine that quality.

In terms of quality, a severe tension arises between the two predominant modes of child care – protective custody versus early childhood education. This tension is brought into sharp relief by the fact that informal child care arrangements with relatives, neighbours, friends and nannies (which comport only weakly or not at all with the early childhood education concept of child care), are so common. With informal arrangements it is difficult to know what *ex ante* entry restrictions are likely to be appropriate or what *ex post* performance disclosure requirements are feasible. Moreover, many of these informal arrangements (especially with relatives) presently involve no or low levels of remuneration. To allow them to qualify for voucher payments would dramatically increase the public costs of child care, while not necessarily substantially increasing the supply of early childhood education. It may be argued that the provision of free or nominally remunerated child care services is an unfair burden that many family members, friends and neighbours (especially women) presently bear and that adequate remuneration would constitute overdue recognition of the social value of child care. However, this is to import a distributional objective on the supply-side that is likely to be sharply at variance with the objective of enhancing the availability and quality of early childhood education.

Given our argument that government support for child care is only justified on the basis of education-based models of delivery, a clear role for government in certifying prospective operators is implicated. Indeed, while many child care providers are currently subject to regulation, it is clear that the current regulatory standards for child care facilities "often fall short of professional recommenda-tions."[74] Barnett and Bergmann suggest that the use of the subsidies could be restricted to designated high-quality facilities.[75] However, we would caution against creating a voucher system that is indistinguishable from supply-side subsidization. If vouchers can only be redeemed at a small number of facilities, parental choice is stifled and competitive pressures fall, obviating two of the main benefits of demand subsidies. Broad supplier eligibility is important not only for maintaining competitive pressures and encouraging parental work force participation, but also because key studies have found that parent satisfaction and employment have reciprocal benefits for early childhood development at least as powerful as early childhood education itself.[76]

> Parenting matters most to the early development of children, so parenting and ECEC services must be complements rather than substitutes – Early learning and care services, particularly when they are of high quality, have important positive effects on children and tend to offset family-based sources of risk. However, parenting *is* a much stronger influence and an enduring one. This is one reason why a system of ECEC services and programs is important – with maternity/parental leave complemented by income and parenting support and by a network of different ECEC services and early childhood development programs in local communities.[77]

Therefore, we would not recommend the elimination of parental leave arrangements, nor would we emphasize quality to the extent that it precludes gainful parental employment. We would instead suggest minimum accreditation requirements designed to ensure that early childhood development is prioritized over simply "warehousing" children. Other unaccredited arrangements would remain permissible but would not attract voucher support. Alternatively, these arrangements might attract a lower level of support (akin to the present child care expense tax deduction or credit in Canada and the US), instead of no support at all. It needs to be acknowledged that in this context vouchers are likely to drama-tically increase public program expenditures, at least if the objective is to increase the availability and quality of early childhood educational opportunities for all preschool children. Increased expenditures are essential if we are to avoid the poor outcomes experienced in Australia.[78] However, if a voucher system is properly implemented competitive pressures should maintain costs far below those levels experienced in jurisdictions such as Denmark.

One of the most important design issues that must be addressed in the context of early childhood education is how to construct a program that minimizes informa-tion failures. In North America many eligible families currently do not take advantage of the child care subsidies that are available to them. The largest barrier is a lack of knowledge – about the existence of the program, the eligibility require-ments, and the program details.

Shlay *et al.* conceptualize information failure as a first-level barrier to subsidy use. "The first level represents barriers created because of knowledge deficiencies, either of subsidies altogether or people's eligibility and opportunities to use them."[79] The pervasiveness of this problem cannot be underestimated. Several studies have found that somewhere between one third to one half of sample respondents are unaware of the existence of child care subsidies.[80] Shlay *et al.* find that among those who said that they need help "Approximately 44 percent incorrectly believed that they were not eligible to receive these subsidies."[81] This suggests that child care subsidy systems may be grossly deficient in informing eligible recipients about their entitlements.

Many parents eligible for subsidies are also misinformed about the program details of child care subsidies. Fuller reports that many mothers believe that "day care" is synonymous with "center" or "preschool."[82] There is also evidence that eligible families have misperceptions about whether or not certain groups had priority in the subsidy system.[83] "Concerns for both efficiency and equity demand that more active steps be taken to inform potential applicants about benefits."[84]

Other information failures arise at the level of quality assessment. Because the consumers of child care (the parents) do not always directly observe the product, monitoring the quality of child care services can be difficult. Even conscientious parental observation is rife with pitfalls. Cryer and Burchinal find that "parents give higher average ratings on every item than do trained observers, by about one standard deviation on average for preschool age classrooms and by about two standard deviations on average for infant-toddler classrooms."[85] One of the major advantages of demand-side subsidies, in general, is that consumers are able to take their business away from low-quality suppliers and move it to high-quality suppliers. If consumers are unable to distinguish between high- and low-quality suppliers, then this benefit is largely lost.

We would suggest that the introduction of a universal system of child care voucher eligibility would have to be accompanied by adequate advertising to ensure program use. Eligible recipients (all parents of young children), could also be identified and informed of eligibility through the income tax return system or through social assistance in the case of unemployed parents. Comprehensive lists of suppliers containing statistics on various quality measures such as staff-to-child ratios, group size and training/certification of staff would be provided to all voucher recipients. The availability of a government hotline for quality complaints and counseling services might also be helpful. Parents of special needs children in particular may require some form of assistance in determining the best child care options.

In sum, we argue that quality in child care provision should be monitored by government accreditation agencies and that voucher support should only attach to those agencies that meet minimum requirements. These accreditation requirements should ensure that early childhood development is the focus of all publicly subsidized child care facilities, while not setting accreditation requirements so high that competitive pressures and parental choice are unduly restricted. More efficient and rigorous quality control will manifest itself in the decentralized decision-making of parents on the placement of their children and the use of their vouchers. In order to protect this form of quality control, an accreditation agency must also collect information on quality measures not required for accreditation. In addition to disseminating information on quality to voucher recipients, this agency must (a) ensure that all parents are aware of their voucher entitlement and encourage participation in the program; and (b) provide an outlet for consumer complaints and a source of government counseling for parents with particularly difficult child care choices to make, preferably through some form of government hotline or, in extreme cases, a formal counseling or referral service. An extensive network of community and government organizations already provides support and counseling for special needs children, and in all likelihood government counseling services would need to do little more than refer parents to an appropriate support group.

Scope of the voucher entitlement

Setting the scope of the entitlement offered by child care vouchers raises three distinct issues: cash payments vs. vouchers; the impact of the introduction of vouchers on the market price for child care; and fixed value vouchers vs. calibrated vouchers. Providing vouchers in lieu of cash payments is a contentious issue in many areas of social assistance. Although the evidence on the comparative costs of various government intervention programs is sparse, there is some data that strongly suggests vouchers are more cost-effective than cash transfers or wage subsidies. In terms of parental participation in the work force, Blau has constructed a model that compares a child care demand subsidy with a wage subsidy and finds that "for a wide range of plausible values of the parameters and variables, an additive child care subsidy that is a given proportion of the child care price generates many more additional hours worked per dollar of government expenditure than an additive wage subsidy of the same proportion of the wage."[86]

In terms of early childhood development, cash transfers are also sub-optimal because of principal–agent problems. Bergmann argues that high-quality child care is a "merit good, something that in our ethical judgment everybody should have, whether or not they are willing or able to buy it."[87] She asserts that the use of cash grants would leave open the possibility that parents would not allocate resources in a way that strives for their children's best interests – and indeed, there is evidence to support this assertion in some jurisdictions.[88] Children are incapable of assuring the effective distribution of these resources and society has an interest in ensuring that children receive high-quality care. Therefore, untied transfers may not be the best means to achieve the goal of improving access to child care. Accordingly, we argue that government subsidy of child care should take the form of demand-side subsidies with bounded parental choice as to the most appropriate service provider. Subsidies should be provided in voucher form rather than as a cash benefit, reducing the use of child care funds for purposes other than quality child care.

Another issue that arises in this context is the value of the voucher entitlement as compared with the current market price of day care services. Depending on the price-elasticity of supply, a broad new voucher entitlement may increase prices for child care in the marketplace dramatically, with the end result that providers are much better off and child care consumers only slightly better off than in the absence of vouchers (as with rent subsidies in the low-income housing sector). There is mixed experience with the effects of the introduction of a new government subsidy on the cost of child care. For instance, there have been reports of increased prices (and price discrimination) in the provision of child care after government subsidies came into effect in Connecticut and Alabama.[89] In a conflicting report, the Council of Economic Advisors states that "the available evidence indicates that the supply of care will rise to meet an increase in demand for care without much of a change in the current price. ... As a result, in the absence of other changes, the benefits of a subsidy accrue to the consumer."[90] Supporting this second assessment is Philip Robins' summary of the available empirical evidence on the price elasticity of supply of child care. Robins states that, "There is some evidence that the supply of child care services can increase by the amount of the increased demand without a corresponding increase in the cost of care."[91] Aside from the anecdotal evidence of program directors in Connecticut and Alabama, it appears that the supply of child care is relatively price elastic. From an *a priori* theoretical perspective, it is not evident that vouchers would increase the market costs of child care by a significant amount given the low barriers to entry for starting up a child care centre. In fact, from a theoretical perspective we can expect that prices, if they spike at all due to voucher-subsidised demand, will quickly adjust downward to reflect the costs of providing child care services.[92]

Finally, a fixed-value voucher for accredited child care centres meeting appropriate early childhood education criteria would be the presumptive norm. However, as we will argue in the case of primary and secondary education, we may need to be sensitive to the special needs of certain children. Children with disabilities and children from disadvantaged backgrounds may require more intensive and expensive care than their relatively advantaged peers. To avoid the negative consequences of cream-skimming in terms of access for needier individuals, these children may require calibrated vouchers to ensure that they have access to care. However, calibration may unduly increase administrative costs and system complexity, and mandatory pooling may be a feasible alternative strategy in this regard. By setting the value of the child care voucher at the cost of providing a quality developmental program of child care to an average child and mandating acceptance of children (or random selections from waiting lists), we could avoid at least some of these cream-skimming problems. Apart from any cream-skimming or price effects, the basic ends of equitable provision are implicated in fixing voucher values. Many relatively poor families might be able to acquire child care, but quality child care could be an entirely different matter.[93] The importance of quality care in capturing positive externalities, and the dangers of negative externalities induced by poor care, cannot be overemphasized.

Cream-skimming is likely to prove problematic in the absence of calibrated vouchers, mandatory pooling or, a third option, extra billing. Extra billing allows the price system to operate as a signal and reward for superior quality, but is likely to compromise equity goals – hence once again the tension between efficiency and equity. Indeed, some studies suggest that the price-signaling function of extra billing may have the perverse effect of discouraging those who are in genuine need of services such as health care (and perhaps child care) from acquiring it.[94] Our preference would be to disallow extra billing by accredited child care facilities. In this way the voice of the politically active would be co-opted in ensuring that the value of vouchers exercisable at accredited child care facilities would be maintained at satisfactory levels for all recipients. Moreover, the typically high ratio of non-profit providers in the child care market[95] should also limit chiseling concerns – alternatively, a strong system for monitoring schools and disseminating results (see discussion of qualified suppliers above and government post-design role below) would discourage for-profit institutions from risking long-term profitability in favour of short-term gains.[96]

On balance, we would also argue against mandatory pooling in the context of child care. Children's needs can be diverse, and specialized services may be necessary in some areas, especially disability services. Mandatory pooling would reduce many of the gains to be made from specialization as well as prove potentially unrealistic as a matter of staffing and training. Instead, calibrated vouchers scaled to both income and other special needs are probably the best way to limit cream-skimming, ensure equity and still allow necessary specialization of services. We would set the value of the child care voucher at the cost of providing a developmental program of child care to an average child, while allowing fluctuations in value by income and needs. Income differentials, for example, could be handled as per Bergmann's proposal. She suggests that above an income cut-off point families would be required to make co-payments representing no more than 30 percent of income earned over the cut-off. The amount of the co-payment would be determined on a sliding scale, thereby increasing the payment as income rises.[97] She stresses that this would help to mitigate the problem of affordability of quality care for middle-income families.

Government's post-design role

The introduction of a child care voucher scheme would almost certainly increase the role of the government in North America, given that in many developed countries governments are not extensively involved in the current provision of child care. Although the government would cease to be a direct provider of child care services (as it is to a limited extent in some North American jurisdictions today), there would be a very large residual role for government to play in the accreditation, regulation, monitoring and funding of child care providers. Governments would also have to be the distributor and financier of the voucher instruments, in addition to being responsible for ensuring that vouchers carry sufficient values to meet minimum access and equity concerns.

Political economy

There is a large and growing demand for affordable, high-quality child care in both Canada and the US. Important participants in debates over child care reform are women's groups that point out the close connection between the ability of women to take an active role in the work force and the availability of affordable, high-quality child care. In addition, many poverty advocates argue that the root of the welfare cycle for many poor families – particularly those headed by single women – is the inability of mothers to work because they cannot afford to pay for adequate child care for their children. In addition, qualified child care providers or prospective providers stand to benefit substantially from any increase in the demand for child care services induced by a voucher system. However, any such initiative is likely to be resisted strongly by many taxpayers and fiscal conservatives opposed to the introduction of any new large-scale government expenditure program. In addition, "family values" advocates argue that private child care facilities are antithetical to traditional families. Consequently, they are likely to dogmatically oppose any publicly financed increase in access to such services.

There are two political arguments for universal child care subsidies that may carry some weight. First, for some families, the stigma associated with participating in a means-tested program serves as a disincentive to seeking aid.[98] This may provide additional support for the arguments of poverty advocates. Second, non-universal programs may lack broad political support because only the poor stand to benefit. Currently, it is estimated in the United States that only about 24 percent of eligible children are receiving subsidies.[99] In Canada, all jurisdictions subsidize child care costs for low-income families but limitations on the number of subsidies available exclude many eligible parents.[100] Universal entitlements, in contrast, are likely to capture more widespread political support, possibly undercutting fiscal conservatives and "family values" traditionalists alike.

Finally, when weighing the benefits and costs of implementing a child care policy based on the private delivery of services, policy-makers should remember two of the key political pitfalls of public systems: entrenched suppliers and unwieldy bureaucracies.[101] Moving towards a publicly provided child care system would almost certainly result in both unionized child care professionals and an administrative oversight body, both highly resistant to reform. If a public child care system were established these entrenched interests would almost certainly militate against necessary reform. In contrast, we currently have no such entrenched interests in North American child care, offering the opportunity to pursue the most optimal policy free from at least one form of political constraint.

Conclusions

Ruth Rose quotes an interesting and perhaps enlightening passage from Katie Cooke's 1986 Canadian *Report of the Task Force on Child Care*. Cooke recalls that prior to the introduction of universal primary education in the nineteenth century, political arguments against the move similar to those heard today in the child care context were commonplace:

> Opponents of the proposed system argued that it would involve enormous expense, the loss of individual choice, and an infringement of religious and language rights. Some questioned the psychological and physical effects of

confining young children to a classroom for long periods of time; others were concerned about the abilities and qualifications of the teachers. There were sharp criticisms regarding the role of the family in the upbringing of their children; parental responsibility and authority would be undermined, family cohesiveness threatened, and the child's well-being jeopardized.[102]

Despite these criticisms, few today would argue against mandatory school attendance to *some* minimum age and most would sanction government funding (although not necessarily direct public provision) of primary education. The positive effects of quality child care are so significant and so far reaching that the case for universal access to early childhood education and care is equally compelling.

More promising still, the North American void in child care provision offers policy-makers a clean slate on which to work. An optimal early childhood education policy can be chalked up comparatively free from the political impediments that often characterize the reform of established government services. This is an opportunity both rare and precious; its value cannot be overemphasized.

Accordingly, we propose that government should support early childhood education and care through demand-side subsidies which offer bounded parental choice among private service providers. These subsidies should be granted in the form of vouchers rather than as a cash benefit and should only be available for government-accredited child care providers. The bar for accreditation must ensure that the focus of every child care program is early childhood education. However, accreditation requirements should not be set so high that competitive pressures and parental choice of workplace are unduly restricted. We also argue that in order to prevent information failures a government agency should collect information on a wide range of quality measures for each accredited provider as well as maintain an outlet for consumer complaints. Information on quality and complaints must be effectively disseminated to all voucher recipients. Further, government counseling or referral services should be available for those parents facing complicated or difficult child care choices. Finally, the value of vouchers should be set at the cost of providing quality early childhood education and then scaled according to income and special needs. This should guard against cream-skimming while simultaneously precluding the need for mandatory pooling or extra billing. We argue that such a system would offer affordable and quality care to families of all socio-economic backgrounds, while maintaining the flexibility necessary for specialized services and providers.

8 Primary and secondary education

Introduction

Ever since Milton Friedman proposed a voucher system for primary and secondary public education in 1955,[1] a vigorous debate has ensued in the US (and to a lesser extent elsewhere) on the virtues of school voucher systems. Recently, limited initiatives and pilot programs in various jurisdictions using vouchers and other choice-oriented initiatives such as charter schools and open enrollment plans have fuelled this debate with results that have spurred divergent analyses and interpretations.[2]

To evaluate the potential of school voucher systems on the quality of educational outcomes, we must first examine the objectives of primary and secondary education and the rationales for government intervention. Against this backdrop, we then consider the various modes for delivery of primary and secondary education, focusing primarily on the conventional public school model of education delivery in which government both owns and operates schools, and then contrast this instrument with a range of different tied demand-side subsidy instruments (including vouchers). In light of the burgeoning international empirical evidence that finds significant educational improvements from the adoption of demand-side subsidy schemes (as against monopoly government provision), we then proceed to evaluate the myriad design challenges entailed by the adoption of educational vouchers so as to ensure that these programs are responsive to legitimate public values.

The ends of primary and second education and the rationales for government intervention

There are two[3] broad approaches to the question of the ends of primary and secondary education. The "skills model" emphasizes the market value of the skills provided by primary and secondary education to the individual student. According to this view, the most important benefits that primary and secondary education confers on students are a range of job-related skills that translate into an increased probability of employment after graduation. These skills can range from basic literacy and numeracy to specialized vocational training and education in critical thinking and problem solving.[4] The second approach, the "citizenship model," is less concerned with the private benefits accruing from education and instead focuses on the solidarity benefits that society derives from having an educated population that can think critically, recognize subtlety and appreciate moral and cultural values. Although this sort of "republican virtue" may, in fact, be of tangible market value, it would be inappropriate to evaluate the success of an educational system based on this model primarily in these terms.[5] Instead, the long-term promotion of the basic values of a society should be evaluated on its own, market-independent terms.

The reality, of course, is that education's promotion of both marketable skills and republican virtue is of value. Further, to some extent, the pursuit of the compe- tencies implied by each of these models will have positive spillover effects on the other. It is for this reason that the basic educational systems in the industrialized democracies seek to educate students in traditional liberal arts subjects such as history, literature and the arts as well as in more obvious skills-oriented areas such as mathematics, science, accounting and computer programming. There is no gainsaying that any successful educational system must pay attention to the many incommensurable values that the system is expected to satisfy.[6]

Given the mixed motivations for primary and secondary education, what is the case for government intervention in this area? There are at least four. First, govern- ment intervention may reflect paternalism considerations that relate to information deficiencies and principal/agent problems that may cause parents to make inappropriate decisions regarding the primary and secondary education of their children. Second, equality concerns arising from the inability of low-income families to borrow against their human capital to finance their education supplies another important rationale for government intervention. Third, the positive externalities emanating from primary and secondary education may cause parents to under- invest in education relative to the levels that are socially warranted, and government intervention is required to correct this under-investment. A fourth and final rationale for intervention relates to government's interest in promoting citizenship and civic virtue values that may be under-supplied or under-demanded by the market.

Paternalism

Government intervention based on paternalism in relation to primary and secondary education is based on concerns that there may be some circumstances in which parents, for a variety of different reasons, fail to make responsible decisions respecting their children's long-term welfare. Parents may fail to make responsible decisions because of a lack of information respecting the benefits and importance of basic education or how to best access it. Alternatively, parental failure to secure a proper education for their children may emanate from a need to enlist the assistance of school-aged children for household tasks or income generation which would be compromised were their children to attend school. These latter problems (really just a species of agency problems where children are principals and parents are their designated agents) are most acute in cases where parents themselves have received a low level of education.[7] These agency problems between parents and children extend beyond the decision as to whether a parent will enroll their child in school and affect the nature of the educational choice that parents may make for their children. The fear is that parents may base their enrollment decisions on convenience for themselves, what is best for the family as a whole or what will be the most cost-effective decision in the short run. In any event, parental failure to make appropriate educational decisions for their children creates life-long and irreversible damage. As a consequence, there is a strong rationale on paternalism grounds for government to intervene so as to limit the scope for this damage to occur.

Having said that there is a strong rationale for intervention on paternalism grounds, it is more difficult to define the appropriate contours of that intervention with precision.[8] On the one hand, considerable expertise is required in order to make good decisions respecting the location and form of schooling that a child will receive and one can argue that government-appointed experts can make these decisions more effectively than parents, or, at least, poorly informed parents. On the other hand, the mode of education of one's children is one of the most important decisions a parent can make. It is a decision infused with sometimes widely divergent yet often reasonable preferences and is likely to be taken very seriously by most (but not all) parents. More than that, while selecting a good school or program requires some understanding of the virtues of different schools, it also requires understanding of the child affected, and it is here that parents are likely to be in the best position to make this choice. Nevertheless, if individual choices are radically self-destructive in their effects on the very individual who makes them or on those for whose well-being they are responsible, there is a strong case for some form of state paternalism.

Equality

Even if parents were strongly inclined to secure the appropriate level and character of basic education for their children, a role for the state in financing or supplying education is still implicated as a result of equality concerns. In particular, the concern is that many parents, particularly those on the margins of society, will not possess the resources to ensure that their children receive an appropriate education in the absence of government assistance, and, as a consequence, their children will be deprived of the opportunities for full and equal participation in society. Although it could be argued that children (or, more realistically, their parents) should be able to borrow to finance their education against their future appreciation in human capital, the existence of endemic imperfections in human capital markets will thwart their ability to do so. Generally speaking, lenders are reluctant to supply funds secured by human capital because of information asymmetry problems which preclude a lender from knowing the dedication of, or value of education to, a potential student borrower *ex ante*. A related concern is the matter of enforcement – slavery is illegal in liberal democratic societies. If a lender did make a loan to a student to finance his or her primary–secondary school education the contract would be entered into when the student is a minor. Lenders would not be able to collect easily (if at all) in the event of default because it would be difficult to convince a court that the child had the capacity to contract at the time of contract formation. Many parents, particularly poorer parents, are, in the absence of state support for basic education, also likely to face these human capital market problems in attempting to borrow on their children's behalf.

Thus, to the extent that some students' families would not be able to afford to pay for private primary and secondary education in a pure market system despite the attractiveness of the investment, a role for government intervention exists for equality reasons. The minimum governmental role in this regard would be to assist in alleviating the borrowing constraint imposed by capital market limitations so that all children would at least potentially have access to primary and secondary education.[9]

Positive externalities

The citizenship model of education emphasizes the positive externalities of education – the benefits that accrue not to the individual directly but to society as a whole. These may take the form of economic benefits such as reduced dependence on social services and reduced crime rates or they may take non-economic forms such as moral development, cultural sophistication and sensitivity, capacity for interaction with members of the community of diverse social and economic backgrounds, and informed participation in democratic institutions and community life. Because individuals cannot internalize all of the benefits of their education, there will be chronic and systemic under-investment in education in a pure market environment.[10] Consequently, government intervention is likely necessary to induce individually rational students and parents to choose to devote resources appropriately to primary and secondary education.

Citizenship values

Any society must take seriously the task of maintaining a cohesive community based on its core values.[11] Hence, the relationship of education to the promotion of social solidarity. However, in liberal democratic societies, it is generally unacceptable for the state to determine coercively how parents should raise their children. Nevertheless, the basic values of respect for individuals, tolerance and the rule of law must be maintained as necessary conditions for the preservation of our society.[12] Thus, parents who choose to educate their children in intolerance and violence present a particularly pointed problem. That is, a completely unfettered market in education may leave society without one of the most important means – public education – by which individuals are currently introduced to a shared culture in which tolerance of diversity is promoted as a positive value. The potential absence of these values in an unconstrained regime of private market education provision arguably introduces scope for some form of government intervention to ensure that such values are introduced to children.

Modes of government intervention

The current primary and secondary education systems in many industrialized democracies are highly heterogeneous. Despite this complexity, the system does admit of some stylized factual assertions about the provision of educational services which, at least, in the United States and Canada, entails a significant role for government-provided education (typically provided by municipal levels of government with varying degrees of financing and oversight emanating from higher levels of government), with a relatively small but stable proportion of students attending private schools. In the United States, for instance, between 10 and 12 percent of students have attended private schools for the past several decades.[13] Private primary and secondary schools in the United States are predominantly sectarian in orientation, with 84.3 percent of private school students attending religiously-oriented schools in 1992.[14] Private primary and secondary schools are markedly less common in Canada. In 1998–9, only 297,798 Canadian students (or 2.77 percent) attended private schools[15] – a rate of about one-half of that in the United States.[16] By way of comparison, in the mid-1980s in the United Kingdom, slightly more than 6 percent of school children attended private schools – also a very minor proportion.[17]

While public schools do not, strictly speaking, have a monopoly on education, it is safe to say that they possess significant market power. If parents desire to send their children to a private school they typically must pay tuition in after-tax dollars for their children directly, with the parent and the school receiving little or no public financial support. In practice the funding of private schools varies dramatically from jurisdiction to jurisdiction. Manitoba is the most generous province in Canada in this regard, providing private schools with approximately 80 percent of the public school expenditure per pupil.[18] Provinces that provide moderate funding are British Columbia, Quebec and Alberta, which provide as much as 60 percent of the per-pupil public funding to private schools.[19] The remaining provinces pursue policies that provide no direct support for independent schools, aligning them closely with the policies that predominate in the United States. At the same time, parents of private school pupils indirectly support the public education system through various taxes, the foremost being property and income taxes. In the absence of strong incentives to remove their children from the public system, such as strong religious beliefs or deeply-rooted concerns with the quality of education publicly available, it is not surprising that parents ordinarily send their children to local public elementary and secondary schools.[20]

Government-owned and operated schools

Despite the dominance of government-provided schools in a number of different countries, this mode of government intervention is not uncontroversial, and many parents (as well as academic commentators) have expressed criticism with the performance of government-run schools, particularly when parents face a dichotomous choice between securing the benefits of state support through attendance of children in public schools or foregoing this benefit entirely by opting for a private school requiring tuition financed out of after-tax income. The criticisms expressed against government delivery can be arrayed in six basic areas, the first two of which concern the content of the education received by individual students, the other four problems relating to the design of the educational delivery system itself. In arraying these criticisms, we wish to emphasize that the over-arching criticism is not one regarding the merits of government intervention in relation to basic education, but rather concern over the precise modality of intervention, and the belief that demonstrable improvements to the system of primary and secondary education could be realized were there greater scope for parental choice in how and where public subsidies were expended. In other words, our discussion is predicated on the view that despite some of the performance failures that have come to be associated with government provision of education, one should not overlook the remarkable contributions that publicly supplied education has historically made in supporting a broad array of public goals.

Low skill levels

One of the strongest criticisms leveled against government schools is the low level of basic skill-acquisition by many students. Major international surveys, for instance, have shown that Canadian and American children enrolled in public schools consistently under-perform students in many other developed countries in core subjects such as mathematics, science and geography.[21] In particular, although Canadian students performed at or above the median of surveyed countries in mathematics at the grade 8 level, they fell well below the median by the time they reached the end of secondary school. American children fared even worse. In science, 10-year-old students from Canada performed above the international median, and American students were at the international median. By the age of 14, however, American students fell well below the median; Canadian results also fell. When students were at the point of completing secondary school, Canada fell below the international median in science and the United States performed extremely poorly.[22] In geography, Canadian students fared poorly against their counterparts in other industrialized countries, and American students were second to last in the industrialized world. These results indicate that the longer children are in the public education system in North America, the farther they fall behind international standards.

Mark Holmes has argued in response to these results that the deterioration in performance at the secondary school level in North America has been exaggerated and that the results do not drop off as precipitously as has been suggested elsewhere. Rather, Holmes argues that the North American educational experience is probably deficient from the earliest grades. "The data in fact suggest that our position is mediocre by age nine, remains so at age fourteen, and is impossible to assess in any legitimate, overall way at the end of secondary school."[23] Thus, there may in fact be no difference in the quality of the education provided to students as they move from primary to secondary schools. An explanation of the drop in performance from primary to secondary school may be that North American children are encouraged not to "drop-out" by an educational establishment that labours under societal pressure to maintain a high graduation rate. In many European countries students are encouraged to follow vocational and apprenticeship paths much earlier than they are in North America.[24] It is thus arguable that in the absence of deliberate sorting activity, poor North American test results can be traced to the disaffection and disinterest of students who would benefit from alternative training and education programming that is less academic in nature.[25]

Insufficient "values" education

Whether it is advocates on the right demanding a return to sectarian education, strict discipline and "family values," or on the left urging a strengthening of the values of cultural diversity, community and tolerance, there are many critics who fault the government-supplied educational system with providing too little in the way of values training. The demands made on the educational system in this regard are deeply problematic. Many parents have less and less time to spend educating their children in their values.[26] This is the result of a long-term trend toward the participation of all adult members of the family in the wage economy. The two-wage-earner family and the single-parent family are increasingly replacing the one-wage-earner, two-parent family. As a result of these pressures, parents increasingly demand that the school system provide the sorts of services that families traditionally provided for themselves – for example, normative training and after-school child minding. However, this has given rise to an intense debate as to the nature of the values that should be instilled in children in public schools. One problem with this criticism of the educational system is that it may not reflect an attainable institutional division of labour. That is, by demanding that our educational institutions perform services as varied as skills training, moral education and cultural enrichment, we may compromise their ability to perform any of these tasks adequately.

Unequal access

Despite the belief that government provision of education should result in a rough equality of educational experience and quality across the system, there is ample evidence that significant and persistent disparities exist within schools across the public system, and further that these disparities reflect underlying differences in the socio-economic status of participating families.[27] This is because the better public schools are usually located in wealthier neighbourhoods. Further exacerbating equity concerns is the fact that it is more expensive to provide the same level of education to poorer children than it is to their wealthier peers, and public schools located in low socio-economic status neighbourhoods do not receive the appropriate level of funding to attend to the needs of students.[28] In the US and in some Canadian provinces, the prominent role played by local property taxes in financing public education, coupled with the ability of more politically articulate upper and middle-class parents to ensure that their local schools receive adequate state support, explains these patterns.[29]

Inflexibility

Some argue that the public school system as it exists today is not sufficiently flexible to adapt to the rapidly changing needs of the marketplace or to the diversity of needs of its students.[30] Because of the cultural and economic diversity in many contemporary industrial societies, as well as the complexity and dynamism of the modern economy, the education system must provide more than just "3 Rs" education to all. It can be argued that what is required is education that is sensitive to the needs of the individual student, given her cultural background, her natural talents and her career goals. Of course, the emphasis placed on flexibility will vary according to the educational model one espouses: adherents of the "citizenship" model will find the system's inflexibility to be less problematic than "skills" model proponents.

Inefficiency

Many argue that the public school system is riddled with a variety of bureaucratic inefficiencies.[31] First, there is the problem of duplication: there are several layers of bureaucracy at state/province, school board, and school levels performing overlapping functions. Further, it is widely claimed that there are too many administrators for too few teachers. Chubb and Moe, in their landmark survey of education in the United States, for instance, argue that high levels of bureaucracy systematically compromise school performance because it limits school autonomy. In particular, they find that: "[a]utonomy has the strongest influence on the overall quality of school organization of any factor that we examined. Bureaucracy is unambiguously bad for school organization."[32] Moreover, as with any non-market-driven resource allocation mechanism, the educational bureaucracy suffers from the difficulty of translating parental and student preferences into concrete programs without the benefits of the price mechanism. That is, without the price mechanism to transmit information between suppliers and consumers, bureaucracies as central planners must gather and assimilate a daunting amount of information in order to make socially desirable decisions. Finally, existing collective bargaining arrangements involving teachers and other educational actors, it is argued, promote a culture in which individual merit and initiative are discounted and complacency, conformity and seniority are rewarded.[33]

Accountability

Another criticism of the publicly delivered system relates to its lack of accountability to parents. Although there are elected school boards and other forms of democratic control over the operation of schools, these are often felt to be too far removed from individual concerns to be effective. A system where credible threats of "exit," actual "exit" and "voice" are available means of feedback to providers has strong appeal to those who feel disenfranchised under the current arrangements in which government-supplied schools are the only institutions that can benefit from public subsidies. As Hirschman argues,[34] one problem with the "exit" option, however, is that those with the greatest ability to discipline through "voice" are often the first to exit. Once they have done so, those who are left may have fewer levers to exercise any control over the system.[35] However, it is the fear of prospective exit that will cause existing institutions (in this case, schools) to seek to correct a deteriorating state of affairs.

Demand-side education subsidies

In light of the various criticisms of government-provided education enumerated above, a number of commentators have argued for the need to instill greater scope for parental (and, where appropriate, student) choice in determining how public funds will be allocated in the system. The claim for enhanced choice, as discussed earlier in Chapter 2, is predicated on the belief that giving citizens greater scope to determine how public funds are spent to advance their interests will ensure greater responsiveness of suppliers (in this case, educators) to their preferences, thereby addressing the accountability concerns discussed above.[36] Of course, enhanced accountability means not only that schools can be expected to be more efficient in how they provide their programs, but that the array of programs (and choices) available to parents can be expected to expand as well, thereby addressing the many other concerns that have been leveled against conventional publicly provided education.

Recent empirical work by Caroline Hoxby[37] has examined the effects of Tiebout choice[38] on school productivity, which is a function of both student learning outcomes and the per-pupil cost of education. While even the richest Tiebout choice contexts in the US do not represent the same range or degree of choice that a voucher regime would entail, Hoxby has found consistent and significant positive impacts on student achievement of even the limited degree of competitiveness that Tiebout choice engenders. Consider the differing degrees of Tiebout choice available in Miami and Boston. The Miami area has only one large school district whereas Boston has 70 school districts within a one-half hour drive of downtown.[39] Clearly, it is much less costly to exercise choice by switching school districts in Boston than it is in Miami. Hoxby's analysis confirms the hypothesis that this greater inter-district competition results in greater school productivity by improving both student learning outcomes and per-student expenditures. Hoxby estimates that test scores in math and reading are between one-quarter and one-half of a standard deviation higher in areas with rich Tiebout choice (such as Boston) than in areas with no Tiebout choice (such as Miami). Moreover, Hoxby finds that the impact of Tiebout choice translates into educational attainment that is 1.4 grades higher and incomes at age 32 that are about 15 percent higher.[40] Encouragingly for the productivity of education in areas with choice, Hoxby found that these improvements in student achievement and performance were associated with *decreased* per-pupil spending on the order of 7.6 to 10.1 percent.[41] The benefits of Tiebout choice seem to be equitably distributed among the population, as well. Hoxby observes that the effects of Tiebout choice are not significantly different for families of low incomes or for minorities.[42] Note, however, that these productivity results are estimated as the effect of moving from one extreme of the Tiebout choice continuum to the other. The actual variation in Tiebout choice between most American cities is not nearly as large as that between Miami and Boston. The degree of Tiebout choice therefore explains a relatively minor proportion of the variation in student achievement and per-pupil spending in the United States. To the extent that Tiebout choice is a weaker, less-dramatic regime of choice than would be associated with school vouchers, the evidence suggests that vouchers might be very effective at both increasing student achievement and reducing costs and therefore improving educational productivity in primary and secondary schools.

Apart from Hoxby's study, there have been a number of other studies that have sought to evaluate the impact of increased school choice on educational outcomes. In a recent study of the results of numerous studies on choice experiments in the United States, Jay Greene concludes that the evidence suggests that school choice increases parental satisfaction, improves the academic performance of students and fosters greater racial integration and greater tolerance towards minorities.[43]

However, as we will discuss, the claim in favour of enhanced choice is not itself uncontroversial. By and large, concern over the prospect of publicly financed school choice turns on the congruence of choice instruments with the values or goals that have traditionally motivated government intervention in this area. It is not that the critics of choice are not prepared to acknowledge the presence of some of the concerns enumerated above, but rather they believe that increased public funding, not increased parental choice, is the appropriate response. Nevertheless, against the claim in favour of increased funding is the relatively poor track-record of a number of marginal reforms (including enhanced funding) to the conventional system that do not offer some scope for increased and meaningful parental choice. It has been demonstrated that reforms such as extending school days, imposing national testing, and school accreditation requirements have "failed to turn around a large-scale decline in education."[44] Although the reasons for this failure are far from clear, some possible explanations are that such reforms induce teachers to "teach-to-the-test," that time is used inefficiently during the school day, and that accreditation requirements are too minimal to ensure adequate educational opportunities. Furthermore, efforts to improve public education through increased funding have proved similarly dismal.[45]

Thus, in light of the generally strong presumptive evidence in favour of increased but nevertheless bounded parental choice, we seek to consider the different ways in which this choice can be effectuated. In particular, we review the experience of several different choice-enhancing experiments that have been adopted in a number of different jurisdictions. We seek to determine whether public subsidization of parental school choice for primary and secondary education can respond to the problems identified for conventional public schools, while respecting received public values and goals that operate in this area. Specifically, we consider open enrollment programs, charter schools, and voucher programs.

Open enrollment

In an open enrollment system, parents are permitted to enroll their children in public schools located in districts other than the one in which they are located. This enables families residing in districts with chronically poorly performing schools to place their children in schools of higher quality without having to change their residence. Regrettably, however, the degree of choice actually conferred on parents in open enrollment systems is not as great as parents would like. It is often the case that the popular schools fill up quickly, and students who do not secure placement in one of these schools will have no choice but to attend an unpopular school. Hoxby notes that "open enrollment programs have such poorly designed funding that programs that are enacted to be universal actually degenerate: preferred districts opt out by ensuring that they never have space to receive students."[46] Similarly, in examining the decision to move to enhanced choice in the New Zealand public school system, Ladd notes that, "successful schools in urban areas had no desire to expand their enrollment. To the contrary, they did everything they could to maintain the mix of students that made them attractive to parents and students in the first place."[47] Thus it seems that in a fully open enrollment system, the schools that are in demand may be resistant to disentangling the linkage between the geographic proximity of nearby students and school enrollment. Not surprisingly, at least part of the resistance to change will emanate from local residents who are fearful that enrollment expansion to accommodate out-of-district students will compromise school quality (as a result of diseconomies of scale or the introduction of a high-needs population into the school without offsetting resources), and this will affect their children's educational experience and the investment value of their homes (where this value reflects, in part, an expectation of access to high-quality schools). While it is possible to mitigate the severity of this resistance to enrollment expansion by requiring schools to take students on a first-come, first-served basis or using lotteries to decide which students are admitted to school, local residents (particularly in close proximity to high-quality schools) can be expected to be no less resistant to the adoption of these models than to open enrollment that requires significant school expansion to exert a meaningful effect on educational outcomes. Further, even if the political resistance from existing stakeholders could be surmounted (by, for instance, allowing for a long transitional period before the changes would take effect), the problem is that open enrollment will be unlikely to introduce a great deal of competition into the public school system because in the absence of surplus capacity, low-quality schools will still have an adequate student base because students who are not admitted to their first choice of schools, due to a lack of places, will be diverted back to lower-quality schools.

Charter schools

Since 1991, the charter school movement has exploded in the United States and abroad.[48] In that year, Minnesota established the first charter school legislation. In 1992, California followed suit. By the end of 1999, charter school enabling legislation had been passed in 42 states, with 37 states supporting a total of 2,695 operational charter schools that serve an estimated 685,000 students.[49] In Canada, one province, Alberta, permits charter schools, and 12 schools have been established.[50] Finally, the Thatcher Government's educational reform program (the "local management of schools" initiative) that was introduced in 1988 in Britain created a number of schools that are operated on a charter model.[51]

Although the exact nature of charter school enabling legislation varies from jurisdiction to jurisdiction,[52] there are several elements that are common to every charter school. As the label suggests, schools that wish to become charter schools, or parties that would like to establish charter schools, must apply for a charter to the government or to its named representative – which is strangely, in some cases, the local school district.[53] Generally speaking, the moving parties must make a written proposal outlining where the school will be located, where it will draw its students from, what grades it will instruct, and what special mandate it is adopting that differentiates it from schools in the public system. Charters are usually initially granted for three to five years. At the end of the charter period, the schools are assessed for adherence to the charter mandate, acceptable student progress and ongoing viability. Renewal of the charter is required if a school is to remain open. Charter schools are publicly funded, but are independent of the school district bureaucracy. Consequently, the governing board of each charter school is responsible for adhering to the terms of the charter that they have been granted and for running and organizing all aspects of the school.[54] Because charter schools receive less money per pupil from government resources, they must manage their budgets effectively in order to put their available finances into school programs, not administrative bureaucracies. This exerts pressure on these schools to offer a high-quality education to prospective students and to do so efficiently. On the demand-side, the charter program experiments are revealing to the extent that they endorse mandatory pooling. Generally any students in a given district are allowed to attend charter schools in that district, and schools cannot discriminate as to whom they will accept. For example, even those charter schools touting themselves as catering to a "gifted" student population cannot categorically deny entry to a student who is not especially gifted, but whose parents believe that she will benefit from attendance at the school.[55] In these terms, while legally independent, the charter school retains a distinctively public character.[56] Indeed, the argument has been made that the charter school, particularly in comparison with the greater flexibility accorded parents in voucher-based models, demonstrates a higher degree of accountability to the public interest.[57]

The empirical data available is supportive of the superior performance of charter schools in relation to conventional public schools. For example, researchers have found that charter school students in Michigan made gains of 1.3 to 2 years in a variety of subjects.[58] This was accomplished despite the fact that the average per-pupil spending in charter schools was $5,783, relative to the average per-pupil spending in public schools of $11,436.[59] Thus, the claim is that charter schools are more efficient than conventional public schools because, in part, of reduced administrative overhead.[60] Researchers have also found improvements in public schools that face competition from charter schools. Hoxby examined student achievement gains in Michigan elementary schools after the introduction of charter schools in the area. She found that schools that faced charter competition raised their annual improvement in achievement by between 1.2 and 2.3 scale points a year in fourth grade reading and between 1.1 and 2.7 scale points in mathematics.[61] Studies have also shown that public schools respond to charter competition not only by increasing the achievement levels of their students, but by increasing their efficiency as well. Hoxby studied the effects of charter schools on public schools in Arizona and found that productivity rose by 0.55 (national percentile points per $1,000 spent) based on the fourth grade reading exam, by 0.7 based on the fourth grade mathematics exam, by 0.38 based on the seventh grade reading exam, and by 0.53 based on the seventh grade mathematics exam.[62] Correspondingly, these schools improved their achievement by 1.4 national percentile points a year in fourth grade reading and 1.39 percentile points in math.[63]

Similarly, Le Grand surveyed the extensive empirical work that has been undertaken on the British educational reform program, and found demonstrable improvements in school performance since the adoption of the decentralization program.[64] Student performance scores on national exams in England went up by 8 percent in a four-year period from 1992/3 to 1996/7.[65] In another study, Howard Glennerester found significant improvements in performance across both good and bad schools. Most arrestingly, he reported that the percentage of students gaining proficiency in math increased from 45 percent to 70 percent in a six-year period (1995 to 2001).[66] These changes occurred during a period in which there was only modest increase in school budgets. Perhaps most significantly, research has indicated that the strength of the performance improvement detected in British schools post-reform is directly correlated with the intensity of the competitive threat faced by schools.[67]

Preliminary studies on the Alberta experience with charter schools are consistent with the data derived from the United States and Britain, and are largely positive.[68] Alberta's students consistently score higher on standardized tests than the Canadian average, even though Alberta spends less than other provinces on education.[69] Finally, the recent experience with charter schools in New Zealand has also been positive. Although the number of new suppliers is not large, there have been some major innovations in the delivery of education programs. For example, there are now about ten independent schools in operation that are targeted towards students who are unmotivated by traditional academic programs and are at risk of dropping out of school.[70] These schools employ various alternative curricula, which focus on activities such as athletics, music, and even military training, while still providing traditional education classes. These schools have enjoyed a great deal of success in increasing the graduation rates of at-risk students. Competition has proved to be useful in that "students alienated by the one-size-fits-all system are staying in school because their schools have been encouraged to innovate."[71] A recent longitudinal study conducted by the New Zealand Council on Educational Research found that "principals and teachers believed that the impact of the educational reforms on children's learning, teaching content, and teaching style was overwhelmingly positive."[72]

It is significant that charter schools have achieved considerable success in spite of the many constraints under which they operate. For instance, even when proven to be successful, charter schools are not generalized throughout the public school system, and, as a consequence, only a small proportion of students in a given area can attend these alternative schools. For example, in Michigan, fewer than 5 percent of school-aged children are eligible to attend charter schools.[73] Further, in many jurisdictions, charter schools face significant entry barriers in the regulatory requirements that must be met before a charter is received. Only Arizona's charter law places no limits on the number of charter schools that can exist and allows almost any person/group meeting specified eligibility criteria to charter a school. Other states' legislation places heavy regulatory and administrative burdens on charter schools, thereby effectively rendering charter schools indistinguishable from public schools. Peterson has found that some states "almost eviscerate the concept by giving the authority to charter schools to local school boards."[74] Similarly, in New Zealand, the government agreed that no new schools may be opened if there is space for students in existing schools.[75] This means that some students will be trapped in poorly performing schools simply because the good schools are filled to capacity. Another barrier confronting charter schools concerns the lack of capital cost funding (even in-kind in the form of access to existing public school facilities) that confront charter school proponents in many jurisdictions.[76] The existence of a number of these barriers to charter schools are not likely the product of a governmental misunderstanding of the optimal conditions for the introduction of a successful experiment in promoting the scope for choice in education, but rather the result of political concessions to various stakeholders (particularly teachers' unions) who are opposed to the prospect of competition, particularly when there is the risk that public resources may be transferred from the existing conventional system to the charter system in response to student or parental choice.

Public voucher programs

Voucher programs differ from charter school models in that the state confers a voucher of some explicit value directly on the parent, who can then apply this voucher in support of their child's enrollment in a broad range of different private schools. In this respect, the voucher, on the surface, appears to be more conducive to enhanced choice than either the open enrollment or charter school models in that the expenditure of the public subsidy is not confined to the broadly conceived public school system. As Hepburn argues, "public vouchers, if administered liberally, have the potential to create a dynamic educational marketplace where educators are encouraged to innovate, to imitate successful practices, and to respond to the needs of their students."[77] Not surprisingly, there are a variety of different design challenges involved in the creation of voucher programs that must be addressed in order to render these programs congruent with the public interest. However, at this point, we focus primarily on the overall performance of these programs based on the experience of several different charter experiments in the United States and abroad, and remit the issue of program design to the next part of this chapter.

MILWAUKEE

The voucher program in Milwaukee was first established in the 1990–1 school year, was only available to families with incomes at or below 175 percent of the federal poverty level, was confined to 1 percent of Milwaukee public school enrolment, and its value was only slightly more than $2,000.[78] In 1993, the limit was increased to 1.5 percent of Milwaukee public school students and eligible students were awarded vouchers by lottery.[79] The vouchers were worth approximately $2,500. In 1998, major changes were made to the program; the voucher amount was raised to about $5,000; 50 percent of the funding for the vouchers began to come from the Milwaukee Public Schools' budget; and the limit was substantially increased to 15 percent of Milwaukee students.[80]

However, even after the 1998 reforms, the program was still beset by several structural defects. First, the scope for choice introduced by the program is modest since only a small number of students can use the vouchers and the majority of students are still confined to public schools. Further, public schools do not stand to lose the entire per-pupil allotment for students that are lost to voucher schools. In 2002–3, the maximum that a school could lose per pupil lost was $2,602.[81] This constitutes an improvement in design over the previously used "hold harmless" policy, which guaranteed that schools would not lose any of their state aid when students took vouchers, and which insulates poorly performing public schools from the threat of competition, thereby dulling any incentive for reform. Second, the voucher amount was still far below the per-pupil government spending for Milwaukee. For instance, in the 2002–3 school year, per-pupil spending averaged $11,436 while the voucher value was capped at $5,783.[82] Third, the design of the program leaves open the possibility that some of the documented improvements in academic achievements discussed below may be the result of self-selection bias. Self-selection bias occurs because "families that are better-off may be more likely to take advantage of school choice than those that are worse off because of better access to information, greater ability to afford transportation, a higher penchant to exercise educational alternatives, and greater generic experience with choice and alternatives."[83] Originally, vouchers were awarded on a first-come, first-served basis, meaning that students who were more eager (or who had more eager parents) would be voucher recipients. However, Goodman argues that, "evaluations of the Milwaukee program and others demonstrate that they are not only enrolling students from low-income families, but they are also enrolling students with below-average scores on achievement exams."[84]

There are three major studies of the performance of the Milwaukee program, conducted by Paul Peterson, Cecilia Rouse, and John Witte. Paul Peterson found that students who received vouchers and remained in the program for three or four years gained 3 to 5 percentage points in reading and 5 to 11 percentage points in math, relative to their public school counterparts.[85] Cecilia Rouse found no significant gains in reading scores, but did find that voucher recipients demonstrated a 1.5 to 2.3 percentage point gain in math scores over their public school counterparts for each year spent in private school.[86] Finally, John Witte found no significant differences in reading and math scores between the control group and the voucher recipients.[87] Several researchers believe that Rouse employed the most sensitive methods of evaluation[88] and that her results are likely the most reliable. Goodman argues that Witte's research may have been subject to selection biases,[89] while Neal has expressed concern over the data collection methods employed by Peterson.[90] Therefore, a conservative conclusion to draw is that the Milwaukee voucher program has produced modest gains in math, but has yet to produce significant gains in reading achievement.

Hoxby argues that the Milwaukee program has generated efficiency gains in the productivity of public schools. She determined the effects of the voucher program on school productivity in three different categories of public schools. "Most treated" schools were those in which at least two-thirds of the student population was eligible for vouchers; "somewhat treated" schools were those in which fewer than two-thirds of the student population was eligible for vouchers; "untreated schools" were public schools that were not located in Milwaukee, were urban, had at least 25 percent of their students eligible for free or reduced-price lunch, and had black students comprise at least 15 percent of the student population.[91] She measured productivity by dividing a school's fourth grade score by its per-pupil spending in thousands of dollars.[92] Her findings demonstrate that productivity, based on math achievement, grew by approximately 0.7 percentile points per thousand dollars between 1996–7 and 1999–2000 in the most treated schools. A similar growth pattern is reported for achievements in science, social studies, language and reading examinations.[93]

In sharp contrast, however, Witte's study of the Milwaukee school voucher experiment found that these purported productivity gains were largely illusory.[94] Some savings were experienced due to lower payroll because of high parental involvement in the early years of the program. Additional savings resulted mainly from the relatively low wages paid to teachers at private schools. As a result of such low wages, however, private schools were largely unable to attract experienced certified teachers and teacher turnover was extremely high – averaging approximately 20 percent per year from 1992 to 1995.[95] If the program were expanded to universal vouchers at present private school salaries, Witte suggests that economic pressures would be likely to drive wages up, thereby reducing the savings that were experienced by voucher-funded schools in the Milwaukee regime. Witte concludes his study of the Milwaukee school voucher experiment with skepticism regarding the promise of greater efficiency by private schools in the following terms:

> [T]here is no consistent and reliable evidence that the Choice students differed in achievement from randomly selected MPS [public school] students or Reject applicants. […] [R]esearchers professing such results [of greater achievement at Choice schools] have a major responsibility to outline the causal mechanism by which these miracles are to be accomplished. Is it only their private school status? Is it only competition? Because, if it is something they do differently and better, those of us who have devoted many years to studying inner-city education in America would like to know exactly what it is.[96]

CLEVELAND

Cleveland's voucher program began as a lottery, but has been expanded in an effort to furnish all low-income families with access to educational vouchers. As with the Milwaukee program, however, the Cleveland program is not funded on a scale that is commensurate with the public school system. For instance, scholarships are worth about $2,250 each as compared with the per-pupil expenditure in public schools of $6,507.[97] There is also a substantial shortage of vouchers relative to the number of eligible applicants, although as the program expands, this shortage is being diminished. One positive aspect of the Cleveland program is the availability of publicly funded transportation for scholarship students.[98] By allowing families who do not reside near a participating school to take advantage of the voucher program, the likelihood of income-based segregation being bolstered is correspondingly reduced.

Greene, Howell and Peterson found that voucher recipients who transferred to a private school for two years demonstrated an 8 percentage point gain in reading scores and a 16 percentage point gain in math scores.[99] However, while Metcalf found that voucher students showed a gain of 6 percentage points in language scores and 4 percentage points in science scores as compared with the public school control group, he found no significant score differences in math, English or social studies.[100] Hansen reports that students using vouchers in Cleveland to attend private schools gained 5 percentile points in reading and 15 percentile points in math relative to the national norm.[101] Although the data is inconclusive in its details, the research teams all agree that the Cleveland voucher program has produced *some* gains in academic achievement for recipients. In light of this performance data, it is not surprising that parents of voucher recipients in Cleveland were much more satisfied with their chosen schools than were non-recipient parents with their public schools. Two-thirds of recipient parents reported that they were "very satisfied" with the academic quality of their private school, as contrasted with the 30 percent of non-recipient parents who reported that they were "very satisfied" with their public school.[102]

One interesting dimension of the Cleveland experiment concerns the impact of the voucher program on racial integration. Greene found that 19 percent of voucher recipients attend private schools that have a racial composition resembling that of the Cleveland area, whereas only 5 percent of public school students attend similarly integrated schools.[103] This suggests that assigning students to schools based on their place of residence has a tendency to group students together on the basis of race as well as income. The Cleveland evidence strongly supports the contention expressed by some voucher advocates that school choice will enhance racial integration.

THE NETHERLANDS

In the Netherlands, approximately 70 percent of school-aged children attend independent schools funded by demand-side subsidies.[104] The state provides funding to public schools and to both religious and secular independent schools on an equal basis. In this system, parents choose the school to which they wish to send their children and the money then follows the parents' choices, albeit in a way that is invisible to parents (they do not receive a paper voucher).[105] In this manner, schools experience the full fiscal benefits of attracting students and the full fiscal losses of losing students. This increases the incentives for schools to respond to competition and improve both the quality of their programs and the efficiency with which they manage their budgets. This feature undergirds Justesen's views that "the principles of free choice and consumer exit are fully implemented" in this system.[106] The cost-efficiency in the Dutch system is evidenced by the fact that the Netherlands per-pupil spending is close to the OECD average. In 1998, it spent US$3,795 on primary education and US$5,304 on secondary education, and the per-pupil cost of public and independent schools does not differ significantly.[107]

Another notable aspect of the Dutch system is that the amount of money allocated per pupil is weighted according to the socio-economic background of each student.[108] As a consequence, there is also evidence that the Dutch system increases socio-economic integration in schools by inducing schools to compete to attract students from the most impoverished socio-economic backgrounds. In this respect, Justesen reports that "the social composition of pupils in independent and public schools does not differ significantly."[109]

Finally, the effectiveness of the education system is evidenced in student achievement levels. The Netherlands has the second highest reading literacy among developed countries.[110] It has been contended that, "this is the major benefit of an education system promoting the principles of 'consumerism' and demand-responsive schools without imposing prohibitive cost on parents."[111]

COLOMBIA

The Colombian voucher system was implemented in 1991 with the intention of aiding low-income families, who had been disproportionately affected by the shortage of places in public secondary schools. The stated goal of the program was to improve student achievement by moving towards a decentralized education system, and was part of a larger effort to expand the private provision of public services.[112] By the beginning of the 1994 school year 90,807 students were using vouchers, which were valued at about US$143. Recipients are limited to "children residing in neighborhoods classified as falling into the two lowest socioeconomic strata (out of 6 possible strata)."[113] Although the program is means-tested, the large number of students awarded vouchers suggests that the negative consequences of government monopoly are mitigated to a large extent. This is further compounded by the fact that private school enrollment as a proportion of total enrollment in Colombia is approximately 2–3 times that in the United States.[114] Therefore, there are enough suppliers to ensure that there are at least moderate competitive pressures in operation. Results from the Angrist *et al.* study show that lottery winners (voucher recipients) score over 0.2 standard deviations higher than lottery losers (program applicants not receiving vouchers), which is roughly the score gain associated with one additional school year.[115]

Other non-academic benefits have been attributed to the voucher initiative. The program has been successful in helping low-income students gain access to private schools, and has also served to reduce overcrowding in the public schools.[116] Researchers at the Massachusetts Institute of Technology found that students who received vouchers had "higher educational attainment, lower grade repetition, an increased probability of taking college entrance exams, higher test scores and a lower probability of teenage marriage"[117] than their non-recipient counterparts. Similarly, Michael Kremer found that voucher recipients were 10 percent more likely to complete eighth grade, were more likely to graduate from high school and scored higher on high school completion and college entrance exams.[118]

Although the results of this program have been largely positive, its introduction has generated increased costs for both the government and for recipient households. It has been estimated that it costs about US$24 more to award a child a voucher than it would to create a space for him or her at a public school.[119] Therefore, unlike the American experience in which private schools are able (or are forced) to educate children with fewer resources than public schools, the Colombian experience has resulted in increased per student expenditures on primary and secondary education. As well, lottery winners spend approximately US$19 more annually on education than lottery losers.[120] This is due to both the tuition fees required in excess of the voucher amount and the wages that are lost when a child devotes more time to school and less time to paid labour. Although these costs may lead one to question the attractiveness of vouchers in the short-run, the long-term benefits greatly outweigh the costs. It has been estimated that voucher recipients can expect to earn US$36–300 more annually than non-recipients.[121]

CHILE

Chile has one of the longest-standing voucher programs for primary and secondary education in the world. It was introduced in 1980 with the goal of improving education through complete decentralization and partial privatization.[122] By the following year 30.4 percent of elementary students and 40.8 percent of secondary students were using vouchers.[123] Prior to these reforms, "the administration of the Chilean school system was fully centralized in the Ministry of Education. The Ministry was not only responsible for the curriculum of the whole education system, but also for the administration of the public schools, which accounted for 80 percent of all schools in the country."[124] Thus, the government had enjoyed a virtual monopoly on education, resulting in both inefficiency and ineffectiveness. The benefits of increased competition in the education market can be readily seen in the Chilean system.

Efforts to improve achievement levels of students included the implementation of a Standardized Performance Examination in 1982. In 1988, scores on this test demonstrated that achievement levels were substantially higher in voucher schools than in the municipal public schools.[125] Contreras found that on an Academic

Aptitude Test (PAA), males attending voucher schools obtain 49 additional points on the math section than those in public schools. The comparable gain for females is 32 points. Gains on the reading portion were 63 points and 55 points, respectively, for males and females.[126] As well, there has been a corresponding increase in the number of years of schooling completed by low-income students and a significant decline in illiteracy levels.[127] It was found that whereas only 50 percent of secondary school-aged children actually attended secondary school in 1970, by 1998 this proportion had risen to 82 percent,[128] evidencing the positive impact that the voucher program has had on enabling children to have access to quality schooling.

Designing a new system

Given the generally supportive empirical data gleaned from a number of different jurisdictions on the performance of education vouchers, we now turn to a discussion of the various subtle design issues that sponsoring governments will need to address if they are to render voucher programs congruent with the legitimate public concerns that have traditionally underpinned government's role in primary and secondary education.

Qualified consumers

One of the first design issues that sponsoring governments will need to address in relation to a proposed educational voucher scheme is citizen eligibility. One option, favoured by a number of commentators, is to make voucher programs in education universally available, and decline to discriminate between different students on the basis of family income or other characteristics (race, ethnicity, academic performance). Yet, operating against widespread adoption of this model is the risk that the introduction of a voucher program will inadvertently but inexorably divert public resources away from low-income families and to higher-income families who come "out of the woodwork" to take advantage of the voucher program (meaning that they will seek to capture the value of the voucher to support their pre-existing enrollment in elite private schools). Unless accompanied by a significant infusion of additional new resources, the creation of a universal voucher system may cause reductions in the quality of the education received by children of low-income families, thereby violating equality values. This problem is more than speculative. In the Cleveland program, for instance, there were few restrictions on student eligibility. Consequently, the majority of students who took advantage of the voucher program were from middle-class families who were committed to receiving Catholic parochial education.[129]

One obvious response to this problem is to target vouchers on a broad class of similarly situated families. Evidence from other choice-oriented schemes shows that without targeting of participants, "choosing families were much more likely to be white, have higher incomes and more educated parents, and be attracted to private schools for religious reasons."[130] The targeting of vouchers also reduces the probability of pervasive cream-skimming. For instance, in the Milwaukee school voucher experiment where only poor, inner-city students were eligible for voucher assistance very little cream-skimming occurred. Children who applied for and received vouchers were largely poor, disadvantaged and suffering in the public system (although their parents had higher than average education levels).[131] These results suggest that the targeting of the program itself plays a large role in the possibility of dramatically reducing both cream-skimming and self-selection of middle- and upper-income students. Witte highlights the difference between targeted and universal programs in the following terms, while cautioning that targeted programs can start an educational system down a slippery political slope toward universality:

> [V]ouchers exemplify a subtle politics that uses a social problem to gain advantages for people well beyond the parameters of that problem; and proponents do so by understanding and successfully manipulating the incremental and pluralist nature of our system. [...] It occurs slowly, continuously taking advantage of the inattention and the inability of opposing groups to maintain constant counter-pressure. [...] I share the view that it is duplicitous and fundamentally perverse for a democratic process to enact a policy with the rationale of helping a population in need, but ending with a policy that in all likelihood will do the opposite.[132]

A practical concern that favours targeted vouchers is that of capacity. Because of the significant start-up time required to establish a new school or to significantly expand existing schools, current capacity at private schools is unlikely to meet the enormous new demand that a universal voucher would be likely to bring to such schools.[133] Of course, under full implementation of a voucher scheme all public schools would be transformed into quasi-private institutions, so system-wide capacity would not necessarily be deficient. It is not unreasonable to expect, however, that many parents exercising choice would prefer to send their children to private schools once this option become more affordable. This practical concern with capacity, however, need not be determinative. There are two alternatives one could use to implement a universal voucher to address this problem. First and most simply, it may be that not every child would be able to attend the first school of her choice – inevitably some students *would be forced* to attend a school that was previously part of the public system.[134] Second, the voucher system could be introduced in stages, with incremental expansion each year in the proportion of students granted vouchers.

Despite the arguments that favour targeted school vouchers, there exist several strong arguments for universality. One is that distributive justice concerns are already addressed through the progressive tax system that exists in most industrialized democracies. It is foreseeable that by forcing the well-off to pay tuition for primary and secondary education, vouchers would become stigmatized as an instrument for the poor (such as with food stamps). Because of the progressive nature of the taxation system, the well-off indirectly currently pay more into the education system than they receive and the less advantaged receive more than they pay. Consequently, we may not need to emphasize further redistribution through targeted vouchers. To the extent that more redistribution is favoured to increase equality, this is a goal that can be met through greater net tax transfers from the well-off to the worse-off and does not need to be dealt with through the deprivation of school vouchers to the well-off.

The second and stronger argument in favour of universality of vouchers is that it creates a collective interest in maintaining the quality of voucher-assisted education by ensuring that the value of the voucher is not degraded over time. With some families in the voucher system and others not, effective political voice in favour of the protection of the system may be attenuated and the values of equality of opportunity and equal citizenship may be compromised through a tiered educational system. "It is better to have the sharp elbows of the middle class on the inside pushing out than to have them on the outside pushing in."[135] However, it may well be the case that we need not fear the diminution of voucher values over time with a targeted program through the loss of the voice of articulate and politically salient citizens. It may be that powerful political forces will lobby for expansion of the program to include the wealthy, not for the diminution of the existing benefits of the program (to the manifest detriment of targeted beneficiaries).[136] The great danger in this direction is that the politically vocal will succeed in expanding a targeted program and scarce education resources will be transferred to wealthy families who previously paid for private education themselves.[137] The best way to prevent such an outcome appears to be the development of strong school-based governance institutions.[138] Reforms might include: mandatory school councils with clear mandates and a cross-section of stakeholders; increasing the responsiveness of regional boards of education; increasing public education on the role and importance of board trustees and school councils; and alter the character of government oversight from a model of "running" school boards to one where government "sets measurable performance obligations and monitors performance."[139] Responsive and efficient school governance might also achieve a more balanced relationship between "voice" and "exit."

Notwithstanding the arguments to the contrary, a universal voucher system is probably preferable to a program with a targeted ambit. If benefits through improvements in student outcomes attend the introduction of choice to a targeted segment of the school-age population, then it is likely that proportionally more benefits will attend the introduction of choice to the entire school-age population. Arthur Hauptman makes precisely this point in the context of higher education, and the analysis equally applies here. "Vouchers that benefit a high percentage of students [and/or] pay a high proportion of the bill are more likely to have an impact on both student and institutional behaviour than programs with a lesser degree of coverage."[140]

Qualified suppliers

One of the critical threshold issues confronting governments in establishing voucher programs, particularly in light of the role for education in promoting citizenship values, is the question of whether sectarian institutions should be eligible for funding. In the United States, this debate has been remitted to the courts in interpreting the scope of the First Amendment's Establishment Clause, which forbids the direct public funding of religious institutions.[141] Since the first voucher programs emerged, there have been several challenges to these programs on Establishment Clause grounds. The Supreme Court, in *Lemon v. Kurtzman*,[142] stated that in order for a statute challenged on these grounds to be deemed constitutional, it must satisfy three criteria. "First, the statute must have a secular legislative purpose; second, its principal or primary effect must be one that neither advances nor inhibits religion … [and] finally, the statute must not foster 'an excessive government entanglement with religion'."[143] Several decisions by the Supreme Court have tended to uphold publicly funded voucher initiatives. For example, the *Mitchell v. Helms*[144] decision firmly established that "when funding is routed to parents and they, in turn, choose religious schools independently of the state, the use of the funds by the schools is irrelevant to the Establishment Clause."[145] This indicates that unless state funding is being directly supplied to religious schools, the Establishment Clause has not been violated. The most recent case involving these issues was *Zelman v. Simmons-Harris*,[146] in which the Supreme Court ruled that the Ohio Pilot Voucher Program did not violate the Establishment Clause. Therefore, although the Establishment Clause has caused hurdles for choice advocates, it does not appear that it will prove to be a decisive factor in the future fate of voucher initiatives in the United States.

Yet, even if sectarian schools are legally permissible, there may be problems with their desirability in principle. Although regulation, and in particular entry controls, should be kept to a minimum in order to avoid the problems of the existing single-provider model, there may be legitimate concerns with a free-for-all of educational suppliers, some of which may be grossly incompetent, socially insidious, or politically subversive.[147] Making actual decisions as to what to tolerate and what to over-ride, however, raises all of the difficult problems of the scope of concepts of externalities and paternalism inherent in the liberal position. How, exactly, this sort of regulation can be carried out is far from clear. Public funding through vouchers of ethnically or religiously separate schools is likely to raise concerns in this regard, particularly on the "citizenship" model of education (above and beyond the constitutional issues outlined above). These concerns are likely to be mitigated only by detailed regulation of school curricula and admissions policies, which is antithetical in important respects to assigning a central role to individual choice, which voucher proponents view as the principal virtue of vouchers. One potential way around this problem is by following the lead of the charter schools in the US, which have avoided concerns of the public funding of religion by being completely non-sectarian.[148] However, it needs to be said that some US empirical evidence suggests that private schools (including religious schools) are more racially integrated than public schools that are tied to residence and housing and promote higher levels of tolerance to minorities.[149]

Another supply-side design issue that needs to be addressed is how to ensure that suppliers are financially healthy. The serious problems[150] involved in the failure of an educational institution may necessitate the existence of regulations to limit entry into the market only to those institutions that have reasonable prospects of remaining in operation over the long-term.[151] In addition, as discussed further below, some on-going quality control may be necessary.

Scope of the voucher entitlement

The implementation of a voucher-based system for education will require public decision-makers to confront a number of vexing design issues concerning the scope and value of vouchers. Should the value of the voucher be the same in all regions of a jurisdiction, irrespective of differences in underlying costs and elasticities of supply? Within a region, should the value of the voucher be set at the costs (fixed and variable) of the most "efficient" school (which will be highly contentious), the current per-pupil public expenditures on education, or some other figure? Finally, support for transportation to and from the best schools is essential in order to avoid having the best schools dominated by those who live nearby, who are usually the wealthiest.[152] Consequently, some have suggested that the inclusion of transportation costs in any proposed voucher is essential to genuine equality of access to education in a voucher program.[153] Although there are few principled reasons against adjusting the value of vouchers on the basis of such criteria, the administrative problems in effectuating this may be considerable. Accordingly, a balance between equity and administrative efficiency must be struck in this area.

Another set of difficult design issues relates to whether vouchers should be of fixed or variable value. If vouchers are of fixed value, then suppliers can be expected to "cream-skim" children who are relatively easy (and less expensive) to educate, while eschewing children who require additional and/or more complex (and hence, more expensive) services because they are gifted, learning disabled or come from disadvantaged socio-economic backgrounds.[154]

One possible response would be to allow for unlimited-value vouchers, but this would generate moral hazard problems on the part of demanders and suppliers, who can externalize the cost of expensive education onto the state. Alternatively, a complex scheme of calibrated vouchers that are adjusted by class of student and carry different but limited values could be created. Most public education systems do, in fact, provide differential subsidies to schools accepting special-needs students, but these values are not explicit and are embedded within the system's operating budget. While rendering these subsidies explicit has the advantage of transparency, it also risks invidious political debates about "pricing (commodifying) the priceless."[155] However, these values could be suppressed by creating different categories of vouchers without making the cost implications explicit.

As discussed in the context of early-childhood education, an alternative mechanism to address cream-skimming is mandatory pooling. If schools were required to enroll every student who wished to attend (or in the case of oversubscription, hold a random lottery for positions), as is the case with charter schools, then it would be more equitable to simply assign a standard voucher value per student that allows for internal cross-subsidization.[156] Instead of trying to deal with the subtleties and nuances of valuation in each individual case, we could rest assured that on average each school is receiving approximately the appropriate level of per-student remuneration. One negative aspect to this standard voucher value regime, however, might be that this may attenuate the emergence of specialized schools oriented towards meeting the needs of higher-cost, more resource-intensive students.

Another possible design response is to preclude for-profit suppliers from participating in the voucher program. The belief is that by limiting participating institutions to those which are organized solely on a non-profit basis, the incentive for cream-skimming will be correspondingly reduced, and, as a consequence, the fixed-value voucher model becomes more plausible. The difficulty, however, is in knowing with certainty that non-for-profit institutions will necessarily be less inclined to cream-skim. Bradford and Shaviro liken the incentive structure of a non-profit organization to a black box, contending that the objective functions of non-profit organizations cannot be modeled accurately.[157] Notwithstanding this view, it is wrong to take it to an extreme. It is unlikely that non-profit institutions are *irrational* – they simply do not respond as predictably to various incentives as profit-seeking organizations. In other words, non-profit organizations have complex utility functions. Nonetheless, non-profit educational institutions likely derive utility, *inter alia*, from providing a high-quality education to as many children as possible while meeting their budget constraints. It is arguable that, consequently, wherever they can save money they will strive to do so – not because they seek to make a higher profit, but because they will be able to educate more students better and thereby better fulfil their mandate. Thus, they may in practice engage in cream-skimming and to a lesser extent, chiselling activities that are often attributed to profit-seeking institutions. Bradford and Shaviro claim that non-profit supply seems to be most successful in areas of traditional contract failure, for example where supplier performance is so hard to monitor that the profit motive reduces, rather than increases, consumer trust.[158] With a strong system for monitoring schools and disseminating results (see the discussion of government's post-design role below), however, it is unlikely (but not impossible) that for-profit schools would mortgage their reputations and their futures by chiselling on costs in the short-run.[159]

It is important to note that not all cream-skimming is socially undesirable. If the goal is to provide an elite education to the most talented students, or perhaps even better than average students, then some element of "cream-skimming" in admissions will be necessary. This would allow for specialized learning adapted to the needs of different sorts of students. On the other hand, it may obviously undermine the values embodied in the "citizenship" model of education. Moreover, this strategy may not work effectively. For example, if gifted students require higher-cost programs to reach their full potential, the incentives presented by a voucher regime may dissuade schools from providing these programs. What may occur is that suppliers will target above-average and gifted students for admission and then deliver their programs at the most cost-effective level. In doing so, providers could reap the benefits of an appearance of a strong program because of the strong results of the gifted students without having to invest additional resources in programs that would push the gifted students to truly excel.

Closely related to the problem of cream-skimming is the problem of extra billing – should we allow education providers to charge an extra fee on top of the face value of the voucher? Extra billing seems to guarantee good-quality education to those who can pay for it, rather than to those who can most benefit from it, which is likely inefficient.[160] Further, allowing those with greater resources to purchase the best educational opportunities undermines equity concerns. It does, however, preserve the autonomy of those who have the resources and are willing to pay for a better education.[161] Moreover, prohibiting extra billing suppresses the price system as both a signal of and reward for differential quality.

Allowing extra billing is likely to prove most problematic with respect to the question of whether to permit vouchers to be used as a credit towards tuition fees charged by schools that are now private. As discussed earlier, one problem with this option is that it might dilute the quality of publicly financed education by spreading the present public education budget more thinly across a larger cohort of students.[162] In addition, it will be argued that allowing vouchers to count as a credit towards private school tuition fees is regressive and may exacerbate inequalities in access to educational opportunities – or at least not change the *status quo*, which is a main motivation of voucher supporters. In fact, this appears to be what would probably have occurred in the Cleveland voucher program if there had not been any controls on who could receive vouchers. A cap of 25 percent of the number of vouchers – first come, first served – was set for current private school students so as to limit the regressive nature of the universality of the program in Cleveland. This limited proportion of vouchers allotted to current private school students was taken up almost immediately. Interestingly, 80 percent of these recipients simply continued on in the same private school that they attended in the previous year, this time with public support.[163]

While economically comfortable families may be able to afford educational opportunities hitherto beyond their means under a voucher program, it will be argued that public resources should be devoted to equalizing educational opportunities for all families, irrespective of means. It may be possible to design educational vouchers in the form of a refundable tax credit that phases out above some income level, but this would mean that wealthier families who are content to send their children to schools that do not extra-bill would also be denied any benefit from the voucher. This would amount to means-testing all voucher recipients and perhaps create additional incentives for wealthier families to opt out of the publicly financed school system altogether and in so doing undermine some of the values embodied in the citizenship model of education, as well as perhaps attenuating the effectiveness of political voice in maintaining the value of voucher entitlements. One solution to this problem would be to require all schools to make a discontinuous election into or out of the voucher system with the former schools accepting a no-extra-billing constraint[164] (in effect, a 100 percent tax on the voucher for parents electing the latter option).

Even if we do not allow extra billing, one might still allow individuals to pay for an education more to their liking entirely at their own cost (as we do at present). If we do this, diversity and civic virtue considerations will be compromised to some extent. However, if we ensure that these individuals continue to pay their fair share of the cost of the publicly financed system, it does not undermine and may actually enhance our ability to provide quality education to the rest of the society. We should keep in mind that it is always, *de facto*, an option for those with sufficient means to go to a jurisdiction where private education is available.

An interesting proposal by Sherry Glied[165] in the context of health care in the United States might be adapted to extra billing in the primary and secondary school voucher context. If we choose to allow extra billing or "topping up," then we are apt to raise concerns that the education afforded by a bare voucher will be substandard and that a multi-tier education system may emerge. However, if we tax the "topping up" portion of tuition fees at a significant rate, say 30 percent, and earmark the funds raised for publicly financed education, then for every dollar paid over and above the voucher face value by those who wish to improve the education provided to their children will lead to improved benefits for the relatively worse off. Exit from a voucher scheme is best seen as being on a continuum where marginal exit is represented by a small "topping up" payment, and complete exit is represented by, for example, sending one's child to a boarding school in another country, where presumably any domestic voucher would be worthless. If we force those who would like to exit the system to pay a proportion of their exit expenditures to those who remain in the system, we can capture their dissatisfaction in explicit tangible monetary terms as an alternative to benefiting directly from their political "voice." For example, rapidly expanding revenue from such a tax would indicate that the value of the basic voucher entitlement should be expanded (and the revenue collected would provide the means to do so). In addition, with the very introduction of this proposal on the political agenda we might capture the voice of those who would prefer to exit the system because, as with the imposition of any tax, there is likely to be intense debate about the amount of tax levied upon extra billing and a recurrent discourse about the face value of the basic voucher.

The extra billing and opt-out issues cast into sharp relief the tension between efficiency and equity in the educational context. Obviously, both provide greater diversity of supply and hence expanded consumer choices. It is also possible that the superior quality of education that they may facilitate will have demonstration effects that translate into political voice by those in the basic voucher system to enhance the value of the voucher. Alternatively, and indeterminately, allowing partial or complete opt-out from the basic voucher system may, while promoting efficiency, also may attenuate political voice in maintaining the value of voucher entitlements and hence compromise equity considerations. Wealthier families may prefer lower taxes, lower-value basic vouchers and greater ability to pay "top up" payments for superior educational services. The challenge of avoiding socially negative "tipping points" in program design is a daunting one.

Government's post-design role

Although governments would not be as involved in the provision of primary and secondary education under a voucher regime as they are under the current system, the government would still need to be involved in the system to make it operate effectively. That is, although the government will be doing more steering than rowing, steering is a demanding and complex task. What will necessarily be involved in the steering role? There are several functions that government will have to assume after a voucher program is in place to ensure its continuing efficacy.

The means of supply-side control we choose is of central importance. If we choose to rely only on *ex ante* government accreditation, this in itself fails to discipline institutions that decline over time. Rather than encouraging educational suppliers to maintain a high quality of service to consumers, *ex ante* accreditation encourages them to meet at first the minimum standards for accreditation but then subsequently to disregard quality for the sake of profit unless periodic re-accreditation requirements were imposed. A more effective incentive system might entail a continuous process of standardized testing even after a school is in operation. Problematically, however, this *ex post* method of evaluation entails high administrative costs and encourages schools to "teach to the test" rather than to innovate or to take risks to provide better education to students.[166]

If we merely require the disclosure of key data about the administration and performance of the school, we take advantage of market pressures on poor providers. Caution must be exercised in this regard, however, because it is possible that schools would be reluctant to take risks by innovating if their short-run results may suffer. Such a situation would have stultifying impacts upon innovation in the school system – a deficiency that a voucher system should counteract, not exacerbate. Another potential difficulty is that for the market to work effectively, we must depend on the sophistication of consumers to discriminate good from bad suppliers. This, of course, is far from assured.[167] The market for primary and secondary education necessarily involves almost everyone. Accordingly, the consumers of this service will be as varied in terms of their capacity to evaluate complex comparative performance data as the population as a whole. Finally, if we make certain results the basis upon which suppliers' performance is measured and compared, then we may create serious perverse incentive or moral hazard problems. That is, if the measure of school success is, for example, the pass rate, then schools will have incentives simply to pass all of their students, regardless of their actual academic achievement. While more sophisticated mandatory performance disclosure requirements can obviously be devised, their complexity is likely to intensify the information-processing burdens faced by the broad spectrum of parents. Compounding this burden on parents is the fact that the actual attributes of education services provided can never be fully known. Because education is to an important extent a "credence" good, rather than an "experience" or "search" good,[168] parents must, to some extent at least, rely on suppliers' claims about the educational services provided – claims that may perhaps be more credible with governmental or private, non-profit provision of educational services.[169]

Michael Fullan has demonstrated that external monitoring (for example, curriculum-based external exit examinations) tends to increase the overall quality of education received by children.[170] One explanation for the mechanism through which this works is that in the absence of an external monitoring arrangement for educational attainment, students and parents have an incentive to select a school that will dispense the highest grades for a given objective level of performance because doing so increases one's chances of acquiring a valuable labour-market signal.[171] Government accreditation, standardized tests, and mandatory disclosure of certain key data about school administration and performance provide some means of disciplining suppliers and providing this external monitoring. However, depending on their design, they will vary greatly in efficacy. For instance the Milwaukee voucher experiment was too lax in this regard. The Milwaukee voucher scheme articulated four criteria, of which schools were required to meet at least one:

1   70 percent of students must advance one grade per year;
2   there must be a 90 percent attendance rate;
3   at least 80 percent of students must make significant academic progress;
4   at least 70 percent of parents must be involved in the life of the school.

If schools were unable to meet any of these criteria, they were given the opportunity to create an alternative criterion of evaluation. Unsurprisingly, no schools ever failed to meet at least one of these criteria[172] – and even if they had, it would have been relatively easy to devise something else that would have sufficed. The consequences were dramatic. One school – the Juanita Virgil Academy – closed within a year of opening. Two other schools – the Milwaukee Preparatory School and Exito – failed while their founders were pursued for fraud and other criminal charges. The former principal of Exito is now serving a prison term on fraud and drug charges.[173] Clearly, a meaningful role for government in maintaining the integrity of a primary and secondary education voucher system is crucial to its success.

Political economy

Primary and secondary education in Canada, the US, and many other countries is a context in which the existing alternative to a voucher-based program is government provision of educational services. Accordingly, it is characterized by entrenched interests that are inclined to resist any significant change in the way that educational services are delivered. First, and most importantly, public school teachers at the primary and secondary level are represented by large and powerful unions. Since the vast majority of teachers at private schools are not unionized, and their wages are often significantly lower than those of public school teachers, there is a strong incentive for public school teachers to resist changes that would threaten their job security and levels of compensation. In addition, there is a large educational bureaucracy that has grown up around the government-run educational system for whom a change from a government-run educational system to a decentralized form of service provision is likely to be perceived as threatening to their employment interests. Another source of potential opposition to school vouchers are parents living in high-quality public school districts, the value of which are imputed into the value of their homes and which could be eroded with a voucher system.

However, there are significant interests lobbying for change in the school system as well. Religious and cultural groups have long argued for increased funding for schools that foster the particular beliefs and customs of their communities. Pluralism in curricula afforded by a voucher program that would leave school choice up to individual parents rather than a single government bureaucracy, if it included sectarian schools, would be appealing to such groups. In addition, educational entrepreneurs would find attractive the opportunities afforded by a private market in educational services with a guaranteed base of consumers armed with government vouchers, and could be expected to argue for an increased role for themselves in the provision of educational services. More importantly, parents – both as individuals and through parent associations – are vitally interested in the quality of their children's education and if widely persuaded that a superior alternative exists to prevailing forms of public provision, are likely to be prepared to invest significant resources, individually and collectively, in promoting such changes. The intensity of most parents' interest in the quality of their children's education stands in marked contrast to the relatively limited interests that they are likely to have, as consumers, in the price and quality of many conventional consumer goods or services that they purchase where their limited stakes are likely to inhibit significant investments in individual or collective action to correct imperfections in these markets. Thus, we are skeptical that collective action problems explain why parents are ineffective in overcoming the political resistance of teachers' unions and the educational bureaucracy to the adoption of a voucher system, *if* it were widely perceived by parents to be a good idea. However, we doubt that parents as a group are widely persuaded of the virtues of an educational voucher system, but rather are often at odds with one another in their interests (e.g. over funding to particular religious groups, communities, or academic programs). Thus, the contentious features of the design of an educational voucher system – admittedly exploited in political discourse by teachers' unions and the educational bureaucracy – are likely at least as much to explain the lack of widespread adoption of educational voucher schemes as the disproportionate political influence of vested supply-side interests.

Conclusions

The primary and secondary education system is a massive and complex system which we, as a society, expect to fulfil a great variety of ends. As we have seen, the primary and secondary education system performs a dual role: (a) providing individuals with economically essential skills and (b) forming citizens who will be contributing members of a democratic society. In furtherance of the first goal, dynamism, innovation, productive efficiency and responsiveness are key requirements. To satisfy the second demand, a well-ordered, equitable, and accountable system is likely to be preferred. Ensuring that each of these goals is met requires complex and contentious judgements about the relative scope of legitimate government action and the free market. Consequently, the convergence of equity and efficiency is not a straightforward consequence of the introduction of school vouchers. Nevertheless, on at least one reading of the limited empirical evidence on school choice to date,[174] school choice not only improves parental satisfaction levels and the academic performance of students, but also fosters greater racial integration and greater tolerance towards minorities – not small achievements – suggesting in turn that we can achieve a better set of trade-offs than our present system of public education provides.

9   Post-secondary education

Introduction

Over the past decade, a number of different industrialized democracies have critically examined the structure and performance of their post-secondary education systems. By and large, the focus of this attention has been on the capacity of the state to support the needs and aspirations of the traditional publicly funded research-intensive university. In the received model, the public research university receives significant levels of funding from the state to support its research and teaching activities, but is subject to some level of state oversight and control so as to render the activities of the institution congruent with the public interest. The level of state intervention in the affairs of the public research university (and its precise form) varies of course from institution to institution, but typically involves some regulation of programs (priority may be placed on education and research programs that are geared to the local economy), tuition fees (typically set at below market rates), and admissions (preferential treatment for in-state versus out-of-state students). In contrast, privately funded research universities (to the extent that they are permitted to operate in jurisdictions supporting public university education) are not subject to the same degree of oversight, but also do not receive the same level and character of public funding.[1]

Concern over the capacity of the publicly funded research university to respond to social needs emanates from a number of different sources. First, given the significant private benefits that are conferred on university graduates (both in terms of their increased social status and enhanced earning power), there is concern over the ability of the publicly funded university system to accommodate the burgeoning interest of students (and their families) in obtaining higher education. In a setting where publicly funded universities enjoy a statutory monopoly on the provision of university education and assuming that the quality of existing programs is to be held constant, any expansion in university enrollment necessarily requires either an increase in the level of state support for the system and/or relaxation of some of the tuition constraints set by government so that students end up bearing more of the costs of their education relative to the benefits received. Concern over capacity constraints in the public university system may also lead the state to consider the scope for entry by private institutions, which in turn raises questions of the appropriate scope for governmental financial support and regulation.

Another concern is with the growing competitive threat posed by elite private universities (particularly in the United States) for the very best students and faculty. To the extent that publicly funded research universities lack the resources or flexibility to attract and retain outstanding faculty and students, the quality of their institutional performance will suffer accordingly. Not surprisingly, the intensity of the threat posed by well-funded private universities to the publicly funded university has spawned a debate over the suitability of relaxing certain constraints that govern the affairs of the public university system.

In this chapter, we consider the appropriate scope for, and efficacy of, modifications to the current funding arrangements for public universities. In addressing this issue, we do not, as in other policy areas, contrast the current system of public funding of universities with a voucher program because in many jurisdictions an embedded voucher program is already in place. Most public universities are funded by the state, at least in part, on the basis of a fixed formula that ties revenue to the number of students enrolled in specific programs, and, as a consequence, institutional funding is determined at least in part by student choice. Accordingly, we focus on how appropriate modifications to the voucher instrument can be designed that would allow for greater flexibility on the part of public universities to increase their sources of tuition revenue, while nevertheless being faithful to legitimate public policy goals (particularly concerning accessibility). Although public universities face a variety of revenue challenges (particularly in relation to funding of basic and applied research), in light of our focus on the various rationales for, and modalities of, the social welfare state, our discussion is restricted to the exploration of the prospects of the voucher instrument in supporting greater tuition pricing flexibility on the part of public universities.

To address this issue, we first examine the desired ends of higher education. We then discuss the various rationales for government intervention. Next we proceed to explore in greater depth the various criticisms and problems of the present arrangements governing publicly funded research-intensive universities throughout the industrialized democracies. Finally, we propose modifications to the current voucher-based model designed to increase the level of private tuition revenue for public universities, but without impairing student equality of opportunity.

The ends of post-secondary education and the rationales for government intervention

There are two quite different but complementary enterprises that motivate the existence of post-secondary institutions.[2] The first is a teaching or educational mandate. As with primary and secondary education, this educational mandate can be understood as having two motivations. The first motivation is that of instilling in students the skills and knowledge that are required to engage in a specific profession or vocation. University professional programs – medicine, dentistry, pharmacy, nursing, law, management, education and engineering – fall squarely into this "skills" portion of the educational mandate. These programs confer substantial private benefits on students in the form of increased human capital. Riddell, for instance, has found most estimates place "average real rates of return to post-secondary education at 6–9 percent for men and 8–10 percent for women, although there are substantial differences across fields of study."[3] The second aim of the teaching mandate is to enable students to mature into effective citizens – fully capable participants in a culturally rich, diverse, democratic society. The fulfillment of this aim is largely the domain of undergraduate arts programs and advanced liberal arts graduate programs, although to some extent all programs contribute to this end. The second enterprise that motivates the existence of post-secondary institutions is the pursuit and amplification of knowledge through rigorous scholarly research. Such research can be conducted at a basic or applied level (or, typically, at both levels), and confers significant benefits on humankind in the form of new understandings of the human condition and the physical environment.[4] In the research-intensive university, neither of these activities can be said to take precedence over the other. Its teaching and research missions fortify and complement one another, and account for its distinctive strengths and longevity.

Given this time-honoured role of the research-intensive university, what is the rationale for government intervention in this area? There are three main rationales that to varying degrees support public involvement in post-secondary education. First, the positive externalities associated with post-secondary education emanating from the civic virtue and citizenship values that are nurtured in students ground a case for public subsidization. So, too, do the positive externalities associated with various types of research activities. Second, there may be a weak paternalism role for government insofar as some students may suffer from informational deficiencies when determining which program of study to pursue at which institution. Third, given the human capital market failures discussed in other educational contexts, there is a strong case for government intervention based on equality of opportunity goals.

Positive externalities

Markets fail to reach efficient outcomes when decision-makers do not experience the full consequences – that is, bear all the costs and reap all the benefits – of their actions. Therefore, a case for government subsidization in the market for post-secondary education is made out to the extent that a significant portion of the benefits of post-secondary education – an enhanced civic culture, valuable research breakthroughs and increased community cohesion – accrue to the public good and not to individual decision-makers alone (i.e. potential students). It makes intuitive economic sense to argue that the government should subsidize the cost of post-secondary education to the extent[5] that society at large reaps the benefits. Concomitantly, individual students should pay the costs of post-secondary education to the extent that they individually reap the private benefits of their post-secondary education. If such a system operated in a world of perfect information and rationality, a socially optimal level of post-secondary education would be "produced" and "consumed" in the marketplace.[6]

Although drawing this dichotomy in the benefits of post-secondary education is overly simplistic and fraught with measurement difficulties, it has utility as a framing idea. Consider the fact that typically post-secondary education that increases a student's future income[7] will increase societal wealth and derivatively government tax revenue, thereby providing concrete benefits to society.[8] In this way, even the most skills-oriented program is likely to generate social benefits. However, the intangible positive externalities – the creation of a robust civic culture and increased community cohesion – associated with post-secondary education in the arts and professions, are probably at least as valuable in the long run as these indirect fiscal dividends.[9] This harkens back to the solidarity-promoting role of the social welfare state. In any event, using the public/private benefit dichotomy we have a *prima facie* case for government intervention in post-secondary education to the extent that mixed private and public funding is required to match the costs of post-secondary education with those garnering the benefits flowing therefrom.

Another related rationale for public intervention in relation to post-secondary education concerns the university's research activities. Because basic (and even applied) research has the character of a public good (its benefits are appropriable by all), it will be under-supplied by the market, and, as a consequence, there is a role for government in subsidizing the production of research. In the absence of this supplementary funding, it is highly unlikely that private parties will dedicate a socially optimal amount of their own resources to research if they will not be able to reap the full range of benefits thereby produced.[10] In the last decade or so, considerable attention has been devoted to the role played by research-intensive universities in spawning industrial innovation. In light of this recognition, governments in a number of jurisdictions have increased the level of public funding keyed to both basic and applied research.[11] Riddell contends that the social benefits of post-secondary education are substantial and may, in fact, approximate the private returns (7–10 percent).[12]

Paternalism

Participation in post-secondary education, unlike participation in primary and secondary education, is not mandatory but optional. Accordingly, one can assume that each individual is making a rational choice to acquire a set of skills or form of learning that will be of significant personal value to them upon graduation. In these terms, government should be understandably wary of exercising a paternalistic role in shaping choices in relation to post-secondary education because the choice of one's vocation is central to one's mode of life and thus to one's very sense of self-fulfillment. Moreover, given that nearly all potential post-secondary students will have already completed about 12 years of formal education before making these choices, they should be regarded as being capable of making rational and informed decisions regarding the appropriate future course of their education.

There may be some modest scope for government intervention grounded on paternalism rationales in the form of a government-mandated disclosure system that would seek to attenuate information asymmetries existing between students and post-secondary institutions, although it is not clear that students themselves are not capable of recognizing the existence of these asymmetries and securing privately produced information (in the form of rankings, university evaluations) that would assist them in making informed choices. Government mandated disclosure would require institutions receiving public funds to publish information respecting the quality of the entering class, the quality and character of the academic program (course offerings, class sizes, faculty/student ratios), student completion rates, faculty research activity, and career placement patterns for graduates.

Equality of opportunity

Although post-secondary education should not be considered a right available to all citizens irrespective of individual merit, true equality of opportunity among equally meritorious citizens (however one defines meritorious in this context) is a benefit of considerable importance. Professional schools play a pivotal "gate-keeper" role in determining access to the corridors of power within a democratic system.[13] The representation of various communities in positions of power and in the professions must be of concern. As such, we should take seriously the broader social consequences of admissions policies in such institutions. However, given the current competitive landscape, and the role of various legal restrictions on dis-criminatory admissions practices, most universities are committed to recruiting the strongest possible student body, and the admissions decision is typically merit driven. The difficulty, however, arises in relation to the capacity of the admitted student to afford the prescribed tuition levels, particularly when, as described earlier in our discussion of primary and secondary education, imperfections in human capital markets constrain the capacity of meritorious students to borrow to finance their education. Consequently, there is a need for government intervention to compensate for these failures and to ensure equality of opportunity for all students.

Modes of government intervention: problems in the present system

As indicated earlier, there is a significant distinction between the private and public university models in terms of the level of institutional flexibility and overall resource support enjoyed by each. However, even within the public university model, there is considerable variation across jurisdictions in the precise way in which funding is transferred to institutions by the state (number of levels of government involved, performance- or non-performance-based funding, tied or untied program funding, degree of tuition pricing flexibility). Of course, there is also considerable variance across jurisdictions in the actual magnitude of state support that is provided to public universities. Yet, despite this variance in the character and level of state support, as indicated earlier, the demands that have been placed on the public university have forced re-examination of the central tenets of government inter-vention in this area. In the following discussion, we briefly highlight some of these defects in order to consider the desirability and design challenges of an alternative model.

Increased demand for higher education

One of the most significant challenges facing the received system of publicly delivered university education emanates from the growing level of student interest in obtaining a university education. Over the last two decades, there has been a steady increase in the demand for university education, both at the undergraduate and graduate levels. This trend reflects, of course, underlying population trends (i.e. the rise in the number of children in the "echo-boom" cohort), but also a secular increase in the demand for higher education programs among the cohort. Further fuelling the demand for higher education in developed countries is the rapidly surging population of students from developing countries who are interested in securing a university education abroad (particularly in OECD countries). In tandem, these demands have placed excessive strain on existing public systems, particularly where enrollment increases require enhanced funding support from sponsoring governments in order to expand programs and facilities.

To the extent that governments have not been able to support program expansion through enhanced public funding, universities have reacted in a number of different ways. Some have simply refused to increase their enrollment base, which means that otherwise qualified students may be deprived of the benefits of higher education. Alternatively, public universities may agree to enroll additional students (as a result of pressure from sponsoring governments), but their decision to do so has come at the cost of reduced program quality, as universities have increased student–faculty ratios or reduced program offerings. Other universities have sought to accommodate enrollment increases by enlisting additional external financial support for the university from private benefaction, industry, or private foundations. In some cases, public institutions have sought and obtained increased governmental support for tuition increases, but typically these are still severely constrained, and often seek to differentiate funding support on student residency (in or out-of-state) or character of program study. In the case of the former, the striking disparities in the level of fees charged by institutions depending on the jurisdiction of the participating student may raise vexing distributional questions when, for instance, the least advantaged students from developing countries are required to pay a substantial tuition premium relative to much more privileged domestic students in developed countries. A further problem with differential student fees relates to the discriminatory impact that this fee structure has on freedom of movement within nations when deployed by lower-level governments.

Regressive subsidization

Another challenge facing the current system of publicly funded universities relates to the highly regressive character of the funding formulas that are typically used to allocate funds to recipient universities. Because public universities are typically funded out of consolidated revenues (on a per-student basis), and because children of higher socio-economic groups participate disproportionately in higher education, the system of flat-based funding constitutes a regressive transfer from poorer to more affluent families.[14] This pattern of public support that perpetuates, rather than attenuates, inter-generational advantages has long been the subject of criticism by commentators from several different political perspectives. Because of this regressive transfer, Nicholas Barr, among others, is highly critical of using general tax revenues to finance higher education: "The taxes of poor families contribute to the consumption by the rich of a university education which helps to keep them rich."[15] Chapman and Greenaway argue that "not only is it the case that graduates receive high returns on average to investment in university there is also no doubt that university students are more likely to come from more privileged backgrounds."[16] The authors argue that the combination of these factors makes a system that does not charge (or minimally charges) students for their post-secondary educations "unquestionably regressive."[17] That is, taxpayers, who do not receive as many benefits from post-secondary education as graduates, are required to finance the majority of others' educations.

Quality

Quite apart from the distributional concerns that are associated with existing systems of public delivery of university education, another set of challenges relates to the quality of programs that public universities can offer, particularly in relation to elite private institutions. At one level, the problem is one of the overall level of resources. Overall expenditure levels at elite private institutions are significantly higher than comparable levels at public universities, particularly when expressed on a per-student basis. This funding advantage reflects the much greater regulatory latitude enjoyed by private institutions in securing tuition fees from students, which are typically only constrained by the market. This tuition revenue advantage is further buttressed by the large accumulated endowments (which generate significant income) and discretionary public research subsidies received by many elite private institutions. In conjunction, the higher levels of revenue enjoyed by elite private institutions confer a significant advantage on these institutions in recruiting and retaining outstanding faculty in an increasingly competitive international labour market, in mounting innovative teaching programs, and in supporting complex and novel research activities.[18] The failure to allow public institutions to secure the funds necessary to create outstanding programs is especially regrettable in light of the large capital investments that states have previously made in these institutions.

Inflexibility

At another level, however, the principal challenge for publicly funded universities increasingly relates to the foregone efficiencies that could be realized from less stringent regulation of their conduct. Tuition price caps, uniform public subsidies that do not differentiate on the basis of institutional (or program) performance (or only crudely track it), limit the incentive and the capacity of institutions to invest in the development of innovative programs that are responsive to student preferences.[19] This lack of differentiation means that students are deprived of the fullest possible range of programs in their home states. It also means that even if there is some realm for meaningful choice in selecting among different publicly funded programs, students will not have access to important price information that, in conjunction with other forms of data, serves as a useful guide to institutional quality. In conjunction, the demand- and supply-side distortions introduced by tuition restrictions and non-differentiated state funding formulas are likely to result in significant efficiency losses.

Attrition

A final challenge confronting publicly funded universities relates to the low levels of student program completion relative to private institutions. The seminal study is by Friedman and Friedman, which compared student attrition rates at representative public and private institutions in the United States, and found that whereas the attrition rate at UCLA (publicly funded) was 50 percent, it was only 5 percent at Dartmouth (privately funded).[20] Canadian evidence supports the linkage of lower tuition fees with higher drop-out rates.[21] The Smith Commission found that 42 percent of students entering Canadian universities in 1985 failed to obtain a degree within five years, and that the attrition rate in graduate programs was lower, but still highly significant, at about one third.[22] The Smith Commission concluded that such statistics are "a symptom of inadequate quality in the organization and delivery of [post-secondary] education."[23] Another explanation may be that tuition fees at publicly subsidized institutions are so low that they do not impress adequately on students the seriousness of the foregone benefits associated with the non-completion of their post-secondary education and the magnitude of the opportunity costs of foregoing workforce participation for several years.

Demand-side experiments

There are several instances where demand-side funding of post-secondary education has been adopted, often as an attempt to address the challenges noted above. The cases discussed below offer examples of failed attempts or at least highly qualified successes, and serve to underline the challenges faced even by reform-minded jurisdictions. In considering the innovations incorporated by Chile and Britain, we emphasize design flaws which we hope to correct in our own proposals for demand-side funding of university education. Ultimately, as noted below, both Chile and Britain made design adjustments which have proved positive.

Chile

Until 1980, Chile had a closed higher education system consisting of only eight universities. In the mid-1970s, levels of enrollment declined significantly, due to "the fiscal shock that Chile's government faced, coupled with the perception that universities were inefficient and offered poor educational services."[24] In response, the Chilean government enacted laws that allowed private providers of post-secondary education to enter the market, and altered the system of financing by reducing institutional grants and making funding student-driven.[25] These reforms were aimed at introducing competition into the higher education sector and encouraging the development of higher-quality programs.[26]

Shortly after these reforms were enacted, the government banned the creation of new institutions (after only three had been established) due to fiscal constraints.[27] Therefore, the desired effects of competition were not realized. Further, the funding formula devised by government encouraged institutions to game the system by increasing the number of students in courses and programs that were inexpensive to provide.[28] Ultimately, the recognition that poor design was having a negative impact led the government to make further changes to the system. Currently, there are 60 universities, 80 professional institutes, and 156 technical training centres in Chile, resulting in creation of competitive incentives. Only 20 universities and 2 institutes receive direct government funding. The privately funded institutions, however, are bound to rely primarily on funding from student contributions, meaning that these institutions are underfunded relative to the social benefits they produce.[29]

United Kingdom

Although Britain boasts internationally renowned post-secondary institutions, funding problems threaten its reputation as one of the world leaders in education. The system has long been beset by poor faculty to student ratios, deteriorating physical facilities and difficulties retaining and recruiting faculty.[30] For many years, universities were not permitted to charge domestic students even nominal levels of tuition. However, over the last decade or so, the government has steadily moved in the direction of increasing the ability of universities to set tuition levels for domestic students, at the same time that a highly modified version of the Higher Education Contribution Scheme was introduced.[31] In 1990, a mortgage-type loan system was introduced, but proved to be highly inefficient: "The loans were designed to replace half of the maintenance support previously covered by the grant but in effect their impact was likely to be smaller than this given that they attracted a zero rate of interest."[32]

Reform measures were first suggested by the National Committee of Inquiry into Higher Education in the 1997 Dearing Report. The thrust of the report was to recommend a gradual shift to a demand-side funding approach.[33] It was anticipated that "if the funding system were driven by student choices, then those choices and the responses by institutions would shape the delivery system."[34] Although the recommendations contained in the Dearing Report were largely disregarded by the government, in 1997, the government did enact some modest reforms. First, "a modest contribution to tuition of 1000 pounds per annum (indexed to the rate of inflation) was introduced, but liability for this was means-tested."[35] A further change was "the switch in the maintenance loan from a mortgage repayment scheme to one in which repayments depend on future income."[36] Although these reforms appeared to be in the right direction, they were not sufficient to alleviate the problems plaguing the post-secondary education sector.

Due to the ineffectiveness of previous reforms, the Labour Government instituted another review of education, which reported in January 2003 (the "Clarke Report").[37] In response to concerns over deteriorating quality, the loss of program competitiveness, and insufficient participation in the university system by students from low-income families, the report proposed substantial (relative to historic conditions) liberalization of tuition pricing by universities. As of 2006, universities will be permitted to set their own student contribution levels within parameters set by the government (the range is set at £0 to £3,000).[38] Further, tuition fees can vary according to the specific courses that students choose to take. In order to assist students in paying these costs, the government is introducing an income-contingent loan system (Graduate Contribution Scheme), as well as a system of grants for disadvantaged students. Ultimately, the House of Commons adopted the Clarke recommendations in February 2004, but only after an intense and protracted political crisis precipitated by concerns over the impact of the reforms on student accessibility.[39]

Designing a new system

In light of the various concerns raised by the existing systems of university education, we argue for a substantial re-orientation of the state's role in supporting public university education. Instead of conferring targeted subsidies to only a handful of public universities that are required to adhere to a number of different regulations in exchange for this support, we propose a more competitive and dynamic university system predicated on the provision of a demand-side voucher calibrated to tuition and reasonable living expenses that would be repayable upon graduation on the basis of earned income (a proposal originally advanced by Milton Friedman[40]). These income-contingent loans should be made available to all students, regardless of parental income or other personal factors. Further, the reliance on income-contingent vouchers would not be inconsistent with the conferral of grant-based scholarships on some students based on merit, disadvantage or other predetermined criteria. With financial assistance being made available universally, tuition fees should be deregulated, allowing universities to determine their own tuition levels. This will allow some universities to offer high-quality programs because they will have the resources necessary to invest in infrastructure, materials and high-salaried professors. It will allow others to gain a competitive advantage by offering programs at a low cost. In such a market, it is necessary that there is relatively unrestricted entry and exit of educational institutions.

The competitive benefits of this system are clear.[41] By relying on the demand-side voucher, consumers of university education will benefit from increased supplier efficiency, enhanced quality of services, and a greater incidence of innovation in the post-secondary education sector. Dohmen comments that "one effect that vouchers might have is to link supply and demand more closely, with demand being based on the interests and needs of the students."[42] When students have true choice among suppliers and supplier income is contingent upon the enrollment decisions of students, it is logical to assume that institutions will be more receptive to student preferences. Those institutions that fail to cater to the interests of the student population will not attract a sufficient number of students to operate. Jongbloed and Koelman state that "Vouchers would enforce the discipline of the market on the providers of education, just as it does on the producers of automatic coffee makers. The introduction of market forces leads to competition and competition will strengthen efficiency, because only the most cost-effective providers will be able to survive."[43] The idea that supply-side financing leads to inefficiency in post-secondary institutions dates back to Adam Smith, who observed that "beyond some point, the higher the level of endowment (subsidy) to any university, the lower its efficiency."[44]

Demand-side financing also increases freedom of choice.[45] Prospective students are often denied the ability to make a free choice, because of cost constraints and a limited number of options being made available. By introducing an income-contingent loan program (ICLP), the barriers associated with cost constraints will be significantly diminished. A loan program is an essential consequence of tuition fee deregulation. As Laidler points out, "government must ensure that lack of access to funds for education does not shut any otherwise qualified and willing participant out of the university system."[46] It is argued that an ICLP is the most efficient and equitable mechanism for achieving this end, because it has the capacity to increase accessibility, despite the higher student contributions required under our system. Since students will not have to repay the loan until they are actually earning income, the low-income status of one's family will not affect one's ability to pay. Calibrating financial obligation to *ex post* realized income rather than *ex ante* financial means is a more effective and equitable mechanism for addressing distributive justice concerns.

Vouchers based on ICLs render the costs of post-secondary education more transparent to students, shift more of the costs of higher education to students, which is appropriate (and more equitable) in light of the significant private benefits associated with university education.[47] Confronting students with the actual costs of their education may also reduce the levels of attrition at post-secondary institutions. Finally, reliance on universal voucher-based ICLs will allow students to realize a higher degree of independence than is possible through existing means-tested loan programs that target financial assistance to those students coming from low-income backgrounds. ICLs mean that "no student need rely on their parents to pay for the cost of their tuition."[48] This can further increase the salience of the value of a post-secondary education to students.

Moreover, there is some evidence that demand-side funding of university education can produce positive results if properly implemented. In addition to the British and Chilean design adjustments, consider the experience of the United States, Australia and New Zealand. The US GI Bill of 1944 and its two descendents (instituted after the Korean and Vietnam wars, respectively) made post-secondary educational vouchers available to all servicemen and women returning from wartime conflict. These measures are often regarded as the most successful implementation of post-secondary education voucher programs and provide useful evidence demonstrating their feasibility.[49] The GI bills made provision for universal vouchers that were awarded regardless of means – every serviceman and woman was entitled to funding for higher education. At its peak in 1947 the GI bill program accounted for over half of all university enrollment with 1.1 million veterans receiving GI bill assistance for higher education.[50] The subsequent incarnations of the program were somewhat less successful, perhaps because the universities were less receptive and accommodating of the special needs of returning veterans.[51] While not as extensive or as influential as the GI bill programs, Pell grants have also been a successful instrument in improving access to post-secondary education for indigent students in the US since their inception in 1972.[52] Subsequent to the passage of the GI Bill in 1944, "one result was an upsurge in enrolments overall, and especially in the Ivy League colleges. Private institutions, which made up most of the top echelon of US colleges, had the largest increase in enrolments."[53] Indeed, the Bill was viewed as being successful both in preparing veterans for participation in the labour market,[54] and in enabling increased numbers of individuals from minority or disadvantaged groups to attend a post-secondary institution.[55]

Australia was one of the first industrialized democracies to adopt a comprehensive ICLP. Prior to the introduction of the program, Australia had experienced surging demand for higher education but limited state capacity to fund required increases for its public universities.[56] Further, higher education was completely free.[57] In 1989, the Higher Education Contribution Scheme (HECS) was created.[58] Under this scheme, students became responsible for a A$1,800 annual charge. This could either be paid up-front with a discount of 15 percent, or a debt could be incurred that would be repaid through the tax system once the individual was earning a minimum of A$30,000.[59] The HECS program is administered by the state and has experienced low administrative costs.[60] Despite the adoption of the HECS program, the Australian university system continued to suffer from underinvestment as a result of continuing restrictions on tuition levels. In 2002, the government instigated a review of higher education in response to concerns over deteriorating quality. As a result of the review process, several reforms have been made to higher educational policy that will allow institutions to determine their own levels of student contributions; a new system of income-contingent loans for students; and the introduction of performance and incentive funding to "encourage universities to differentiate their missions and to achieve reform in the areas of learning and teaching, equity, workplace productivity, collaboration and quality."[61] Importantly, empirical review of the HECS program (and related regulatory changes) reveals that "the socioeconomic make-up of the higher education student body was about the same in the late 1990s as it was before HECS was introduced."[62]

Following Australia's lead, New Zealand implemented an ICLP in 1991, which operates by making loan repayments dependent on an individual's income. Payments are collected through the tax system and there is a progressive percentage rate of collection as income rises beyond the threshold.[63] Despite their operational similarity, the New Zealand system differs from the Australian system in a number of key respects. First, "the loans are designed to cover both university fees and some living expenses."[64] This is an important difference. For many students, living expenses constitute a significant out-of-pocket expense that they will incur in attending a post-secondary institution, and the failure to ensure that students have sufficient access to loans to cover these expenses will discourage attendance in programs that students deem to be first best given their interests and aptitudes. Second, the scheme originally applied a market rate of interest to the loans.[65] Third, universities are allowed to set their own tuition levels.[66] Thus, universities can charge fees that are higher or lower than those at other institutions, and can also charge varying fees for different courses.[67] It is also worth noting that "there are no limitations under the scheme related to the parents' income."[68]

In 2000, the government introduced a zero nominal rate of interest for the period that a student was enrolled at a post-secondary institution, and allowed for variations to the real rate of interest depending on graduates' employment circumstances. These changes have increased the administrative complexity and costs of the loan regime.[69] However, the program is regarded as successful and, in particular, has demonstrated that reliance on the tax system as the collection mechanism is effective.[70]

In light of the demonstrated prospects of the voucher instrument to support increased choice and accessibility goals in relation to post-secondary education in a number of different jurisdictions, we elaborate on this proposal, and discuss several critical design issues. Again, as in the case of other policy contexts, it is our view that although the state's role would change significantly in this model, its involvement and support is still fundamental for achieving a more equitable and efficient system of university education than is presently available in those states relying on the traditional model of delivery or demand-side models suffering from flawed design.

Qualified consumers

One of the first design issues that policy-makers would have to confront in establishing this voucher-based model of university education is the scope of student eligibility. As we have discussed above, under the current system of publicly funded university education, each student who enrolls in a publicly funded university attracts a non-transparent state subsidy which is unrelated to the student's underlying characteristics (e.g. socio-economic status). Again, it is this feature of the current system of public education which renders it vulnerable to criticism on distributional grounds. One option therefore in designing a new system is to make income-contingent loans available only to those students demonstrating financial disadvantage. The case in favour of this approach is clear: given the propensity of students from more advantaged backgrounds to enroll in university and to be able to secure the funds from family sources to support their enrollment, relatively scarce public funds should be concentrated on students from lower-income backgrounds who not only have less access to family resources, but who are also less likely to enroll in university in the first place.

However, means-tested income-contingent vouchers in the post-secondary education context suffer from several defects. In contrast to other policy contexts where means-testing of benefits is necessary because of the substantial costs involved in program delivery, there is now significant experience with income-contingent loans at the university level that demonstrates that, if properly designed, the social costs of these programs are not significant. Specifically, the relatively low costs of these programs reflects their loan-based nature and the significant cost savings that arise from state administration. In respect of the latter, by relying on collection through the tax system, the administrative costs of collecting on active and also defaulted loans would be reduced (and would probably even reduce the incidence of defaults – given that the negative repercussions of tax evasion are high). Evidence from the United States suggests that the administrative costs of using the tax system for collecting on loans would be relatively insignificant. In a 1982 experiment, the Internal Revenue Service withheld income tax refunds from tax payers who had outstanding non-tax federal debt or who had defaulted on spousal or child support payments. The marginal costs of collecting using this process were less than one cent per dollar.[71] By contrast, the current collection system for Canadian Student Loans that are in default results in marginal costs per dollar recovered of between 19 and 28 cents. Thus, the fact that the state can ensure loan repayment by relying on the income tax system constitutes a significant cost saving. The benefits of state administration are further enhanced by the pooling benefits of enrolling a large student population in the program.

The costs of designing and implementing a principled means-tested income-contingent loan program for university students are not likely to be trivial. As in other policy contexts, the state will be required to amass reliable information on family income and assets bearing on the question of the degree of neediness. This is complicated enough in situations where the only financial information required relates to the program applicant or her young children, but much more complex when dealing with university-age students. When is a student no longer dependent on his or her family for financial support? Does this dependence exist only for the first university degree or for subsequent degrees as well? Is this dependence real or imputed? That is, how should the state deal with student claims of estrangement from family members, particularly as the student's age increases? How should the state address dynamic family circumstances (such as family dissolution) in allocating responsibility for student support? Even assuming that this information could be gathered and assimilated in a principled manner, other daunting implementation issues confront means-testing of ICLs. How should the state calibrate the vouchers to recognize different degrees of financial disadvantage? In other words, should the state seek to create a cash-deductible portion of every income-contingent loan conferred reflecting differential advantage, and, if so, what factors other than socio-economic circumstances should be used to determine the magnitude of the deductible portion (e.g. number of children enrolled in university, membership in a minority ethnic, racial or religious group that has been the subject of historic discrimination)?

Brief enumeration of the various design issues involved in the creation of a means-tested loan program indicates that public resolution of these issues is bound to be normatively contentious and politically destabilizing as disappointed program applicants challenge both the *ex ante* criteria and their *ex post* application to specific cases, creating significant costs without offsetting benefits. Moreover, to the extent that there are significant positive externalities associated with university education, a case for partial state subsidization of students from all family backgrounds can be made. For these reasons, we do not believe that means-testing of income-contingent loans should be deployed in this setting.

Having argued in favour of broad eligibility for participation in the ICL voucher program, it is worth recalling that the state still possesses the ability to provide targeted assistance to certain students in the form of grant-based vouchers that would reduce the lifetime cost to the student of the income-contingent loan. For instance, the state could confer grants on students from certain groups (however defined) that are under-represented in university relative to their percentage in the relevant population base in order to encourage their enrollment in university. However, it should be emphasized that the rationale for this assistance is based on the state's role in promoting equality of opportunity, and not on any adverse impact of the ICL plans on students from low-income backgrounds. Since, by definition, ICL programs contemplate repayment solely on the basis of post-graduation income, students from all income backgrounds should have no rational basis for declining to assume the responsibility for education-based debt. Given that the magnitude and pacing of loan repayment will turn on income, the risk of delayed (or defaulted) repayment is borne by the state or, perhaps more narrowly, by all participating students. Thus, concerns over the innate debt aversion of students from low-income backgrounds are not implicated under the ICL program we are proposing.

Qualified suppliers

As we have indicated, at the heart of our proposed voucher system is the promotion of increased responsiveness, innovation and differentiation by university suppliers, and the belief that this conduct is best achieved through heightened institutional competition for students. This competition will emanate not only from existing institutions, but from new entrants as well. Thus, a necessary part of policy reform will be the removal of barriers to entry by new or existing out-of-state institutions. The question remains, however, whether inherent information asymmetries between consumers and suppliers of university education require a role for the state in determining which institutions are eligible to receive the ICL vouchers, and, if so, in what manner the state should vindicate this role.

Traditionally, the state has played an important role in certifying universities, although this role has changed in many jurisdictions as of late. The argument for intervention is based on the inability of students (and their families) to ascertain the quality of a university education *ex ante* because it is alleged to be an experience good, and the fear that students will be unwittingly lured to institutions or programs whose educational benefits (however defined) are not commensurate with the costs entailed. By establishing clear criteria for recognition, the state will be able to bond the quality of institutions operating in its jurisdiction, thereby attenuating the risks of disappointed student expectations. Further, by ensuring that all institutions operating in a given jurisdiction meet minimum quality standards, the risk of negative spillover effects arising from the under-performance or failure of one institution to other institutions in the same jurisdiction is attenuated.

Like all forms of industry entry regulation, the certification regime used to approve new entrants into the field of university education is subject to abuse as a result of pressure from incumbent suppliers who wish to restrict the level of local competition. Although the objective function of the non-profit university is difficult to model, there is little doubt that institutional stakeholders in incumbent institutions benefit from having a stronger faculty and student base, and competitive entry risks the strength of their franchise. These concerns are heightened when existing institutions are publicly funded and regulated and, therefore, less able to respond to competitive threats than their private peer group. Publicly funded institutions may also resist new entry because of the fear that scarce public resources earmarked for public university education will ultimately be distributed more broadly across the population of institutions. This concern is not without a rational basis. Given the many advantages that incumbent public institutions have (in terms of existing physical and reputational capital), new entrants and their prospective students (and their taxpaying parents) will attempt to persuade the legislature to provide at least a modicum of funding support for students who opt for programs in private institutions.

It is our view that the normative case in favour of according the government a significant role in regulating entry into the university market has never been strong, and has been further weakened with the passage of time. As in the case of other experience-based goods, suppliers will find credible ways to signal their quality to prospective students, and to overcome innate informational asymmetries. Institutions can (and do routinely) disclose data respecting their student body, faculty quality, range of programs, and placement rates to prospective students. These data, while not a perfect proxy for institutional performance, are strongly indicative of it, particularly given the associational benefits of university education. Collection, assimilation and assessment of this information by credible third-party organizations (public or private) further attenuates the existence of informational asymmetries between suppliers and consumers, especially when their public assessments are enhanced by privately collected qualitative data. Indeed, it can be argued that the level of private donations received by institutions (either current or historic) constitutes another way of signaling institutional quality to prospective students. By contributing to their alma mater, graduating students register their appreciation of the experience they have received, and the life-long benefits that it has conferred on them. In these terms, institutions who are dependent upon these contributions for their program offerings, will be loath to jeopardize future tuition income or alumni contributions by chiseling on the quality of their current offerings.

Thus, given the existence of strong innate interests on the part of existing and prospective suppliers to bond their performance, coupled with the capacity of student consumers aided by informational intermediaries to ascertain accurately the quality of programs prior to entry, we would argue for a relatively light-handed level of regulation in determining which resident institutions should be eligible for ICL vouchers. Generally, students will not be likely to make irrational choices in this setting, particularly when one considers the costs of university education in terms of their foregone income during university, as well as the responsibility they will ultimately bear for repaying student debt, albeit on an income-contingent basis. Having said that, we would not go so far as to abandon entirely the scope for some minimal core of entry regulation. Sponsoring governments will have legitimate concerns over entry by nefarious or illegitimate operators who seek to exploit certain disadvantaged population groups (for instance, recent immigrants) by overstating the putative benefits of their programs to students, particularly where these institutions do not have any sunk reputational or physical capital investment in the jurisdiction. Governments will fear that where students are insulated from confronting any of the current costs of their university program (other than the opportunity costs of foregone income), certain vulnerable students will be induced to pay excessively high tuition levels (particularly in relation to the long-term benefits realized from the program) to these institutions financed by government-backed loans. Apart from governmental certification of institutions and ongoing regulatory review (perhaps, as we discuss below, primarily in the form of mandatory disclosure of information), another possible response to this moral hazard problem is for governments to impose some of the costs of loan defaults back onto participating universities by, for instance, reducing their loan proceeds from the vouchers tendered by future students so as to reflect historical loan-servicing experience. However government decides to proceed, the critical design issue is to ensure that the regulatory regime that is established to govern entry be insulated from capture by incumbent institutions, and further that regulation not deter dynamic entry.

Should the premium on broad-based citizen access to the higher education marketplace extend to out-of-state institutions? The eligibility of foreign institutions to participate in the voucher program of a sponsoring state is a difficult one. Allowing students to secure state loan assistance for participation at out-of-state institutions will obviously be welfare enhancing for the affected students because it allows them to access a broader array of programs and university offerings than if they were confined solely to the local marketplace. Further, to the extent that the motivation for government provision of the ICL voucher program is based on various distributional concerns, there would appear to be little reason to deprive citizens of the benefits of state assistance for higher education simply because the student affected wishes to pursue a program abroad. This position is strengthened by noting the evolving character of university educational programming. Although there is strong reason to believe that the residential-based university experience will persist well into the future, the rise of large internet-based universities (which require lower physical capital investments as a prerequisite to effective entry) virtually guarantees that foreign institutions will be an important competitor in the local education marketplace.[72] On the other hand, funding students in foreign programs creates more daunting monitoring challenges because governments will typically have less information respecting the character of the institutions than those in their own jurisdiction, increasing the scope for students and others to defraud the state. Further, because foreign-educated students are less likely to return home after graduation, the risk of loan non-repayment is increased.

Scope of the voucher entitlement

As discussed above, the voucher we are proposing would be geared to tuition levels and reasonable living expenses and repaid on the basis of *ex post* realized incomes. In Friedman's original conception of the university voucher, however, graduates would pay a percentage of their future taxable income (above a certain threshold) based on the amount that they originally borrowed to finance their education. Thus, the government's contribution would not so much be a loan as it would be an equity investment in an individual's human capital that reaps dividends throughout a beneficiary's life and throughout each year as employers withhold mandatory payments with income taxes. However, a program designed on this model introduces certain incentive problems. Students who anticipate earning high incomes post-graduation will refrain from participating in the program because they fear that government will appropriate too large a share of the value of their enhanced human capital, and will, if they can, seek to secure loans from other sources who offer funding on more conventional terms, although to the extent that education-based loan markets are underdeveloped, their capacity to do so may be constrained. Alternatively, as Riddell notes, economically prosperous graduates may seek to exit to other states having lower effective levels of taxation, so that they avoid the repayment obligation.[73] Although sponsoring governments could seek to impose an exit tax on graduating students when they leave their home jurisdiction equal to the amount of the outstanding student debt, such taxes are enormously difficult to implement and also have pernicious effects on individual liberty and societal wealth creation.

In any event, Friedman's scheme is not the only proposal that could be considered. As an alternative, the government could operate a true loan program in much the same way. Borrowers would pay a minimum percentage of their taxable income (that would be withheld at source along with their income taxes) toward their loan liability and the accrued interest until they have fully paid it off. This would allow students to pay off their loans at a pace that they could manifestly and demonstrably handle – higher payments in years of high income, and lower payments in years of lower income – and would not disproportionately place the burden of funding post-secondary education on the most successful, ambitious, or financially fortuitous graduates – as Friedman's scheme may.

Of course, under this alternative system some post-secondary education borrowers would never pay off the full amount of their loan because of premature death, the difficulty and costs of tracking persons who leave the jurisdiction, or because, for whatever reason, they do not engage in monetarily rewarding employment. To the extent that money is borrowed and never repaid, the loan scheme would subsidize post-secondary education in a way that Friedman's regime would not, as his assumption is that the dividend rate on the equity investment would be set so as to reduce (if not eliminate) the prospect of systemic subsidization. The same could be done for a true loan program, but high interest rates and the rigours of the compounding on liabilities would probably make this policy unattractive. For this reason, there might be some pressure to introduce interest rates lower than comparable market rates. However, this would introduce incentive problems into the system. With sub-market interest rates students would have an incentive to borrow as much money as possible and reinvest whatever borrowed funds were superfluous to their needs at market interest rates. Consequently, if the degree of subsidization associated with a true income-contingent loan program with an at-market interest rate were thought insufficient, we might maintain some transfers directly to institutions. However, they would be reduced in direct proportion to the amount of subsidization that the income-contingent loan program provides.

To the extent that citizenship or civic virtue considerations favour participation by students in undergraduate and graduate liberal arts programs that in themselves offer limited income-earning prospects after graduation, income-contingent loan programs will by design take this into account in determining post-graduation repayment obligations. If this is thought to be an insufficient response to citizenship and civic virtue concerns, modest universal per capita subsidies to all students admitted to first degree non-professional programs may be justified. For those attending vocationally-oriented community college programs where citizenship considerations are less salient, an income-contingent loan program should sufficiently address distributional concerns. Although some scholars actually advocate reducing or eliminating the level of government support to universities,[74] the economic and social importance of higher education[75] militates against this view. Those who recommend a reduction in government support argue that this will introduce market discipline into higher education, thereby weeding out mediocre faculty and students, and producing a better system in the long run. The benefits of market discipline, however, can still be gained without such drastic measures. First, the case for public funding of research is not related to the efficiency benefits of a pricing scheme for education that reflects its market value. Furthermore, we also have strong reasons to maintain substantial government support for students. We should support the public benefits of post-secondary education such as the promotion of citizenship values, economic growth, the development of a robust civic culture, and the wide dissemination of society's stock of knowledge. Thus, government should intervene in and fund post-secondary education to a significant extent. Consequently, it is not the *fact* of the current intervention and subsidization that is at issue, but the *nature* of the current subsidization and support that is problematic.

Government's post-design role

Ongoing government intervention in the market for post-secondary education should be limited to remedying the problems identified in the first part of this chapter. That is, the government should finance the public portion of the benefits of post-secondary research and education and guarantee access to loans for all students, regardless of familial means,[76] so as to facilitate access to higher education. It is sometimes argued that reducing barriers to entry to allow private post-secondary institutions to operate freely will allow substandard suppliers to enter the marketplace and that this will have negative spillover effects that threaten the educational standards of established institutions.[77] However, the precise mechanism through which these negative spillovers would reduce educational quality is unclear. If many of the same instructors remain with incumbent institutions and strive to improve their performance in the face of new competition, it is difficult to see what factors would lead to a decline in educational quality. Competitive credential inflation might play a role in a diminution of quality, but there is no inherent necessity behind educational quality worsening even if and when grades do inflate.[78] Nicholas Barr argues that external evaluation mechanisms can guard against a degradation of education quality in incumbent institutions that may be engendered by low-quality entrants.[79] Barr suggests that one effective method "to protect standards is to monitor quality and publish the results."[80] Douglas Auld prefers the idea of accreditation through a self-regulatory body or perhaps through an organ of government.[81] Notwithstanding this putative problem and its proposed solutions, the ultimately more sensible and intuitively satisfying prediction from an economic standpoint is that the provision of education in the system as a whole will improve with reduced barriers to entry as institutions are forced to compete directly with each other for student-controlled resources and research funding.[82]

Political economy

The post-secondary education sector is very different in most industrialized democracies from the United States. In the former, for the most part, universities and colleges are fully public institutions. Although they have begun to rely more heavily on private support (e.g. tuition revenue) in the provision of certain limited professional educational services, they remain largely public institutions with highly subsidized tuition for all students. In the United States, by contrast, there is much greater diversity. Although there are many public post-secondary institutions, there are far more that are private. Outside the United States, the most important challenge is to overcome the institutional culture of the academy that is antithetical to greater reliance on private support and to entry by private institutions. Allowing the creation of new universities and colleges, while allowing existing universities and colleges to determine their own fee schedules, is likely to engender substantial resistance for several reasons. As in primary and secondary education, many university and college instructors and administrators who work within the present system are likely to resist the introduction of a more competitive, more differentiated post-secondary educational sector for fear of loss of job security and lower levels of compensation, at least for less-accomplished faculty members.[83] This resistance to change would be unlikely to be politically decisive if students and their parents were widely persuaded of the virtues of such a change. However, in many cases, they are likely to resist the substitution of income-contingent loans and mandatory repayment schemes as mechanisms for ensuring access for the regressive redistribution entailed in prevailing low-cost universal access financing arrangements.

In the US, more aggressive movement in this direction is unlikely to encounter the same resistance, simply because the status quo already exhibits many of these features. More expansive and widely available income-contingent loan programs, underwritten by government, are likely to engender resistance from many taxpayers and fiscal conservatives concerned over increases in government expenditures, but this opposition may well not be decisive if the programs are, in the long run, largely financially self-sustaining, and to the extent that they are not, entail some reallocation of the already substantial level of government subsidies to post-secondary education and research to such a program.

Conclusions

Vouchers, as we argued above, are not a novel public policy instrument in the post-secondary education context. For decades, governments in industrialized democracies have funded public universities on the basis of their enrollment levels, but have only accorded limited scope for these institutions to rely on student tuition to support program quality. The voucher proposal that we canvassed in this chapter is meant to protect, and, indeed, promote, access to universities by students from financially disadvantaged families while simultaneously improving program quality. It does so by creating an explicit demand-side voucher that would consist of two components: means-tested grants for students from financially disadvantaged families and income-contingent loans for tuition and related expenses for all students. Further, to promote institutional innovation, differentiation, and quality we argue that institutions receiving these vouchers ought to enjoy increased flexibility in relation to tuition pricing, and that barriers to entry by new institutions be relaxed (subject to an appropriate *ex ante* certification regime and *ex post* requirements for information dissemination). In tandem, we believe that these reforms are likely to create a far more dynamic university system, while steadfastly protecting accessibility goals.

10 Labour market training

Introduction

With growing and shifting patterns of international trade, increasingly large and destabilizing international capital flows, the potentially adverse impact of rapid technological change on lower-skilled workers, and an OECD standardized unemployment rate that more than doubled from just over 3 percent in 1973 to 7.3 percent in 1997,[1] governments world-wide are increasingly preoccupied with the devastating social and private costs of unemployment.[2] The classically prescribed macroeconomic remedy – Keynesian demand-side economic stimulus – has attracted diminishing support because of government deficit and debt levels and doubts as to its efficacy – qualms that were exacerbated by the "stagflation" experienced by many economies in the 1970s and early 1980s.[3] Because of the lagging support for this default policy, various alternatives have been promoted. One such alternative strategy consists of a supply-side policy that emphasizes the importance of systemic deregulation and liberalization of labour markets – thereby reducing the costs of, and simultaneously increasing the demand for, labour. However, this strategy, if unaccompanied by targeted transitional assistance to displaced workers, attracts concerns that it will increase income inequalities, threaten job security and more generally reintroduce the problems that supply-side labour market regulations were initially designed to address.[4] Another option is the adoption of microeconomic-oriented active labour market policies (ALMPs) that focus on job search facilitation, job training and remedial education. Many governments have endorsed ALMPs as their preferred policy in addressing unemployment. Given the mixed evidence of the effectiveness and successes of such strategies to date,[5] increased consumer choice and the infusion of competitive pressures facilitated by voucher instruments may be the stimuli that ALMPs require to respond effectively to the challenges of unemployment.

This chapter begins by briefly adumbrating the goals of, and rationales for, labour market training programs. Next, we outline the modes and problems of current government intervention in the labour market, as well as some promising experiments in voucher program intervention. Finally, we outline ways to design a voucher regime that may address the problems that currently plague labour market training, while at the same time presenting a more attractive efficiency–equity trade-off than currently dominates government policy in most Western jurisdictions.

The ends of job-training and the rationales for government intervention

The outlook, attitudes and psychological well-being of many members of society are influenced both directly and indirectly by the state of the labour market. For those who are unemployed, the state of the labour market, for obvious reasons, plays a constant and direct role in their lives. For those who are employed, unemployment rates often influence worries about job security, economic self-sufficiency, and the well-being of family members. In times of extremely high unemployment, the measures taken to improve the performance of the labour market are important for almost everyone's sense of hope, well-being and security.

The primary goals of labour market training programs and other forms of government intervention are relatively uncontroversial – to increase labour market participation (i.e. to induce discouraged workers to return to the labour market) and to increase employment rates (i.e. to employ a higher percentage of the labour market). Morley Gunderson has described the goals of labour market training in these terms:

> [T]he objectives of government sponsored training [are] to increase productivity and hence growth, to reduce unemployment, inflation and income disparities, and to provide workers with better-paid, steadier and more satisfying employment, and to provide business with skilled labour.[6]

This basis for labour market policy is supplemented by two key ends of government intervention: providing for a more equitable distribution of resources and building social solidarity. Although redistribution can also be consistent with efficiency, equity can, and we would argue should, stand alone as a fundamental principle of a liberal society.[7] The aim of equitable redistribution in this case is humanitarian: "to assist the more disadvantaged and vulnerable groups in society."[8]

Social solidarity is quite distinct from redistributive ends. There are few aspects of modern life so central to social participation as employment. Meaningful occupation, in all its various forms, has a long history in Western civilization and philosophy as a fundamental source of the personal fulfillment and self-respect vital for civic participation. Not surprisingly, taxpayers (viewed as participating citizens) prefer to contribute to social programs which bring the unemployed back into the fold, so to speak.[9] Welfare recipients (non-participants) also tend to prefer such programs, troubled by the "stigma" that flows from dependency.[10] Moreover, labels like taxpaying "participant" and unemployed "non-participant" often carry the taint of "fault," an elusive concept as Gunderson notes and one that undermines social solidarity.

While social solidarity and equitable distribution of income are not directly equivalent to reduced unemployment rates, a reduction in unemployment is a *de facto* step forward for both – and therefore ties together a comparatively neat package of government ends. The widespread agreement on what labour market training programs should seek to do makes analyzing and determining the optimal way of going about achieving the desired ends less complicated than in contexts in which there are multifarious and sometimes conflicting goals. However, despite this pervasive consensus on what the outcomes should be, both the rationales for government intervention and the characteristics of the labour market which underpin these rationales are complex and multifaceted.

There is a close relationship between the character of modern unemployment and the rationales underlying the ends of government intervention in the labour market. Individuals are unemployed for a variety of reasons. For the sake of simplicity, we may group the causes of unemployment into three broad categories: cyclical unemployment, frictional unemployment, and structural unemployment.[11] Individuals who are without jobs because of a downturn in the business cycle are cyclically unemployed. For cyclical unemployment, unemployment insurance (for income smoothing) and growth-encouraging macroeconomic policy (to expedite the transition to macroeconomic expansion) are the most appropriate tools of assistance. Frictional unemployment includes individuals who are unemployed because they are "between jobs." For frictional unemployment, various inter-mediary strategies that may help match employers looking for new employees with unemployed individuals with the requisite skills is the most appropriate form of government intervention. The third and most problematic category of unemploy-ment from a societal standpoint – structural unemployment – is comprised of those unemployed persons who are unable to find employment because they lack the skills necessary for available job opportunities. Structural unemployment cannot be dealt with by macroeconomic policy because the structurally unemployed (by definition) are unlikely to find lasting employment without the acquisition of skills that enhance their productivity and abilities.

The modern unemployment dilemma is, increasingly, a dilemma of structural unemployment and wage pressures on low-skilled workers. Unemployment figures have been on a long-term rise in most OECD countries.[12] Indeed, in all countries except Canada, the United States and Japan, unemployment levels in the early 1990s reached their highest levels since the Great Depression. Currently, North America's unemployment figures compare favourably with most European countries. Part of the explanation for this inter-continental difference is that although Canada's over-all unemployment rate is considerably higher than that in the United States, both countries boast structural unemployment figures that are roughly one-quarter of what they are in most of Western Europe.[13]

Despite North America's advantage with regard to the rate of structural unemployment, there are several reasons to be dissatisfied with the employment situation. The unemployment rate has not risen as sharply for low-skilled work in North America as it has elsewhere in the OECD, but this is largely a function of the substantial drop in real wages for the low-skilled component of the workforce.[14] (However, this decline in real wages has recently shown signs of reversing.)[15] In addition to the number of actual unemployed, there are also many who are employed part-time but who would prefer full-time work (the underemployed), and many welfare recipients who have given up looking for work altogether (discouraged workers). Pressures on low-skilled workers reflect to some degree the increasing international division of labour with a shift in low-skilled manufacturing jobs to low-wage developing countries and to a greater degree technological change and lower levels of unionization.[16] Globalization has resulted in an essentially bifurcated labour market. Reliable sources of offshore low-skilled labour have increased significantly, placing severe pressure on low-skilled workers in industrialized states. The result is typically increasing numbers of low-skilled and therefore structurally unemployed workers, or wage pressures such as will permit the less skilled to retain a semblance of employment on condition of sharply reduced circumstances.

Even more troubling, key demographic groups often face disproportionate losses. For instance, in Canada and the United States as well as in the OECD overall, the youth unemployment rate is roughly double the aggregate figure.[17] In addition, women in North America face an unemployment rate 1.36 times higher than that of men. Recent immigrants are also typically among the most unemployed, in some cases as a result of poor skill assessment by employers rather than limited skills per se.[18] Although unemployment rates vary greatly across different education levels, the disparity in unemployment levels between the best-educated quartile and the worst-educated quartile has grown steadily across the OECD.

Structural unemployment poses a complex problem for the underlying rationales for government intervention – and is thus primarily responsible for framing our focus as one of government intervention in labour market *training*. As a starting premise, in the acquisition and development of job-related skills, employers should be willing to pay for training that is firm specific and employees should be willing to pay for the acquisition of general human capital.[19] There are several reasons, however, for assuming that employers and employees will be unable to make optimal decisions about investments in training – thus providing a rationale for government intervention. First is the existence of bargaining failures between employer and employee as to who will bear the costs of training and in what amount. Second, the problem of human capital market failure also arises in this context much as it does in the primary, secondary and post-secondary education contexts.[20] Third, there are externalities associated with training that are unlikely to be captured fully by the private investor. Finally, several government policies cause market-based labour market training decisions to be sub-optimal, and may therefore make government intervention through ALMPs a "second-best" response.

Bargaining failure

There are several important complications that can lead to the benefits of training not accruing to those who have incurred the costs of training. First, most job training programs provide participants with increases to both their firm-specific and general human capital. Because it is very difficult for employers and employees to accurately measure or apportion the shares of general and firm-specific learning that will emerge from a particular type of training, it may prove difficult to reach agreement on who should bear the costs of training.[21] Second, even if employers and employees can arrange training such that they each pay for the benefits that they will receive, employers face a poaching problem to the extent that other employers, given that they have not had to incur training costs that have yielded industry-relevant benefits, can afford to entice trained employees away from their original employer with higher wages.[22] As Gunderson notes, "To avoid losing their trained employee, the firm that provided the training would have to pay the higher competitive wages. As such, they would double pay by paying for the training and paying the higher wage to keep the trained employee."[23] Consequently, employers are likely to under-invest in training that has some benefits that accrue solely to the employee and similarly employees are likely to under-invest in training that has some benefits that accrue solely to the employer. Third, employees may have good incentives to bear the burden of general training (through wage reductions recognizing employer expenditures on general training, for example), but may simply be unable to do so. There are a variety of reasons for this: because of the difficulty of disentangling general and specific training, employees may be reluctant to accept wage cuts for what may seem little return; regulations setting wage rates, such as minimum wage laws, may make it difficult to lower wages in exchange for training; and finally, human capital market failures may simply make wage cuts or other employee expenditures unaffordable.[24]

Failures in human capital markets

The human capital market problem as it arises here is largely the same as in the primary and secondary education and post-secondary education contexts discussed earlier. Individual workers who wish to upgrade their skills may find it difficult to borrow money to finance training because they cannot post their anticipated increase in human capital as collateral to finance debt. This explains government intervention in the post-secondary loan market, frequently by guaranteeing student loans or providing them directly. The parallel between post-secondary government loans and labour market training is of course quite close. To the extent that this human capital market failure prevents individuals from undertaking cost-justified investments in training programs, there is a role for government in either guaranteeing loans made to those in training by private providers, or by engaging in the direct provision of financial support to trainees.

Externalities

Reducing unemployment inevitably results in positive by-products for the public at large. This is usually because government acts as a "provider of last resort" in a variety of areas, ranging from the obvious social assistance and employment insurance schemes to the less obvious health care facilities, drug treatment centres, disability payments, and even crime prevention programs and prisons.[25] When unemployment falls, government spending on these and other programs is reduced along with dependency, depression, crime, substance abuse and the inevitable family difficulties that accompany any long-term unemployment, particularly in one-income households. Many of these externalities, such as a reduction in welfare payments, are clearly identifiable as direct savings for the taxpayer. Others, such as the prevention of child or spousal abuse, are more difficult to measure but unquestionably result in savings for the state. Ultimately, however, these are benefits that individuals and businesses find difficult to internalize, and therefore any market investment in labour training will be sub-optimal.

"Second-best" intervention

Government involvement in the job training function may constitute a "second-best" response to incentive distortions induced by other public policies, such as unemployment insurance, social assistance benefits, and minimum wage laws. These public policies tend to weaken the incentives for the unemployed to seek work. Thus, embarking on a job search or obtaining training is less attractive than it would be in the absence of these policies. Government involvement in job training may also be a second-best response to the inadequacies of the primary and secondary education system (shortcomings which are discussed in Chapter 8 of this book). To the extent that the primary and secondary school system does not prepare some students adequately for employment either through teaching them the wrong set of skills or passing them even though they are functionally illiterate (which would be a failure of the "skills" model of education), government has a responsibility to remedy this failure.

Modes of government intervention

Modern government intervention aimed at ameliorating structural unemployment has typically taken three forms: Passive Labour Market Policies (PLMPs) such as unemployment insurance, government run Active Labour Market Policies (ALMPs) as supply-side subsidies, and competitively delivered ALMPs, in some cases financed by government vouchers (demand-side subsidies). Modes of government intervention vary significantly from jurisdiction to jurisdiction, but some general trends are evident. These are, most notably, the failure of PLMPs to address high structural unemployment, the limited utility of supply-side ALMPs and, finally, encouraging results from demand-side ALMP experiments.

Passive labour market policies

PLMPs are simply labour market interventions that provide income support. A wide range of policy options can be viewed as PLMPs, including: employment insurance or welfare plans; government subsidies to faltering businesses or regions; and wage-fixing policies such as minimum wage, living wage, or pay equity.[26] PLMPs can be conceptualized as a safety net – "one that would catch people and prevent them from 'hitting bottom'."[27]

PLMPs also have a tendency to produce perverse incentive effects. A non-exhaustive list includes:

increasing the incidence and duration of unemployment; fostering layoffs as opposed to other forms of downside adjusting such as labor hoarding or reduced hours or wages; fostering seasonal work; encouraging labor force participation to build eligibility for UI; fostering large spikes in weeks of employment at the minimum weeks necessary to be eligible for UI: and discouraging labor mobility in the direction of market forces – out of high unemployment regions and into low unemployment ones.[28]

The more generous the benefits, the stronger these incentive effects become. The most basic difficulty with PLMPs, however, is that they target the symptom of unemployment, a lack of income, rather than the cause, a lack of marketable skills.[29]

Originally developed to provide temporary assistance to the *cyclically* unemployed, PLMPs have, not surprisingly, been unable to address *structural* unemployment. To the extent that structurally unemployed workers are receiving PLMPs, this is unlikely to have any discernable impact on their employment prospects. Income maintenance alone provides no incentive to pursue training. Although most countries still spend a larger proportion of resources on PLMPs, the trend is one of decreased proportions of money allocated to such measures accompanied by a corresponding increase in the resources devoted to ALMPs.[30]

Government-run active labour market policies: supply-side subsidies

In contrast to PLMPs, "the intent of active labor market policies … is to act like a trampoline to facilitate those who fall to bounce back into the labor market."[31] Existing ALMPs may be divided into four broad types: job search assistance, short-term classroom training, on-the-job training (i.e. subsidized employment), and long-term remedial training. Evaluating the net impact of each of these types of ALMPs is methodologically complex. In addition to direct costs and benefits, evaluation involves taking into account deadweight losses (program participants who would have found employment without the program), substitution losses (program participants who find jobs that would have been filled by non-participants), and displacement losses (program participants displacing currently employed non-participants), all of which defy accurate measurement.[32] Notwithstanding the complicated nature of accurate program evaluation, there is growing evidence from the United States and Canada respecting the efficacy of the various types of ALMPs. Kluve and Schmidt report that, "training measures and job search assistance are more likely than subsidy-type schemes to display a positive impact on program participants."[33] In contrast, almost all evaluations of job creation and employment subsidies in the public sector report that these initiatives fail to deliver.[34] Other studies suggest that the results of ALMPs have been mixed.[35] It is to the problems associated with the implementation of ALMPs that we now turn.

Job search assistance (JSA)

In both Canada[36] and the United States,[37] government-administered job posting and placement programs help individuals to find jobs for which they are qualified. In some cases, these programs have roughly the same success rates as job-training programs and at much lower cost.[38] Evaluations of the JSA element of the Job Training Partnership Act (JTPA) in the United States have found that "these programmes have also been successful in reducing social assistance receipt, although they do not typically eliminate it."[39] Meyer surveyed five ALMP experiments in the United States and found that "job search monitoring and assistance together significantly reduce the duration of claims."[40] Further, the OECD reports that, "Intensified job placement and counselling programmes, aimed at encouraging effective job search by the unemployed, have proved especially cost-effective."[41] Some commentators also believe that JSA is superior to training programs because "it ensures that disadvantaged individuals receive jobs rather than only providing them with job training and then assuming employment will follow."[42] While debatable, this conclusion does highlight an important issue for policy-makers: not every unemployed worker requires extensive training or education.

The success of JSA measures, therefore, is a function of the type of unemployment problem at hand. For frictional unemployment this strategy is appropriate. With frictional unemployment, all that is required is to gather and provide enough information for qualified workers and employers to find one another. For structural unemployment, however, mere job search assistance will not be effective because it does not address the fundamental problem – even with full information about the employment market, individuals without the requisite skills will remain unemployed. Since job search assistance programs and job training programs are directed at different problems, we should not see them as substitutes, but rather as complements.

Short-term classroom training

In the United States,[43] welfare-to-work[44] classroom-training programs are highly decentralized. Nevertheless, for the purposes of this analysis, we may categorize them by the groups to which they are addressed – poor single parents, disadvantaged adults, and disadvantaged youth. A large percentage of the participants[45] in each of these sorts of programs have not completed high school. There is little difference, however, in the net results of each program. In each case, there is only a marginal increase in employment levels and only a marginal (if any) decrease in dependence on social assistance by participants.[46] The US Comprehensive Employment and Training Act (CETA), which was enacted in 1973, relied on contracting with public organizations to provide classroom and on-the-job training and was widely viewed as ineffectual. The Job Training Partnership Act (JTPA), enacted in 1982, sought to shift to output-based contracting with private organizations, but pervasive cream-skimming of the more readily re-employed has substantially attenuated its effectiveness.[47] Indeed, recent studies indicate that job-training programs such as

JTPA have had only a marginally positive effect on dislocated workers. Further, there is evidence that job training programs can have a negative effect on the economically disadvantaged due to the tendency of such programs to nurture unrealistic employment expectations among participants.[48] Targeted short-term classroom training programs for specific subgroups of the unemployed (e.g. female labour market re-entrants) have generally proven more effective than the provision of classroom training to broad classes of unemployed.[49]

Evidence of the success or failure of programs outside of the United States is far from voluminous. Nonetheless, it is possible to offer some generalizations about comparative experience. In Canada, although both classroom and on-the-job training have enjoyed only moderate success, on-the-job training has been shown to be relatively more effective than classroom training in improving an individual's relative employability.[50] Job-training strategies in Canada have historically been highly centralized, which is problematic because bureaucratic processes are, for the most part, ineffective at allocating scarce resources as efficiently as are market-oriented arrangements. It is understandably difficult, for instance, for administrators of centrally organized programs to know exactly what training programs will be in primary demand in coming months or years in various geographical areas, and what types of programs would particularly suit the talents, ambitions and interests of incoming participants. Consequently, centrally arranged contracts with providers of training, such as community colleges, which make provision for a certain number of students in certain courses, are likely to be grossly inefficient. Put another way, centrally devised allocation methods are likely to result in systemic and pervasive misallocation of resources. Decentralized, market-based decision making about job-training on the other hand, as is common in the United States, is likely to result in fewer systemic errors of this nature.

In Europe, and particularly Sweden, classroom training is more often coupled with on-the-job training than in North America.[51] Sweden's classroom training programs have often been cited as examples of effective labour market training, although it has been found that those individuals who acquire practical, on-the-job training in the Swedish program are more successful than those who receive only classroom instruction. Both programs, however, have only modestly positive effects on labour market attractiveness for participants.

On-the-job training

Subsidized employment, or on-the-job training, is already part of the government job-training strategy in both Canada and the United States and some studies argue that it is superior to classroom training. The OECD argues that the Canadian Employability Improvement Programme (CEIP) "appears to derive much of its success from well-targeted measures, both to the individual and to local labour market needs."[52] Policy recommendations include keeping "programmes small in scale and well-targeted so that they can cater to a relatively homogeneous group of the unemployed."[53] Evidence from the US Employment Service suggests that the individual-treatment approach shortened unemployment duration and yielded benefits that greatly exceeded the higher costs of targeted programs.[54] Martin finds that programs receiving positive evaluations are typically those that have the following three characteristics: tight targeting; small-scale delivery; and strong on-the-job components.[55] Finally, the US National JTPA (Job Training Partnership Act) study, conducted by Abt Associates, provides further support for increasing use of on-the-job programs. The study found that, "adults recommended for classroom training in occupational skills experienced no significant gains in earnings, but adults recommended for on-the-job training achieved significant gains."[56]

However, certain problems are evident in these programs. First, most programs have been structured without the possibility of flexible adjustments to reflect changing labour market demands. Thus, programs have been instituted to instruct individuals in certain skills even when there may be little demand for them. Leaving the choice of skills acquired up to the individual worker would be a more efficient method of allocation. Second, there are strong incentives for firms to spend very little on training or simply do away with training altogether. Firms also have an incentive to exploit the opportunity to hire unskilled workers (whom they may have hired and trained in any event) and train them with government funding at little or no extra cost to themselves. Consequently, wage subsidy programs have often been plagued by high deadweight, substitution and displacement losses. In addition, public employment programs have tended to result in temporary "make-work" stints with marginal effects on the future employability of participants.[57]

Long-term remedial education

Although not strictly a job-training concern, the lack of high school education has been found[58] to be the most serious impediment to employment for recipients of aid to families with dependent children (AFDC, i.e. welfare) in the United States. As John Martin argues, "It cannot be overemphasised that if young people leave the schooling system without qualifications and a good grounding in the 3Rs, it is well nigh impossible for labour market programs to overcome these handicaps later on."[59] Indeed, the evidence suggests that job-training efforts cannot be pursued in isolation from other considerations such as primary and secondary education and adult literacy programs.

A Fraser Institute study recently concluded that government-sponsored training programs in the United States have been largely unsuccessful in reducing unemployment, increasing earnings, and reducing welfare dependency among disadvantaged groups (i.e. poor single parents and youths who are high school drop-outs).[60] The study indicates that US programs targeting single parents raised per-week earnings between US$2.18 and US$19.96.[61] "In half of all cases, these training programs did not result in reductions in AFDC receipts, and when they did, reductions ranged from 1.1 to 5.2 percentage points."[62] It is difficult to justify the sizeable public expenditures on such programs (US$689 to $4,895 per program recipient) given the minor benefits accruing to participants.[63] The results are equally discouraging in the context of ALMPs aimed at disadvantaged adults and out-of-school youths.

The Fraser Institute study argues that the failure of the US training programs reflects the low educational levels of program participants.[64] As many as 82.9 percent of disadvantaged adults participating in the training programs had fewer than 12 years of formal schooling.[65] Job training programs, either in the classroom or on-the-job, in many cases prove ineffectual because the participants are functionally illiterate. Long-term remedial training is necessary in such circumstances.

OECD countries have often discounted the importance of remedial training in structuring their ALMPs. In developed economies, "workers are expected to do a wider range of tasks both horizontally at the same level of complexity (i.e. job enlargement) and vertically at different levels of complexity (i.e. job enrichment)."[66] Highly functional literacy and the resultant skill of "learning how to learn" are critically important attributes in today's work environment. The importance of remedial education in equipping the under-educated among the unemployed has been substantiated in other studies as well. A 1997 regional case study following mass lay-offs in a single-industry Northern Ontario mining town found that training programs as a whole offered minimal benefits to laid-off workers. Longer duration programs at the college level proved to be much more effective.[67]

Competitive active labour market policies

Competitive ALMP experiments have proved fruitful in a number of jurisdictions, and the competitive model of choice has increasingly become a demand-side model: the voucher system. Under such systems the government offers vouchers to unemployed individuals who choose an ALMP provider from amongst a competitive pool. The provider then redeems the value of the voucher from the government. However, the introduction of competitive pressures into the provision of labour market training has been incremental and very few governments have completely abandoned the public provision of ALMPs. Instead, most offer some range of publicly provided services in addition to vouchers or allow vouchers to be redeemed on a competitive basis at either private or public institutions. A review of the competitive experiences of three countries, Chile, Sweden, and Australia, is illustrative. Chile offers an example of an early struggle to utilize competitive pressures, only partially successful in the absence of a voucher model. Sweden demonstrates some of the gains to be made from market contestability, as well as a common attachment to publicly delivered services – even in the face of gains from competition. Australia, the most progressive country in the OECD on the private delivery of labour market training,[68] provides a useful model for voucher delivery.

Chile

Following the ousting of the Socialist Government in the mid-1970s, "Chile initiated a series of comprehensive institution reforms aimed at creating a market-oriented and open economy."[69] Against this broader background of privatization, a competitive market for training services emerged. This included decentralization of services, diversification in the supply of technical and vocational education and training (TVET), and more market involvement in work-related education and training.[70] Reforms required the Ministry of Education to withdraw from its role as a direct provider and instead set training standards and allocate subsidies.[71]

Chile subsidizes enterprise-based programs (training services provided by employers to their employees) through tax rebates, thus reducing the financial burden of training on companies. For workers who do not have access to enterprise programs, such as low-skilled labour, the unemployed and youth, the government finances "public" training programs, which are selected on a competitive basis through public tenders. While these programs are referred to as "public training programs," they are actually provided by private agencies. Providers include both training agencies and businesses, the latter of which offer on-the-job training. Follow-up studies on enterprise-based on-the-job programs show that "the post-training placement rate is over 70 percent."[72] The main problem with the Chilean system is its reliance on supply-side subsidies rather than demand-side subsidies. Indeed, distortions include "inefficient behavior of enterprises in their training decisions induced by subsidies, a lack of information and the diversity of the training services supplied, both in terms of content and quality."[73] Chile, then, has introduced some competition into the labour training market but failed to take the plunge into a voucher system. Programs such as Chile's also tend to be more prone to cream-skimming, as discussed in more detail below.[74]

Sweden

Sweden has a long-standing tradition of emphasizing the use of ALMPs over PLMPs, and until the economic downturn of the early 1990s had one of the lowest unemployment rates of OECD countries.[75] Government employment offices provide information on labour training programs and eligibility requirements, as well as playing a role in assigning participants to courses.[76] In 1993, the training market was made fully contestable, incorporating both private and public providers. By 1995, the market share of government-run labour market training centres fell from 75 percent to 36 percent, while the share held by private providers climbed to 45 percent.[77] Further, the average course cost per participant fell by 20 percent – meaningful competition resulted in a significant reduction in government expenditures.[78] Unfortunately, international comparisons are less flattering. Per-capita expenditure on training is approximately $7,500 in Sweden, while this figure is between $2,000 and $3,000 in the United States.[79]

Although publicly run training centres compete with profit-oriented as well as non-profit organizations, most courses are operated by the state.[80] This difference seems particularly relevant in distinguishing vocational training from "classroom" training, and indeed participants may follow courses in the regular school system on top of their labour market training program.[81] Given the savings already realized by increased competition, it seems likely that costs could be further reduced by the introduction of more private participation. There appears to be a (not uncommon) bias in favour of public service provision in areas more traditionally associated with "education" than labour market training, even when the distinction is of little utility and the benefits of private provision may be considerable. Funding for both ALMPs and PLMPs in Sweden comes primarily from the state budget, with a small contribution from unemployment insurance society membership fees.[82] Any further reduction in costs would therefore result either in better services, expanded services, or lower taxes.

Australia

Prior to 1998, private job-placement agencies were active, but the dominant share of the market was held by public employment agencies run by the Commonwealth Employment Service (CES). In 1998, "the CES was abolished and replaced by the Job Network (JN), in which practically all public employment services were contracted out to private or community organizations."[83] Three types of services are now contracted out to private providers through a tender process: job-matching, job-search training and intensive assistance (IA) programs. A newly formed agency, Centrelink, is responsible for administering income support as well as registering unemployed persons, assessing eligibility, and determining in which of the three programs an unemployed person should take part. The main aims of these reforms are to

> bring about a national approach to training; ensure that there is competition between training providers; and make training demand-driven (rather than supply-driven), so that enterprises (industry/business) are in partnership with the Government to improve the relevance, effectiveness and efficiency of training.[84]

Individual consumers are free to choose which of the approved private suppliers they approach for services. After receiving government referral to one of the three services types, "job-seekers may choose individually among the suppliers already approved in a competitive tendering process."[85] While the range of suppliers is admittedly limited through the tendering process, approved clients are able to exercise choice among these suppliers.

Government referral constitutes a voucher by any other name and the Australian approach is, *de facto*, a voucher system. Job-matching agencies receive a stipulated amount for each jobseeker.[86] JSA agencies receive payment for each unemployed person who signs onto the job-search plan. For Intensive Assistance providers (those that provide education and training programs in addition to JSA), three payments are made at different points of the process: "The up-front portion is made to the provider on referral; an interim payment is made if the jobseeker significantly reduces drawings on social security; and a final payment is made if benefit cessation or reduction continues over a further 13 consecutive weeks."[87] The profitability of an agency is therefore contingent upon its ability to attract a large number of clients and to produce a desired outcome. The money follows the client and clients have free choice among suppliers.

Although the reforms are still new, early evaluations suggest that they have produced benefits for recipients and savings for the government. The previous

"Jobs Club" system, which provided services similar to the new JSA programs, cost A\$2,510 per unsubsidized employment outcome. In contrast, the JSA programs cost A\$1,118 per unsubsidized employment outcome.[88] The voucher programs are also more effective. "The most prominent difference is that 31.7 percent of Job Club participants were in 'further assistance' three months after leaving the program, compared to just 4.7 percent for those assisted by the contracted providers."[89] These results are encouraging and suggest that the introduction of market mechanisms has already begun to achieve the desired effects.

Intensive Assistance results are more difficult to evaluate, principally because the resources devoted to each participant and program are highly variable. However, preliminary data suggests that IA is more cost-efficient than its predecessors. IA providers receive approximately A\$9,000 for successfully placing a client from the hardest-to-place category. If it is assumed that these providers have the same success rates as the old providers (and therefore do not receive full payment for all clients), then the average payment received per client from the most disadvantaged group is A\$4,550.[90] In contrast, the old JobSkills program had a per-client cost of A\$7,105 and the New Work Opportunities program had a per-client cost of A\$10,009.[91] Therefore, it seems likely that IA is substantially more cost-effective.

The OECD estimates that the cost of Australian AMLP programs represented 0.8 percent of GDP in 1995/1996, but only 0.4 percent of GDP in 1998/1999.[92] These figures suggest that preliminary findings of cost-effectiveness are not illusory, although other factors such as an improved economy may weaken the argument. Clients also appear to be satisfied with the services. A nationwide jobseeker satisfaction survey administered in 1999 indicated that over 75 percent of jobseekers were satisfied with their providers and believed that their job prospects had improved as a result of their participation in the program.

Designing a new system

Based on the experience surveyed above, we believe that there is reason to consider enhanced reliance on vouchers for the delivery of government-supported labour market training activities. Having said that, we are anxious not to overstate the case for voucher programs: experiments with market contestability in the training sector have tended to produce mixed results. One consistent outcome, however, has been that "the existence of private providers tends to put pressure on the PES [Public Employment Service] to adopt methods and practices which have proved successful in the private sector."[93] Therefore, even if private providers do not themselves necessarily deliver higher-quality training, they appear to have the positive effect of introducing the competitive incentives required for public providers to improve the quality of their services.

The theoretical basis for this claim is simple and well supported. PES monopolies, like other monopolies, tend towards inefficiency and quality homogeneity. Administrative inefficiency is a case in point: Martin finds that "in 1996, the average OECD country devoted 21 per cent of active spending to PES administration."[94] In order to improve the efficiency with which training and placement agencies are run, he suggests that policy-makers, "explore ways of making the PES more effective by giving greater play to the role of market signals."[95] The OECD echoed this recommendation in their 1994 Jobs Strategy report.[96]

US analysts have also questioned the efficacy of state-run programs. According to Hattiangadi,

> numerous studies find that many of the 163 federal employment and training programs are redundant, costly, and produce very limited results. With a $20 billion price tag to taxpayers, these results are quite discouraging.[97]

Alternatively, "evidence suggests that privately provided services yield significantly higher rates of return on human capital investments."[98] Market competition offers benefits such as "a greater range of approaches being tested, leading to innovation, a higher rate of improvement in service quality and cost effectiveness, and a greater responsiveness to client needs."[99]

A voucher system, then, has the capacity to increase the range of choices available to unemployed individuals in terms of job-finding strategies (e.g. search strategies, training options, exposure to new approaches and ideas, etc.). It also has the capacity to foster competition on the supply-side so that job search and training services are continuously improved. If the potential of a voucher scheme is even partially realized in these dimensions, it is very likely that reliance on social assistance will decrease dramatically – perhaps leading to an overall reduction of expenditures by the state on unemployment reduction initiatives. The key is careful design. The OECD emphasizes four essential elements of a privatized training market:

> a sufficient number of private and public suppliers; free market access for new suppliers at any time; a purchasing (or fee-setting) agency which is independent from the public supplier; and random assignment of clients to the suppliers or free and informed choice of the clients.[100]

At base, the OECD is identifying the hallmarks of a contestable market system capable of producing strong competitive incentives. In the following section we outline our own criteria for a well-designed voucher system. Note the emphasis on three persistent design problems: information failure, mandatory participation and cream-skimming.

Qualified consumers

Both distributive justice and social externalities (such as reduced crime rates, drug abuse, improved economic growth, and increased social cohesion and solidarity) suggest that all unemployed individuals who do not possess the wherewithal to mount a successful job search and/or who lack the personal resources to fund cost-justified training should be eligible for some form of public assistance in finding appropriate employment. In order to maintain the effectiveness of such an initiative we would ideally be able to target the resulting programs specifically to these disenfranchised individuals. The additional costs of means-testing the unemployed for limited forms of job search assistance may well exceed the benefits. Means-testing may be cost-justified only for more expensive job training programs. A voucher program that is implemented in stages (with hopefully high rates of program attrition due to placement), which first provides basic job search assistance, then provides classroom and on-the-job training and ultimately offers remedial education for the longer-term unemployed, would be more appropriate. In this way, we would avoid at least some of the deadweight losses associated with providing training to the frictionally unemployed (who do not need it) while still providing job-training to those who suffer from structural unemployment (who do).

Indeed, not only should a staged voucher program be made *available* to all the longer-term unemployed, there is a strong argument to be made that in many cases the programs should be *mandatory*. In this way, we may mitigate the operation of substitution and income effects,[101] which reduce the incentives to seek work and increase unemployment rates. Empirical evidence suggests that mandatory programs have a stronger positive impact on unemployment levels than voluntary programs.[102]

In Scandinavian countries, where compulsion to participate is high, studies suggest that mandatory programs have a stronger positive impact on employment levels than do voluntary programs.[103] The British "New Deal," a mandatory program aimed at reducing the incidence of unemployment among young adults, has also been successful. Unemployed individuals between the ages of 18 and 24 are first given extensive JSA services.[104] Those who are unable to secure employment must then choose one of four options: training/education, a wage subsidy to an employer, voluntary work, or government-provided employment.[105] If an individual does not choose an option, then he or she suffers a benefits sanction: "Initially, sanctions take the form of withdrawal of benefit for two weeks, and further refusals may result in repeated four-weekly withdrawals."[106] The implementation of this program has resulted in a decreased incidence of unemployment among young people[107] and produced an estimated annual net social benefit of more than £57 million.[108] The British Restart interview initiative, also administered on a semi-mandatory basis, has shown distinct improvements for those required to participate.[109]

However, results from the United States' welfare-to-work programs have not been as promising, or have at least varied significantly depending on the underlying population that is sought to be assisted. Milhar and Smith find that while disadvantaged single parents experienced moderate employment and wage gains, participants classified as disadvantaged adults and disadvantaged youth did not demonstrate similar gains. Overall, increases in earnings ranged from $0 to $19.96 per week, increases in employment levels ranged from 0 percent to 13.6 percent, and the only group to show a (slightly) decreased reliance on government aid was the single parent group.[110] However, one must be cautious when interpreting these results. These programs are classroom-training programs with generally lower success rates. US outcomes, then, may be attributable to other aspects of faulty system design and are atypical for mandatory programs.

Accordingly, we believe that after some given period of unemployment, participation in the labour market training voucher system should be required as a condition for continuing receipt of unemployment benefits. Further, incentives should be established in order to encourage good-faith efforts on the part of participants to leverage their program participation into employment. In particular, government benefits such as unemployment insurance should not be available upon completion of the program but should only be available after a substantial requalifying period of employment. In this way, participants will have incentives to search out the most effective program and to make good-faith efforts to succeed. This should reduce the relevance of some studies which have found that ALMPs have increased unemployment, "possibly because they were seen by the participants to be a better alternative than searching for regular jobs."[111] Of course, for humanitarian reasons, basic welfare should still be available to those who are absolutely unable to find work, as it would be once unemployment benefits had run out even in the absence of a comprehensive ALMP.

Qualified suppliers

Significant private sector participation is essential to the success of a national labour market strategy. In the case of job search assistance, it is likely that a centralized public information system on job vacancies, perhaps supplemented with a mandatory obligation on employers to post vacancies, would be most effective.[112] There would be no good reason to forbid competition in the job placement market even if some of the intermediary functions of job placement services were displaced by the establishment of a centralized public information system on job vacancies. Assistance in preparing job applications, résumés and preparing for job interviews could be provided to all unemployed workers in the form of a modest voucher set at the government's avoidable cost of providing such a service itself. The voucher could be made exercisable either with government agencies or private sector job placement agencies.

As for classroom training, not only public colleges and vocational schools, but also accredited private colleges and academies should be entitled to provide classroom training. In the latter category, considerations similar to those discussed in our earlier treatment of post-secondary education are applicable. Private suppliers of classroom training provide an incentive to public agencies to improve their services. In addition, unemployed persons have good reason to choose the most effective provider of classroom training, especially when such training is mandatory and unemployment benefits are not available after the training period without a requalifying period of employment. In such a system, there is strong reason to believe that the private choices of individuals will be the most effective resource allocation mechanism, subject to an appropriate accreditation regime that guards against provision by nefarious operators. For central planning of labour market needs to be as effective as market ordering, there would need to be an enormous devotion of public resources to analyzing every industry and sector of the domestic and international economy, and a strong mechanism for determining the capabilities and interests of trainees. Even so, it is highly unlikely that central planning could ever evaluate trainees well enough or predict the eclectic and dynamic needs of the economy long enough in advance or flexibly enough to meet demand satisfactorily. In abandoning the idea of central planning in favour of market-based choice, we can avoid the costly and ultimately futile exercise of trying to predict labour-market needs or worker preferences and abilities.

With respect to wage subsidies granted to industries providing on-the-job training (which would follow worker choice), a balance is required between allowing only those industries to qualify that can provide genuinely valuable skills training and allowing a considerable degree of flexibility in the choice of program to individuals and supplying firms. Experience suggests that some form of labour–industry partnership may be the most appropriate way of identifying and certifying qualifying industries with future employment growth prospects.[113] This may still leave some room for strategic behaviour on both sides,[114] but if unemployment benefits are not available on completion of the on-the-job training program without a substantial requalifying period of employment, the unemployed will have strong incentives to search out effective programs. Employers will have similarly strong incentives when recruiting employees to offer credible assurances regarding the future prospects of employment.

Once we are sure that consumers both have relative freedom to choose their own training program and that the incentives to choose effective programs exist, we must ensure that they are well informed about the relative merits of the different programs. Information failure is implicated for two reasons: (1) a general lack of consumer information and (2) consumers of employment training are often disadvantaged members of society who may lack the ability to assimilate the available information. If consumers simply select providers at random, then the rationale for introducing consumer choice is subverted. Jurisdictions offering some form of voucher program have struggled with this issue in different ways.

Australia has attempted to address information failures by setting training standards.[115] Although this ensures that consumers are provided with a basic minimum standard of service, it does not really address the problem of information failure: studies found a significant variation in performance (successful employment of program participants) among Australian labour training providers.[116] Australia responded by supporting high-profile advertising campaigns and other initiatives designed to disseminate information.[117] While these activities will doubtless increase awareness of choice among consumers, it does not necessarily address the key problem: lack of specific information on the relative performance of service providers.

The United Kingdom uses "Restart" interviews before election of a voucher program to ameliorate information failures.[118] At these interviews voucher recipients meet government counselors who provide information about the various programs – with some success in reducing structural unemployment.[119] Similarly, Denmark has established a system of advisory meetings at which "individual action plans are drawn up . . . either at the request of the individual after the first 6 months of unemployment or on a mandatory basis after 20 months of unemployment."[120] These initiatives are arguably better-suited to ameliorating information failures, but run the risk of force-feeding programs preferred by the bureaucracy to consumers (exactly the sort of centralized resource allocation we oppose) and thus reducing genuine consumer choice. However, an alternative perspective might argue that the structurally unemployed are often less educated and more vulnerable than the average consumer. Some degree of mentorship may in fact be necessary to facilitate truly informed market decision making.

Accordingly, we should require full disclosure of the nature of the training and the agency's or employer's past success rates measured against various indicia. Such information could be delivered either without mentorship or through restart interviews or advisory meetings, depending on the relative costs and benefits of funding mentorship programs. Structured in this way, the market – by way of vouchers – may prove a more effective mechanism for the allocation of job-training programs to those in need than the public sector administered programs that have hitherto been dominant in North America and many industrialized countries.

Scope of the voucher entitlement

As discussed above, a voucher scheme for labour market training should be staged to reduce the deadweight losses associated with training those who do not need to be trained. The first stage would include a relatively low-cost voucher that would be provided to all unemployed workers to defray all or most of the costs of job-placement services. The second-stage voucher, for the longer-term structurally unemployed, would be a fixed-value voucher provided to all those who remain unemployed after a certain period of search. This second-stage voucher could be exercised, at the participant's option, for classroom training, on-the-job training, or some combination of the two. The choice would be mandatory in the sense that unemployment benefits would cease to be payable if an election were not made. Prudent choice of a job-training strategy would be encouraged in that payment of unemployment insurance benefits would terminate upon completion of the job-training program if the participant does not engage in a period of requalifying employment. The third stage of the voucher program – longer-term remedial training – would be reserved for those who are structurally unemployed because of functional illiteracy, or for those who would prefer to make a larger investment in human capital than would be possible through a short-duration classroom or on-the-job training program. For longer-term remedial training that focuses on teaching the 3Rs to the functionally illiterate, a case similar to that discussed in the context of primary and secondary education can be made for public funding of fixed-value vouchers. Long-term training that takes the form of purely vocational instruction could be facilitated through income-contingent loan programs similar to those that would be available for post-secondary education.

Cream-skimming has proven to be a major problem with private sector involvement in job-training programs.[121] Where private sector providers have been remunerated by government on the basis of subsequent placement rates for participants, this has created incentives only to enroll the easiest-to-place participants, who are least in need of job-training. By shifting the subsidies to the demand-side, these incentives will likely be somewhat muted. However, with fixed-value vouchers there will still be perverse incentives for private providers to seek out those unemployed that present the lowest costs or risks to the providers – ironically the ones among the unemployed who are the least in need of assistance. In some cases, other perverse incentives have developed. For example, Cockx examined the incentives faced by program administrators in the Social Employment (SE) program in Belgium. This program was administered by local welfare agencies, which were also responsible for paying out unemployment benefits. The SE program was designed as a "temporary subsidized public sector work experience program"[122] that was aimed at reintegrating welfare recipients into the labour market. However, the local welfare agencies were also responsible for the provision of community services, and viewed the SE program as an opportunity to purchase cheap labour from program participants. These agencies had incentives to use recipients to provide various community services rather than to encourage their reintegration into the normal labour market.[123] These perverse incentives resulted in an ineffective program, with only 6 percent of participants being encouraged to apply for other work.[124] Further, most participants were engaged in low-skilled jobs such as dishwashing and cleaning. This latter form of cream-skimming is precisely the kind of problem best addressed by a voucher system: given a choice, voucher recipients will not participate in a program that exploits their patronage while offering no discernible improvement in their long-term employment prospects. But perverse incentives will still persist under voucher systems and have been addressed by different jurisdictions in different ways.

In Australia a number of successful safeguards have been implemented to reduce cream-skimming. For Intensive Assistance (IA), the most expensive training program offered, the payment structure is such that successful outcomes for the most disadvantaged jobseekers are more lucrative than those for relatively more advantaged jobseekers.[125] This encourages suppliers to target assistance to the most disadvantaged individuals. It is also mandatory for suppliers to accept IA referrals. Therefore, any cream-skimming that would occur would manifest itself in providers devoting more resources to those disadvantaged clients that appeared to have higher chances of success – an outcome not suggested by the data. Dockery and Stromback find that

> in terms of sex, age, unemployment duration, level of education and special target groups, the profile of jobseekers placed in jobs through basic matching activities of the Job Network is very similar to that of jobseekers placed in jobs by the public employment service in 1996–1997.[126]

The evidence also suggests that commencement rates in these programs are higher for the very long-term unemployed and for those with lower levels of education.[127]

Other countries have been less successful. Studies of the JTPA in the United States have found evidence of cream-skimming.[128] Yet it is possible that this is the result of consumer self-selection. Perhaps only those who believe that they are likely to experience returns on training will apply. This is likely to occur regardless of whether or not consumer co-payments are required: participation in a program will involve non-monetary costs such as time, as well as possible monetary costs associated with transportation, child care etc. If co-payments are required for participation, then this effect will be even more pronounced.

The Australian system, essentially risk-adjusting the value of the vouchers, might be the best option, although it would introduce major additional complexities into the system that may not be cost-justified. Another way to address the cream-skimming problem might be to implement mandatory pooling, whereby all training facilities would have to accept all candidates who present vouchers. By setting the voucher value at the approximate cost of training an average individual, most training centres would presumably receive close to the appropriate level of funding. Unfortunately, in so doing we may incur significant decreases in the potentially valuable development of specialization and expertise. One might also permit extra-billing for job placement, short-term classroom training and longer-term remedial education, utilizing the price system as a signal of and reward for superior quality services, and allow the additional costs to be financed by participants from income-contingent loan programs, especially for longer-term remedial education. The best design choice in this area may be the Australian system, but supporting evidence developed through additional careful studies across multiple jurisdictions would give us more confidence in this conclusion.

One possible way of addressing the perverse incentive properties of government-financed vouchers would be to make payment to a JSA or training agency contingent on success. Under such a system providers could be reimbursed for each client whom they successfully reintegrate into the labour market or who stops receiving unemployment benefits. The drawbacks of such a system include: increased incentives for suppliers to engage in cream-skimming behaviour; increased risk and therefore reluctance to enter the market by suppliers; and reduced incentives to respond to clients' needs – that is, to ask: is this job in my *client's* best interest? Finding a system in which a balance can be struck between increased participation in the labour force and promoting equality and individual well-being is a challenging task. In a fully contingent system, however, the disadvantages are daunting, and would subvert government's objectives in this area. A funding scheme, however, in which payment is partially contingent upon the ability of agencies to attract clients and partially contingent upon the outcomes generated by these agencies, is clearly superior to a system without performance incentives.

Government's post-design role

The government's post-design role in the labour market training context will be substantial. Mechanisms will have to be set up to channel (or at the very least track), unemployed persons through the three stages of the voucher program. At the first stage, the government's role would be quite minor, limited to sending out job-search vouchers along with a list of agencies that are available to redeem the voucher. The most cost-effective way to distribute these vouchers would probably be with unemployment insurance benefit payments. Because of the limited value of job-search vouchers there would probably be no need for any proactive ongoing monitoring of facilities that offer the job-search function. However, government would need to be sensitive to complaints about agencies that provide egregiously inadequate service or refuse to redeem vouchers for high-cost individuals – a flouting of the mandatory pooling requirement for job-search facilitators. The tender process in the Australian system serves this function well. By establishing a Customer Service Line through which consumers could make complaints about providers and using this information in the re-tendering process, authorities were able to "select among the market participants, thereby removing the poorest performing ones."[129]

At the second stage of the process, there will be a role for government to play in distributing vouchers, but also in collecting and disseminating information to participants about the various classroom and on-the-job training programs available. Participants will have strong incentives to identify and select effective training programs. There may also be a role for government in accreditation.

At the third stage of the program, the government would have to maintain involvement in the job-seeking process by setting up a mechanism through which individuals can take stock of their needs and abilities and enter either a remedial 3Rs education program or pursue a longer-term more vocationally-oriented program, perhaps at a community college. A further role for government at the third stage could include extending the income-contingent loan program, initially set up for those engaged in post-secondary education (described in Chapter 9) for labour market trainees pursuing vocational education.

Political economy

In both Canada and the United States, a mixture of public and private organizations already provide labour market training. While the efficacy of existing programs appears to be mixed or poor, reforms that entail higher levels of government expenditures are likely to be resisted by many taxpayers, while those who stand to benefit directly from labour market training – the unemployed or potentially unemployed – are politically marginalized and do not have a significant voice in public policy debates. In order to enhance the public appeal of a broad-based voucher program for labour market training, it is likely that reforms will need to be widely perceived as beneficial to society as a whole and not simply the unemployed, and as well will mostly entail the redeployment of existing public resources rather than their augmentation. One means by which the scope of appeal of voucher-oriented reforms to labour market training programs might be broadened is to tie these reforms to existing trends in social policy reform. Many of the goals of welfare reform are consistent with the structure of voucher-oriented labour market training programs. The importance of individual responsibility for training choices and time limits on transfer payments as incentives to pursue job-training opportunities more effectively are goals that might best be pursued through a joint strategy that eliminates welfare-dependency (and the social pathologies that often accompany it) and increases the general skill levels of unemployed workers.

Conclusions

A voucher program that pays sufficient attention to key design challenges may represent a major step forward in the amelioration of unemployment. Such a program could both increase the range of options available to the unemployed and foster competition on the supply-side so that job search and training services are continuously improved. If the full potential of a voucher scheme can be tapped, or even approximated, reliance on social assistance will decrease dramatically – with significant savings for the state.

We envision that participation in some form of AMLP would be mandatory for all individuals who have been receiving unemployment benefits for between 6 and 8 months. At that time, every participant would be required to meet with a government employment counselor who would assist in needs assessment. The counselor would also provide information on different programs. There are both costs and benefits to a government counseling service. Ultimately, however, we argue that there is a role for government counseling because the unemployed are a vulnerable group and information asymmetries are likely to compromise the quality of individual choices. The structurally unemployed, in particular, may be less equipped to make informed decisions in the absence of counseling, and in any case the plethora of options available to participants in a fully contestable system are likely to prove bewildering even to the most discerning of consumers – much like selecting a university or college. That said, a successful voucher system must take care to ensure that the flaws of other labour training models do not creep into the design. Government counselors must help participants understand their choices, not make those choices for them. Any form of counseling which advocates cookie-cutter solutions or pushes participants towards favoured programs as a matter of administrative convenience would undercut the competitive gains that we expect from a voucher system.

The needs assessment would determine if the participant's unemployment was frictional or structural. If unemployment is deemed to be frictional, the participant would be given a voucher representing the average cost of a JSA program, with a specified period of time within which to use the voucher. Benefits sanction would result if the voucher is not used in the allotted period of time. If the participant fails to obtain employment, further assessments would be made. If unemployment is deemed to be structural, the participant would require a more comprehensive program. Specific skills-shortages would be assessed and the counselor would discuss the relevant options with the individual. Varying voucher amounts would be available for those requiring on-the-job skills training, short-term classroom training, or long-term remedial training. For those who may require some combination of assistance measures, vouchers would be made available on a progressive basis, preventing the waste of resources while ensuring that services are still made available to those who require more intensive assistance.

On the supply-side, we argue that the market for JSA and training services should be made contestable, allowing public, private for-profit, and private non-profit agencies to compete for vouchers. The virtues of competition need not be restated. In order to mitigate potential problems, it may be necessary for providers to be government-accredited in order to be reimbursed through the voucher scheme. This would ensure a minimum standard of quality for participants, enhancing their chances for employment. Further, independent evaluations of agencies could be undertaken by an independent government-sponsored agency on a regular basis, perhaps, as suggested earlier, on the basis of mandatory disclosure of performance information. This would allow both government and consumers to have the best possible information on the effectiveness and efficiency of different providers. In order to promote equality and ensure that the positive redistribution effects of these vouchers are realized, the state will also have to enact regulations on the acceptance of clients and the payment structure for providers. In order to ensure that these clients are being served effectively, as well as to ensure that public resources are having the desired social effects, we argue that reimbursement should reflect both (1) levels of client disadvantage and (2) successful outcome. While risk-adjusting adds complexity and increases costs, it also provides a strong incentive to avoid cream-skimming and may, given the Australian experience, be justified.

We anticipate that these reforms will increase the effectiveness of active measures directed at the unemployed as well as increase the efficiency with which such programs are delivered. Under a voucher system, society can more fully realize both the private and social returns of labour market training.

11 Conclusion

Introduction

We commenced this book with a challenge: what would the state look like if governments were to rely almost exclusively on vouchers to deliver public goods and services across the broad spectrum of activities that comprise the modern welfare state? We sought to address this issue by considering how governments actually deliver public goods and services in a range of different policy areas, being particularly attentive to the normative rationales for intervention in each of these areas, to the instrument mix currently being used by government to realize public goals, and to their performance. It is against this backdrop that we considered the prospects for the voucher. In case after case, we argued that, providing that sponsoring governments are steadfastly attentive to demonstrating fidelity to public goals and values through their design, implementation and monitoring of voucher programs, the voucher possesses considerable promise as an instrument of public policy. Vouchers can, we believe, achieve a more satisfactory optimization of efficiency and equity goals than many competing instruments.

Nevertheless, despite the demonstrated promise of the voucher in a number of different policy contexts, the various challenges for government in creating publicly accountable and normatively robust voucher programs ought not to be underestimated. We have seen that the design, implementation and monitoring responsibilities that governments must vindicate in the creation and support of these programs are not trivial either in normative or political terms. In terms of the former, it is inconceivable that normatively defensible voucher programs can be created without confronting a series of difficult and often contentious issues relating to the scope, scale and operation of the proposed program. In terms of the latter, vouchers, particularly where they displace existing modes of public delivery, cannot help but elicit strong stakeholder antipathy. It is here that ideas and interests are intimately linked. To the extent that vouchers force a wrenching and normatively contentious consideration of core public interests and goals in a discrete policy area, this is likely to serve as fodder for the innate stakeholder opposition to the proposed policy reforms. After all, stakeholders having vested interests in the perpetuation of the status quo will enjoy much greater political traction when they appeal to public goals and values that are congruent with their personal interests, rather than simply relying on strenuous and naked assertions of their narrowly defined self-interest. The intensity of this combination of entrenched and salient interests and normatively vexing design, implementation and monitoring issues explains why government by voucher on the scale we have envisaged has yet to arrive. Put simply, governments have only a limited amount of political capital to invest in any major policy reform initiative, and the normative and political challenges of vouchers dictates that these initiatives can only be done in an incremental, piecemeal fashion. Thus, in considering the promise of the voucher instrument, it is clear that both *ideas* and *interests* matter,[1] and one should avoid the temptation of assigning a weight to one or the other that over-determines their role in the policy process. We elaborate briefly on different schools of thought on the relative roles of ideas and interests in the policy process in liberal democracies.

Ideas

According to an oft-cited claim of John Maynard Keynes, sooner or later, it is ideas, not vested interests, which are dangerous for good or evil.[2] While not denying the importance of self-interest in the political process, Steven Kelman argues[3] that the economist's (Public Choice) view of the political process dramatically under-estimates the role of what he calls "public spirit" or "civic virtue" or simply non-self-interested ideas in the political process. He invokes many examples to substantiate this view, such as the enactment of extensive consumer protection and environmental legislation in the 1960s and early 1970s in the US and many other countries over the protestations and resistance of concentrated and entrenched interests, and de-regulation, privatization, and tax reform in the late 1970s and 1980s in the US and many other countries, again over the protestations of many powerful and deeply entrenched interests. Indeed, the so-called paradox of voting – why so many citizens choose to vote in national elections at some cost to themselves and usually with minimal chance of influencing the outcome – suggests a powerful notion of civic virtue at work. In this respect, ideas or values that are likely to be influential will extend well beyond maximizing the total social surplus and correcting for market failures in a welfare economics framework, and are likely to include notions of distributive justice, corrective justice, communitarianism, gender and racial equality, due process, etc. To attempt to reduce civic commitments to these ideas or values to direct or indirect pursuit of self-interest is often quite unpersuasive. For example, some argue, on quasi-Marxist grounds, that the reason why a majority of citizens in most industrialized countries favour various forms of social safety nets, such as social assistance and unemployment insurance, when many of them face a very remote probability of ever having to resort to these systems, is that this is an attempt by a well-endowed majority to negate the possibility of civil insurrection by an impoverished minority which might threaten the formers' endowments. This seems intuitively a completely unpersuasive explanation of why most citizens are committed to some notion of distributive justice, even if they do not perceive themselves as likely to be direct material beneficiaries of these policies.

Thus, in Kelman's view, politics, to an important extent, is as much about what are thought to be good ideas as what are thought to be salient political interests. In other words, persuasion has important currency in the political process, in a reciprocal sense: voters, interest groups, scholars and policy commentators may persuade politicians, bureaucrats and regulators of the virtues of a position or idea; similarly political leaders, bureaucrats, or regulators, may persuade interest groups and voters of the wisdom of an idea (a form of civic republican view of government). Just as in private markets where entrepreneurs engage in a ceaseless process of innovation and attempt to persuade consumers of the virtues of their innovations, which necessarily assumes that preferences are not innate and immutable, it seems equally plausible that preferences are not fixed and immutable in the political process. It is an odd irony that political economists, who stress the dynamic qualities of private markets and forces of innovation and new entry in breaking down entrenched market positions (the "perennial gale of creative destruction" in Joseph Schumpeter's famous words[4]), are inclined to view the political process in such static terms and the role for policy innovations and policy entrepreneurs as so limited.

Notwithstanding the attractions of these arguments about the salience of ideas in the policy-making process, it seems obvious that ideas cannot be abstracted from particular political and historical contexts. Nor can "political market failures" of the kind emphasized by Public Choice theory be discounted in many contexts. In particular, ideas need a congenial political context if they are to take root. In other words, ideas without supportive and salient political interests are likely to be doomed to political oblivion. Thus, an appropriate conjuncture of both ideas and political context is required if ideas are to be an important agent of change.

Interests

Public choice theory holds that the various classes of participants in collective decision-making processes (politicians, bureaucrats, regulators, interest groups, the media, and voters) should not be viewed as involved in the common and selfless pursuit of some agreed set of public interest goals, but rather that collective or government decision-making should be viewed as a kind of implicit market involving intricate sets of exchanges between or among self-interested actors.[5] That is to say, actors will be similarly self-interested whether they are acting in economic or political markets. Thus, for example, in order to attain or retain political office politicians will find it rational to fashion policies that exploit various political asymmetries: between marginal voters (uncommitted voters in swing ridings) and infra-marginal voters; between well-informed and ill-informed voters; and between concentrated and diffuse interest groups facing differential political mobilization costs (collective action problems). Bureaucrats will be motivated to promote policies that maximize their power, pay, and prestige. Regulators will seek a quiet life by coming to accommodations with the interests they are suppose to be regulating, and perhaps also enhancing their prospects of employment in the regulated industry after their tenure as regulators (the "capture" theory of regulation). The media, in order to maximize readership or viewing audiences and thus enhance advertising revenues, will trivialize complex policy issues, sensationalize mishaps unreflective of systemic policy failures, and turn over issues at a rapid rate with minimal investigative follow-up in order to cater to readers' and viewers' limited attention spans (rational ignorance).

On this view of the policy-making process, the iron triangle of self-interested politicians, bureaucrats/regulators, and rent-seeking special interest groups (and the media) would seem to be largely impervious to policy change. Whatever set of policies currently obtains represents a form of "efficient" political equilibrium, no matter how inefficient from a conventional welfare economics perspective.[6] In other words, there are no "big bills left on the sidewalk" because somebody would have already picked them up.[7]

However, the conventional claim by many Public Choice theorists of the disproportionate influence of concentrated interest groups in the political process raises major puzzles. The trends observable in many countries over the past two decades or so towards economic deregulation (including trade liberalization) and privatization and the introduction of competition into hitherto monopolized sectors, in most cases have generated substantial benefits for consumers,[8] but consumers are the quintessential example of diffuse interests, who in these contexts seem to have triumphed over concentrated incumbent producer interests, contrary to the predictions of Public Choice theory. Similarly, the dramatic growth in environmental, health and safety, and other forms of social regulation in recent years again appears to reflect the triumph of consumer, environmental, worker, and related racial and gender interests over concentrated producer interests. Thus, in our view, Public Choice theory does not have a well-developed dynamic account of what sorts of forces disrupt existing political equilibria and lead over (often relatively short periods of) time to non-incremental policy changes.[9]

Government by voucher as an idea

Our conclusions are perhaps not surprising. Once we move beyond mere aphorisms or sloganeering, the detailed design of voucher systems raises technically complex and normatively contentious issues. Moreover, these design issues are likely to elicit substantially different responses and different efficiency–equity trade-offs from one programmatic context to another. These conclusions are best under-scored by briefly reviewing our tentative and no doubt highly contestable design proposals in each of the programmatic areas that we have surveyed against the major design issues which we identified at the outset of this book.

The case for redistribution and its form

Both the case for redistribution in general and the case for redistribution in kind are inherently highly contestable normative issues. Any voucher system implicitly provides an affirmative answer to both questions. In the programmatic areas reviewed, primary and secondary school education and child care seem principally to implicate the distributive justice, social and political externalities, and incomplete capital markets rationales for vouchers, and somewhat less strongly the paternalistic rationale. Post-secondary education and job-training programs principally implicate the distributive justice and incomplete capital markets rationale, much less strongly the social and political externalities rationales, and weakly, if at all, the paternalism rationale. Health care and long-term care strongly implicate the distributive justice, political externalities, and incomplete insurance markets rationales, less strongly the social externalities rationale. Because of information asymmetries between patients and physicians, there is a paternalistic rationale for regulating service quality in this market. Legal aid implicates principally the distributive justice and incomplete insurance markets rationales, but also to a significant extent the social externalities rationale (in terms of promoting respect for the rule of law), and only weakly the paternalistic rationale. Food stamps and low-income housing programs principally implicate the distributive justice rationale, but evidence of the near cash equivalence for voucher programs in these contexts suggest a weak functional basis for tied as opposed to cash transfers.

Qualified consumers

Here the central issue is likely to be, in many contexts, whether the entitlement should be universal or means-tested. Inadequacy of endowments as a rationale for a voucher system will tend to favour the latter, while social and political externalities, incomplete insurance markets, and paternalism may favour the former. In our programmatic contexts, the case for universal entitlements is strongest with respect to primary and secondary education and child care because of social and political externalities and citizenship, social solidarity and equality of opportunity concerns. The case for universal entitlements is much weaker in the case of the subset of students with the aptitude and desire for post-secondary education, because of the high private returns to such education and the strongly regressive nature of universal entitlements in this context. However, distributive justice and incomplete capital market concerns justify some form of means-tested demand-side assistance, ideally in the form of income-contingent loans where repayment obligations are calibrated to post-graduation economic success (rather than pre-program financial means) and grants that are responsive to concerns with accessibility for debt-averse students from low-income families. Further, to the extent that income-contingent loan programs can largely be self-financing and do not generate excessive administrative costs, there is a strong argument for making that component of the voucher program universally available. With respect to job-training programs for unemployed adults, the social externalities associated with unemployment may argue for limited forms of universal entitlements. On the assumption that most unemployed individuals lack means, distributive justice concerns may militate in the same direction. For long-term classroom or remedial re-training for the subset of long-term unemployed, arguably distributive justice and incomplete capital market considerations dominate and call for similar forms of means-tested financial assistance (e.g. income-contingent loans) as would apply more generally in the post-secondary educational sector. With respect to health care, conventional social externalities and paternalism arguments have limited force in this context in supporting universal entitlements, while distributive justice concerns would argue for some form of means-tested assistance, thus ensuring access by all citizens to essential health care services. However, a major concern relates to incomplete private insurance markets which may preclude access to coverage for high-risk consumers, whatever their means, and may justify mandatory pooling through some form of social health insurance scheme. Another concern relates to political externalities with respect to a Rawlsian primary good (like primary and secondary education). The exit option in this context is likely to attenuate substantially the effectiveness of the voice option in maintaining the quality of health care services in the entitlement market. In these respects, decisions by wealthier citizens to opt out of the entitlement system entails substantial negative political externalities for those who have no choice but to remain in the entitlement market. The US health care market well exemplifies the effect of these externalities, compared with the universal entitlement systems that exist in most other developed countries. With respect to legal aid, social externalities associated with respect for the rule of law require that citizens should be able to ascertain the law that relates to them in their various activities that engage the legal system, thus distinguishing legal services from many other essential services that citizens require. However, the demands of the rule of law do not require that government pay for legal services for all. Rather, when coupled with the demands of distributive justice, it simply requires that when individuals need them and lack the means to purchase these services themselves, the government should provide them with the means to do so, thus implying a means-tested entitlement. In the case of food stamps and low-income housing programs, ensuring access by all citizens to basic necessities of life implies means-tested entitlements that satisfy distributive justice concerns.

Qualified suppliers

Obviously, one of the principal virtues of voucher systems is the competition that they are intended to elicit on the supply-side of voucher-assisted markets, thus requiring a significant number of competing providers and relatively free entry. Most of the rationales for any form of government intervention at all in the programmatic sectors under review are implicated in determining what restrictions, if any, should be placed on qualifying suppliers and new entrants (i.e. distributive justice, social externalities, and paternalism). With respect to primary/secondary education and child care (at least if viewed as early childhood education), social externalities/citizenship social solidarity values in particular, and to a much lesser extent paternalistic values may argue for some restrictions on qualifying suppliers in order to screen out grossly incompetent and more importantly socially insidious or politically subversive providers. Paternalism concerns might be largely addressed by various *ex post* mandatory disclosure requirements as to relative school performance rather than relying excessively on *ex ante* screening (depending on one's assessment of the ability of most parents to utilize this information effectively), but these will not address social externalities concerns that are reasonably raised by racist, segregationist, or subversive educational ideologies. Public financing of religious schools is also likely to raise analogous concerns, especially in jurisdictions having constitutional prohibitions on public support for religious institutions. Thus, we do not see how the state can avoid performing some *ex ante* screening function, while recognizing how sensitive and contentious this exercise is likely to prove. Distributive justice concerns are also implicated to the extent that voucher entitlements can be used as a credit towards private school tuition fees, thus further enabling wealthier families to purchase superior quality education, and spreading more thinly, and diluting the impact of, existing public education budgets. While allowing parents to opt out entirely of the entitlement system by sending their children to private schools at their own expense (an option that cannot realistically be foreclosed) may also pose political risks to the quality of educational services provided in the entitlement system, we should not go out of our way to foster a two-tier or multi-tier child care and primary/secondary educational system closely correlated with wealth if we are committed to genuine equality of opportunity. With respect to post-secondary education, social externality and paternalism concerns seem to provide a much less compelling case for extensive restrictions on qualifying suppliers; similarly in the case of job-training programs for unemployed adults. With respect to health care services, individual health care professionals would remain subject to existing licensing and certification regimes and hospitals and other health-related institutions to existing licensing or accreditation regimes. However, there seem compelling virtues in managed competition models of the health care market, where private health plans or fund-holders compete with each other in the provision of prescribed essential services to citizens holding universal capitated vouchers for these services. Relative to other delivery models the managed competition model appears to present individual consumers with more tractable information problems (which can be mitigated further by mandatory disclosure requirements of comparative plan performance against prescribed criteria), enable efficiencies to be realized from vertical integration and other tailored contractual arrangements with plan personnel and facilities, and are likely to contain substantially moral hazard and hence externalities problems on both the supply- and demand-sides of the health care market entailed in more individualized fee-for-service state subsidized health care provision. With respect to legal aid, legal aid providers would typically be licensed lawyers, although we envisage a form of organizational competition between the private bar, staff offices, and community clinics (where scale and specialization, along with more efficient use of para-legal personnel, may reduce costs and enhance quality), with legally aided clients given the choice as to where to acquire legal aid services.

The scope of voucher entitlements

No sensible voucher system can provide an unlimited claim to the costs of goods or services to which it relates without creating massive moral hazard problems on both the supply- and demand-sides of the market (i.e. running up bills at taxpayers' expense). On the other hand, a capped or fixed-value voucher, depending both on its value and supply-side elasticities, may lead to under-provision of needed services for many consumers. With respect to child care and primary/secondary education, we contemplate presumptively a fixed-value voucher, although it may be difficult to avoid the need to adjust the value of the voucher to accommodate the special needs of, for example, children with learning or other disabilities or disadvantages or special transportation requirements. Even here, in order to avoid moral hazard problems, additional voucher increments would need to be capped by class of student need, unavoidably introducing significant additional complexity into the design of the voucher system. Alternatively, some form of mandatory pooling would be necessary, such as first-come, first-served, or allocation of school placements by lottery where demand exceeds supply. With respect to post-secondary education and job-training, the case for scaling the value of vouchers by reference to different categories of recipients does not seem as obvious, recognizing that income-contingent loan programs can be designed with sufficient flexibility to accommodate the varied circumstances of student recipients. With respect to health care services, a single fixed-value (capitated) voucher presents a particularly acute problem in that the widely varying health status of individual citizens entails equally widely varying costs and risks to health care providers. In the absence of some attempt to develop a calibrated, risk-adjusted array of vouchers by reference to the health status of classes of recipients, or elaborate regulations enforcing mandatory pooling of disparate risks, the problem of cream-skimming and the distributional consequences thereof are likely to prove severe. With respect to legal aid, the task of determining the value of vouchers per class of case is also problematic. A lump-sum voucher creates incentives for providers to plead clients guilty in criminal matters or to settle civil cases early and for low value, whether justified or not, whereas an hourly tariff, even if limited, creates incentives to protract matters unjustifiably, perhaps arguing for a fixed hourly tariff per class of matter up to some capped limit, although recognizing that this will still create incentives to attenuate effort once this limit has been reached, even though the complexity of the matter in question may genuinely require more time and effort on the part of the supplier.

Extra billing (topping up)

With fixed-sum or capped voucher systems, the question of whether suppliers should be permitted to "extra bill" consumers on top of the value of the voucher raises highly problematic issues. With respect to child care and primary/secondary education, allowing day-care centres and schools to extra bill on top of vouchers is likely to violate distributive justice, social solidarity and equality of opportunity concerns in that it will permit families with greater private resources to acquire a better quality of education than families with fewer private endowments. We recognize, of course, that wealthier families always have the option of sending their children to private schools entirely at their own expense – an option that we would not, of course, foreclose – but to permit extra billing may seriously exacerbate existing inequalities of educational opportunities as well as compromising citizenship values that emphasize the importance of all children inculcating norms of equal and effective citizenship. Hence we favour a prohibition or at least a tax on extra billing or "top-up" payments. With respect to post-secondary education and classroom job-training, citizenship concerns have less salience, given that participation in post-secondary programs is not mandatory. Hence, efficiency considerations should be given more weight by allowing institutions offering a superior service to price it accordingly, with the price system serving as both a signal of and reward for superior quality, leaving distributional concerns to be addressed through income-contingent loan schemes coupled with means-tested grants. With respect to health care services, which like primary/secondary education, can be viewed as an essential service for all members of the population (and hence a primary good in Rawlsian terms), extra billing poses the same threat to universal access to similar quality essential health care services as means-tested entitlements and is quickly likely to lead to a two-tier or multi-tier health care system in terms of quality. Thus, for essential health care services covered by the entitlement system, we favour a prohibition or at least a tax on extra billing, although we would not foreclose complete opt-out from the entitlement system at the individual's own expense. With respect to legal aid, given the means-tested nature of the entitlement, it seems inappropriate, and largely pointless, if eligibility criteria are designed to identify recipients lacking capacity to pay for legal services, that lawyers providing legal aid services should be able to attempt to extra bill clients presumptively lacking the means to be able to afford the services in the first place, although in order to induce lawyers in private practice to provide legal aid services, legal aid fees will need to be highly sensitive to commercial fee levels. If eligibility criteria were more relaxed, then it may be more appropriate for legal services to be paid for, in some cases, through a combination of vouchers and personal means of the recipient. With respect to food stamps and rent vouchers, eligibility criteria take account of the financial capacity of recipients in setting the value of the voucher, given prevailing market prices for food or accommodation, so that it is assumed that suppliers will simply charge market prices and be paid partly by voucher and partly from the recipient's personal means.

Cream-skimming

If vouchers are designed with a fixed or capped value (as they must be if massive moral hazard problems are to be avoided), this will create incentives for suppliers to minimize their costs by screening or selecting out citizens who pose special risks or costs to them, even though these citizens may be amongst the most disadvantaged or needy members of the constituency at which the voucher system is directed. With respect to child care and primary/secondary education, cream-skimming is likely to be a significant problem with respect to children with learning disabilities, physical or mental handicaps, recent immigrants who speak English as a second language, and children from severely disadvantaged homes who require special attention. A calibrated or risk-adjusted voucher system would partially address this problem but is unlikely to solve it completely. The only other plausible strategy is detailed state regulation of admission policies of participating schools or facilities by compelling some form of mandatory pooling, although this would be a substantial intrusion into the autonomy of schools and how they organize themselves and their curricula, which voucher proponents view as one of the principal virtues of the voucher system, as well as posing major challenges in effective regulatory design and enforcement. In the case of post-secondary education, however, cream-skimming is of the essence of admission policies to superior educational institutions. Moreover, it provides efficient incentives for both institutions and prospective students to aspire to greater levels of achievement. Given that participation in post-secondary education is not mandatory and that social externalities/citizenship values are less centrally implicated in its provision, efficiency considerations would seem strongly to favour permitting cream-skimming, leaving distributional concerns to be addressed through income-contingent loan programs and means-tested grants. With respect to job-training programs (both classroom and on-the-job), fixed or limited value vouchers are likely to create incentives for providers to screen out the hard-to-train or hard to place, even though these individuals may be amongst the most disadvantaged and most in need of assistance. The severity of this problem is again likely, in large part, to be a function of the value of the vouchers and supply-side elasticities. Otherwise, the only mechanisms for alleviating the cream-skimming problem is to calibrate the value of vouchers by class of displaced worker (or for longer-term training to mitigate these effects through income-contingent loans), or to regulate closely admissions policies for classroom and on-the-job training programs by compelling mandatory pooling, raising similar problems of regulatory design and enforcement as noted above in connection with primary and secondary education. With respect to health care services, cream-skimming by health care providers is likely to be a severe problem with fixed-value or limited vouchers. Again, calibrating the value of vouchers by reference to the health status of classes of participants would substantially ameliorate, but probably not eliminate the problem; alternatively, admission conditions for joining competing health care plans would need to be tightly regulated in order to effect some form of mandatory pooling. With respect to legal aid, fixed or limited value vouchers will also lead to a problem of cream-skimming, by creating incentives for legal aid lawyers to avoid taking cases of such complexity or contentiousness that the hours and effort required are likely to exceed the cap. While adjusting the value of the voucher in some cases would alleviate this problem, containing countervailing moral hazard problems is likely to be intensive in its demands on administrative resources.

The politics of vouchers

Our book has predominantly been concerned with the normative properties of government by voucher as an *idea* in a wide variety of contexts. However, we have also attempted to address the positive politics of government by voucher in these contexts. It is now over 30 years since Milton Friedman first proposed the voucher concept in the context of primary and secondary school education, but it has yet to gain wide acceptance in this context.[10] In Friedman's view, this is a case where a good idea has been subverted by entrenched special interests, in particular teachers' unions and the educational bureaucracy, whose material self-interest is likely to be adversely affected by a more competitive environment for the provision of educational services.[11] Is it the case that government by voucher is invariably a good idea, but is destined to languish as a result of the disproportionate political influence of vested interests? In this book, we have sought to show that, depending on how various critical design issues are resolved, government by voucher is not an unambiguously good idea in all the service contexts in which it has been proposed. Similarly, we would argue that where it is a good idea, the power of special interests is unlikely to be so overwhelming that, deterministically, it can be assumed that they will always subvert the idea. Thus, in evaluating why government by voucher has not been adopted in various contexts, attention is required both to the soundness of the *idea* and the salience of vested political *interests* in explaining the persistence of prevailing policies and their resilience to change.

With respect to the politics of vouchers, the most important point to be made is that there is no single politics of vouchers.[12] Each programmatic context considered in this study is likely to yield its own particular configuration of political interests favouring or opposing the adoption of voucher schemes. To the extent that generalization is possible, it seems likely that the politics surrounding the introduction of new government expenditure programs through utilization of the voucher concept, in contexts where the government has previously played no or a limited role (e.g. child care, long-term care), will tend to differ from contexts where the government has previously played a major expenditure and delivery role and is contemplating the substitution of a voucher scheme for pre-existing delivery modalities. In the first class of case, groups on the traditional left of the political spectrum may well favour the introduction of voucher systems, while forces on the political right are likely to resist the additional government expenditures required to finance such programs. In the second class of case, forces on the political right may well favour the adoption of voucher schemes, on the grounds of their perceived superior efficiency in terms of the cost and quality of services, while forces on the political left may see such schemes as threatening political interests with whom they identify (e.g. unionized public sector employees). However, while these factors may suggest the general configuration of political interests that one might expect to find arrayed for and against voucher schemes in particular contexts, an evaluation of which set of political forces is likely to prevail requires a context-specific analysis.

Conclusions

To sum up the major implications of our study of government by voucher, in contemplating voucher reforms in the social services sector, policy-makers need to squarely address three constellations of issues – efficiency, equity, and political feasibility. Efficiency largely engages the likely operation of markets for social services within the market paradigm itself. Is such a market likely to be structurally competitive? Is it likely to be affected by serious information asymmetries? Is it likely to generate serious negative social externalities? Can governments identify policies that are likely to mitigate any of these potential forms of market failure that will not themselves induce even more costly market distortions? Equity largely engages the distribution and value of demand-side entitlements. It is important to emphasize that voucher concept itself does not provide any new normative purchase or insights on these issues, and hence there is much to be said in designing voucher systems for taking long-standing patterns of entitlements largely as given or at least not seriously negating or derogating from existing entitlements if the politics of voucher reform are not to be rendered unnecessarily intractable. Political feasibility, for existing programs, engages the political influence and mobilization capacity of incumbent interests, and the countervailing possibilities of mobilizing a relatively common front of typically more diffuse demand-side and new supply-side interests. For new programs (e.g. child care, long-term care for the elderly and disabled), the power of incumbency is a less significant political factor, although citizens themselves may be conflicted as to the fiscal prudence of major new social spending programs, on which voucher proponents will carry a substantial burden of political persuasion.

With respect to these three sets of issues, two clear conclusions emerge from this study. The first is that there is nothing simple or normatively uncontentious in the design of any voucher system, despite the superficially attractive congruence between efficiency and/or equity that proponents of such schemes claim on their behalf. This is not to discount the considerable potential for voucher systems for enhancing the efficiency and/or equity properties of existing arrangements for providing many social services, but rather to argue that better trade-offs rather than happy congruence may be the most we can reasonably aspire to. The second conclusion is that the claim that by invoking the discipline of market-driven exit vouchers offer an escape from the messy and unprincipled compromises of politics and the frailties of voice as a disciplining mechanism is largely an illusion. Under voucher schemes, supply-side interests, especially but not only incumbents, have strong incentives to lobby to maintain or erect restrictions on entry in order to avoid competitive pressures on job security, wages, and benefits, and to argue for unlimited or expansive vouchers. In turn, demand-side interests (demand-side politics have received much less attention than warranted in the voucher literature) with widely divergent understandings of equity (and their own self-interests) will also be conflicted over qualifying suppliers, qualifying consumers, the value of the voucher, extra billing (top ups), opt-out, and cream-skimming. All of these issues will require political resolution. Markets never exist in a state of nature but in an endless and uneasy embrace with politics. It is not clear that "steering" is politically less problematic than "rowing." While the state would have withdrawn from its role as direct provider, its roles as financier and regulator may attract no less political intensity. The American writer H.L. Mencken once remarked, "For every complex problem there is a solution that is neat, plausible, and wrong." Our conclusions as to the prospects for voucher systems attempt to take seriously this cautionary wisdom. Nevertheless, with this caution in mind, avoiding the temptation of easy sloganeering and paying close attention to detailed design issues, we conclude that voucher systems have the potential to revolutionize – generally for the better –

many aspects of the welfare state. We hope that this book will better inform the debates that we predict we will inevitably confront about the role and design of voucher systems in the future welfare state.

Notes

1 Introduction

1 See Albert Hirshman, *Exit, Voice and Loyalty: Responses to Decline in Firms, Organizations and States* (Cambridge, MA: Harvard University Press, 1970).
2 See discussion in Julian Le Grand, *Motivation, Agency and Public Policy* (New York: Oxford University Press, 2003).
3 Arthur Okun, *Equality and Efficiency: The Big Trade-off* (New York: Brookings Institution, 1975).
4 Gordon Cleveland and Susan Colley, "The future of government in supporting early childhood education and care in Ontario," *Report to the Panel on the Role of Government in Ontario* (2003), p. 93.
5 Editorial, "Choice politics," *The Wall Street Journal* (eastern edition) 15 October, 1993.
6 David W. Kirkpatrick, "Teacher unions and educational reform: the view from inside," *Government Union Review* (Vienna, Ca.) 19 (2000) 2, p. 1.
7 "Choice bandwagon," *Wall Street Journal* (eastern edition) January 29, 1999, p. 1.
8 Andrew Coyne, "Vouchers by another name," *National Post* (May 11, 2001), p. A15.
9 Ibid.; Robert Benzie and Les Perreaux, "Rebates spell end to public schools," *National Post* (May 10, 2001), p. A11.
10 Caroline Malan, "Tax aid for private schools under fire," *Toronto Star* (May 11, 2001), p. A1.
11 Tom Blackwell, "Watchdog fears racist schools in Ontario: tax credit opens door to 'ghettoizing' education," *Ottawa Citizen* (May 18, 2001), p. A5.
12 Rebort Benzie, "Opposition predicts exodus from public schools: tax credits are not US-style vouchers, Flaherty says," *National Post* (May 11, 2001), p. A6.
13 Sarah Lyall, "Europe weighs the unthinkable: high college fees," *New York Times* (December 25, 2003), p. A3.
14 Innes Willox, "Minister says full fees were unis' idea," *The Age (Melbourne)* (April 9, 1997), 7; Margalit Edelman, "Blair falling on sword of education reform?" *Christian Science Monitor* (January 26, 2004), p. 9.
15 Luke Slattery, "Student anger over university fees is deep, broad and here to stay," *The Australian* (April 11, 1997), p. 13.
16 Ibid.
17 Guy Healy, "NTEU generals chart striking battle campaign," *The Australian* (October 8, 1997), p. 27.
18 Aisha Labi, "Blair government proposes raising tuition, angering many in Britain," *Chronicle of Higher Education* (January 23, 2004).
19 "Less drama please," *The Economist* (January 29, 2004).
20 Amy Goldstein, "Bush's housing policy proposal," *Washington Post* (April 16, 2003), p. D3. Under the program, beneficiaries are expected to contribute no more than 30 percent of their income to rent, and the federal government through 2,600

regional and local housing agencies will pay the difference between this amount and market rents.

21   "Cuomo: HUD budget an 'historic victory'," *US Newswire* (October 21, 1998), 1.

22   William Raspberry, "Transforming public housing, a pit of despair," *The Record* (June 10, 1998), p. A13.

23   Kevin Diaz, "Once-heralded deal to demolish projects now faces criticism," *Star Tribune* (August 15, 1999), p. A1.

24   Ibid.

25   Erin J. Aubry, "Housing vouchers draw tenants' fire," *Los Angeles Times* (February 19, 1995), p. 10.

26   Julia Neuberger, "Welcome them: the asylum bill is unfair," *The Guardian* (November 9, 1999), p. 19; BBC News, "Asylum voucher sparks protest," *BBC News* (April 3, 2000).

27   Jeremy Hardy, "Bedpan humour," *The Guardian* (July 29, 2000), p. 16.

28   BBC News, *supra* note 26.

29   Alan Travis and Patrick Wintour, "Jay attacks union chief in asylum row," *The Guardian* (April 15, 2000), p. 1.

30   Richard Ford, "Blunkett row over Asian arranged marriages," *The Times* (February 8, 2002), p. 1.

31   Vernellia R. Randall, "Does Clinton's health care reform proposal ensure [e]qual[ity] of health care for ethnic Americans and the poor?" *Brooklyn Law Review*, 60 (1994).

32   Ibid.

33   Ibid.

34   David Rogers and Hilary Stout, "'Single-payer' concept for health-care plan is alive and well despite downgrading by Clinton," *Wall Street Journal* (eastern edition) December 31, 1993. See also: David. Rogers, "Pressured by the right, GOP moderate Chafee clings to Clinton's goal of universal health care," *Wall Street Journal* (eastern edition) March 3, 1994.

35   Rick Wartzman, "Advertising war over health reform heats up, with confused Americans caught in crossfire," *Wall Street Journal* (eastern edition) July15 , 1994; Cyndee Miller, "Ads are huge weapons in the battle of health care reform," *Marketing News* (Chicago) 28 (September12 , 1994), 19, pp. 1–3.

36   "Prognosis, poor: vocal lobby groups stall President Clinton's bid to offer affordable health insurance," *Maclean's* (Toronto) 107 (March 14, 1994), 11, p. 20.

37   Michael E. DeBakey, "Health care: report from the trenches: prescription for disaster," *Wall Street Journal* (eastern edition) June 23, 1994.

38   *Supra* note 9.

39   Robert J. Blendon, John Marttila, John M. Benson, Matthew C. Shelter *et al.*, "The beliefs and values shaping today's health reform debate," *Health Affairs* (Chevy Chase) 13 (Spring 1994) 1, p. 274.

40   Ibid.

41   "However it may be ignored or camouflaged, I believe that redistribution is at the heart of the health care debate. The concept of insurance, particularly health insurance, involves the sharing of common risk. Major health care reform inevitably will require a significant degree of personal and political commitment to sharing resources. So the ultimate issue may be whether after a decade of focusing on self-interest the voting public and their elected officials are willing to sacrifice and share enough to assure health coverage for all Americans. The polls remain open on this." Edward G. Grossman, "Comparing the options for universal coverage," *Health Affairs* (Chevy Chase) 13 (Spring 1994) 2, p. 84.

42   Milton Friedman, "The role of government in education," in R.A. Solo (ed.) *Economics and the Public Interest* (New Brunswick, NJ: Rutgers University Press, 1955).

43   Doug Owram, "Economic thought in the 1930s: the prelude to Keynesianism," in Raymond B. Blake and Jeff Keshen (eds) *Social Welfare Policy in Canada: Historical Readings* (Toronto: Copp Clark, 1995), p. 178.

44   T.H. Marshall, *Social Policy in the Twentieth Century*, 4th edn (London: Hutchinson, 1975), p. 25.

45   T.H. Marshall (ed.) *Citizenship and Social Class and Other Essays* (Cambridge: Cambridge University Press, 1950), p. 24.

46   Marshall, *supra* note 44, p. 26. With regards to Germany, see Christoph Butterwegge, *Wohlfahrtsstaat im Wandel: Probleme under Perspektiven der Sozialpolitik*, 2nd edn (Opladen: Leske u. Budrich, 1999), p. 24; Hans Pohl (ed.), "Einführung," *Staatliche, städtische, betriebliche und kirchliche Sozialpolitik vom Mittelalter bis zur Gegenwart* (VSWG.-B. 95) (Stuttgart: Franz Steiner Verlag, 1989), p. 19; and Heinz Lampert, *Sozialpolitik, I: staatliche*, in Willi Albers *et al.* (eds) *Handwörterbuch der Wirtschaftswissenschaft*, vol. 7 (Stuttgart: Vandenhoeck and Ruprecht, 1977–83), p. 73. With regards to France, see Timothy B. Smith, *Creating the Welfare State in France, 1880–1940* (Montreal and Kingston, Ontario: McGill-Queen's University Press, 2003).

47   Christian Marzahn, "Das Zucht- und Arbeitshaus. Die Kerninstitution frühbürger-licher Sozialpolitik," in Christian Marzahn and Hans-Günther Ritz (eds) *Zähmen und Bewahren. Die Anfänge bürgerlicher Sozialpolitik* (Bielefeld: AJZ, 1984), p. 67. Quoted in Christoph Butterwegge, *Wohlfahrtsstaat im Wandel*, p. 25.

48   Albert Weale, "Equality, social solidarity and the welfare state," *Ethics*, 100 (1990), p. 477.

49   Marshall, *supra* note 44, p. 23.

50   *Historical Statistics of the United States, Colonial Times to 1970*, Bicentennial edn, Bureau of the Census, Department of Commerce (Washington, DC: US Government Printing Office, 1975), part 2, p. 1140, series Y. Quoted in Theda Skocpol, "America's first social security system: the expansion of benefits for Civil War veterans," in Skocpol, *Social Policy in the United States*, p. 42, n. 16.

51   Skocpol, ibid., p. 37, with statistics from *Report of the Commissioner of Pensions* in *Reports of the Department of the Interior for the Fiscal Year Ended June 20, 1910*, vol. 1 (Washington DC: Government Printing Office, 1911), pp. 146, 149; and US Bureau of the Census, *Historical Statistics of the United States*, Bicentennial edn, part 1 (Washington, DC: Government Printing Office, 1975), 15, series A, p. 133.

52   Skocpol, ibid., p. 44.

53   Marshall, *supra* note 44, p. 83.

54   David A. Moss, *When All Else Fails: Government as Ultimate Risk Manager* (Cambridge, MA: Cambridge University Press, 2002); Andrew Green, "The evolution of government as risk manager in Canada," Panel on the Role of Government Research Paper Series, RP(4), October 2002.

55   Kenneth F. Arrow, "Uncertainty and the welfare economics of medical care," *American Economic Review*, 53 (1963), pp. 941–73; and Kenneth J. Arrow and Robert C. Lind, "Uncertainty and the evaluation of public investment decisions," *American Economic Review*, 60(3) (1970). For a good overview of the economics of insurance, see Nicholas Barr, *The Economics of the Welfare State*, 3rd edn (Stanford, CA: Stanford University Press, 1998), chap. 5.

56   For studies on misperception of risk, see Daniel Ellsberg, "Risk, ambiguity, and the savage axioms," *Quarterly Journal of Economics*, 75(4) (1961), 643; Paul J.H. Schoemaker, "The expected utility model: its variants, purpose, evidence, and limitations," *Journal of Economic Literature*, 20(2) (1982); Jens Beckert, "What is sociological about economic sociology? Uncertainty and the embeddedness of economic action," *Theory and Society*, 25(6) (1996), p. 802. An insightful paper by George A. Akerlof and Janet L. Yellen, "Rational models of irrational behavior," *American Economic Review*, 77(2) (1987); Papers and Proceedings, deals with how human decision-making, far from being scientific, depends on simple "shorthand" heuristic devices that can often lead to predictable biases. On this latter point, see also Amos Tversky and Daniel Kahneman, "Judgment and uncertainty: heuristics and biases," *Science*, 185 (1974), p. 1124; Ola Svenson, "Are we all less risky and more skillful than our fellow drivers?,"

Acta Psychologica, 47 (1981), p. 143; Neil D. Weinstein, "Why it won't happen to me: perceptions of risk factors and susceptibility," *Health Psychology*, 3(5) (1984), p. 431; A.J. Rothman, W.M. Klein, and N.D. Weinstein, "Absolute and relative biases in estimations of personal risk," *Journal of Applied Social Psychology*, 26(14) (1996), p. 1213; Neil D. Weinstein, "Unrealistic optimism about susceptibility to health problems: conclusions from a community-wide sample," *Journal of Behavioural Medicine*, 10(5) (1987), p. 481.

57 Cass R. Sunstein and Richard H. Thaler, "Libertarian paternalism is not an oxymoron," AEI-Brookings Joint Center for Regulatory Studies, Working Paper No. 03–02, available on the Social Science Research Network Electronic Paper Collection at http://ssrn.com/abstract_id=405940. See also Christine Jolls, Cass R. Sunstein and Richard Thaler, "A behavioural approach to law and economics," *Stanford Law Review*, 50 (1997–8), p. 1471.

58 Doug Owram, "Economic thought in the 1930s," in Blake and Keshen (eds) *Social Welfare Policy in Canada*, see note 43.

59 For the classical view that considered the economy as naturally tending towards equilibrium, see Alfred Marshall, *Principles of Economics, an Introductory Volume*, 8th edn (London: Macmillan, 1927). See also W.C. Clark, "Business cycles and the depression of 1920–1," *Queen's University Bulletin of the Departments of History and Political and Economic Science*, 40 (August, 1921); and Wesley Mitchell, *Business Cycles: The Problem and its Setting*, National Bureau of Economic Research Series, General Series, vol. 10 (New York: National Bureau of Economic Research, 1928).

60 See for instance, O.D. Skelton, "Current events," *Queen's Quarterly*, 16(4) (April, 1909); Bryce Stewart, "The problem of unemployment," *Social Welfare*, 3(8) (March 1921); and J.B. Alexander, "Business depressions," *Canadian Bankers*, 34(4) (July, 1927).

61 Marshall, *supra* note 44, p. 79.

62 T.H. Marshall, "Citizenship and social class," in T.H. Marshall (ed.) *Citizenship and Social Class and Other Essays* (Cambridge: Cambridge University Press, 1950), p. 43.

63 Marshall, *Citizenship and Social Class*, p. 47.

64 Ibid., p. 14.

65 Howard Glennerster, *British Social Policy Since 1945* (Oxford: Blackwell, 1995), pp. 35–8.

66 *Beveridge Report*, p. 6.

2   The case for vouchers

1 Hart, O., Shleifer, A. and Vishny, R., "The proper scope of government: theory and an application to prisons," *Quarterly Journal of Economics* (November, 1997), pp. 1127–8.

2 Milton Friedman, *Capitalism and Freedom* (Chicago, IL: University of Chicago Press, 1962), ch. 6, pp. 85–107.

3 Mark Blaug, "Education vouchers – it all depends on what you mean," in J. Le Grand and R. Robinson (eds) *Privatisation and the Welfare State* (London: Allen & Unwin, 1984) p. 160.

4 Wiseman, J., "The economics of education," *Scottish Journal of Political Economy*, 6(1) (1959), pp. 48–58. Reprinted in Blaug, Mark (ed.) *Economics of Education 2* (Middlesex: Penguin, 1969) pp. 360–72.

5 Blaug, 1984, p. 160.

6 Ibid.

7 Bradford, D.F. and Shaviro, D.N., "Economics of vouchers," in Steuerle, Ooms, Peterson and Reischauer (eds) *Vouchers and the Provision of Public Services* (Washington, DC: Brookings Institution Press, 2000), p. 43.

8 Blaug, 1984, p. 164.

9 Barr, Nicholas, *The Economics of the Welfare State*, 3rd edn (Stanford: Stanford University Press, 1998), pp. 347–8; see also Barr, p. 96 (reproduced in Table 2.1, this volume).

10 Bradford and Shaviro, p. 45.

11 Bridge, Gary, "Citizen choice in public services: voucher systems," in Emanuel Savas (ed.) *Alternatives for Delivering Public Services* (Boulder, CO: Westview Press, 1977), p. 54.

12 Osbourne, D. and Gaebler, T., *Reinventing Government* (Reading: Addison Wesley, 1992), p. xxi.

13 Ibid.

14 Andrei Shleifer, "State versus private ownership," *The Journal of Economic Perspectives*, 12(4) (Autumn, 1998), p. 148.

15 See Le Grand and Estrin, especially "An equitarian market socialism," by Peter Abell, pp. 78–99.

16 Martha Minow, "Public and private partnerships: accounting for the new religion," *Harvard Law Review*, 116 (March, 2003).

17 Ronald A. Cass, "Privatization: politics, law, and theory," *Marquette Law Review*, 71(449) (1988), p. 488.

18 See, for instance, Alan Walker "The political economy of privatisation," in J. Le Grand and R. Robinson (eds) *Privatisation and the Welfare State* (London: Allen & Unwin, 1984), pp. 19–44; and, more recently, Martha Minow, "Public and private partnerships: accounting for the new religion," *Harvard Law Review*, 116 (2003), p. 1229. For a response to Prof. Minow's article, see also M. Trebilcock and E. Iacobucci, "Privatization and accountability," *Harvard Law Review*, 116(5) (2003), pp. 1422–53.

19 Hart *et al.*, *supra* note 1.

20 See Michael J. Trebilcock, *The Prospects of Reinventing Government* (Toronto: CD Howe Institute, 1994), pp. 7–8; Michael Jensen and William Meckling, "Theory of the firm: managerial behavior, agency costs, and ownership structure," *Journal of Financial Economics*, 3 (1976), p. 305; and Michael Jensen and Clifford Smith, "Stockholder, manager, and creditor interests: applications of agency theory," in Edward Altman and Martin Subrahmanyan (eds) *Recent Advances in Corporate Finance* (Homewood, IL: Richard D. Irwin, 1985), p. 38.

21 Friedman, pp. 1–36.

22 Trebilcock, p. 8; Jensen and Smith, "Stockholder," p. 38.

23 Trebilcock, p. 8.

24 Trebilcock, pp. 9–10.

25 Minow, p. 1270; see also Martha Minow, *Partners, Not Rivals: Privatization and the Public Good* (Boston, MA: Beacon Press, 2002), especially pp. 150–6.

26 Trebilcock and Iacobucci, p. 1449.

27 Jody Freeman, "Extending public law norms through privatization," *Harvard Law Review*, 116(5) (March, 2003), p. 1285.

28 Situations where funds are allocated by a different jurisdiction than the one which actually contracts for services can create further contractual complications. In Canada, for instance, a large portion of health care funding takes the form of transfer payments from the federal government to the provincial health ministries, and conflicts often arise over how much control the federal authorities should be able to exercise over the funding decisions of individual provinces. In this case, concerns about federalism and regional sovereignty create another array of principal-agent problems..

29 Trebilcock and Iacobucci, p. 1426.

30 Trebilcock and Iacobucci, pp. 1427–8.

31 Trebilcock and Iacobucci, p. 1427; Trebilcock, p. 11.

32 Stiglitz, Joseph E., *Economics of the Public Sector*, 3rd edn (New York: Norton, 2000), p. 80; for a more general discussion of market failure due to incomplete markets, see pp. 76–85; see also Harvey Rosen, *Public Finance* (Homewood, IL: Richard D. Irwin, 1985), pp. 60–3; and Barr, pp. 80–3.

33 Stiglitz, p. 205; however, for a more qualified account, including a discussion of some of the putative managerial advantages of direct government, see Christopher Leman, "Direct government," in L. Salamon (ed.) *The Tools of Government: A Guide to the New Governance* (Oxford: Oxford University Press, 2002), pp. 48–79.

34 Stiglitz, pp. 208–9.

35 Evan Davis, *Public Spending* (London: Penguin, 1998) furnishes a commonsensical preliminary discussion of the economic advantages and potential drawbacks of contracting-out; see especially pp. 208–31.

36 Hrab, Roy, *Privatization: Experiences and Prospects*, Ontario Panel on the Role of Government, University of Toronto Faculty of Law (2003), p. 8. See also J.S. Vickers and G.K. Yarrow, *Privatization: An Economic Analysis* (Cambridge: MIT Press, 1988).

37 Shleifer, p. 137.

38 Megginson, W.L. and Netter, J.M., "From state to market: a survey of empirical studies on privatization," *Journal of Economic Literature*, 39 (2001), p. 331.

39 Trebilcock and Iacobucci, *supra* note 18, p. 1428.

40 Ibid., p. 1429.

41 Hrab, p. 5.

42 Hart, Shleifer and Vishny, *supra* note 1, p. 1128.

43 Trebilcock, p. 15; Oliver Williamson, "The logic of economic organization," *Journal of Law, Economics and Organization*, 4 (1988), p. 77.

44 Hart *et al.*, p. 1128; see also John Donahue, *The Privatization Decision: Public Ends, Private Means* (New York: Basic Books, 1989), pp. 79–98.

45 Stiglitz, pp. 190–7.

46 Williamson, Oliver, *The Economic Institutions of Capitalism* (New York: Free Press, 1985), chap. 13.

47 Demsetz, Harold, "Why regulate utilities?," *Journal of Law and Economics*, 11 (1968), p. 55.

48 Chapter 3 of this volume discusses the cash equivalence of food stamp programmes in more detail. See also Robert A. Moffitt, "Lessons from the food stamp program," in Steuerle *et al.*, pp. 131–5.

49 Mill, John Stuart, "On liberty," in Robert M. Stewart (ed.) *Readings in Political and Social Philosophy* (New York: Oxford University Press, 1996), p. 126.

50 Friedman, p. 178.

51 Yale University Press, 1999.

52 John Richards, *Retooling the Welfare State* (Toronto: C.D. Howe Institute, 1997), p. 257 contends that ALMPs are merely synonymous with "workfare" and "tough love" measures; however, we favour an expanded definition of ALMPs as programmes which tie the receipt of benefits to participation in direct employment, education and placement programmes which aim to reintegrate underemployed persons into the labour market and to increase the incentive for and access to gainful employment as opposed to reliance on income transfers as a principal source of revenue.

53 Richards, p. 258.

54 Richards, p. 261.

55 Richards, *op. cit.*

56 Albert Hirshman, *Exit, Voice and Loyalty* (Cambridge, MA: Harvard University Press, 1970).

57 Bradford and Shaviro, *op. cit.*

58 Bradford and Shaviro, *op. cit.*

59 "Experience goods" are goods whose full attributes are only revealed by usage; "credence goods" are goods whose attributes are never fully observable by the user and entail reliance on the supplier's claims about them; search goods are those whose attributes are fully observable on prior inspection: see Phillip Nelson, "Advertising and information," *Journal of Political Economy*, 82 (1974), p. 729; Nelson, "Information and consumer bahavior," *Journal of Political Economy*, 78 (1970), p. 311.

60   The specific problem of supply-side market inelasticity is discussed in greater detail in Chapter 4.

61   For a detailed study of the interplay of interests and norms, see Graham Mayeda, "Who's calling the shots? Balancing the role of norms and interests through a historical approach to the process of social policy formation," unpublished manuscript (2002).

62   Nicholas Mercuro and Steven G. Medema, *Economics and the Law: From Posner to Postmodernism* (Princeton, NJ: Princeton University Press, 1997), p. 88. See also James D. Gwartney and Richard E. Wagner, "Public choice and the conduct of representative government," in James D. Gwartney and Richard E. Wagner (eds) *Public Choice and Constitutional Economics* (Greenwich, CT: JAI Press, 1988), p. 7.

63   Michael J. Trebilcock, Douglas G. Hartle, J. Robert S. Prichard and Donald N. Dewees, *The Choice of Governing Instrument* (Ottawa: Minister of Supply and Services Canada, 1982), pp. 15–17.

64   Mercuro and Medema, *Economics and the Law*, pp. 91–4; Trebilcock *et al.*, *Choice of Governing Instrument*, pp. 10–17.

65   Nicholas Barr, *The Economics of the Welfare State*, 3rd edn (Stanford, CA: Stanford University Press, 1998), pp. 89–90.

66   Steven Kelman, "A case for in-kind transfers," *Economics and Philosophy*, 2 (1986), p. 55.

67   Gøsta Esping-Andersen, *The Three Worlds of Welfare-state Capitalism* (Cambridge: Polity Press, 1990), p. 15.

68   Esping-Andersen, *Three Worlds of Welfare State Capitalism*, pp. 17–18. For a fuller explanation of the class-coalition theses, see M. Weir and Theda Skocpol, "State structures and the possibilities for 'Keynesian' responses to the Great Depression in Sweden, Britain, and the United States," in P. Evans, P. Rushemayer and T. Skocpol (eds) *Bringing the State Back In* (New York: Cambridge University Press); P. Gourevitch, *Politics in Hard Times* (Ithaca, NY: Cornell University Press, 1986); G. Esping-Andersen, *Politics Against Markets* (Princeton, NJ: Princeton University Press, 1985); G. Esping-Andersen and R. Friedland, "Class coalitions in the making of West European economies," *Political Power and Social Theory*, 3 (1982).

69   Gary S. Becker, "A theory of competition among pressure groups for political influence," *The Quarterly Journal of Economics*, 98 (1983), p. 371.

70   Clifford Winston, "Economic deregulation: Days of reckoning for microeconomists," *Journal of Economic Literature*, 41 (1993), pp. 1263, 1267. Winston points out that "[a]ccording to Peltzman (1989), the implications of the Chicago theory are that compact, well-organized groups (frequently but not always producers) will tend to preserve a politically optimal distribution of rents across this coalition of well-organized groups," p. 1267; see also Sam Peltzman, "The economic theory of regulation after a decade of deregulation," *Brookings Pap. Econ. Act.: Microeconomics* (1989), p. 1.

71   See John Rawls, *Political Liberalism* (New York: Columbia University Press, 1993), p. 47ff. for a discussion of the contrast between rationality and reasonableness. See also Jürgen Habermas, *Between Facts and Norms* (Cambridge, MA: MIT Press, 1996; originally published in 1992 by Suhrkamp as *Faktizität und Geltung.Beiträge zur Diskurstheorie des Rechts und des demokratischen Rechtsstaats*), in which he explains that politically binding decisions, because they are made in the interests of the public, must have reference back to the discourse of rights: "The constitutionally organized political system is … specialized for generating collectively binding decisions. […] [I]n virtue of its internal relation to law, politics is responsible for problems that concern society as a whole. It must be possible to interpret collectively binding decisions as a realization of rights such that the structures of recognition built into communicative action are transferred, via the medium of law, from the level of simple interactions to the abstract and anonymous relationships among strangers," p. 385.

72 Michael Trebilcock, "The choice of governing instrument: a retrospective," forthcoming, p. 5.
73 Ninette Kelley and Michael Trebilcock, *The Making of the Mosaic: A History of Canadian Immigration Policy* (Toronto: University of Toronto Press, 1998), p. 9.

3 Food stamps

1   Super, D. and Lewis, C., "Introduction to the Food Stamp Program," *Clearinghouse Review* (November, 1991), p. 905.
2   Kuhn, B., Dunn, P.A., Smallwood, D., Hanson, K., Blaylock, J. and Vogel, S., "Policy watch: the Food Stamp Program and welfare reform," *Journal of Economic Perspectives*, 10(2) (Spring, 1996), p. 191.
3   Though it is true that some sub-groups receive proportionally more benefit from the program than others, it is the over-representation of these sub-groups in the low-income category that explains this outcome and not a particular targeting practice of the program.
4   Christina Tuttle, of Mathematica Policy Research, Inc., for the USDA Office of Analysis, Nutrition and Evaluation, "Characteristics of food stamp households: fiscal year 2001" (July, 2001), available at: http://www.mathematica-mpr.com.
5   Robert Moffitt, "Lessons from the food stamp program," in Steuerle *et al.* (eds) *Vouchers and the Provision of Public Services* (Washington, DC: Brookings Institution Press, 2000), p. 119.
6   Ibid.
7   Butler, J.S. and Raymond, J.E., "The effect of the food stamp program on nutrient intake," *Economic Inquiry*, 34 (October, 1996), p. 78.
8   Kohrs, Czajka-Nairns, Davis and Guthrie, cited in Butler and Raymond, *supra* note 7, p. 784.
9   Basiotis, P., Kramer-LeBlanc, C. and Kennedy, E., "Maintaining nutrition security and diet quality: the role of the Food Stamp Program and WIC," *Family Economics and Nutrition Review*, 11(1) (1998), p. 12.
10 Ibid.
11 Douglas Besharov, *Washington Post* (December 8, 2002), p. B01.
12 Basiotis *et al.*, *supra* note 9.
13 Peter K. Eisinger, *Toward An End To Hunger In America* (Washington, DC: Brookings Institution Press, 1998), p. 42.
14 Ibid.
15 Ibid., p. 41.
16 Moffitt, *supra* note 5, p. 3. The program served approximately 4 million persons annually.
17 Eisinger, *supra* note 13, p. 3.
18 Ibid., p. 39.
19 Ibid., pp. 4–5.
20 Ibid., p. 43.
21 This section draws substantially on James Ohls and Harold Beebout, *The Food Stamp Program: Design Tradeoffs, Policy, and Impacts* (Urban Insitute, 1993), Robert Moffit's "Lessons from the Food Stamp Program" (*supra* note 5) as well as the USDA Food and Nutrition Service, "A Short History of the Food Stamp Program," available at: http://www.fns.usda.gov/fsp/rules/Legislation/history.htm.
22 USDA. *supra* note 21.
23 Ibid.
24 Ibid.
25 Ibid.

26 Bolen, E., "A poor measure of the wrong thing: the food stamp program's quality control system discourages participation by working families," *Hastings Law Journal*, 53 (November, 2001), pp. 213–41.

27 For a comprehensive historical account, see Maurice MacDonald, *Food, Stamps, and Income Maintenance* (New York: Academic Press, 1977).

28 The term paternalism often carries negative connotations (i.e. restricting autonomy and choice of the beneficiary). However, if we interpret efficiency in its broadest sense, looking at both those subsidized and those who are subsidizers, then paternalism may actually move towards efficiency. Paternalistic actions can be characterized as efforts "to target specific needs and adopt the most efficient method of achieving an equity goal." See C. Eugene Steuerle, "Common issues for voucher programs," in Steurle *et al.* (*supra* note 5, pp. 3–39) for such an argument.

29 USDA, *supra* note 21.

30 Simple cost-benefit analysis would dictate that the government adopt the policy which minimizes costs. For example, if the cost to decrease fraud is more than the loss from fraud, the economically prudent solution is to ignore the practice.

31 Critics of welfare payments invariably use such extreme illustrations in order to draw attention to welfare abuse.

32 Robert Moffitt, "Incentive effects of the US welfare system: a review," *Journal of Economic Literature*, 30(1) (March, 1992), p. 14.

33 Ibid.

34 Ibid.

35 This is of course assuming there are no illicit activities such as selling stamps for other goods or cash.

36 Although an argument can be made that the consumption of food does not necessarily mean the consumption of healthy food. The consumer is free to consume non-nutritious items.

37 Breunig, R., Dasgupta, I., Gundersen, C. and Pattanaik, P., *Explaining the Food Stamp Cash-Out Puzzle* (April, 2001), p. 1, available at: http://www.ers.usda.gov. Document ID 'fanrr12'.

38 For a representative characterization of this model, see especially Southworth, H., "The economics of public measures to subsidize food," *Journal of Farm Economics*, 68(1) (1945), pp. 37–43.

39 For complete discussion on the extent to which vouchers are cash-equivalent see David F. Bradford and Daniel Shaviro, "The economics of vouchers," in C. Eugene Steuerle, Van Doorn Ooms, George Peterson and Robert D. Reischauer (eds) *Vouchers and the Provision of Public Services* (Washington, DC: Brookings Institution Press, CED, Urban Institute Press, 2000), pp. 53–54.

40 Kuhn, *supra* note 2, p. 193.

41 Ibid., p. 194.

42 Breunig *et al.*, *supra* note 37.

43 World Bank Policy Research Report, *Assessing Aid: What Works, What Doesn't, and Why* (New York: Oxford University Press, 1998), p. 62.

44 Fraker, T., *The Effects of Food Stamps on Food Consumption: A Review of the Literature*, USDA Food and Nutrition Service, available at: http://www.mathematica-mpr.com.

45 Ibid.

46 Bishop, J.A., Formby, J.P. and Zeager, L.A., "The effect of food stamp cashout on undernutrition," *Economics Letters*, 67 (2000), p. 84.

47 Breunig *et al.*, *supra* note 37, p. iii.

48 Ibid., p. 4.

49 Tuttle, *supra* note 4, p. 5.

50 Ibid., p. 3.

51 Ibid., p. 2.

52 Ibid.

53 Although we choose not to engage in a lengthy discussion of the precise definition of "food inadequacy" – for our purposes, we assume that the level of food inadequacy increases as the wealth of a household decreases – Eisinger, *supra* note 13, pp. 11–20, provides an excellent analysis of the definitional problems with words such as hunger and food inadequacy.

54 Within the Temporary Assistance to Needy Families (TANF) legislation, there exists a provision that food stamps will be terminated after an aggregate of three months of assistance in any 36-month period for individuals falling in the age bracket of 18–50 who are not disabled, raising children, working at least 20 hours a week, or participating in job training programs.

55 Moffitt, *supra* note 32, pp. 1–3. See also Moffitt, R. and Kehrer, K., "The effect of tax and transfer programs on labor supply: the evidence from the income maintenance experiments," in Ronald Ehrenberg (ed.) *Research in Labor Economics*, vol. 4 (Greenwich, CT: JAI Press, 1981), pp. 103–50.

56 Moffitt, *supra* note 32.

57 Richard D. Coe, "Nonparticipation in the welfare programs by eligible households: the case of the food stamp program," *Journal of Economic Issues*, 17 (December, 1983), p. 1036.

58 Marlene Kim and Thanos Mergoupis, "The working poor and welfare recipiency: participation, evidence, and policy directions," *Journal of Economic Issues*, 31(3) (September, 1997), p. 708.

59 Eisinger, *supra* note 13, p. 50.

60 Ibid., p. 52.

61 Coe, *supra* note 57, p. 1038.

62 Eisinger, *supra* note 13, p. 52.

63 Ibid.

64 Ibid.

65 Moffitt, *supra* note 5, p. 126.

66 Ibid.

67 These comments regarding trafficking are based on Moffitt, ibid.

68 Daniel S. Hamermesh and James M. Johannes, "Food stamps as money: the macroeconomics of a transfer program," *Journal of Political Economy*, 93(1), p. 206.

69 Ibid.

70 Kuhn, *supra* note 2, p. 195.

71 Ibid., p. 190.

72 A verbal formula is:
Value of food stamps = Cost of nutritionally adequate low-cost diet – 0.30 (net income)
The cost of nutritionally adequate low-cost diet = f(size of family).

73 Kuhn, *supra* note 2, p. 190.

74 Ibid. In 1993, the average monthly benefit per participant was $68 (Kuhn, *supra* note 191).

75 Tuttle, *supra* note 4.

4 Low-income housing

1 See e.g., Toronto Disaster Relief Committee, *Homelessness in Toronto-State of Emergency Declaration: An Urgent Call for Emergency Humanitarian Relief and Prevention Measures* (Toronto: Toronto Disaster Relief Committee, 1998).

2 C. Theodore Koebel, "Housing conditions of low-income families in the private, unassisted housing market in the United States," *Housing Studies*, 12(2) (1997), p. 201.

3 Ibid.

4   McCrone, G. and Stephens, M., *Housing Policy in Britain and Europe* (London: UCL Press, 1995).

5   Pete Malpass, "Housing tenure and affordability: the British disease," in G. Hallett (ed.) *The New Housing Shortage* (London: Routledge, 1993), p. 68.

6   Howenstine, E.J., "The new housing shortage: the problem of housing affordability in the United States," in G. Hallett, *supra* note 5, p. 25.

7   Ibid.

8   Ibid., pp. 25–6.

9   van Weesep, J. and van Kempen, R., "Low income and housing in the Dutch welfare state," in G. Hallett, *supra* note 5, pp. 179–206.

10   Shlomi Feiner, "Getting our housing in order: the privatization of public housing in Ontario," Centre for the Study of State and Market WPS #35 (Toronto: University of Toronto, 1997), pp. 6–7.

11   "Taking responsibility for homelessness: an action plan for Toronto" (January, 1999) Report of the Mayor's Homelessness Action Task Force, 56 [hereinafter the Golden Report].

12   Micheal E. Stone, *Shelter Poverty: New Ideas on Housing Affordability* (Philadelphia, PA: Temple University Press, 1993), p. 2.

13   See, for instance, Materu, J.S., "Housing for low-income groups: beyond the sites-and-services model in Tanzania," *Ekistics*, 61(366–7) (May–August, 1994), pp. 223–31; Sivam, A. and Karuppannan, S., "Role of state and market in housing delivery for low-income groups in India," *Journal of Housing and the Built Environment*, 17 (2002), pp. 69–88.

14   *The Japan Almanac 2001* (Tokyo: Asahi Shimbun, 2001).

15   Ontario Affordable Housing Program Queen's Printer for Ontario, 2002, p. 4.

16   McCrone and Stephens *supra* note 4, p. 14.

17   Materu *supra* note 13, p. 223.

18   While it is certainly possible to make the case that housing investment also constitutes a means of regulating public morality and of insuring individual risk, such arguments are seldom advanced or influential, and hence will not be examined in detail here.

19   For a comprehensive theoretical discussion of the relationships between civic engagement and social solidarity, see James Coleman's influential "Social capital in the creation of human capital," *American Journal of Sociology*, 94 (1988), pp. 95–120, as well as his *The Foundations of Social Theory* (Cambridge, MA: Harvard University Press, 1990), pp. 300–21. A more recent discussion of civic engagement and American political life is found in Robert Putnam, "The prosperous community: social capital and public life," *American Prospect*, 13 (1993), pp. 35–42; "Bowling alone," *Journal of Democracy*, 6(1) (January, 1995), pp. 65–78; and in his more recent book *Bowling Alone: The Collapse and Revival of American Community* (New York: Simon & Schuster, 2000). See also Alexis de Tocqueville's classic, *Democracy in America* (Maier, J.P., ed.; Lawrence, G., trans.) (Garden City, NY: Anchor Books, 1969), especially pp. 513–17. Finally, see also Jane Jacobs, *The Death and Life of Great American Cities* (New York: Random House, 1961).

20   Cohen, L. and Swift, S., "A public health approach to the violence epidemic in the United States," *Environment and Urbanization*, 5(2) (October, 1993), pp. 50–66.

21   Castells, Manuel, *The City and Grass Roots: A Cross-Cultural Theory of Urban Social Movements* (London: Edward Arnold, 1983).

22   Modibo Coulibaly, Rodney D. Green and David M. James, *Segregation in Federally Subsidized Low-income Housing in the United States* (Westport, CT: Praeger, 1998), pp. 112–13.

23   Ibid., p.113. Of the 7,073 projects indicated, 15 percent housed only one racial group. In 1,010, blacks were the only tenants, while 789 were exclusively white.

24   *Gautreaux v. Chicago Housing Authority*, 296 F. Supp. 907, 915 (N.D. Ill., 1969).

25 Seliga, J., "Comment: 'Gautreaux' a generation later: remedying the second ghetto or creating the third?," *Northwestern University Law Review*, 94(3) (2000).

26 HABITAT (United Nations Centre for Human Settlements) *An Urbanizing World: Global Report on Human Settlements 1996* (London: Oxford University Press, 1996), p. 106.

27 Ibid., p.107.

28 Pugh, Cedric, "The role of the World Bank in housing," in B. Aldrich and R. Sandhu (eds) *Housing the Poor: Policy and Practice in Developing Countries* (London: Zed, 1995).

29 HABITAT, *supra* note 26, p. 109.

30 Ibid.

31 International Centre for the Prevention of Crime (ICPC), Workshop on Urban Violence, 9th UN Congress on Crime Prevention, Cairo, February, 1995.

32 Robert Chambers, "Editiorial introduction: vulnerability, coping and policy," in *Vulnerability: How the Poor Cope, IDS Bulletin*, 20(2) (April, 1989), pp. 1–7.

33 HABITAT, *supra* note 26, p. 108.

34 Escobar-Latapí, A. and González de la Rocha, M., "Crisis, restructuring and urban poverty in Mexico," *Environment and Urbanization*, 7(1) (April, 1995), pp. 57–75.

35 HABITAT, *supra* note 26, p. 118 (Box 3.6).

36 Materu, *supra* note 13, pp. 223–4; Abrams, C., *Man's Struggle for Shelter in an Urbanizing World* (Cambridge, MA: MIT Press, 1964); Drakakis-Smith, D., *Urbanization, Housing and the Development Process* (London: Croom Helm, 1981); Grimes, O., *Housing for Low-Income Urban Families* (Baltimore, MD: Johns Hopkins University Press, 1976).

37 Ch. 1, p. 12.

38 Ch. 1, p. 12.

39 HABITAT, *supra* note 26, p. xxviii.

40 McCrone and Stephens, *supra* note 4.

41 Ibid., p. 2.

42 Quoted in Howenstine, *supra* note 6, p. 44.

43 Margaret Jane Radin, "Residential rent control," *Philosophy & Public Affairs*, 15 (1985), pp. 350–80. Radin challenges the classic economic assumption of treating housing as an ordinary market commodity. She argues that residential rent control is separated conceptually from price control because there exists a normative distinction between rented residences and other rented and sold commodities.

44 *Universal Declaration of Human Rights*, Article 25.

45 *The Rights Revolution: 2000 CBC Massey Lecture Series* (Toronto: House of Anansi Press, 2000).

46 Hallett, *supra* note 5, p. 2.

47 Balchin, P., "Introduction to social housing," in P. Balchin (ed.) *Housing Policy in Europe* (New York: Routledge, 1996), p. 69.

48 Ibid.

49 Ibid., p. 70.

50 Ibid., p. 73.

51 Ibid., p. 173.

52 Ibid., p. 192.

53 Barlow, J. and Duncan, S., *Success and Failure in Housing Provision: European Systems Compared* (London: Pergamon, 1994), p. 52.

54 Ibid., p. 45.

55 Ibid., p. 53.

56 Ibid., p. 29.

57 Dieneman, Otto, "Housing problems in the former German Democratic Republic and the 'New German States'," in Hallett, *supra* note 5, p. 129.

58 Ibid., p. 137.

59 Ibid.

60 Ibid.

61　Ibid., p. 138.
62　Ibid., p. 139.
63　Bengt Turner, "Sweden," in P. Balchin (ed.) *supra* note 47, p. 107.
64　Agus, Mohammed Razali, "The role of state and market in the Malaysian housing sector," *Journal of Housing and the Built Environment*, 17 (2002), pp. 49–67; Sheng, Yap Kioe, "Housing, the state and the market in Thailand: enabling and enriching the private sector," *Journal of Housing and the Built Environment*, 17 (2002), pp. 33–47; Harris, Richard and Wahba, Malak, "The urban geography of low-income housing: Cairo (1947–96) exemplifies a model," *International Journal of Urban and Regional Planning*, 26(1) (March, 2002), pp. 58–79.
65　McCrone and Stephens, *supra* note 4, p.87.
66　Ibid., p. 139.
67　Tomann, Horst, "Germany," in P. Balchin (ed.) *supra* note 47, p. 54.
68　Ibid., p. 6.
69　Schaefer, Jean-Pierre, "Housing affordability in France," in Hallett, *supra* note 5, pp. 151–78.
70　Ontario Affordable Housing Program, *supra* note 15, p. 6.
71　Malpezzi, Stephen and Vandell, Kerry, "Does the low-income housing tax credit increase the supply of housing?," *Journal of Housing Economics*, 11 (2002), pp. 360–80, p. 361.
72　Malpezzi and Vandell, *supra* note 71, pp. 363–4.
73　Michael Murray, "Subsidized and unsubsidized housing starts: 1961–1977," *Review of Economics and Statistics*, 64 (1983), pp. 590–7; Murray, "Subsidized and unsubsidized housing starts: 1935–1977: crowding out and cointegration," *Journal of Real Estate Finance and Economics*, 18 (1999), pp. 107–24; also William Strange, *The Unintended Consequences of Housing Policy* (Toronto: C.D. Howe Institute, Backgrounder No. 75, September, 2003), p. 3.
74　Malpezzi and Vandell, *supra* note 71, pp. 364–5.
75　Howenstine, *supra* note 6, p. 22.
76　Ibid.
77　Susin, Scott, "Rent vouchers and the price of low-income housing," *Journal of Public Economics*, 83 (2002), pp. 109–52, p. 110.
78　Ibid.
79　Ibid.
80　Peterson, G., "Housing vouchers: the U.S. experience," in C.E. Steuerle, Van Doorn Ooms, G. Peterson, and R.D. Reischauer (eds), *Vouchers and the Provision of Public Services* (Washington, DC: Brookings Institution Press, 2000), p. 154.
81　Seliga, *supra* note 25.
82　Susin, *supra* note 77, p. 110.
83　Susin, *supra* note 77, p. 109.
84　Ibid., p. 145.
85　Ibid., p. 146.
86　Ibid.
87　Ibid., pp. 146–7.
88　Malpezzi and Vandell, *supra* note 71.
89　Stephen Mayo, "Source of inefficiency in public housing programs: a comparison of US and German experience," *Journal of Urban Economics*, 20 (1988), pp. 229–49.
90　Peterson, *supra* note 80, pp. 169–70.
91　Iacobucci, Edward, "Rent control: a proposal for reform," *Ottawa Law Journal*, 27 (1995–6), p. 320.
92　William S. Strange, *The Unintended Consequences of Housing Policy* (Toronto: C.D. Howe Institute, Backgrounder No. 75, September, 2003).
93　Priemus, Hugo, "Housing vouchers: a contribution from abroad," in Steuerle *et al. supra* note 80, p. 191.

5 Legal aid

1 The highly negative consequences that follow from a conviction for even a minor criminal offence suggest that moral hazard in the form of covered individuals engaging in more criminal activity because they are assured of representation would not seem to be a major issue.

2 Legal Action Group, "The Scope of Legal Services," in T. Goriely and A. Paterson (eds) *A Reader on Resourcing Civil Justice* (Oxford: Oxford University Press, 1996) p. 75.

3 Ibid.

4 Griffiths, John, "The distribution of legal services in the Netherlands," in ibid., p. 83.

5 Luban, David, "The right to legal services," in ibid., pp. 39–65.

6 See, for instance, John Rawls, "Justice as fairness," *Philosophical Review*, 67(2) (April, 1958), pp. 164–94, and his "A Kantian conception of equality," *Cambridge Review*, 96(2225) (February, 1975), pp. 94–9.

7 Michael Ignatieff, "Rights, recognition and nationalism," in *The Rights Revolution* (Toronto: House of Anansi Press, 2000), p. 125.

8 This section is largely based on Dyzenhaus, David, "Normative justifications for the provision of legal aid," *Report of the Ontario Legal Aid Review: A Blueprint for Publicly Funded Legal Services, vol. I* (Toronto: Ontario Government, 1997), p. 475.

9 See especially Thomas Hobbes, *The Leviathan* (Chapter 6, §. 140): "[T]he Command of the Common-wealth, is Law only to those, that have means to take notice of it."

10 Legal Services Corporation, "Suggested list of priorities for LSC recipients," *Federal Register*, 61(104) (May 29, 1996), p. 26935.

11 Spiro Agnew, "What's wrong with the Legal Services Program," *American Bar Association Journal*, 58 (1972), p. 930.

12 See Patricia Hughes, "The gendered nature of legal aid," in F.H. Zemans, P.J. Monahan and A. Thomas (eds) *Report on Legal Aid in Ontario: Background Papers* (North York, Ontario: Osgoode Hall Law School, 1997), and Mary Jane Mossman, "Gender, equality, family law and access to justice," *International Journal of Law and the Family*, 8(357) (1994), pp. 365–7.

13 See Janet Mosher, "Poverty law: a case study," *Report of the Ontario Legal Aid Review: A Blueprint for Publicly Funded Legal Services* (Toronto: Government of Ontario, 1997).

14 Griffiths, *supra* note 4.

15 For a discussion of the different structures of legal aid in various countries and jurisdictions, see David Crerar, "A cross-jurisdictional study of legal aid: governance, coverage, eligibility, financing, and delivery in Canada, England and Wales, New Zealand, and the United States," *Report of the Ontario Legal Aid Review: A Blueprint for Publicly Funded Legal Services* (Toronto: Government of Ontario, 1997), p. 1071.

16 Consider, as a further example, the differences between the legal aid systems in the Canadian provinces of Alberta and Saskatchewan. In Alberta, nearly all (99 percent) of legal aid is delivered by private firms, whose fees are paid with certificates issued by the state to clients who meet a means test. In direct contrast, in Saskatchewan almost 100 percent of legal aid is delivered directly by provincially employed staff lawyers. Ibid., p. 1155. In the US, there are also variations within individual states. For example, New York operates its legal aid system on a county basis, with some counties employing public defenders and some using an assigned counsel system. See Martin L. Friedland, "Governance of legal aid schemes," *Report of the Ontario Legal Aid Review: A Blueprint for Publicly Funded Legal Services* (Toronto: Government of Ontario, 1997), pp. 1017, 1043.

17 Charendoff, S., Leach, M. and Levy, T., "Legal aid delivery models," *Report of the Ontario Legal Aid Review: A Blueprint for Publicly Funded Legal Services* (Toronto: Government of Ontario, 1997), p. 546.

18   Alan Paterson, "Financing legal services: a comparative perspective," in Paterson and Goriely, *supra* note 2, p. 252.
19   Ibid., p. 253.
20   Menkel-Meadow, quoted in ibid.
21   Charendoff *et al.*, *supra* note 17.
22   Ibid.
23   Ibid.
24   New Zealand Annual Report on Legal Aid 2001–2002, p. 12.
25   Lord High Chancellor of Northern Ireland, "The future of legal aid in Northern Ireland," Crown Copyright, 2000.
26   Ibid., p. 25.
27   Jeremy Cooper, "The United States: the struggle to control policy," *Public Legal Services* (London: Sweet & Maxwell, 1982), p. 58.
28   Ibid.
29   Ibid.
30   Ibid., p.49.
31   Ibid.
32   Ibid.
33   "Access to justice in South Africa: legal aid transformation and paralegal movement," available at: http://www.case.org.za/htm/legal3.htm, p. 4.
34   Ibid., p. 8.
35   Alan W. Houseman, "Recent developments: civil legal assistance in the United States," available at: http://faculty.law.ubc.ca/ilac/Papers/09%20Houseman.html, p. 4.
36   Jeremy Cooper, "A concluding analysis," *supra* note 27, p. 285.
37   Jeremy Cooper, "The United Kingdom: cautious beginnings," *supra* note 27, p. 39.
38   LSC, *supra* note 10, pp. 26934–5.
39   Cappelletti, M. and Garth, B., "The worldwide movement to make rights effective," in Paterson and Goriely, *supra* note 2, p. 102.
40   Cooper, *supra* note 27.
41   Tamera Goriely, "Legal aid delivery systems: which offer the best value for money in mass casework? A summary of international evidence," available at: http://www.lcd.gov.uk/research/1997/1097es.htm, p. 3.
42   Ibid., p. 4.
43   Ibid.
44   Paterson, *supra* note 18, p. 250.
45   Weikel, quoted in ibid., p. 251.
46   Paterson, *supra* note 18, p. 251.
47   Ibid.
48   Francis Regan, "The Swedish legal services policy remix," *Journal of Law and Society*, 30(1) (March, 2003), pp. 49–86.
49   Matthews, R.C.O., "The economics of professional ethics: should the professions be more like a business?," *Economic Journal*, 101 (1991), p. 737.
50   Gwyn Bevan, "Has there been supplier-induced demand for legal aid?," *Civil Justice Quarterly*, 15 (April, 1996), p. 103.
51   Ibid., p.105.
52   Blankenberg, E., "Comparing legal aid schemes in Europe," *Civil Justice Quarterly*, 11 (1992), p. 106.
53   Gray, A., Rickman, N. and Fenn, P., "Professional autonomy and the cost of legal aid," *Oxford Economic Papers*, 51 (1999), p. 556.
54   Ibid.
55   Ministry of the Attorney General of Ontario, Ontario Legal Aid Review, chapter 7: "The choice of delivery models for legal aid," available at: http://www.attorneygeneral.jus.gov.on.ca/English/about/pubs/olar/ch7.asp, p. 22.

56   Ibid., p. 22.
57   Gray, Rickman and Fenn, *supra* note 53, p. 557.
58   Ontario Ministry of the Attorney General, *supra* note 55, p. 5.
59   See Goriely, *supra* note 2, p. 1.
60   South Africa, *supra* note 33, p. 8.
61   Ibid., p. 2.
62   Ibid., p. 3.
63   Ibid., p. 3.
64   National Council of Welfare, Legal Aid and the Poor, available at: htpp://www.ncwcnbes.net/htmdocument/reportlegalaid/reportlegalaid.htm, p. 33.
65   Ibid., p. 33.
66   Ibid., p. 35.
67   Ibid., p. 35.
68   Ibid., p. 35.
69   The United Kingdom Law Society, The Future of Publicly Funded Legal Services (2003), p. 54.
70   Ibid., p. 54.
71   Frank H. Stephen, Reform of Legal Aid in Scotland. University of Strathclyde research paper, p. 9.
72   Ibid., p. 9.
73   Regan, *supra* note 48, p. 52.
74   Regan, *supra* note 48.
75   Ibid., p. 63.
76   See Wydrzynski, Hildebrandt and Blonde, "The CAW prepaid legal services plan: a case study of an alternative funding and delivery method for legal services," *Windsor Yearbook of Access to Justice*, 22 (1991).
77   Griffiths, J., *supra* note 4.
78   Goriely, T. and Paterson, A., "Introduction," in *supra* note 2, p.10.
79   Ibid.
80   Ibid., p.12.
81   Blankenberg, *supra* note 52, p. 108.
82   National Council of Welfare, *supra* note 64, p. 23.
83   Blankenberg, *supra* note 52, p. 108.
84   It may be desirable to restrict the range of choice available for legal aid clients for representation at some standard proceedings. For example, it may be wise to mandate that duty counsel be used in specific circumstances where clear economies of scale exist such as at bail hearings or adjournments. See Ontario Legal Aid Review, *supra* note 55, pp. 120, 133.
85   A full discussion of these quality monitoring and control mechanisms for the delivery of legal aid services from which this summary is adopted is contained in the *Report of the Ontario Legal Aid Review, supra* note 55, pp. 129–32. Also valuable is the background study prepared for the same report, Sandra Wain, "Quality control and performance measures," *A Blueprint for Publicly Funded Legal Services* (Toronto: Government of Ontario, 1997), p. 609.
86   Albert Klijn, "The Dutch 1994 Legal Aid Act as a new incentives structure" (1998), available at: http://faculty.law.ubc.ca/ilac/Papers/12%20Klijn.html, p. 5.
87   Ibid., p. 6.
88   Ibid.
89   Ibid.
90   Peter van den Biggelaar, "Legal aid in the Netherlands" (1998), available at: http://faculty.law.ubc.ca/ilac/Papers/01%20biggelaar.html, p. 1.
91   Ibid., p. 1.
92   Martin Friedland, "Governance of legal aid schemes," *Ontario Legal Aid Review, supra* note 55.

93 Ibid., p. 1067.
94 Ibid.
95 Ibid., p. 1068.
96 Ibid., pp. 1031–2.

6 Health care

1 World Health Organization, *Charter* (New York: World Health Organization, 1974).
2 See John Rawls, *A Theory of Justice* (Cambridge, MA: Harvard University Press, 1971).
3 The concern for the necessary conditions for free choice is one of the principal features that distinguish liberalism (of, say, John Rawls, *supra* note 2) and Ronald Dworkin, *Taking Rights Seriously* (Cambridge, MA: Harvard University Press, 1976) from libertarianism (of, say, Robert Nozick, *Anarchy, State and Utopia*) (New York: Basic Books, 1974).
4 John Rawls, *supra* note 2, argues that a liberal theory of justice demands that any inequalities in a social framework must work to the advantage of the least well off (the difference principle) and that the necessary conditions for autonomous choice are guaranteed for all.
5 At least, those disadvantages that are the result of poor health which does not, itself, result from unwise choices made by the individuals themselves. There might be an argument for the provision of health care services to those who have suffered as a result of their own poor choices, but it will be of a different kind.
6 See R.G. Evans, M.L. Barer and T.R. Marmor (eds) *Why Are Some People Healthy and Others Not?: The Determinants of the Health of Populations* (New York: Aldene De Gruyter, 1994).
7 See e.g. *Garlarsillio v. Schocter* 2 S.C.R. 119 (1993), p. 135.
8 G.F. Anderson and J.P. Poullier, "Health spending, access, and outcomes: trends in industrialized countries," *Health Affairs*, 18(3) (1999), p. 179.
9 Sherry Glied, *Chronic Condition: Why Health Care Reform Fails* (Cambridge, MA: Harvard University Press, 1997), p. 5.
10 Anderson and Poullier, *supra* note 8.
11 For a detailed analysis of health care spending trends in the OECD member countries see Anderson and Poullier, *supra* note 8, pp. 178–92. See also S. Smith *et al.*, "The next decade of health spending: a new outlook," *Health Affairs*, 18(4) (1999), pp. 86–95.
12 Ibid.
13 R. Grad, "Health care reform in Canada: is there room for efficiency?," *Health Law in Canada*, 20(2) (1999), p. 17.
14 Colleen Flood, *International Health Care Reform: A Legal, Economic and Political Analysis* (London and New York: Routledge, 2000), p. 16.
15 Anderson and Poullier, *supra* note 8, p. 188.
16 See Colleen Flood and Tom Archibald, "The illegality of private health care in Canada," *Canadian Medical Association Journal*, 164(6) (2001), p. 825.
17 See A. Blomquist, "Conclusion: themes in health care reform," in A. Blomquist and D.M. Brown (eds) *Limits to Care: Reforming Canada's Health System in an Age of Restraint* (Toronto: C.D. Howe Institute, 1994), pp. 399, 416.
18 See Nadeem Esmail and Michael Walker, *How Good is Canadian Health Care? 2004 Report: An International Comparison* (Vancouver: Fraser Institute, 2004), p. 16.
19 See G.L. Stoddart, M.L. Barer, R.G. Evans and V. Bhatia, "Why not user charges? The real issues – a discussion paper" (Ontario: The Premier's Council on Health, Well-Being and Social Justice, 1993), p. 5; Morris Barer, Robert Evans, Kimberlyn McGrail, Bo Green, Clyde Hertzman and Samuel Sheps, "Beneath the calm surface:

the changing face of physician-service use in British Columbia 1985/86 Versus 1996/97," *Canadian Medical Association Journal*, 170 (2004), p. 803.

20　See Julian Le Grand, *Motivation, Agency and Public Policy: Of Knights, Knaves, Pawns and Queens* (Oxford: Oxford University Press, 2003), Chapter 7.

21　Ibid.

22　See Colleen Flood, "The structure and dynamics of Canada's health care system," in J. Downie and T. Caulfield (eds) *Canadian Health Law and Policy* (Toronto: Butterworths, 1999), p. 33.

23　This list of problems with the incentive structure of hospital financing comes from John F. Marriott and Ann L. Marble, *The Hospital Sector: Reform Initiatives*, Discussion Paper 94–13 (Kingston, Ontario: School of Policy Studies, 1994), p. 11.

24　Flood, *supra* note 22, p. 38.

25　C. Fooks, "Will power, cost control, and health reform in Canada, 1987–1992," in F. Powell and A. Wesson (eds) *Health Care Systems in Transition: An International Perspective* (Thousand Oaks, CA: Sage Publications, 1999), pp. 151, 162.

26　Flood, *supra* note 22, p. 9.

27　Ibid.

28　S. Dunlop, P. Coyte and W. McIsaac, "Socio-economic status and the utilisation of physicians' services: results from the Canadian National Population Health Survey," *Social Sciences and Medicine*, 51 (2000), pp. 123–33.

29　Canada, Commission on the Future of Health Care in Canada, *Building on Values: The Future of Health Care in Canada* (Ottawa: Canada Communications Group, 2002) (Commissioner Roy Romanow) and Canada, Commission on the Future of Health Care in Canada, *The Health of Canadians – The Federal Role: Interim Report: Volume Two – Current Trends and Future Challenges* (Ottawa: Canada Communications Group, 2002a).

30　Ibid.

31　Flood, *supra* note 22, p. 88.

32　S. Giaimo and P. Manow, "Institutions and ideas into politics: health care reform in Britain and Germany," in C. Altenstetter and J.W. Björkman (eds) *Health Policy Reform, National Variations and Globalization* (New York: St Martin's Press, 1997), pp. 175, 177.

33　Flood, *supra* note 22, p. 93.

34　Ibid., p. 94.

35　Ibid.

36　Giaimo and Manow, *supra* note 32.

37　P. Day and R. Klein, "Britain's health care experiment," in F. Powell and A. Wesson (eds) *Health Care Systems in Transition: An International Perspective* (Thousand Oaks, CA: Sage Publications, 1999), pp. 281, 283.

38　Ibid., p. 285.

39　Ibid., p. 287.

40　Department of Health White Paper, *Working for Patients* (CM 555; January, 1989).

41　*The National Health Service and Community Care Act* (UK) 1990, c.19.

42　Giaimo and Manow, *supra* note 32.

43　Day and Klein, *supra* note 37, p. 288.

44　Note that the distinction between Directly Managed Units (DMUs) and NHS Trusts has become irrelevant as by 1997 all hospitals and community units had applied for and become trusts, shedding their DMU status. J. Appleby, "The reforms of the British national service," in F. Powell and A. Wesson (eds) *Health Care Systems in Transition: An International Perspective* (Thousand Oaks, CA: Sage Publications, 1999), pp. 305, 310.

45　Giaimo and Manow, *supra* note 32.

46　Flood, *supra* note 22, p. 98.

47　Giaimo and Manow, *supra* note 32, p. 178.

48　Flood, *supra* note 22, p. 98.

49 C.H. Tuohy, *Accidental Logics: The Dynamics of Change in the Health Care Arena in the United States, Britain, and Canada* (Oxford and New York: Oxford University Press, 1999), p. 169.
50 Ibid., p. 171.
51 Ibid.
52 Ibid., p. 170.
53 Day and Klein, *supra* note 37, p. 288.
54 C. Paton, "The politics and economics of health care reform: Britain in comparative context," in C. Altenstetter and J.W. Björkman (eds) *Health Policy Reform, National Variations and Globalization* (New York: St Martin's Press, 1997), pp. 175, 177.
55 Ibid.
56 Flood, *supra* note 22, p. 101.
57 Carolyn Hughes Tuohy, "Agency, contract and governance: shifting shapes of accountability in the health care arena," *Journal of Health Politics, Policy and Law*, 28 (2003), p. 207.
58 R. Klein and J. Dixon, "Cash bonanza for NHS: the price is centralization," *British Medical Journal*, 320 (2000), pp. 889–90.
59 Alain C. Enthoven – the principal proponent of managed competition in America – summarises the development of this view in "The history and principles of managed competition," *Health Affairs*, 12 (1993, Supp.), p. 24.
60 In the spring of 1993, more than 40 million Americans (15 percent of the population) lacked health insurance. Although the uninsured are provided with some basic health care services, these services are substantially more limited than those provided to individuals who are covered – routine care is generally forgone, and more serious illnesses tend to be dealt with later in their course when doctors can do less to treat them. See Glied, *supra* note 9, p. 5.
61 Ibid., p. 8.
62 Flood, *supra* note 22, p. 50.
63 The Alliances would negotiate on behalf of everyone except those on Medicare and employees in firms with over 5,000 employees.
64 Flood, *supra* note 22, p. 52.
65 Ibid.
66 See Colleen Flood, *supra* note 14, Chapter 8. The American system, as it exists now, is allocatively inefficient. Although overall life expectancy is not exceptionally high in the United States, the life expectancy for those over eighty is the highest in the world. That is, a disproportionate amount of resources are spent on prolonging the end of life, and much less are going toward preventive and primary services. See G. J. Scheiber *et al.*, "Health system performance in OECD countries, 1980–1992," *Health Affairs*, 13(4) (Fall, 1994), pp. 100, 106, Exhibit 4, from OECD data and their own estimates.
67 R. Klein and J. Dixon, "Cash bonanza for NHS: the price is centralization," *British Medical Journal*, 320 (2000), pp. 889–90.
68 Paul Belien, "Patient empowerment in Europe," *Fraser Forum* (Vancouver: Fraser Institute, February, 1998).
69 Martin Pfaff and Dietmar Wassener, "Germany," *Journal of Health Politics, Policy and Law*, 25(5) (2000), p. 911.
70 European Observatory on Health Care Systems, Health Care Systems in Transition: Germany (2000), available at: http://www.observatory.dk, pp. 52–3. As of 1997, Germany spent US$2,364 per-capita on health care, which was second only to Switzerland among WHO countries. As of 1998, Germany ranked first among WHO countries in terms of health care spending as a percentage of GDP, with expenditures at 10.7 percent of GDP.
71 Ibid., p. 47.
72 Ibid., p. 96.

73 Ibid., pp. 114–15.

74 Belien, *supra* note 68.

75 Pfaff and Wassener, *supra* note 69, pp. 909–10.

76 Belien, *supra* note 68.

77 Hans Maarse and Aggie Paulus, "Has solidarity survived? A comparative analysis of social health insurance reform in four European countries," *Journal of Health Politics, Policy and Law*, 28(4) (2003), p. 597.

78 Ibid.

79 Ibid.

80 Ibid.

81 Eddy van Doorslaer and Frederik T. Schut, "Belgium and the Netherlands revisited," *Journal of Health Politics, Policy and Law*, 25(5) (2000), p. 879.

82 Maarse *et al.*, *supra* note 77, p. 601.

83 Our proposal for a tax-based user fee is based largely on S. Aba, W. Goodman, and J. Mintz, "Funding public provision of private health: the case for co-payment contribution through the tax system," C.D. Howe Institute Commentary #163, May, 2002.

84 M. Stabile, "The role of benefit taxes in the health care sector," p. 60 (Research Paper No. 14, Panel on the Role of Government, 2003); Robert Evans, "Raising the money: options, consequences, and objectives for financing health care in Canada," Discussion Paper No. 27 for the Commission on the Future of Health Care in Canada (Romanow Commission), October, 2002.

85 Ibid.

86 E. Forget, R. Deber and L. Roos, "Medical savings accounts: will they reduce costs?," *Canadian Medical Association Journal*, 167(2) (2002), pp. 143–7. Studies find that high usage of medical services in the previous year is the best indicator of future usage; see Stabile (2003). Under this system, diabetics and other individuals with chronic medical conditions will owe the difference between the medical allowance and catastrophic coverage each year. The persistent nature of health care usage leads some critics to argue that any form of demand-side health care tax is simply a tax on the sick. See also Romanow (2002), pp. 29–30.

87 See *supra* note 83.

88 Ibid.

89 See discussion in Stabile *supra* note 84; and Romanow *supra* note 29.

90 Colleen Flood, *supra* note 14, pp. 243–5.

91 U. Gerdtham, J. Sogaard, F. Andersson and B. Jonsson, "Econometric analysis of health expenditure: a cross-section study of the OECD countries," *Journal of Health Economics*, 11 (1992), pp. 63–84. However, studies done in aggregate are difficult to interpret and may exaggerate a correlation between FFS and higher spending when other factors play a role.

92 Stabile, *supra* note 84, p. 59.

93 Le Grand, *supra* note 20, Chapter 7.

94 Colleen Flood, *supra* note 14, pp. 245–6.

95 M. Gaymor and M. Gertler, "Moral hazard and risk spreading in partnerships," *Rand Journal of Economics*, 26(4) (1995), pp. 591–613.

96 These studies are reviewed in S. Glied, "Managed care," in Culyer and Newhouse (eds) *Handbook of Health Economics* (New York: Elsevier, 2000).

97 A. Scott, "Economics of general practice," in Culyer and Newhouse (eds) *Handbook of Health Economics* (New York: Elsevier, 2000), pp. 1175–200.

98 See generally, M. Grignon, V. Paris, D. Polton in collaboration with A. Couffinhal and B. Pierrard, "Influence of physician payment methods on efficiency of the health care system," *Romanow Commission on the Future of Health Care in Canada*, Background Paper 35 (2002), pp. 12–13. See also A. Krasnik, P. Groenwegen and

P.A. Pederson, "Changing remuneration system: effects on activity in general practice," *British Medical Journal*, 300 (1990), pp. 1698–701.

99   *Red Book* (2002), available at: http://www.nhs.uk/redbook/2.htm.

100   Grignon *et al.* (2002) (discussing the UK).

101   Grad, *supra* note 13, p. 19.

102   Flood, *supra* note 22, p. 156.

103   See, for example, Morris L. Barer, Clyde Hertzman, Robert Miller and Marina V. Pascali, "On being old and sick: the burden of health care for the elderly in Canada and the United States," *Journal of Health Politics, Policy and Law*, 17(4) (1992); Alison Evans Cuellar and Joshua M. Wiener, "Can social insurance for long-term care work? The experience of Germany," *Health Affairs*, 19(3) (2000); World Health Organization, "Home-based long-term care," *WHO Technical Report Series*, 898 (2000) (Geneva).

104   See Edward C. Norton and P. Joseph, "Policy options for public long-term care insurance," *Journal of the American Medical Association*, 271(9) (1994). The authors state that the US, Germany, Belgium and France are countries with spend-down requirements. Several other countries do not rely on means testing, but do require substantial co-payments, which often end up depleting an individual's assets. Examples of the latter include Canada, Australia, Denmark, the Netherlands and Sweden.

105   Judith Feder, Harriet L. Komisar, and Marlene Niefeld, "Long-term care in the United States: an overview," *Health Affairs*, 19(3) (2000).

106   James Davies, "Social and economic risks to seniors," *Paper for the Role of Government Panel* (2003), pp. 2–3.

107   Ibid.

108   Ibid.

109   Ibid.

110   Ibid.

111   European Observatory on Health Care Systems, *supra* note 70, p. 69.

112   Ibid.

113   See, for example, Morris L. Barer, Clyde Hertzman, Robert Miller and Marina V. Pascali, "On being old and sick: the burden of health care for the elderly in Canada and the United States," *Journal of Health Politics, Policy and Law*, 17(4) (1992); Alison Evans Cuellar and Joshua M. Wiener, "Can social insurance for long-term care work? The experience of Germany," *Health Affairs*, 19(3) (2000); World Health Organization, "Home-based long-term care," *WHO Technical Report Series*, 898 (2000) (Geneva).

114   Ibid.

115   Edward C. Norton and Joseph P. Newhouse, "Policy options for public long-term care insurance," *Journal of American Medical Association*, 271 (1994), p. 1524. Also note that there are other countries, such as Germany, that utilize both the health care system and the social insurance system in the financing of institutional care. However, it is not necessarily the case that the individual (or social assistance system) will be responsible for housing costs. Individuals have a certain level of entitlement that is derived from LTC insurance benefits. Any amount in excess of this entitlement must be paid by the individual, unless he or she qualifies (on a means-tested basis) for social assistance.

116   Johan Hjertqvist, "Swedish health-care reform: from public monopolies to market services," available at: http://www.iedm.org/library/Hjertqvist_en.html.

117   Jacqueline S. Zinn, "Market competition and the quality of nursing home care," *Journal of Health Politics, Policy and Law*, 19(3) (1994), p. 556.

118   Ibid., p. 556.

119   Scott Miyake Geron, "The quality of consumer-directed long-term care," available at: http://www.asaging.org/generations/gen-24–3/qualitycons.html.

120   Ibid.
121   Although government officials dismiss the notion that there are significant numbers of Canadians travelling south due to lack of proof, at the same time they make no effort to compile the information. See Grad, *supra* note 13, p. 21.
122   Glied, *supra* note 9, p. 220.

7   Early childhood education

1   Between 1977 and 1993 the number of children under five years of age in non-parental care with mothers in the paid labour force in the United States nearly tripled to almost 10 million. See Council of Economic Advisors, "The economics of child care" (December, 1997), available at: http://clinton3.nara.gov/WH/EOP/CEA/html/childcare.html. Similarly, as of 1998, in Canada approximately 60 percent of children under the age of six – or nearly 1.4 million children – had mothers who participated in the paid labour force. For more detailed information, see Child Care Resource and Research Unit, *Early Childhood Care and Education in Canada: Provinces and Territories 1998*, 4th edn (Toronto: University of Toronto, 2000), p. 95.
2   Martha Friendly, "What is the public interest in child care?," *Policy Options*, 18(3) (1997), p. 6. Public spending on early childhood education in both the United States and Canada is lower than in most OECD countries, at a little above 0.2 percent of GDP as compared with 0.4–0.6 percent in Europe, while Australia and Denmark are the unusual outliers at levels as low as 0.1 percent of GDP and as high as 0.8 percent respectively. See Gordon Cleveland and Susan Colley, "The Future of Government in Supporting Early Childhood Education and Care in Ontario," Report to the Panel on the Role of Government in Ontario (2003), p. 13, available at: http://www.law-lib.utoronto.ca/investing/reports/rp24a.pdf. Organization of Economic Cooperation and Development, *Education at a Glance: OECD Indicators* (OECD: Paris, 2003), p. 209. Denmark was spending as much as 1.1 percent of GDP on child care prior to 2003.
3   Cleveland and Colley, *supra* note 2, p. 20.
4   Ibid., p. 7.
5   Ibid., p. 24.
6   Ibid.
7   D.L. Reeves, *Child Care Crisis* (Santa Barbara, CA: ABC-CLIO, 1992), p. 28. However, they may also be some negative externalities of child care. For example at page 29, child psychologist Jay Belsky is quoted as arguing that evidence shows that "infants in day care are more likely to develop insecure attachments to their parents … show more serious aggression, less co-operation, less tolerance of frustration, more misbehaviour, and at times social withdrawal." The National Center for Clinical Infant Programs has taken the position that these negative consequences are more closely associated with poor-quality child care than with high-quality, stimulating child care environments, and that quality child care is associated with thriving children and families rather than these negative outcomes.
8   David Blau, "The quality of child care: an economic perspective," in David Blau (ed.) *The Economics of Child Care* (New York: Russell Sage Foundation, 1991), p. 147.
9   Sheila B. Kamerman, Michelle Neuman, Jane Waldfogel and Jeanne Brooks-Gunn, *Social Policies, Family Types and Child Outcomes in Selected OECD Countries* (Paris: OECD, 2003), p. 28.
10   Ibid., pp. 28–9.
11   Ibid., p. 28.
12   For example, "Head Start," a federally funded US program that seeks to enroll low-income children from the age of three to five in high-quality child care environments,

has been found in several studies to be ineffectual in improving the *long-run* academic achievement, emotional adjustment, graduation rate, teen pregnancy rate, crime rate or employment rate of Head Start children *vis-à-vis* non-participants. Patrick Basham, "Head start or false hope? Lessons in early childhood education," *Fraser Forum*, 5 (September, 2000), p. 6. A subsequent study found that poor long-run outcomes were largely the result of later experiences with poor-quality primary and secondary schools, responsible for "offsetting" the "initial positive effects of Head Start." See Cleveland and Colley, *supra* note 2, p. 31. Moreover, many positive outcomes persisted, including a 20 percent increase in the likelihood of white Americans completing high school, a 20–8 percent increase in college attendance for the same group, and a 12 percent drop in the likelihood of engaging in criminal activity among African-Americans.

13   Organization for Economic Co-operation and Development, *Starting Strong: Early Childhood Education and Care* (Paris: OECD, 2001), p. 26.

14   Marcia K. Meyers and Theresa Heintze, "The performance of the child-care subsidy system," *Social Service Review*, 73(1) (1999), p. 39.

15   Bruce Fuller, Sharon L. Kagan, Gretchen L. Caspary and Christiane A. Gauthier, "Welfare reform and child care options for low-income families," *The Future of Children*, 12(1) (2002), p. 101, available at: www.futureofchildren.org/usr_doc/tfoc12–1f.pdf.

16   Robert J. Lemke, Ann Dryden Witte, Magaly Queralt and Robert Witt, "Child care and the welfare to work transition," NBER Working Paper No. 7583 (2000), p. 17, available at: http://www.nber.org/papers/w7583.

17   David Blau and Erdal Tekin, "The determinants and consequences of child care subsidies for single mothers," NBER Working Paper No. 9665 (2003), p. 7, available at: http://www.nber.org/papers/w9665.

18   Ibid., p. 20.

19   Magaly Queralt, Ann Dryden Witte and Harriet Griesinger, "Changing policies, changing impacts: employment and earnings of child-care subsidy recipients in the era of welfare reform," *Social Service Review*, 74(4) (2000), p. 594.

20   Sheila B. Kamerman, "Early childhood education and care: an overview of developments in the OECD countries," *International Journal of Educational Research*, 33 (2000), p. 9.

21   In doing so, Haskins implicitly minimizes the public benefits that attend child care as well as the private benefits that accrue directly to children and not to their parents.

22   Ron Haskins, "What day care crisis?," *Regulation*, 13(2) (1998).

23   Susan Prentice, "The deficiencies of commercial day care," *Policy Options*, 18(1) (1997), p. 43.

24   Ellen Kisker and Rebecca Maynard, "Quality, cost and parental choice of child care," in David Blau (ed.) *The Economics of Child Care* (New York: Russell Sage Foundation, 1991), p. 130.

25   Michael Krashinsky and Gordon Cleveland, "Rethinking the rationales for public funding of child care," *Policy Options*, 18(1) (1997), p. 16.

26   Lisa M. Powell, "Family behaviour and child care costs: policy implications," *Policy Options*, 18(1) (1997), p. 13.

27   Gordon Cleveland and Douglas Hyatt, "Subsidizing child care for low-income families: a good bargain for Canadian governments?," *Choices: Family Policy*, 4(2) (1998), p. 11.

28   Gordon Cleveland and Michael Krashinsky, "The benefits and costs of good child care," working paper (Toronto: University of Toronto at Scarborough, Department of Economics, 1998), p. 16, available at: www.childcarecanada.org/pubs/other/benefits/bc.pdf.

29   Friendly, *supra* note 2, p. 4.

30 For a recent study that links quality child care with impressive reductions in later criminal activity, see Newman *et al.*, *America's Child Care Crisis: A Crime Prevention Tragedy* (Washington, DC: "Fight Crime: Invest in Kids," 2000).

31 See also Karoly *et al.*, who performed a cost savings analysis of the Perry Preschool Project, which was an intensive early childhood intervention experiment. It is important to note that this analysis measures only the financial costs and savings, and disregards intangible benefits. The program cost was US$12,148 per child. The projected savings, which comprised reduced special education costs, increased taxes on earnings, decreased welfare payments, and decreased criminal justice costs, totaled US$25,335. This represents an average savings to the government of US$13,187. Found in David M. Blau, "Child care subsidy programs" NBER Working Paper 7806 (2000), pp. 60–1, available at: http://www.nber.org/papers/w7806.

32 For a discussion of the empirical evidence supporting this assertion, see Richard Tremblay and Christa Japel, "The long-term impact of quality early child care," *Policy Options*, 18(1) (1997).

33 Prentice, *supra* note 23.

34 Cleveland and Colley, *supra* note 2, p. 8.

35 Ibid., p. 37.

36 Ron Haskins, *supra* note 22, p. 20.

37 Internal Revenue Code section 129(a) 1995; see more generally, Mary L. Heen "Welfare reform, child care costs and taxes: delivering increased work-related child care benefits to low-income families," *Yale Law and Policy Review*, 13 (1995), p. 192.

38 See *Income Tax Act*, Revised Status of Canada 1985, c.1, s.63.

39 In May of 2001, the federal government also concluded an Early Childhood Development Initiatives agreement with all provinces and territories (except Quebec), which stipulated increased federal funding in exchange for provincial development of child care services. In 2003 this was supplemented by an additional $1 billion in federal investment in early childhood learning. For Ontario, this increased funding has mostly resulted in a Network of Early Years Centres. These Centres focus almost entirely on support services for parents, and then mostly on healthy development or special needs programs – all desperately needed and worthy initiatives, but limited as tools for early childhood education. Cleveland and Colley, *supra* note 2, pp. 23, 50–1.

40 Ibid., pp. 11, 65. Quebec also expects to more than double the number of child care spaces available by 2005–6. In some quarters, the Quebec program has been suggested as a potential model for Canada.

41 Ibid., pp. 74, 76–78. Finland, Sweden and Portugal all fit within this category. Norway guarantees universal access to child care from birth to six years of age.

42 Ibid., p. 78. The United Kingdom also offers free public child care for all children aged three to four.

43 Frances Press and Alan Hayes, "OECD thematic review of early childhood education and care policy: Australian background report," paper prepared for the Commonwealth Government of Australia (2000), p. 37; OECD, *supra* note 2.

44 Ibid. Denmark also uses demand-side subsidies, as will be discussed in more detail below.

45 Rachel Connolly, "The importance of child care costs to women's decision making," in David Blau (ed.) *The Economics of Child Care* (New York: Russell Sage Foundation, 1991), p. 87.

46 Cleveland and Colley, *supra* note 2, pp. 65, 71.

47 Alanna Mitchell, "Vouchers raise doubts about universal care," *Globe and Mail* (November 21, 1995), p. A8. See also ibid., p. 45. In Ontario, for example, student parents must declare their loans as income, Registered Retirement Savings Plans are treated as liquid assets, assets over $5,000 precludes eligibility, and in any case

subsidy assistance is typically contingent on exhausting all assets. Despite these criteria, long waiting lists of fully eligible parents persist.

48   Moreover, caps placed on the maximum expenditures that are deductible from taxes are problematic in that better quality child care – the kind we should seek to encourage – often exceeds these caps, thereby providing an added incentive to parents to select child care options that are of lower quality but are fully within the tax-deductible range.

49   Cleveland and Colley, *supra* note 2, pp. 45, 66, 115.

50   Ibid., p. 66.

51   Ibid., p. 67. As in Quebec, for example. In order to finance extensive public child care services, Quebec revoked provincial tax deductions related to child care expenses. Quebec is trying to correct the problem of "atypical" parental needs, but as yet no action has been taken.

52   Ibid., p. 76.

53   Ministry of Health, Welfare and Sport, and Ministry of Education, Art and Science, "Early childhood education and care policy in the Netherlands," *Background Report to the OECD Project* (2000), p. 58. See also ibid., pp. 75–6. Child care in the Netherlands is typically private for children aged 0 to 3 years, but publicly co-funded by vouchers. Parental fees are set at about 44 percent of the costs while government and employers account for the remainder. Fees are also determined on a sliding scale, with higher-income families paying a significantly greater proportion of the costs than low-income families; 50 percent of families use employer-funded day care centres while an additional 20 percent use child care centres.

54   Cleveland and Colley, *supra* note 2, p. 80.

55   For a discussion of this connection see Gillian Doherty *et al.*, *Child Care: Canada Can't Work Without It* (Toronto: Child-Care Resource and Research Unit, University of Toronto, 1995), p. 8.

56   Cleveland and Colley, *supra* note 2, p. 14.

57   Ibid., pp. 34, 42.

58   Cleveland and Colley, *supra* note 2, pp. 42–3, 65–6. It is important to note that these measures may not accurately reflect the quality of care in Quebec, as the study was completed before the institution of reforms. Quebec now requires that two-thirds of staff at child care centres have early childhood education training from a college or university; all family care providers, service units often attached to the centres, must now have a minimum of 45 hours of training.

59   Ibid., pp. 42–3, 48. These findings have been disputed by some provinces. Ontario, for example, dismisses the data entirely but has not been able to offer an alternative analysis. A government agency established in 1998 to assess child care services has not completed its work, leaving parents and caregivers with few means to accurately assess quality and no means to ensure accountability.

60   Ibid., p. 80.

61   OECD, *supra* note 13, p. 164.

62   Ibid., p. 163.

63   Connolly, *supra* note 45. See also Alison P. Hagy, "The demand for child care quality: an hedonic price theory approach," *Journal of Human Resources*, 33(3) (1998), p. 684.

64   Cleveland and Colley, *supra* note 2, pp. 73–4, 77, 78.

65   Ibid., p. 58.

66   Ibid.

67   Ibid., p. 86.

68   Fuller *et al.*, *supra* note 15, p. 107.

69   Cleveland and Colley, *supra* note 2, p. 16.

70   Press and Hayes, *supra* note 43, p. 32.

71   Ibid., p. 33.

72   Ibid., p. 18.

73 Cleveland and Colley, *supra* note 2, p. 73.
74 Hagy, *supra* note 63.
75 Blau, *supra* note 31, pp. 65–6.
76 Cleveland and Colley, *supra* note 2, pp. 16–17.
77 Ibid., p. 17.
78 According to some experts "no less than 1 percent of the gross domestic product of the countries should be spent on the ECE system." Wolfgang Tietze and Debby Cryer, "Current trends in European early child care and education," *Annals of the American Academy of Political and Social Science*, 563 (1999), p. 191.
79 Anne B. Shlay, Marsha Weinraub, Michelle Harmon and Henry Tran, "Barriers to subsidies: why low-income families do not use child care subsidies," Temple University Institute for Survey Research (2002), p. 5, available at: www.temple.edu/cpp/content/reports/Barriers_To_Subsidies.pdf.
80 Ibid., p. 5.
81 Ibid., p. 17.
82 Fuller *et al.*, *supra* note 15, pp. 110–11.
83 Shlay *et al.*, *supra* note 79, p. 24.
84 Meyers and Heintze, *supra* note 14, p. 60.
85 Blau, *supra* note 31, p. 20.
86 Ibid., p. 28.
87 Ibid., p. 21.
88 Cleveland and Colley, *supra* note 2, p. 76.
89 Douglas J. Besharov and Nazinin Samari, "Child care vouchers and cash payments," in C. Eugene Steuerle, Van Doorn Ooms, George Peterson and Robert D. Reischauer (eds) *Vouchers and the Provision of Public Services* (Washinton, DC: Brookings Institution Press, CED, Urban Institute Press, 2000), p. 200. Several day care centres were reported to be price discriminating by offering lower prices to those who were not benefiting from government subsidization.
90 Council of Economic Advisors, *supra* note 1.
91 Philip K. Robins, "Child care policy and research: an economist's perspective," in David Blau (ed.) *The Economics of Child Care* (New York: Russell Sage Foundation, 1991), p. 37.
92 If prices increase because providers have turned to providing higher-quality services, we should not be concerned. Such quality increases would probably be a very worthwhile government expenditure given the high positive externalities associated with high-quality child care. The trouble in this regard is that it is often quite difficult to evaluate the quality of child care programmes, and higher prices may indicate anti-competitive behaviour, collusion amongst suppliers (unlikely given the ease of entry and large number of suppliers), or the implementation of worthwhile and needed quality improvements.
93 W. Steven Barnett and Leonard N. Masse, "Funding issues for early childhood care and education programs," in D. Cryer (ed.) *Early Childhood Education and Care in the USA* (Baltimore, MD: Paul H. Brookes, 2003), pp. 8–14.
94 Joseph P . Newhouse and The Insurance Experiment Group, *Free For All? Lessons from the RAND Health Insurance Experiment* (Cambridge, MA: Harvard University Press, 1993), pp. 40, 79.
95 Cleveland and Colley, *supra* note 2, p. 8.
96 For an extended discussion, see Chapter 7 on primary and secondary education.
97 Barbara R. Bergmann, "Making child care 'affordable' in the United States," *Annals of the American Academy of Political and Social Science*, 563 (1999), pp. 214–15.
98 Blau, *supra* note 31, p. 42.
99 Blau, *supra* note 31, p. 12.
100 "The state of early childhood education and care in Canada: an overview" (date unknown), available at: http://www.childcarecanada.org/ECEC2001/overview_fedrole_aboriginal.pdf.

101   See Chapter 8 on primary and secondary education.
102   Ruth Rose, "For direct public funding of child care," *Policy Options*, 18(1) (1997), p. 33.

8   Primary and secondary education

1   Milton Friedman, "The role of government in education," in R.A. Solo (ed) *Economics and the Public Interest* (New Brunswick, NJ: Rutgers University Press, 1955).
2   See, for example, John Witte, *The Market Approach to Education: An Analysis of America's First Voucher Program* (Princeton, NJ: Princeton University Press, 2000), p. 133, and J.P Greene, P.E. Peterson and J. Du, "School choice in Milwaukee: a randomized experiment," in P.E. Peterson and B.C. Hassel (eds) *Learning from School Choice* (Washington, DC: The Brookings Institution, 1998), p. 335. Witte compares his analysis of the Milwaukee data – finding no significant improvement in either reading or mathematics compared with the control group – to those of others (such as Greene *et al.*) who have found positive outcomes for voucher students *vis-à-vis* non-choice students. As further evidence of the gulf in findings between voucher supporters and critics, see E. Muir and F.H. Nelson, "Social science examinations of the Milwaukee voucher experiment," American Federation of Teachers Research Department, available at: http://www.aft.org/research/vouchers/mil/rouse/rouse.htm. For a positive review of the evidence see Jay P. Greene, "A survey of results from voucher experiments: where we are and what we know," in Claudia R. Hepburn (ed) *Can the Market Save Our Schools?* (Vancouver: Fraser Institute, 2001).
3   There are, of course, other approaches. One important variant shares with the skills model the view that education is primarily a private good. It differs, however, in emphasizing its role in human flourishing, rather than as a means to greater long-term earning potential. Education that is pursued for these sorts of reasons (i.e. as personal fulfilment) is perhaps least deserving of public support.
4   Economic Council of Canada *Education and Training in Canada* (Ottawa: Canadian Communications Group, 1992), p. 8 outlines the goals of education in much greater detail. Rather than two basic approaches, the report sets out four sets of goals: (1) academic goals, such as literacy and numeracy, problem-solving and the ability to think critically; (2) vocational goals more closely focused on direct application in a particular career; (3) social, civic and cultural goals such as citizen participation, moral development, awareness of one's own culture and a sensitivity to the diversity of other cultures; and (4) personal goals of emotional and physical well-being, creativity and self-realization.
5   Business leaders often say that classicists, not MBAs, make the best managers. This may or may not be true. However, the point is simply that the value of a "liberal" education is to be measured in other terms. [This "classical" defence of liberal education transcends divisions over the particular value that theorists give to cultural diversity. In favour of cultural diversity are Martha Nussbaum, *Cultivating Humanity: A Classical Defence of Reform in Liberal Education* (Cambridge University Press, 1998), and Amy Gutmann, *Democratic Education* (Princeton, NJ: Princeton University Press, 1987); famously against such diversity is Allan Bloom, *The Closing of the American Mind* (New York: Touchstone Books, 1988).]
6   See, for example, Cass Sunstein, *Free Markets and Social Justice* (Oxford: Oxford University Press, 1997) Chapter 3; Charles Taylor, *Philosophy and the Human Sciences: Philosophical Papers 2* (Cambridge: Cambridge University Press, 1985) Chapter 9; and Peter Drucker, *The New Realities: In Government and Politics, In Economics and Business, In Society and World View* (New York: Harper & Row, 1989), especially Chapter 2, "No more salvation by society."
7   Economic Council of Canada, *supra* note 4, p. 26.

8   See Michael Trebilcock, *The Limits of Freedom of Contract* (Cambridge, MA: Harvard University Press, 1993), Chapter 7.

9   For a more extensive discussion of this issue centred on post-secondary education, see Nicholas Barr, *The Economics of the Welfare State*, 3rd edn (Stanford, CA: Stanford University Press, 1998), p. 353.

10   This will be the outcome so long as the screening hypothesis does not strictly hold. The screening hypothesis states that although education beyond a certain point (e.g. literacy and numeracy) is *associated* with higher incomes later in life, the education itself is not the *cause* of the higher income. The screening hypothesis views more than a basic education as being an expensive and burdensome signal of ability that employers and others use as a guide to select talented individuals from the labour market. For a discussion, see ibid., p. 324.

11   For a discussion of the role of government in promoting social solidarity and maintaining core values in the context of the welfare state, see Albert Weale, "Equality, social solidarity, and the welfare state," *Ethics*, 100(3) (1990), p. 473.

12   Mark Holmes, *The Reformation of Canada's Schools: Breaking the Barriers to Parental Choice* (Montreal: McGill-Queen's University Press, 1998), p. 244.

13   Witte, *supra* note 2, p. 30.

14   Ibid.

15   Statistics Canada, "Enrolment in elementary and secondary schools," *Catalogue No.81–229-XIB*. The relevant table is available as a digital document at: http://www.statcan.ca/english/Pgdb/educ01.htm.

16   This difference is probably partly due to the fact that Ontario and Quebec, Canada's two most populous provinces, provide public funding for Roman Catholic schools, thereby reducing demand for private Catholic schools relative to the United States.

17   Barr, *supra* note 9, p. 337.

18   Holmes, *supra* note 12, p. 32.

19   Federation of Independent Schools in Canada, "Provincial funding of independent schools" (1999), available at: http://www.direct.ca/fisa/fisc/funding.htm.

20   Many families make decisions about where to live based on their perception of the quality of the schooling that their children will receive in the local primary and secondary schools.

21   See Chapter 2 of the Economic Council of Canada, *supra* note 4, from which the data in the following paragraph are taken.

22   Economic Council of Canada, *supra* note 4, p. 16.

23   Holmes, *supra* note 12, p. 116.

24   Ibid., pp. 129–30.

25   This "winnowing" explanation cannot, of course, be complete. Because North American results from the early stages of elementary school (where presumably there is no winnowing) are not competitive with the results of the most successful countries, there is undoubtedly room for improvement in our the provision of at least primary education and most probably secondary education, as well.

26   On this question generally, see Judith Maxwell, "The social role of the state in a knowledge-based economy," in P. Grady, R. Howse and J. Maxwell (eds) *Redefining Social Security* (Kingston, Ontario: Queen's University School of Policy Studies, 1995), pp. 1–45. In particular, she points out that 35–40 percent of children do not live with both biological parents because of divorce or separation; a majority of mothers work outside the home.

27   It is perhaps for this reason that a majority (73 percent) of minority parents are in favour of some form of voucher program [statistic from Rose, Lowell C., Alec M. Gallup and Stanley M. Elam, 29th "Annual Phi Delta Kappa-Gallup poll of the public's attitudes toward the public schools", in *Phi Delta Kappan* (September, 1998), pp. 41–58, quoted in John H. Bishop, "Privatizing education: lessons from Canada and Europe," in C. Eugene Steuerle, Van Doorn Ooms, George Peterson and Robert

D. Reischauer (eds) *Vouchers and the Provision of Public Services* (Washington, DC: Brookings Institution Press, CED, Urban Institute Press, 2000), p. 292]. We should not confuse this issue with the racial integration of schools, however. John Witte points out that inner city school districts are already 90 percent non-white. There simply are very few white children to integrate with the non-white population, see Witte *supra* note 2, p. 6.

28   See Centre for the Study of Public Policy, "Education vouchers," in *Education Vouchers: From Theory to Alum Rock* (Homewood, IL: ETC Publishing, 1972), p. 178.

29   See Jonathan Kozol, *Savage Inequalities: Children in America's Schools* (New York: Harper Perennial, 1992), Chapter 6.

30   John Chubb and Terry Moe, *Politics, Markets and America's Schools* (New York: Brookings Institution, 1990), pp. 171–3 have suggested that inner city school districts are averse to change because of the high level of political pressure exerted upon them. Witte, *supra* note 2, p. 115 argues that such school districts are, in fact, the most dynamic as a result of these pressures. They engage in a great deal of experimentation and publicize it regularly. On the other hand, others criticize this "experimentation" as being part of the problem and have dubbed the process "policy churning." Frederick Hess states that, "Reform, rather than being the remedy to what ails urban schools, has generally been a distraction and a hindrance ... The irony of school reform is that the sheer amount of activity – the fact that reform is the status quo – impedes the ability of any particular reform to have a lasting effect." See F.M. Hess, "Policy churn and urban school reform," in P.E. Peterson and B.C. Hassel (eds) *Learning from School Choice* (Washington, DC: Brookings Institution, 1998), p. 121.

31   For an example from the US context, see Chubb and Moe, ibid., pp. 167–9. A Canadian perspective and criticism of bureaucratic inefficiency is forcefully argued by Mark Holmes, *supra* note 12, Chapter 3.

32   Chubb and Moe, ibid., p. 183.

33   For a forceful example of this position, see David Denholm, "The impact of unionism on the quality of education," available at: http://www.psrf.org/issues/impact.jsp. Denholm argues that the criticism of the role of unions in education should not necessarily be translated into a criticism of teachers; "A careful examination of the role of unions [in education] might bring one to the conclusion that rather than saying that being anti-union is not being anti-teacher, it would be more correct to say that being anti-union is being pro-teacher."

34   See Albert Hirschman, *Exit, Voice and Loyalty* (Cambridge, MA: Harvard University Press, 1970).

35   Hirschman also argues, however, that exit enhances voice for those who remain in the system. The problem is that those who have the ability (or savoir-faire) to exercise voice may be the first to leave, leaving suppliers who are more open to dialogue and reform without any incentive or impetus to reform due to a lack of organized opposition or dissenting "voice."

36   Keith Syler, "Parental choice v. state monopoly: mother knows best – a comment on America's schools and vouchers," *University of Cincinnati Law Review*, 68 (2000), p. 1345.

37   Caroline Hoxby, "Does competition among public schools benefit students and taxpayers?," *American Economic Review*, 90(5) (2000), p. 1209; also Hoxby, "Analyzing school choice reforms that use America's traditional forms of parental choice," in Claudia R. Hepburn (ed) *Can the Market Save Our Schools?* (Vancouver: Fraser Institute, 2001).

38   Tiebout choice, as used by Hoxby in the school choice context, refers to the idea that when households make decisions regarding where exactly to reside in a given city, they pay attention to the quality of the local school districts and the property taxes that are imposed for their financing. The seminal paper describing the Tiebout

model is C.M. Tiebout, "A pure theory of local expenditures," *Journal of Political Economy*, 64(5) (1956), p. 416.

39   See Hoxby, 2000, *supra* note 37, p. 1215.

40   Ibid., p. 1228. According to Hoxby, these estimated effects are all significant at the 5 percent level except for the educational attainment figure, which is significant at the 10 percent level.

41   Ibid., pp. 1230–1.

42   Ibid., p. 1237.

43   Greene, in Hepburn, *supra* note 2, pp. 143–4.

44   Matthew Ladner and Matthew J. Brouillette, "The impact of charter schools and public school choice on public school districts in Wayne County, Michigan," *Howard Law Journal*, 45 (2002), p. 399.

45   For instance, some of the best funded public school systems in the United States are among the worst performing. Take, for example, the District of Columbia, which spends $8,000 per pupil, relative to the national average of $6,000, while its student performance is among the worst in the nation. John G. Goodman, "School choice vs. school choice," *Howard Law Journal*, 45 (2002), p. 379. On a nationally administered math test, eighth grade DC students ranked 41st among the 50 US states, and fourth grade students ranked 40th on the nationally administered reading test. In a 1996 report, the District of Columbia Financial Responsibility and Management Assistance Authority remarked that "the longer students stay in the District's public school system, the less likely they are to succeed." However, Reschovsky and Imazeki speculate that this discrepancy between input and output may be due to, "a set of factors outside the control of local school districts that require some districts to pay higher salaries than others in order to attract teachers with similar qualifications to carry out similar teaching assignments." They claim that factors such as, "the racial and ethnic composition of the student body, land costs, and a range of variables that influence the attractiveness of any geographical area, such as weather conditions and crime rates" will have a large impact on the expenditures that will be required to attract and keep teachers in particular schools. Therefore, the higher expenditures in districts such as Washington DC may simply reflect the higher salaries demanded by teachers. Andrew Reschovsky and Jennifer Imazeki, "Achieving educational adequacy through school finance reform," *Journal of Education Finance*, 26:4 (2001), p. 377.

46   Caroline M. Hoxby, "School choice and school competition: evidence from the United States," working paper, p. 46, available at: post.economics.harvard.edu/faculty/hoxby/papers/sweden.pdf.

47   Helen F. Ladd, "School vouchers: a critical view," *Journal of Economic Perspectives*, 16(4) (2002), pp. 7–8.

48   For an international review of the charter school movement see T.R. Williams, "Educational governance: a paper prepared for the panel on the role of government," Report to the Panel on the Role of Government in Ontario (2003), available at: http://www.law-lib.utoronto.ca/investing/reports/rp46.pdf.

49   See United States Charter Schools, "Overview of charter schools" (October, 1999), available at: http://www.uscharterschools.org/pub/uscs_docs/o/index.htm.

50   Williams, *supra* note 48, p. 32.

51   See the extensive discussion on this experience in Julian Le Grand, *Motivation, Agency and Public Policy* (New York: Oxford University Press, 2003), Chapter 8. The 1988 Education Reform Act transferred significant operating authority from local governments directly to schools. School governing bodies were given significant responsibility for all aspects of a school's operations. Funding for the schools was determined on the basis of student enrollment, and schools were required to accept as many students as their physical capacity would allow.

52   Charter schools differ in character based primarily on the enabling legislation of the jurisdiction in which they operate.

53   It is strange to have local school boards act as a charter-granting institution because the local bureaucracy often has strong interests in favour of job security and the integrity of the public school system that run directly counter to encouraging the flourishing of an alternative school system. In fact, this is what has typified the Alberta charter school experience, where only two of twelve charter schools were supported by local school boards. The remaining charters had to be considered and renewed directly by the Minister of Education. For a full discussion, see Lynn Bosetti *et al.*, *Canadian Charter Schools at the Crossroads* (Kelowna, BC: Society for the Advancement of Excellence in Education, 2000), p. 113; also Lynn Bosetti, "The Alberta charter school experience," in Claudia R. Hepburn (ed.) *Can the Market Save Our Schools?* (Vancouver: Fraser Institute, 2001), pp. 101–20.

54   Ibid., 2000, p. 113.

55   Ibid., p. 10.

56   Edwin G. West, "Education vouchers in practice and principle: a world survey," Human Capital Development and Operations Policy – Working Papers (February, 1996), available at: http://www.worldbank.org/html/extdr/hnp/hddflash/workp/wp_00064.html. See also Ladner and Brouilette, *supra* note 44, p. 396.

57   Claudia Rebanks Hepburn, "The case for school choice: models from the United States, New Zealand, Denmark, and Sweden," Fraser Institute Critical Issues Bulletin (1999), available at: http://www.fraserinstitute.ca.

58   Ibid., p. 10.

59   Caroline M. Hoxby, *supra* note 46, p. 4.

60   However, Lin reports that charter schools devote an average of 30 percent of their revenues to business and administration as compared with 12 percent for non-charter public schools. Qiuyun Lin, "An evaluation of charter school effectiveness," *Education*, 122(1) (2001), p. 171.

61   Caroline M. Hoxby, *supra* note 46, p. 35.

62   Ibid., p. 61.

63   Ibid., p. 60.

64   Le Grand, *supra* note 51, Chapter 8.

65   Ibid., p. 109.

66   Ibid., p. 110.

67   Le Grand, *supra* note 51, p. 113.

68   Beverly Lynn Bosetti *et al.*, *Canada's Charter Schools: Initial Report* (Kelowna, BC: Society for the Advancement of Excellence in Education, 1998), available at: http://www.excellenceineducation.ca/publications/A_002_AAA_MID.php.

69   Arthur Sweetman, "Ontario's kindergarten to grade 12 education system: some thoughts for the future," Report to the Panel on the Role of Government in Ontario (2003), available at: http://www.law-lib.utoronto.ca/investing/reports/rp25.pdf.

70   Hepburn, *supra* note 57, p. 20.

71   Ibid.

72   Ibid., p. 18.

73   Ladner and Brouilette, *supra* note 44, pp. 397–8.

74   Paul E. Peterson, "School choice: a report card," *Virginia Journal of Social Policy and the Law*, 6 (1998), p. 52.

75   Hepburn, *supra* note 57, p. 17.

76   Lin, *supra* note 60.

77   Hepburn, *supra* note 57, p. 30.

78   Caroline M. Hoxby, *supra* note 46, p. 22.

79   Ibid.

80   Ibid., p. 23.

81   Ibid.

82   Ibid., p. 4.
83   H.M. Levin, "Educational vouchers: effectiveness, choice, and costs," *Journal of Policy Analysis and Management*, 17(3) (1998), p. 379.
84   John Goodman, *supra* note 45, p. 388.
85   Ibid.
86   Ibid., p. 383.
87   Ibid.
88   Helen F. Ladd, *supra* note 47, p. 10.
89   John Goodman, *supra* note 45, p. 383.
90   Derek Neal, "How vouchers could change the market for education," *Journal of Economic Perspectives*, 16(4) (2002), p. 30.
91   Caroline M. Hoxby, *supra* note 46, pp. 25, 57.
92   Ibid., p. 59.
93   Ibid., p. 37.
94   Witte, *supra* note 2, p. 105.
95   Ibid., p. 93.
96   Ibid., pp. 142–3, 151.
97   Jay P. Greene, William G. Howell, and Paul E. Peterson, "An evaluation of the Cleveland voucher program," Program on Education Policy and Governance (1997), available at: http://www.schoolchoices.org/roo/cleveland1.htm.
98   Ibid.
99   John Goodman, *supra* note 45, p. 385.
100 Ibid.
101 Suzanne Hansen, "School vouchers: the answer to a failing public school system," *Hamline Journal of Public Law and Policy*, 23 (2001), p. 89.
102 Robert Holland and Don Soifer, "How school choice benefits the urban poor," *Howard Law Journal*, 45 (2002), p. 349.
103 John Goodman, *supra* note 45, p. 392.
104 Mogens Kamp Justesen, "Learning from Europe: the Dutch and Danish school systems," *Adam Smith Institute* (London, 2002), p. 17, available at: www.adamsmith.org/policy/publications/pdf-files/learning-from-europe.pdf.
105 Ibid., p. 21.
106 Ibid., p. 17.
107 Ibid., p. 20.
108 Ibid., p. 21.
109 Ibid., p. 22.
110 Arthur Sweetman, *supra* note 69, Table 8.
111 Mogens Kamp Justesen, *supra* note 104, p. 23.
112 Joshua D. Angrist, Eric Bettinger, Erik Bloom, Elizabeth King and Michael Kremer, "Vouchers for private schooling in Colombia: evidence from a randomized natural experiment," NBER Working Paper no. 8343 (2001), p. 4, available at: http://www.nber.org/papers/w8343.
113 Ibid.
114 Ibid., p. 3.
115 Ibid., p. 14.
116 Edwin G. West, *supra* note 56.
117 John Goodman, *supra* note 45, p. 386.
118 Michael Kremer, "Randomized evaluations of educational programs in developing countries: some lessons," available at: post.economics.harvard.edu/faculty/kremer/webpapers/Randomized_Evaluations.pdf.
119 Angrist *et al.*, *supra* note 112, p. 17.
120 Ibid., p. 24.
121 Ibid., p. 25.

122   See Dante Contreras, "Vouchers, school choice and the access to higher education," Center Discussion Paper No. 845 (2002), available at: www.econ.yale.edu/growth_pdf/cdp845.pdf.

123   Edwin G. West, *supra* note 56.

124   Dante Contreras, *supra* note 122, p. 4.

125   Edwin G. West, *supra* note 56.

126   Dante Contreras, *supra* note 122, p. 21.

127   Edwin G. West, *supra* note 56.

128   Dante Contreras, *supra* note 122, p. 14.

129   Witte, *supra* note 2, p. 74. Note that the inclusion of erstwhile private school students in a voucher regime dilutes the per-student funding of those who were in the public system for the entire time, while at the same time putting pressures on the voucher system for increased funding.

130   Ibid., p. 196.

131   See Peterson, *supra* note 74.

132   Witte, *supra* note 2, pp. 191–2.

133   Isabel V. Sawhill (with Shannon L. Smith), "Vouchers for elementary and secondary education," in C. Eugene Steuerle, Van Doorn Ooms, George Peterson and Robert D. Reischauer (eds) *Vouchers and the Provision of Public Services* (Washington, DC: Brookings Institution Press, CED, Urban Institute Press, 2000), p. 261.

134   The suggestion is that, with a one-time introduction of a voucher programme, erstwhile private institutions may be highly oversubscribed while schools that were previously part of the public system may be undersubscribed. Upon allocation of places in each school, some students would inevitably have no alternative other than to attend a previously public institution. This alternative might not, as a matter of fact, be a poor one once the erstwhile public school is set in a different institutional environment with much stronger incentives to perform. Psychologically and symbolically, however, parents most concerned about the quality of their child's school will most likely seek schools that were previously private.

135   Weale, *supra* note 11, p. 484.

136   Witte, *supra* note 2, pp. 197–9.

137   Ibid., pp. 7, 18.

138   Such as those suggested by the Panel on the Role of Government, *Investing In People: Creating a Human Capital Society for Ontario* (Toronto: Queen's Printer for Ontario, 2004), p. 14.

139   Williams, *supra* note 48, pp. 21–2.

140   Arthur Hauptman, "Vouchers and American higher education," in C. Eugene Steuerle, Van Doorn Ooms, George Peterson and Robert D. Reischauer (eds) *Vouchers and the Provision of Public Services* (Washinton, DC: Brookings Institution Press, CED, Urban Institute Press, 2000), p. 363.

141   This, along with the question of the state-to-state constitutionality of school vouchers for private religious primary and secondary education, is the most important legal issue in the voucher debate in America. For a discussion, see Joseph P. Viteritti, "School choice and state constitutional law," in P.E. Peterson and B.C. Hassel (eds) *Learning from School Choice* (Washington, DC: Brookings Institution, 1998), p. 409.

142   *Lemon v. Kurtzman*, 403 US 602 (1971)

143   *Lemon v. Kurtzman*, pp. 612–13. Quoted in Elisha Winkler, "Simmons-Harris v. Zelman," *American University Journal of Gender, Social Policy and the Law*, 10 (2002), p. 758.

144   *Mitchell v. Helms*, 530 US 793, 845 (2000).

145   Frank R. Kemerer, "Reconsidering the constitutionality of vouchers," *Journal of Law and Education*, 30 (2000), p. 443.

146   *Zelman v. Simmons-Harris*, 122 S. Ct. 2460 (2002).

147 In the Alberta charter school context, another problem has arisen in this regard. The Alberta legislation was designed under the assumption that there would be co-operation between local school boards and charter schools. Consequently, the legislation called on local school boards to grant and renew charters. However, school boards have felt threatened by charter schools and the Minister of Education in Alberta has had to step in to grant and renew charters to all but one of the charter schools in the province. See Bosetti *et al.*, *supra* note 53, pp. 170, 113.

148 See United States Charter Schools, *supra* note 49. For another solution, consider David M. Beatty, *The Ultimate Rule of Law* (New York: Oxford University Press, 2004), pp. 177–81. Beatty advocates a "proportional funding" approach, based on the Hungarian model. The Hungarian constitutional courts have ruled that "the state must fund private schools 'in proportion to their undertaking the state's programmes'." This avoids forcing religious citizens to subsidize public education they disdain, while supporting the goals of the state in religious schools to the precise extent that state curricula is taught. Beatty further suggests, following India's Supreme Court, that the state may also regulate the quality of education in religious schools and takes reasonable steps to prevent intolerance and bigotry. Such a system would preserve fundamental state interests, while avoiding the differential treatment of secular and religious communities – a "rule which calls on the church and state to co-operate where their interests overlap."

149 See Greene, in Hepburn, *supra* note 2, p. 137.

150 For example, the loss of a valuable school year to pupils, additional stress, disruption of lifestyle, and dislocation from one's peers and social group.

151 In Milwaukee, this sort of school failure actually took place, causing the students of the Juanita Virgil Academy to lose a year's education. Ernest L. Boyer, *School Choice* (Princeton, NJ: Carnegie Foundation, 1992), p. 67.

152 Jerome J. Hanus and Peter W. Cookson, *Choosing Schools – Vouchers and American Education* (Washington, DC: American University Press, 1996), p. 160.

153 See Greene *et al.*, "Lesson from the Cleveland scholarship programme," in P.E. Peterson and B.C. Hassel (eds) *Learning from School Choice* (Washington, DC: Brookings Institution, 1998), pp. 357–92.

154 To the extent that students' learning is monitored, it will be advantageous to have gifted children in attendance and to treat them as ordinary students. Thus, the moral hazard problem involved here is not that schools will not want gifted students, but that they will not provide specialized programs that would benefit the gifted.

155 Guido Calabresi and Philip Bobbitt, *Tragic Choices* (New York: W.W. Norton, 1978).

156 This arrangement would have the added benefit of ensuring that schools do not explicitly cream-skim or engage in any overt forms of discrimination. There would not be any "fall back" reasons, for instance, to explain covert racially or ethnically discriminating policies. This mandatory pooling arrangement is what predominates in most charter schools. For an example, see Bosetti *et al.*, *supra* note 53, p. 10.

157 Bradford, David F., and Daniel Shaviro, "The economics of vouchers," in C. Eugene Steuerle, Van Doorn Ooms, George Peterson and Robert D. Reischauer (eds) *Vouchers and the Provision of Public Services* (Washinton, DC: Brookings Institution Press, CED, Urban Institute Press, 2000), p. 86.

158 Ibid., p. 53. As an illustration of this idea they suggest that donors, students and faculty of a for-profit university would be suspicious that decisions might not be made to maximize the quality of teaching or research, but instead to maximize payments to the shareholders. This fear may not disappear, but would at least diminish if the university were a non-profit institution.

159 Fly-by-night schools seeking to maximize profit in the short-run are more likely with extremely lenient government *ex ante* accreditation. The greater the barriers to entry to opening a school, the less likely such perverse behaviour by for-profit schools will be. There is an obvious trade-off involved, however, because the greater the barriers to entry, the less competitive the education system as a whole will be.

160   It is suggested that extra billing would be inefficient because social efficiency might militate in favour of an alternate distribution of educational resources. Allocating scarce educational resources as according to *ex ante* ability to pay does satisfy a *prima facie* utilitarian efficiency condition, but if those who are willing to pay the most are not the most able to benefit from education, long-run efficiency might not be obtained.

161   This trade-off between equity and efficiency is brought out clearly in the differences between the school voucher proposals of Friedman, *supra* note 1 and C. Jencks, *Education Vouchers: A Report on the Financing of Elementary Education by Grants to Parents* (Cambridge, MA: Cambridge Center for the Study of Public Policy, 1970). Friedman advocates setting the value of the basic voucher at the average per-student cost of state education (or a proportion thereof) and granting schools the ability to extra-bill freely. Jencks' scheme is more concerned with distributive justice and would therefore set the basic voucher at the full per-student average cost of state education and would provide an additional increment on the vouchers of poor student. The Jencks scheme would not allow extra billing or topping up at all, so that schools with a higher proportion of poor students would have better per-student funding.

162   This is the "duplicity" that Witte points to in his criticism of the politics behind the Milwaukee school voucher programme. It was introduced as a targeted means of helping poor inner city children, but has developed into a broad-based programme that may help middle-income families to the detriment of poor families. See Witte, *supra* note 2, p. 192.

163   Ibid., p. 74.

164   A no-extra-billing constraint would have to be made credible by mechanisms to guard against disguised extra billing via mandated or "expected" charitable contributions.

165   Sherry Glied, *Chronic Condition: Why Health Care Reform Fails* (Cambridge, MA: Harvard University Press, 1997), p. 220.

166   For a discussion of standardized testing see Janice Stein, *The Cult of Efficiency – The Massey Lecture Series* (Toronto: House of Anansi Press, 2001), Chapter 4, in particular pp. 154–68. However, there is some evidence that standardized testing in Canada tests to the curriculum more effectively than is often the case in American schools. Standardized testing, then, may be appropriate where tests designs facilitate rather than complicate the development of human capital. See Panel on the Role of Government, "Voice and choice in education," *Staff Report: Creating a Human Capital Society for Ontario* (Panel on the Role of Government, 2004), available at: http://www.law-lib.utoronto.ca/investing/staff/staffch2.pdf.; and Sweetman, *supra* note 69.

167   J. Douglas Willms and Frank H. Echols, "The Scottish experience of parental school choice," in Edith Rasell and Richard Rothstein (eds) *School Choice: Examining the Evidence* (Washington, DC: Economic Policy Institute, 1993), p. 49. The authors found that parents who exercised choice were "more highly educated and had more prestigious occupations than those who sent their children to the designated school."

168   For a definition of "credence" goods, see Richard Posner, *An Economic Approach to the Law of Evidence* (1999), p. 51. *Stanford Law Review*, 1477, p. 1489.

169   It may be possible to get around this credibility problem of for-profit suppliers misrepresenting the quality of their service in two different ways. The first would be by having an independent organization – perhaps most credibly government – engaged in information gathering, analysing and dissemination processes. To the extent that education is a pure "credence" good in the aggregate, however, this effort may be frustrated. The second way might emerge spontaneously – parents might monitor acceptance rates into key universities, thereby learning much about the experts' view of particular schools or programmes.

170   Michael Fullan, *The New Meaning of Educational Change*, 3rd edn (New York: Teachers College Press, Columbia University, 2001). See also Panel on the Role of Govern-

ment, *supra* note 138, p. 14 and Sweetman, *supra* note 69.

171 The "high marks" signal is valuable at the secondary school level because it can lead to admission at a more prestigious university and the consequent acquisition of an even more valuable market signal. The same sort of incentive exists for students in universities to select courses that are graded more leniently so that they can gain access to subsequent education resources more easily – for example, spots in graduate schools, medical schools and law schools. Of course, to the extent that others engage in this strategy, it increases the incentive for each individual student to search out less-demanding courses as well.

172 Witte, *supra* note 2, pp. 45–6.

173 Ibid., p. 108.

174 Greene, in Hepburn, *supra* note 2, p. 137.

9 Post-secondary education

1 The boundary between public and private universities should not, however, be drawn too starkly. Many elite private institutions receive significant levels of state support in the form of competitively allocated research grants and student-based financial aid assistance, which mutes the difference between these two modes of provision.

2 For a general discussion, see Douglas Auld, *Expanding Horizons: Privatizing Universities* (Toronto: University of Toronto, 1996), Chapter 1.

3 W. Craig Riddell, "The role of government in post-secondary education in Ontario," Report to the Panel on the Role of Government in Ontario (2003), p. 49, available at: http://www.law-lib.utoronto.ca/investing/reports/rp29.pdf. Riddell notes that these private returns have remained high despite considerable increases in the number of educated workers over the last several decades. Riddell further notes that the impact of education on earnings is causal, i.e. workers are more productive as a result of education rather than education being simply a means of signaling worker quality.

4 Somewhat more broadly, there is a literature showing that, particularly in a human capital economy, university research contributes significantly to societal wealth. See Anna-Lee Saxenian, *Regional Advantage: Culture and Competition in Silicon Valley and Route 128* (Cambridge, MA: Harvard University Press, 1994).

5 By the term "extent" it is suggested that the state, which is the ultimate beneficiary of the public benefits, should bear a proportion of the costs of higher education relative the overall benefits of higher education. In this way, the rates of return for both the private and the public expenditures on post-secondary education would be equalised, without privileging either.

6 The fact that the benefits to society and to the individual are largely intangible and probably impossible to measure accurately does not undermine the theoretical cogency of this argument. A system that at least *attempted* to do this would probably reach a more efficient outcome than our system does at present.

7 Some have argued that university education does not actually cause one's income to be higher. The screening hypothesis argues that post-secondary education may just be a signal of some other attributes to which employers assign value. See Nicholas Barr, *The Economics of the Welfare State*, 3rd edn (Stanford, CA: Stanford University Press, 1998), p. 324.

8 For a further discussion of this idea, see Barr, ibid., p. 325.

9 Even more than at the primary and secondary levels, the positions of Martha Nussbaum, *Cultivating Humanity: A Classical Defence of Reform in Liberal Education* (Cambridge: Cambridge University Press, 1998), Amy Gutmann, *Democratic Education* (Princeton, NJ: Princeton University Press, 1987), and Allan Bloom, *The Closing of the American Mind* (New York: Touchstone Books, 1988) are important. That is, it is

at the university level that they are most concerned with promoting a vision of liberal education as formative of a certain character and way of experiencing the world, not merely as imparting marketable skills.

10   In actual fact, even with government subsidization, investment in research will probably be deficient because research does not have guaranteed payoffs and most investors are risk averse. That is, a guaranteed return is to some extent preferred to a higher expected, but more variable return. Note that investment in applied research will probably be less deficient than investment in pure research because of the greater prospect of appropriating the benefits therefrom via patents.

11   See, for instance, Robert J. Barro, "Human capital and growth," *American Economic Review*, 91(2) (2001), pp. 12–17 and Robert J. Barro and Eaverier sala-i-Martin, *Economic Growth* (New York: McGraw-Hill, 1995).

12   Riddell, *supra* note 3, p. 24.

13   Ronald Dworkin, "DeFunis v. Sweatt," in Marshall Cohen, Thomas Nagel and Thomas Scanlon (eds) *Equality and Preferential Treatment* (Princeton, NJ: Princeton University Press, 1977), p. 63.

14   In the US, private universities often pursue "need-blind" admissions policies and then provide varying degrees of student assistance to those who are in financial need. The net result is that education is means-tested at private American universities. Another way to describe this policy, however, is to say that private American schools engage in a system of price discrimination that is designed to extract the maximum amount of money from each student. Given that private universities in the US are non-profit institutions interested in educating the strongest students possible, from an equity standpoint this regime of price discrimination is not necessarily repugnant, but at worst benign and perhaps even desirable. It serves as a way for students from wealthier families to cross-subsidize students with a lower ability to pay, while ensuring that only the most able applicants are granted admission. Many private universities supplement the federally sponsored loan program with internal income-contingent repayment plans (ICRPs) for loans that they grant to students in need of financial aid. The price discrimination regimes combined with ICRPs make access to education relatively equitable at private universities – despite the high tuition fees – for students confronting affordability problems. In terms of accessibility, then, private universities are arguably well ahead of their public counterparts.

15   Barr, *supra* note 7, p. 347.

16   Bruce Chapman and David Greenaway, "Learning to live with loans? Policy Transfer and the funding of higher education," paper for the Internationalism and Policy Transfer Conference, Tulane University (2003), p. 8. See also O. Mehmet, *Who Benefits from the Ontario University System: A Benefit–Cost Analysis by Income Groups* (Toronto: Ontario Economic Council, 1978), p. 45: "The principal net gainers from the university system are the middle and upper-income groups at the expense of lower-income groups. In this sense, the university system is a large public expenditure program in which the relatively poor groups tend to subsidize the relatively rich."

17   Chapman and Greenaway, ibid., p. 8.

18   In extreme, some public institutions confront a combination of caps on faculty salaries, mandatory salary disclosure and tuition fee restrictions which make it increasingly difficult for these institutions to attract and retain the most sought-after professors. For instance, in 1980 in the US the average gap in salary between full professors at public and private universities was $1,300. By 1998, this gap had widened to $21,700. "United States: the gap widens," *The Economist* (April 22, 2000).

19   This lack of flexibility is perhaps most evident in relation to the relatively poor response of public universities to the growing needs of mature and part-time students. Whereas only 27 percent of US college students were 25 or older in 1970, by 1991 this segment of the student body had risen to constitute 45 percent of students. Entrepreneurial private institutions in the United States that cater to mature and part-time students through an array of online correspondence and other materials

have begun to fill the void left by slowly moving public and well-established private institutions. New opportunities will arise as technology becomes more reliable, more interactive and more ubiquitous. However, it is not clear that public institutions have been nearly as responsive to these needs.

20 Milton Friedman and Rose Friedman, *Free to Choose* (New York: Harcourt Brace Jovanovich, 1980), pp. 176–7.

21 An alternate explanation may be that high tuition rates dissuade high-risk students from attending universities with high tuition. Instead high-risk students prefer to attend where they can make a lower-valued investment in their post-secondary education (and therefore have less to lose in the case of abandonment).

22 Commission of Inquiry on Canadian University Education, *Report* (Ottawa: AUCC, 1991), p. 105.

23 Ibid., p. 106.

24 Dave Guerin, "Entitlements in education: empowering student demand," Education Directions Ltd (August 1997), p. 43, available at: http://www.ed.co.nz/docs/entitle.pdf.

25 Ibid.

26 Ben Jongbloed and Jos Koelman, "Vouchers for higher education? A survey of the literature commissioned by the Hong Kong University Grants Committee" (2000) Center for Higher Education Policy Studies, p. 36.

27 Guerin, *supra* note 24, p. 44.

28 Ibid.

29 Ibid.

30 Kate Galbraith, "Britain's sinking fleet of universities," *Chronicle of Higher Education* (March 21, 2003). See also: "Who pays to study?," *The Economist* (January 22, 2004).

31 Chapman and Greenaway, *supra* note 16, p. 15.

32 Ibid., p. 16.

33 Guerin, *supra* note 24, p. 45.

34 Ibid.

35 Chapman and Greenaway, *supra* note 16, p. 16.

36 Ibid.

37 House of Commons Education and Skills Committee, "The future of higher education" (London: The Stationery Office, 2003), p. 5, available at: http://www.parliament.the-stationery-office.co.uk/pa/cm200203/cmselect/cmeduski/425/425.pdf.

38 Ibid., p. 85.

39 See Kate Galbraith, "Bill to increase tuition in Britain passes its first test, narrowly," *Chronicle of Higher Education* (February 6, 2004).

40 Milton Friedman, *Capitalism and Freedom* (Chicago, IL: University of Chicago Press, 1962), p. 105.

41 Unsurprisingly, many commentators have argued that the threatened or actual entry of private post-secondary institutions creates competitive pressures that spur public suppliers to improve. Roger Geiger, "The private alternative in higher education," *European Journal of Education*, 20(4) (1985), p. 397.

42 Dieter Dohmen, "Vouchers in higher education – a practical approach," paper presented at the Education and Socio-economical Research and Consulting Conference 2000 (September, 2000), p. 24, available at: http://www.ceserc.com/forum_004.pdf.

43 Jongbloed and Koelman, *supra* note 26, p. 12.

44 Edwin G. West, "Education with and without the state," *HCO Working Papers* (date unknown), p. 6v available at: http://www.worldbank.org/html/extdr/hnp/hddflash/workp/wp_00061.html.

45 Jongbloed and Koelman, *supra* note 26, p. 11.

46   David Laidler, "Renovating the ivory tower: an introductory essay," in David Laider (ed.) *Renovating the Ivory Tower: Canadian Universities and the Knowledge Economy* (Toronto: C.D. Howe Institute, 2002), pp. 29–30.

47   Hessel Oosterbeek, "Innovative ways to finance education and their relation to lifelong learning," *Education Economics*, 6(3) (1998), p. 8.

48   House of Commons Education and Skills Committee, *supra* note 37, p. 52.

49   Arthur Hauptman, "Vouchers and American higher education," in C. Eugene Steuerle, Van Doorn Ooms, George Peterson and Robert D. Reischauer (eds) *Vouchers and the Provision of Public Services* (Washington, DC: Brookings Institution Press, CED, Urban Institute Press, 2000), p. 346.

50   Ibid., p. 122.

51   Ibid.

52   Ibid., p. 125.

53   Guerin, *supra* note 24, p. 37.

54   Jongbloed and Koelman, *supra* note 26, p. 27.

55   Guerin, *supra* note 24.

56   Peter Karmel, "Higher education at the crossroads: response to an Australian ministerial discussion paper," *Higher Education*, 45 (2003), pp. 3–4.

57   Edwin G. West, *Ending the Squeeze on Universities: Canada in a World Perspective* (Ottawa: Carlton University, 1993), p. 28, available at: www.ncl.ac.uk/egwest/pdfs/ending%20the%20squeeze.pdf.

58   Chapman and Greenaway, *supra* note 16, p. 11.

59   Ibid., p. 12.

60   Ibid.

61   "Policy paper," *Our Universities: Backing Australia's Future* (2003), available at: http://www.backingaustraliasfuture.gov.au/policy_paper/1.htm.

62   Chapman and Greenaway, *supra* note 16, p. 13.

63   Ibid., p. 13.

64   Ibid., p. 14.

65   Ibid.

66   Ibid.

67   West, *supra* note 57, p. 28.

68   Ibid., p. 26.

69   Chapman and Greenaway, *supra* note 16, p. 14.

70   Ibid.

71   E.G. West, *Ending the Squeeze on Universities* (Ottawa: Institute for Research on Public Policy, 1993), p. 26.

72   Despite large start-up costs that have traditionally attended the opening of a new post-secondary institution, the internet has started to reduce the large capital requirements that have hitherto acted as a significant barrier to entry for new universities. Physical infrastructure, staffing, housing, food services, recreation and athletics are vital to traditional post-secondary institutions, but are relatively unimportant considerations for setting up a post-secondary educational institution on the World Wide Web, where both teaching and learning are done *in absentia*. In addition, the increased competition arising from the ability of geographically diverse incumbent universities to compete directly for the same students is a potentially very valuable instrument in weeding out poor suppliers of internet-based education.

73   Riddell, *supra* note 3, p. 71. It is hard to quantify the magnitude of this risk. In a setting of integrated labour markets, inter-jurisdictional tax differentials always pose a risk to retention of high-income earners. However, the mobility of taxpayers in response to tax differentials should not be overstated given the range of connections that individuals have to their home jurisdictions.

74   See, for example Reuven Brenner, *The Future of Higher Education* (Toronto, Centre for the Study of State and Market, 1996).

75   See, for example, G.S. Becker, K.M. Murphy and R. Tamura, "Human capital,
      fertility and economic growth," *Journal of Political Economy*, 98(5) (1990); G.
      Psacharopoulos, "The contribution of education to economic growth: international
      comparisons," in J.W. Kendrick (ed.) *International Comparisons of Productivity and Causes
      of the Slowdown* (Cambridge, MA: Ballinger, 1984), p. 335.

76   Removing the means-test requirement is beneficial in two ways. First, students do
      not have to rely on the support of their parents (or rebut a "presumption of support")
      and can be self-sufficient from the moment that they leave the family home. Second,
      there will be a gain in administrative efficiency as resources will not have to be
      devoted to evaluating and processing means-testing portions of applications.

77   Barr, *supra* note 7, p. 352.

78   For instance, graduate programs in North American universities have high average
      grades – most graduate students have an "A" average upon graduation, whereas
      undergraduate programs have much lower average grades – virtually always only a
      minority of students graduate with "A" averages. Few people would take this as an
      indication that graduate students learn less than undergraduate students. It is simply
      widely accepted that graduate students should earn higher grades than under-
      graduates do and this expectation is built into the evaluation process.

79   Barr, *supra* note 7, p. 352.

80   Ibid. Some monitoring of institutions will be done by society at large. Students will
      want to attend strong institutions so that they have ready access to labour markets
      and the top graduate and professional programmes. Employers will engage in
      monitoring so that they hire personnel who are well educated and capable.

81   Auld, *supra* note 2, pp. 44, 52.

82   Ibid., p. 62. Institutions will likely compete especially vigorously in terms of their
      ability to exploit technology and innovate in the utilization of their existing human
      capital.

83   It is unlikely, however, that job security would be reduced for the existing professoriate.
      Labour demand for incumbent academics would likely increase significantly.

10 Labour market training

1   John P. Martin, "What works among active labour market policies: evidence from
     OECD countries' experiences," Labour Market and Social Policy Occasional Paper
     No. 35 (Paris: OECD, 1998), p. 5.

2   Concern in North America is lower than it is elsewhere in the OECD at present as
     the unemployment rate is near a 30-year low. According to the *US Bureau of Labor
     Statistics* as of June 2000 the unemployment rate in the US was 4.0 percent – US
     Bureau of Labor Statistics, "The employment situation: June 2000" (July 7, 2000),
     available at: ftp://ftp.bls.gov/pub/news.release/History/empsit.07072000.news.
     Similarly, according to *Statistics Canada*, the unemployment rate in Canada in June
     2000 was 6.6 percent, also at a 30-year low. Statistics Canada, "The daily: labour
     force survey June 2000" (July 7, 2000), available at: http://www.collectionscanada.ca/
     eppp-archive/100/201/301/daily/daily-h/2000/00–07/00–07–07/d000707a.htm.
     Elsewhere in the OECD, however, unemployment figures are not as sanguine and
     pose a continuing cause for concern.

3   This is not to say, however, that macroeconomic policy writ large is unimportant in
     reducing unemployment. Rather, prudent growth encouraging fiscal and monetary
     policy should be considered a foundational requirement for embarking upon
     microeconomically-oriented employment strategies.

4   Andrew Bernstein and Michael Trebilcock, "Labour market training & retraining,"
     Working Paper No.4 (Toronto: Center for the Study of State & Market, University
     of Toronto, 1996), p. 23.

5 For an evaluation of many recent ALMPs among OECD countries see Martin, *supra* note 1. For an earlier and in some ways more thorough analysis, see Robert G. Fay, "Enhancing the effectiveness of active labour market policies: evidence from programme evaluations in OECD countries," Labour Market and Social Policy Occasional Paper No. 18 (Paris: OECD, 1996). See also Bernstein and Trebilcock, ibid.

6 Morley Gunderson, "Training in Canada: progress and problems," in Barrie O. Pettman (ed) *Government Involvement in Training* (Bradford: MCB Publications Limited, 1978), p. 127.

7 Morley Gunderson, "Active labour market adjustment policies: what we know and don't know ," report to the Panel on the Role of Government in Ontario (2003), p. 16, available at http://www.law-lib.utoronto.ca/investing/reports/rp33.pdf.

8 Ibid., p. 15.

9 Ibid., p. 8.

10 Ibid., p. 9.

11 There are others, most notably seasonal unemployment in sectors such as fishing and construction.

12 Organisation for Economic Co-operation and Development, *The OECD Jobs Study: Facts, Analysis, Strategies* (Paris: OECD, 1994) p. 9.

13 Ibid., Table 1. Long-term unemployment, which is usually attributable to structural features, as of 1994 constituted 42.2 percent of the unemployment rate in the European Union, compared with a comparably minor 11.2 percent in Canada and the United States.

14 See Richard B. Freeman, "Are your wages set in Beijing?," *The Journal of Economic Perspectives*, 9(3) (1995), p. 18. Freeman claims that real wages in the US for males with 12 years of education dropped 20 percent in real terms between 1979 and 1993. For further evidence of the erosion of real wages over the same period of time in the US see William Cline, *Trade and Income Distribution* (Washington, DC: Institute for International Economics, 1997), p. 23. See also Philippe Aghion and Jeffry G. Williamson, *Growth, Inequality and Globalization* (Cambridge: Cambridge University Press, 1998), p. 36.

15 See US Department of Labour Council of Economic Advisors, *20 Million Jobs: January 1993 to November 1999* (December 3, 1999), available at: http://clinton4.nara.gov/media/pdf/20miljobs.pdf. According to the report at page 6, "The resumption in real earnings growth since 1996 has been especially evident among low-wage workers [... and] compared with the 1980s expansion, the growth in earnings has been much more evenly distributed."

16 Cline, *supra* note 14, pp. 32–3.

17 OECD, *supra* note 12, Table 1. In 1993, the OECD average for youth unemployment stood at 15.1 percent (*vs.* aggregate of 7.8 percent); in Canada, the youth unemployment level was roughly 17.8 percent.

18 Jeffrey G. Reitz, "Occupational dimensions of immigrant credential assessment," in Charles Beach, Alan Green and Jeffrey G. Reitz (eds) *Canadian Immigration Policy for the 21st Century* (Kingston, Ontario: Jun Deutsch, 2003).

19 In practice, however, the split between firm-specific and general human capital is very blurred. One aspect of training may apply only to the operation of a very specialised machine, for instance. This is *prima facie* a firm-specific investment. However, such a skill may have general human capital aspects. For example, such a skill may be considered general human capital within the industry if competing firms use similar machines.

20 Much of the following discussion on the rationales for government intervention in alleviating structural unemployment in the labour market is adapted from M. Gunderson and C. Riddell, "Training in Canada," in A. Barry (ed.) *Labour Market Policy in Canada and Latin America: Challenges of a New Millennium* (The Hague: Kluwer

Academic Publishers, forthcoming). See also John Donahue, *The Privatization Decision: Public Ends, Private Means* (New York: Basic Books, 1989), pp. 189–96.

21 Of course, this agreement does not need to be explicit. It may be easier for employers to implicitly impute some of the costs of employee training on to employees through reduced wages or benefits, for instance.

22 Gunderson, *supra* note 7, p. 14. The degree to which this poaching problem exists will in large part depend on how firm-specific and how extensive the training has been. If the skills that the employer has equipped employees with are of value only to that particular employer, which is unlikely, then the poaching problem will not exist. In the same way, if the training that the employer has put the employee through has been of extremely short duration, then poaching will also be only a minor issue. On the other hand, with extensive and portable training, poaching may become a major problem for sponsoring employers.

23 Ibid.

24 Ibid.

25 Ibid., pp. 14–15.

26 Ibid., p. 4.

27 Ibid., p. 3.

28 Ibid., p. 18.

29 Ibid., p. 7.

30 Ibid., p. 6.

31 Ibid., p. 3.

32 Fay, *supra* note 5, p. 43.

33 Jochen Kluve and Cristoph Schmidt, "Can training and employment subsidies combat European unemployment?," *Economic Policy*, 17(35) (2002), p. 438.

34 Ibid., p. 439. See also Organisation for Economic Co-operation and Development, *OECD Economic Surveys: Canada* (Paris: OECD, 2001), p. 144.

35 See Fay, *supra* note 5. See also Robert J. Lalonde, "The promise of public sector sponsored training programs," *Journal of Economic Perspectives*, 9(2) (1995), p. 149; Duane E. Leigh, *Assisting Workers Displaced by Structural Change* (Kalamazoo, MI: Upjohn Institute, 1995); and Duane E. Leigh, *Does Training Work for Displaced Workers?* (Kalamazoo, MI: Upjohn Institute, 1990).

36 In Canada, the National Employment Service acts as a labour market intermediary by providing assistance to the unemployed through employment centres, by the provision of job-finding education and through the operation of "job clubs."

37 In the United States, there are a variety of different state and local placement programs.

38 Fay, *supra* note 5, p. 23.

39 Organization for Economic Co-operation and Development, *The OECD Jobs Strategy: Enhancing the Effectiveness of Active Labour Market Policies* (Paris: OECD, 1996), p. 11.

40 In John Van Reenen, "Active labour market policies and the British new deal for the young unemployed in context," NBER Working Papers No. 9576 (2003), p. 11.

41 OECD, *supra* note 12, p. 37.

42 Anita U. Hattiangadi, "Welfare changes accentuate the need for job training reform," *Fact & Fallacy: Contemporary Issues in Employment and Workplace Policy*, 3(4) (1997), available at: http://www.epf.org/pubs/newsletters/1997/ff3–4.asp.

43 One feature of US programs that distinguishes them from most others is that they are mandatory. Results here should be understood in that light.

44 These are programs designed to bring individuals into the labour market. They are distinct from programs designed to increase the skills-level of those already employed.

45 From 41.3 percent to 65.4 percent of single parents, from 27.9 percent to 82.9 percent of disadvantaged adults, and 48.4 percent or more of disadvantaged youth failed to graduate from high school. Figures are reported in Fazil Milhar and M.

Danielle Smith, *Government-Sponsored Training Programs: Failure in the United States, Lessons for Canada* (Vancouver: Fraser Institute, 1997), pp. 4–7.

46   Results were best for single parents, who were at the top of the spectrum in each category. The other two groups experienced virtually no gains in any of the categories. Over-all, earnings increased from nothing to as much as $19.96 per week; employment levels by a maximum of 13.6 percent and as little as nothing, dependence on government aid fell slightly among single parents, but not at all among the other two groups. These figures are from Milhar and Smith, ibid., p. 5.

47   See Donahue, *supra* note 20, pp. 179, 198.

48   Burt S. Barnow, "Vouchers for federal targeted training programs," in C. Eugene Steuerle, Van Doorn Ooms, George Peterson and Robert D. Reischauer (eds) *Vouchers and the Provision of Public Services* (Washinton, DC: Brookings Institution Press, CED, Urban Institute Press, 2000), p. 245.

49   Fay, *supra* note 5, pp. 27, 60.

50   W. Craig Riddell, "Human capital formation in Canada: recent developments and policy responses," in Keith Banting and C. M. Beach (eds) *Labour Market Polarization and Social Policy Reform* (Kingston, Ontario: School of Policy Studies, 1995), p. 162. "When classroom training works, it seems to work best for youths and females re-entering the labour market."

51   See P. Treh'rning, *Measures to Combat Unemployment in Sweden* (Stockholm: Swedish Institute, 1993); Swedish Institute, *Fact Sheets on Sweden – Swedish Labour Market Policy*, (Stockholm: Swedish Institute, 1994).

52   OECD, *supra* note 39, p. 10.

53   Ibid., p. 43.

54   Organization for Economic Co-operation and Development, *The OECD Jobs Study: Implementing the Strategy* (Paris: OECD, 1995), p. 29.

55   Martin, *supra* note 1, p. 17.

56   Hattiangadi, *supra* note 42.

57   Fay, *supra* note 5, p. 22.

58   Results reported in Milhar and Smith, *supra* note 45.

59   Martin, *supra* note 1, p. 20.

60   Mihlar and Smith, *supra* note 45.

61   Fazil Mihlar and M. Danielle Smith, "Government-sponsored training programs not a solution for unemployed Canadians," *The Fraser Institute* (December, 1997), available at: http://oldfraser.lexi.net/publications/forum/1998/january/release.html.

62   Ibid.

63   Ibid.

64   Ibid.

65   Ibid.

66   Gunderson and Riddell, *supra* note 20.

67   David Leadbeater and Peter Suschnigg, "Training as the principal focus of adjustment policy: a critical view from Northern Ontario," *Canadian Public Policy*, 23(1) (1997), pp. 14–15.

68   Robert G. Fay, "Making the public employment service more effective through the introduction of market signals," OECD Labour Market and Social Policy Occasional Paper No. 25 (Paris: OECD, 1997), p. 3.

69   Eduardo Martinez Espinoza, "Chile: experiences in a market-oriented training system" (1997), p. 2, available at: http://www.ilo.org/public/english/employment/skills/training/publ/chile.htm.

70   Ibid.

71   Ibid., p. 5.

72   Ibid., p. 13.

73   Ibid., p. 9.

74   See the Belgian experience as discussed below.
75   Organisation for Economic Co-operation and Development, *Implementing the OECD Jobs Strategy: Member Countries Experience* (OECD: Paris, 1997) p. 36.
76   Daniela Andren and Thomas Andren, "Assessing the employment effects of labor market training programs in Sweden," Working Papers in Economics No. 70 (2002), p. 4.
77   Fay, *supra* note 68, p. 11.
78   Ibid.
79   James J. Heckman, Robert J. LaLonde and Jeffrey A. Smith, "The economics and econometrics of active labor market programs," in A. Ashenfelter and D. Card (eds) *Handbook of Labor Economics, Volume III* (Amsterdam: Elsevier Science, 1999), p. 1874. Note, however, that the Swedish figures include stipends for participants while the US figures do not.
80   Andren and Andren, *supra* note 76, pp. 5 and 14.
81   Ibid., p. 5.
82   The Swedish Institute for Social Research and ECOTEC Research and Consulting, "Labour Market Studies: Sweden" (1996), p. 92. Membership fees accounted for 3 percent of total unemployment insurance benefits in 1996.
83   Alfred M. Dockery and Thorsten Stromback, "Devolving public employment services: preliminary assessment of the Australian experiment," *International Labour Review*, 140(4) (2001), p. 435.
84   William Hall, "Australia in transition," International Labour Organization (1997), available at: http://www.ilo.org/public/english/employment/skills/training/publ/aus.htm.
85   Jens Lundsgaard, "Competition and efficiency in publicly funded services," OECD Economics Department Working Paper no. 331 (2002), p. 21.
86   Dockery and Stromback, *supra* note 83, p. 436.
87   Ibid., p. 437.
88   Ibid., p. 441.
89   Ibid., pp. 439–40.
90   Ibid., p. 441.
91   Ibid.
92   Organization for Economic Co-operation and Development, *Innovations in Labour Market Policies: The Australian Way* (Paris: OECD, 2001), p. 13.
93   OECD, *supra* note 39, p. 26.
94   Martin, *supra* note 1, p. 18.
95   Ibid., p. 28.
96   OECD, *supra* note 12, p. 47.
97   Hattiangadi, *supra* note 42.
98   Ibid.
99   Dockery and Stromback, *supra* note 83, p. 432.
100 OECD, *supra* note 39, pp. 27–8.
101 The substitution effect lowers the opportunity cost of choosing leisure as one's earning potential drops. The income effect lowers the incentive to work as one's income rises. In this particular instance, income is rising because of more generous government assistance, and the opportunity costs of not working are low because those with low skill levels have little prospect for gaining highly remunerated positions.
102 Scandinavian schemes that are coupled with a high degree of compulsion to enter them have been the most successful. See OECD, *supra* note 12 or OECD, *supra* note 75, pp. 85–6.
103 Ibid. See also OECD, *supra* note 75, pp. 85–6.
104 Van Reenen, *supra* note 40, p. 1.
105 Ibid., p. 2.
106 Ibid., p. 8.

107   See ibid., pp. 13–18 for a full account.
108   Ibid., p. 19.
109   Peter Dolton and Donal O'Neill, "Unemployment duration and the restart effect: some experimental evidence," *Economic Journal*, 106(435) (1996), p. 390.
110   Milhar and Smith, *supra* note 45, pp. 4–7.
111   OECD, *supra* note 75, p. 82.
112   The strategy of requiring all job vacancies to be posted to government-run job banks may constitute undue labour market regulation and be a deterrent to hiring. The question of how large of a deterrent such a policy would be is an empirical one, and must be balanced against the efficiency gains associated with having a central repository of all job openings.
113   Leigh, 1995, *supra* note 35, p. 188.
114   For example, employers might simply use unskilled, cheap labour without providing any training, and employees may look for the least skills-intensive job without having to go through any training.
115   Hall, *supra* note 84, p. 12.
116   OECD, *supra* note 92, p. 222.
117   "Job network ad costs $1.3m," *Courier-Mail* (November 11, 2003).
118   OECD, *supra* note 75.
119   Ibid., p. 84.
120   OECD, *supra* note 39, p. 31.
121   See Donahue, *supra* note 20, p. 198.
122   Bart Cockx, "The design of active labour market policies: what matters and what doesn't?," Institut de Recherches Economiques et Sociales and the Université Catholique de Louvain Department of Economics (1998), p. 8.
123   Ibid., p. 10.
124   Ibid., p. 11.
125   Dockery and Stromback, *supra* note 83, p. 437.
126   Ibid., p. 444.
127   Ibid.
128   Heckman, LaLonde and Smith, *supra* note 79.
129   Lundsgaard, *supra* note 85, p. 21.

11 Conclusion

1   See Michael J. Trebilcock, "Lurching around Chicago: the positive challenge of explaining the recent regulatory reform agenda," in Richard M. Bird, Michael J. Trebilcock and Thomas A. Wilson (eds) *Rationality in Public Policy: Retrospect and Prospect, A Tribute to Douglas Hartle* (Toronto: Canadian Tax Foundation, 1999), Chapter 11; Michael Trebilcock and Ron Daniels, "Journeys across the institutional divides: reinterpreting the reinventing government movement," Working Paper, University of Toronto Law School (2000).
2   J.M. Keynes, *The General Theory of Employment, Interest & Money* (London: Macmillan, 1936), p. 384.
3   Steven Kelman, *Making Public Policy: A Hopeful View of American Government* (New York: Basic Books, 1987).
4   Joseph Schumpeter, *Capitalism, Socialism and Democracy* (New York: Harper Row, 1975), p. 87.
5   See e.g. Dennis Mueller, *Public Choice II* (Cambridge University Press, 1989); Douglas Hartle, Michael Trebilcock, J.R.S. Prichard and Don Dewees, *The Choice of Governing Instrument* (Economic Council of Canada, 1982); Andrei Schleifer and Robert Vishny, *The Grabbing Hand* (Cambridge, MA: Harvard University Press, 1998).

6   See George Stigler, "Law or economics?," *Journal of Law and Economics*, 35 (1992) 455; Gary Becker, "A theory of competition among pressure groups," *Quarterly Journal of Economics*, 98 (1983), p. 372.

7   Mancur Olson, "Big bills left on the side-walk: why some nations are rich and others poor," *Journal of Economic Perspectives*, 10 (1996), p. 3.

8   See e.g. C. Winston "Economic deregulation," *Journal of Economic Literature*, 31 (1993) 1263; R. Crandall and J. Ellig, "Economic deregulation and customer choice," (Washington, DC: George Mason University, Centre for Market Processes, 1997).

9   See Trebilcock, "Lurching around Chicago," *op.cit.*

10 Milton Friedman, *Capitalism and Freedom* (Chicaco, IL: University of Chicago Press, 1962), pp. 85–107.

11 See Milton and Rose Friedman, *Free to Choose* (New York: Harcourt Brace Jovanovich, 1980), p. 157.

12 See Burdett Loomis, "The politics of vouchers," in C. Eugene Steuerle, Van Doorn Ooms, George Peterson and Robert Reischauer (eds) *Vouchers and the Provision of Public Services* (Washinton, DC: Brookings Institution Press, CED, Urban Institute Press, 2000).

Index

eBooks

eBooks – at www.eBookstore.tandf.co.uk

A library at your fingertips!

eBooks are electronic versions of printed books. You can store them on your PC/laptop or browse them online.

They have advantages for anyone needing rapid access to a wide variety of published, copyright information.

eBooks can help your research by enabling you to bookmark chapters, annotate text and use instant searches to find specific words or phrases. Several eBook files would fit on even a small laptop or PDA.

NEW: Save money by eSubscribing: cheap, online access to any eBook for as long as you need it.

Annual subscription packages

We now offer special low-cost bulk subscriptions to packages of eBooks in certain subject areas. These are available to libraries or to individuals.

For more information please contact webmaster.ebooks@tandf.co.uk

We're continually developing the eBook concept, so keep up to date by visiting the website.

www.eBookstore.tandf.co.uk